Federal Appropriations Law

Note to Students:

Changes in Public Laws pertaining to acquisition procedures occur regularly. If portions of this textbook have been affected by recent changes, you may ask your instructor to update them orally as needed. Portions of this text include public domain materials from the Principles of Federal Appropriations Law, also known as the Red Book, a multi-volume treatise on federal fiscal law created by the U.S. Government Accountability Office, as well as other GAO materials.

GMIG

Palmdale, California

www.gmig.org

© 2016 Gonzales-McCaulley Investment Group, Inc.

ISBN-13: 978-1533241078
ISBN-10: 1533241074

This page intentionally left blank

Table of Contents

This page intentionally left blank

Chapter 1: Introduction

A. Congress and the Constitutional Power of the Purse

"Money is, with propriety, considered as the vital principle of the body politic; as that which sustains its life and motion, and enables it to perform its most essential functions."

The Federalist No. 30 (Alexander Hamilton).

A necessary corollary of Hamilton's thesis is that the body that controls the government's money also wields great power to shape and control the government itself by determining, for example, the purpose for which government may use money or the amounts that are available for its endeavors.

Through the Constitution, the framers provided that the legislative branch—the Congress—has power to control the government's purse strings. As James Madison explained, the framers vested Congress with the power of the purse for two primary reasons. The Federalist No. 58 (James Madison). First, this arrangement ensured that the government remained directly accountable to the will of the people: "power over the purse may, in fact, be regarded as the most complete and effectual weapon with which any constitution can arm the immediate representatives of the people, for obtaining a redress of every grievance, and for carrying into effect every just and salutary measure." Id. Second, Congress through its power of the purse holds a key check on the power of the other branches, allowing it to reduce "all the overgrown prerogatives of the other branches of government." Id. Indeed, a later observer described the power of the purse as "the most important single curb in the Constitution on Presidential power."

The framers vested Congress with the power of the purse by providing in the Constitution that "no Money shall be drawn from the Treasury, but in Consequence of Appropriations made by Law." U.S. Const., art. I, § 9, cl. 7. Time and again, the Supreme Court has reaffirmed that this clause means exactly what its straightforward language suggests: "no money can be paid out of the Treasury unless it has been appropriated by an act of Congress." Cincinnati Soap Co. v. United States, 301 U.S. 308, 321 (1937). This principle, when stated differently, reveals a tenet that is of critical importance to every agency, every officer, every employee of the federal government:

> "The established rule is that the expenditure of public funds is proper only when authorized by Congress, not that public funds may be expended unless prohibited by Congress."

United States v. MacCollom, 426 U.S. 317, 321 (1976).

This quintessential axiom animates the entire body of appropriations law. As James Madison and subsequent constitutional scholars have recognized, the congressional power of the purse is a key element of the constitutional framework of checks and balances. Accordingly, Congress's power of the purse does not manifest as a reservation of congressional authority to disapprove of federal expenditures. Rather, the Constitution vests in Congress the power and duty to affirmatively authorize all expenditures. Regardless of the nature of the payment—a salary, a payment promised under a contract, a payment ordered by a court—a federal agency may not make such a payment and, indeed, may not even incur a liability for such a payment, unless

Congress has made funding authority available. Indeed, a federal agency is a creature of law and can only carry out any of its functions to the extent authorized by law. See, e.g., Atlantic City Electric Co. v. Federal Energy Regulatory Commission, 295 F.3d 1, 8 (D.C. Cir. 2002). See also B-323449, Aug. 14, 2012; B-288266, Jan. 27, 2003. Therefore, agencies must operate not only in accordance with the funding levels Congress has permitted, but also in accordance with their authorizing statutes.

The axiom that obligations and expenditures are permitted only in accordance with an appropriation made by law is not limited to funds drawn from the so-called "general fund" of the Treasury, which is where the government deposits the bulk of its tax receipts. Instead, any government obligation or expenditure whatsoever—whether it is derived from the general fund, from fees arising from the government's business-like activities, or from any other source—may be made only as authorized by an appropriation. Some government activities are financed by permanent appropriations, and some of these derive their funds from fees rather than taxes. Congress need not appropriate funds for these activities on an annual basis to ensure their continued operation.

Nevertheless, such activities are financed using appropriated funds, and absent any statute stating otherwise, such activities are subject to the limitations imposed by law upon the use of all appropriated amounts. Whenever "the Congress specifies the manner in which a Federal entity shall be funded and makes such funds available for obligation and expenditure, that constitutes an appropriation, whether the language is found in an appropriation act or in other legislation." B-193573, Dec. 19, 1979.

The Constitution does not detail how Congress is to implement its constitutional power of the purse, but provides Congress with the power to enact statutes to protect and exercise this power. U.S. Const., art. I, § 9, cl. 7 (Congress may make all laws "necessary and proper" for carrying into effect Congress's legislative powers). Congress has done this through, among other ways, the annual budget and appropriations process and through a series of permanent statutes that establish controls on the use of appropriated funds. As one court has put it:

> "[The Appropriations Clause] is not self-defining and Congress has plenary power to give meaning to the provision. The Congressionally chosen method of implementing the requirements of Article I, section 9, clause 7 is to be found in various statutory provisions."

Harrington v. Bush, 553 F.2d 190, 194–95 (D.C. Cir. 1977). E.g., Walker v. Department of Housing & Urban Development, 912 F.2d 819, 829 (5th Cir. 1990).

There were few statutory funding controls in the early years of the nation and abuses were commonplace. As early as 1809, one senator, citing a string of abuses, introduced a resolution to look into ways to prevent the improper expenditure of public funds. In 1816 and 1817, John C. Calhoun lamented the "great evil" of diverting public funds to uses other than those for which they were appropriated. Executive abuses continued into the post-Civil War years. "Funds were commingled. Obligations were made without appropriations. Unexpended balances from prior years were used to augment current appropriations."

The permanent fiscal statutes, found mostly in title 31 of the United States Code, implement Congress's power of the purse and are designed to combat these and other abuses. These statutes form the legal framework for appropriations law. They did not spring up overnight, but have evolved over the span of more than two centuries. Nevertheless, when viewed as a whole, they form a logical framework that governs the collection and use of public money. We may regard them as pieces of a puzzle that fit together to form the larger picture of how Congress exercises its power of the purse. As Hamilton explained, nearly any action government takes requires money; therefore, the statutes governing the use of public money ultimately affect every government activity, whether monumental or minute. Some of the key statutes in this scheme, each of which is discussed elsewhere in this publication, are:

- A statute will not be construed as making an appropriation unless it expressly so states. 31 U.S.C. § 1301(d).

- Appropriations may be used only for their intended purposes. 31 U.S.C. § 1301(a). This is known as the purpose statute.

- Appropriations made for a definite period of time may be used only for expenses properly incurred during that time. 31 U.S.C. § 1502(a). This is known as the bona fide needs statute.

- Time-limited appropriations that are unobligated at the end of their period of availability are said to "expire" and are no longer available for new obligations. 31 U.S.C. § 1552. This statute is known as the account closing law and it specifies the limited uses for which expired funds remain available.

- Agencies may not spend, or commit themselves to spend, in advance of or in excess of appropriations. 31 U.S.C. § 1341. This is known as the Antideficiency Act.

- Unless authorized by law, an agency may not keep money it receives from sources other than appropriations, but must deposit the money in the Treasury. 31 U.S.C. § 3302(b). This is known as the miscellaneous receipts statute.

- All obligations that an agency incurs must be supported by documentary evidence and must be properly recorded. 31 U.S.C. § 1501. This is known as the recording statute.

This publication discusses the body of decisions and opinions, especially from the courts and GAO, that interpret and apply these statutes. Collectively, the clauses of the Constitution pertaining to Congress's power of the purse, the statutes protecting and exercising this power, and the decisions interpreting this power constitute the body of what is known as appropriations law. This body of law gives flesh and force to one of the key pillars of democracy that the framers incorporated in the Constitution. Appropriations law is not only about ensuring that federal agencies follow a set of rules that Congress has enacted. These laws also help ensure that government carries out the will of, and remains accountable to, the American people.

B. The Role of GAO and its Predecessors

In furtherance of its constitutional responsibilities to control and oversee the use of public money, Congress has vested GAO with several statutory functions. Because some of these functions were carried out by other government officers before Congress created GAO in 1921, a brief discussion of these predecessors to GAO will help illuminate the contours of GAO's responsibilities.

1. Accounting Officers Prior to 1921

Since the early days of the republic, Congress, in exercising its oversight of the public purse, has utilized administrative officials for the settlement of public accounts and the review of federal expenditures.

a. Prior to 1894

Throughout most of the nineteenth century, the accounting officers consisted of a series of comptrollers and auditors. Starting in 1817 with two comptrollers and four auditors, the number increased until, for the second half of the century, there were three co-equal comptrollers (First Comptroller, Second Comptroller, Commissioner of Customs) and six auditors (First Auditor, Second Auditor, etc.), all officials of the Treasury Department. The jurisdiction of the comptrollers and auditors was divided generally along departmental lines, with the auditors examining accounts and submitting their settlements to the appropriate comptroller.

The practice of rendering written decisions goes back at least to 1817. However, very little of this material exists in published form. (Until sometime after the Civil War, the decisions were handwritten.)

There are no published decisions of the First Comptroller prior to the term of William Lawrence (1880–85). Lawrence published his decisions in a series of six annual volumes. After Lawrence's decisions, a gap of 9 years followed until First Comptroller Robert Bowler published a single unnumbered volume of his 1893–94 decisions.

The decisions of the Second Comptroller and the Commissioner of Customs were never published. However, volumes of digests of decisions of the Second Comptroller were published starting in 1852. The first volume, unnumbered, saw three cumulative editions, the latest issued in 1869 and including digests for the period 1817–69. Three additional volumes (designated volumes 2, 3, and 4) were published in 1884, 1893, and 1899 (the latter being published several years after the office had ceased to exist), covering respectively, the periods 1869–84, 1884–93, and 1893–94. Thus, material available in permanent form from this period consists of Lawrence's six volumes, Bowler's single volume, and four volumes of Second Comptroller digests.

b. 1894–1921: Comptroller of the Treasury

In 1894, Congress enacted the so-called Dockery Act, actually a part of the general appropriation act for 1895 (ch. 174, 28 Stat. 162, 205 (July 31, 1894)), which consolidated the functions of the First and Second Comptrollers and the Commissioner of Customs into the newly created Comptroller of the Treasury. (The title was a reversion to one that had been used before 1817.)

The six auditors remained, with different titles, but their settlements no longer had to be automatically submitted to the Comptroller.

The Dockery Act included a provision requiring the Comptroller of the Treasury to render decisions upon the request of an agency head or a disbursing officer. (Certifying officers did not exist back then.) Although this was to a large extent a codification of existing practice, it gave increased significance to the availability of the decisions. Accordingly, the first Comptroller of the Treasury (Robert Bowler, who had been First Comptroller when the Dockery Act passed) initiated the practice of publishing an annual volume of decisions "of such general character as will furnish precedents for the settlements of future accounts." 1 Comp. Dec. iv (1896) (Preface).

The Decisions of the Comptroller of the Treasury series consists of 27 volumes covering the period 1894–1921. Comptroller of the Treasury decisions not included in the annual volumes exist in bound "manuscript volumes," which are now in the custody of the National Archives, and are, thus, unavailable as a practical matter.

2. GAO's Authority to Settle Accounts and Issue Decisions

When the Budget and Accounting Act, 1921, created the General Accounting Office, the offices of the Comptroller of the Treasury and the six Auditors were abolished and their functions transferred to the Comptroller General. Among these functions was the issuance of legal decisions to agency officials concerning the availability and use of appropriated funds. Thus, the decisions GAO issues today reflect the continuing evolution of a body of administrative law on federal fiscal matters dating back to the Nation's infancy.

Under the Budget and Accounting Act, the Comptroller General "shall settle all accounts of the United States Government." 31 U.S.C. § 3526(a). Often the term "settle" means "compromise," particularly when used in a litigious context. Here, however, "settle" means an administrative determination of the state of the account and the final amount due. Illinois Surety Co. v. United States ex rel. Peeler, 240 U.S. 214, 219-221 (1916). Accountable officers bear personal pecuniary liability for the loss of funds in their accounts. For example, certifying officers bear personal liability for the amount of any illegal or improper payments resulting from their certifications. 31 U.S.C. § 3528(a)(3); B-301184, Jan. 15, 2004; B-307693, Apr. 12, 2007. Therefore, when the Comptroller General settles an account, he determines the amount due to the government for any funds that have been lost. The account balance the Comptroller General certifies is conclusive on the executive branch. 31 U.S.C. § 3526(d); St. Louis, Brownsville & Mexico Railway Co. v. United States, 268 U.S. 169 (1925); 54 Comp. Gen. 921 (1975); 33 Op. Atty. Gen. 268 (1922).

Integral to the Comptroller General's duty to settle the government's accounts is his authority to issue advance decisions to disbursing officers, certifying officers, and to heads of agencies and agency components. 31 U.S.C. § 3529. Such decisions may concern either a payment the head of the agency will make, or a voucher presented to a certifying official for certification. Id. Decisions of the Comptroller General under 31 U.S.C. § 3529 bind him when he settles an account containing the payment. 31 U.S.C. § 3526(b). Therefore, "the Comptroller General in an audit of agency obligations and expenditures may not legally object to particular financial transactions that he has already decided under section 3529 are in accordance with law." B-

288266, Jan. 27, 2003. Thus, though the work of an accountable officer brings a formidable burden of personal pecuniary liability, advance decisions afford accountable officers a measure of protection and counsel.

A decision regarding an account of the government is binding on the executive branch. 31 U.S.C. § 3526(d); see also United States ex rel. Skinner & Eddy Corp. v. McCarl, 275 U.S. 1, 4 n.2 (1927); St. Louis, Brownsville & Mexico Railway Co. v. United States, 268 U.S. 169, 174 (1925); United States v. Standard Oil Co. of California, 545 F.2d 624, 637–38 (9th Cir. 1976). However, it is not binding on a private party who, if dissatisfied, retains whatever recourse to the courts he would otherwise have had. The Comptroller General has no power to enforce decisions. Ultimately, agency officials who act contrary to Comptroller General decisions may have to respond to congressional appropriations and program oversight committees.

a. Procedures

For many years the Comptroller General had authority to administratively and conclusively settle and adjust all claims against the United States. In 1995, Congress transferred a number of GAO's claims settlement duties to other agencies. However, accounts settlement authority remains vested in the Comptroller General. Though the Comptroller General no longer issues decisions regarding claims settlement, he continues to perform his statutory duty to issue decisions regarding the legal availability of appropriations. B-327146, Aug. 6, 2015.

There is no specific procedure for requesting a decision from the Comptroller General. A simple letter is usually sufficient. The request should, however, include all pertinent information or supporting material and should present any arguments the requestor wishes to have considered. GAO, Procedures and Practices for Legal Decisions and Opinions, GAO-06-1064SP (Washington, D.C.: Sept. 2006). GAO will also receive requests for decisions by email. To submit a request by email, refer to the "Appropriations Law Decisions" page of GAO's website at www.gao.gov/legal/appropriations-law-decisions/faqs.

A request for an advance decision submitted by a certifying officer will usually arise from "a voucher presented . . . for certification." 31 U.S.C. § 3529(a)(2). At one time, GAO insisted that the original voucher accompany the request and occasionally declined to render the decision f this was not done. See, e.g., 21 Comp. Gen. 1128 (1942). The requirement was eliminated in B-223608, Dec. 19, 1988:

> "Consistent with our current practice, submission of the original voucher need not accompany the request for an advance decision. Accordingly, in the future, the original voucher should be retained in the appropriate finance office. A photocopy accompanying the request for decision will be sufficient. Language to the contrary in prior decisions may be disregarded."

Even if no voucher is submitted, GAO will most likely render the decision notwithstanding the absence of a voucher if the question is of general interest and appears likely to recur. See, e.g., 55 Comp. Gen. 652 (1976); 53 Comp. Gen. 429 (1973); 53 Comp. Gen. 71 (1973); 52 Comp. Gen. 83 (1972).

Often, requests for decisions will require factual development, and GAO will contact the agency as necessary to establish and document relevant facts. It is the usual practice of GAO to obtain the legal positions and views of the agency or agencies involved in the request for a decision or opinion.

An involved party or agency may request reconsideration of a decision. The standard applied is whether the request demonstrates error of fact or law (e.g., B-184062, July 6, 1976) or presents new information not considered in the earlier decision. See B-306666.2, Mar. 20, 2009; B-271838.2, May 23, 1997. While the Comptroller General gives precedential weight to prior decisions, a decision may be modified or overruled by a subsequent decision. In overruling its decisions, GAO follows the approach summarized by the Comptroller of the Treasury in a 1902 decision:

> "I regret exceedingly the necessity of overruling decisions of this office heretofore made for the guidance of heads of departments and the protection of paying officers, and fully appreciate that certainty in decisions is greatly to be desired in order that uniformity of practice may obtain in the expenditure of the public money, but when a decision is made not only wrong in principle but harmful in its workings, my pride of decision is not so strong that when my attention is directed to such decision I will not promptly overrule it. It is a very easy thing to be consistent, that is, to insist that the horse is 16 feet high, but not so easy to get right and keep right."

8 Comp. Dec. 695, 697 (1902).

b. Matters Not Considered

There are a number of areas in which, as a matter of law or policy, the Comptroller General will generally decline to render a decision.

Effective June 30, 1996, Congress transferred claims settlement authority under 31 U.S.C. § 3302 to the Director of the Office of Management and Budget (OMB). The Director of OMB delegated claims settlement authority to the agency from whose activities the claim arose. See, e.g., B-302996, May 21, 2004 (GAO no longer has authority to settle a claim for severance pay); B-278805, July 21, 1999 (the International Trade Commission was the appropriate agency to resolve the subject claims request).

Other areas where the Comptroller General will decline to render decisions include questions where the determination of another agency is by law "final and conclusive." Examples are determinations on the merits of a claim against another agency under the Federal Tort Claims Act (28 U.S.C. § 2672) or the Military Personnel and Civilian Employees' Claims Act of 1964 (31 U.S.C. § 3721). See, e.g., B-300829, Apr. 4, 2004 (regarding the Military Personnel and Civilian Employees' Claims Act). Another example is a decision by the Secretary of Veterans Affairs on a claim for veterans' benefits (38 U.S.C. § 511). See 56 Comp. Gen. 587, 591 (1977); B-226599.2, Nov. 3, 1988 (nondecision letter).

In addition, GAO has traditionally declined to render decisions in a number of areas that are specifically within the jurisdiction of some other agency and concerning which GAO would not be in the position to make authoritative determinations, even though the other agency's determination is not statutorily "final and conclusive." Thus, GAO will not "decide" whether a given action violates a provision of the Criminal Code (title 18 of the United States Code) since this is within the jurisdiction of the Justice Department and the courts. If the use of public funds is an element of the alleged violation, the extent of GAO's involvement will be to determine if appropriated funds were in fact used and to refer the matter to the Justice Department if deemed appropriate or if requested to do so.

Other examples of areas where GAO has declined to render decisions are antitrust law, political activities of federal employees under the Hatch Act, and determinations as to what is or is not taxable under the Internal Revenue Code.

GAO avoids opining on an issue that is the subject of current litigation, unless the court expresses an interest in receiving GAO's opinion. GAO's policy with respect to issues that are the subject of agency administrative proceedings is generally similar to its litigation policy. See 69 Comp. Gen. 134 (1989) (declining to render an opinion on the propriety of an attorney's fee award being considered by the Equal Employment Opportunity Commission). See also B-259632, n.2, June 12, 1995.

Another long-standing GAO policy concerns the constitutionality of acts of Congress. As an agent of Congress, GAO recognizes that it is neither our role nor our province to opine on or adjudicate the constitutionality of duly enacted statutes. See, e.g., B-326013, Aug. 21, 2014; B-323449, Aug. 14, 2012; B-321982, Oct. 11, 2011. Such laws come to GAO with a heavy presumption in favor of their constitutionality and, like the courts, GAO will construe statutes narrowly to avoid constitutional issues.

Immigration & Naturalization Service v. St. Cyr, 533 U.S. 289, 299, n.12 (2001); B-300192, Nov. 13, 2002 (regarding a provision in the fiscal year 2003 Continuing Resolution, Pub. L. No. 107-229, § 117, 116 Stat. 1465, 1468 (Sept. 30, 2002), prohibiting the use of appropriations to acquire private sector printing and specifically prohibiting the use of appropriations to pay for printing the President's Budget other than through the Government Printing Office: "Given our authority to settle and audit the accounts of the government . . ., we will apply laws as we find them absent a controlling opinion that such laws are unconstitutional."). GAO will, however, express its opinion, upon the request of a Member or committee of Congress, on the constitutionality of a bill prior to enactment. E.g., B-360241, Mar. 18, 2003; B-228805, Sept. 28, 1987.

3. Program Evaluations and Financial Audits, Investigations, and Account Settlement

In addition to GAO's authority to settle the accounts of the United States and to issue decisions on matters involving the use of public money, Congress has also vested GAO with authority to investigate and evaluate agency activities and to audit financial transactions. GAO's audit and evaluation authority is rooted in many statutory provisions. One such provision is in the Budget and Accounting Act, 1921, and vested the Comptroller General with the authority to investigate the receipt, disbursement, and application of public funds, reporting the results to Congress; and to make investigations and reports upon the request of either house of Congress or of any congressional committee with jurisdiction over revenue, appropriations, or expenditures. He was also directed to supply such information to the President when requested by the President. The mandates in the 1921 legislation, together with a subsequent directive in the Legislative

Reorganization Act of 1946 to make expenditure analyses of executive branch agencies with reports to the cognizant congressional committees, have played a large part in preparing Congress to consider the merits of the President's annual budget submission.

The Accounting and Auditing Act of 1950 authorized the Comptroller General to audit the financial transactions of most executive, legislative, and judicial agencies; and to prescribe, in consultation with the President and the Secretary of the Treasury, accounting principles, standards, and requirements for the executive agencies suitable to their needs. In addition, the Legislative Reorganization Act of 1970 expanded the focus of GAO's audit activities to include program evaluations as well as financial audits.

In carrying out its various responsibilities to examine the financial, management, and program activities of federal agencies, and to evaluate the efficiency, effectiveness, and economy of agency operations, GAO reports to Congress both objective findings and recommendations for improvement. Recommendations are addressed to agency heads for action that the agency is authorized to take under existing law. Matters for consideration are addressed to Congress.

Under section 236 of the Legislative Reorganization Act of 1970, 31 U.S.C. § 720(b), whenever GAO issues a report that contains recommendations to the head of a federal agency, the agency must submit a written statement of the actions taken with respect to the recommendations to (1) the Senate Committee on Governmental Affairs and the House Committee on Government Reform, not later than 60 days after the date of the report and (2) the Senate and House Appropriations Committees in connection with the agency's first request for appropriations submitted more than 60 days after the date of the report. As GAO pointed out in a letter to a private inquirer (B-207783, Apr. 1, 1983, nondecision letter), the law does not require the agency to comply with the recommendation, merely to report on the "actions taken," which can range from full compliance to zero. The theory is that, if the agency disagrees with the GAO recommendation, Congress will have both positions so that it can then take whatever action it might deem appropriate.

The term "agency" for purposes of 31 U.S.C. § 720 is broadly defined to include any department, agency, or instrumentality of the U.S. government, including wholly owned but not mixed-ownership government corporations, or the District of Columbia government. 31 U.S.C. § 720(a). See also B-114831-O.M., July 28, 1975.

4. Publication of Decisions

Between July 1921 and September 1994, decisions that the General Counsel determined had wide applicability were published annually in hardbound volumes entitled Decisions of the Comptroller General. These decisions are cited by volume, page number on which the decision begins, and the year. For example: 31 Comp. Gen. 350 (1952). All other decisions were filed at GAO and available publicly upon request. There is no legal distinction between a decision published in Decisions of the Comptroller General and an unpublished decision. 28 Comp. Gen. 69, 71 (1948).

Many of GAO's decisions (published and unpublished) prior to 1994, and all decisions since 1994, are available on the GAO internet site, www.gao.gov. Unpublished decisions prior to 1994, and all subsequent decisions, are cited by file number and date. For example: B-193282,

Dec. 21, 1978. The present file numbering system ("B-numbers") has been in use since January 1939. From 1924 through 1938, file numbers had an "A" prefix. Some of the computerized legal research systems (e.g., Lexis, Westlaw) carry Comptroller General decisions. GAO's Office of General Counsel will assist researchers who have difficulty locating a copy of GAO decisions.

5. Other GAO Publications

GAO expresses its positions in many forms. Most of the GAO materials cited in this publication are decisions of the Comptroller General. While these constitute the most significant body of GAO positions on legal issues, the editors have also included, as appropriate, citations to the following items:

Legal opinions to Congress—GAO prepares legal opinions at the request of congressional committees or individual Members of Congress. Congressional opinions are prepared in letter rather than decision format, but have the same weight and effect as decision. The citation form is identical to that for decision. As a practical matter, except where specifically identified in the text, the reader will not be able to distinguish between a decision and a congressional opinion based on the form of the citation.

Office memoranda—Legal questions are frequently presented by other divisions or offices within GAO. The response is in the form of an internal memorandum, formerly signed by the Comptroller General, but now, for the most part, signed by the General Counsel or someone on the General Counsel's staff. The citation is the same as for a B-numbered decision, except that the suffix "O.M." (Office Memorandum) has traditionally been added. More recent material tends to omit the suffix, in which case our practice in this publication is to identify the citation as a memorandum to avoid confusion with decisions. Office memoranda are usually not cited in a decision. Technically, an office memorandum is not a decision of the Comptroller General as provided in 31 U.S.C. § 3529, does not have the same legal or precedential effect, and should never be cited as a decision. Instead, office memoranda represent the views of the General Counsel or members of the General Counsel's staff. Notwithstanding these limitations, we have included selected citations to GAO office memoranda, particularly where they provide guidance in the absence of formal decisions on a given point, contain useful research or discussion, or have subsequently been followed in practice.

Audit reports—A GAO audit report is cited by its title, date of issuance, and a numerical designation. Up to the mid-1970s, the same file numbering system was used as in decisions ("B-numbers"). From the mid-1970s until October 2000, the designation for an audit report consisted of both a "B-number" and an identifier consisting of the initials of the issuing division, the fiscal year, and the report number. GAO no longer assigns a "B-number" to audit reports; now the designation includes only the fiscal year and the report number.

Several audit reports are cited throughout this publication either as authority for some legal proposition or to provide sources of additional information to supplement the discussion in the text. To prevent confusion stemming from different citation formats used over the years, our practice in this publication is to always identify an audit report as a "GAO report" in the text, in addition to the citation.

All new GAO reports are published on GAO's website at www.gao.gov.

In addition to the reports themselves, GAO publishes a number of pamphlets and other documents relating to its audit function. See, e.g., GAO, Standards for Internal Control in the Federal Government, GAO-14-704G (Washington, D.C.: Sept. 2014) (known as the "Green Book"); GAO, Government Auditing Standards, GAO-12-331G (Washington, D.C.: Dec. 1, 2011) (known as the "Yellow Book"). References to any of these will be fully described in the text where they occur.

Nondecision letters—On occasion, GAO may issue letters, signed by some subordinate official on the General Counsel's staff, usually to an individual or organization who has requested information or who has requested a legal opinion, but is not entitled by law to a formal decision. Their purpose is basically to convey information rather than resolve a legal issue. Several of these are cited in this publication, either because they offer a particularly clear statement of some policy or position, or to supplement the material found in the decision. Each is identified parenthetically. The citation form is otherwise identical to an unpublished decision. As with the office memoranda, these are not decisions of the Comptroller General and do not have the same legal or precedential effect.

Circular letters—A circular letter is a letter addressed simply to the "Heads of Federal Departments and Agencies" or to "Federal Certifying and Disbursing Officers." Circular letters, although not common, are used for a variety of purposes and may emanate from a particular division within GAO or directly from the Comptroller General. Circular letters that announce significant changes in pertinent legal requirements or GAO audit policy or procedures are occasionally cited in this publication. They are identified as such and often, but not always, bear file designations similar to unpublished decision. See B-275605, May 17, 1997 (announcing changes resulting from the transfer of claims settlement and other related functions).

GAO's Policy and Procedures Manual for Guidance of Federal Agencies—Originally published in 1957 as a large loose-leaf volume, this was, for many years, the official medium through which the Comptroller General issued accounting principles and standards and related material for the development of accounting systems and internal auditing programs, uniform procedures, and regulations governing GAO's relationship with other federal agencies and private parties. The title of particular relevance for federal appropriations law is Title 7, "Fiscal Procedures." Researchers can access Title 7 on GAO's website, www.gao.gov/products/149099.

6. Standard Budgetary Terms

A Glossary of Terms Used in the Federal Budget Process, GAO-05-734SP (Washington, D.C.: Sept. 2005), contains standard definitions of fiscal and budgetary terms. As required by law, GAO publishes this guide in cooperation with the Secretary of the Treasury and the Directors of the Office of Management and Budget and the Congressional Budget Office. 31 U.S.C. § 1112(c). It is updated from time to time. Definitions used throughout Principles of Federal Appropriations Law are based on the Glossary unless otherwise noted.

7. Informal Technical Assistance

GAO also offers informal technical assistance regarding matters of appropriations law. Submit requests for assistance to redbook@gao.gov. Informal opinions expressed by GAO officers or employees may not represent the views of the Comptroller General or GAO and are in no way controlling on any subsequent formal or official determinations by the Comptroller General. 56 Comp. Gen. 768, 773–74 (1977); 31 Comp. Gen. 613 (1952); 29 Comp. Gen. 335 (1950); 12 Comp. Gen. 207 (1932); 4 Comp. Gen. 1024 (1925).

C. An Analytical Framework

"I'm very glad," said Pooh happily, "that I thought of giving you a Useful Pot to put things in."

A.A. Milne, Winnie-The-Pooh, Chapter 6.

This publication contains an analytical framework that the reader can use to analyze most appropriations law problems. Questions in appropriations law are easier to resolve after one spots the key issues and classifies the problem into the appropriate aspect of an overarching framework.

Every appropriation contains limitations upon its availability; that is, federal agencies may spend appropriated amounts only in accordance with the conditions that Congress has placed upon the appropriation. These conditions may be classified in three ways: purpose, time, and amount. For an example, examine the following appropriation for the Marshals Service for fiscal year 2015:

"For necessary expenses of the United States Marshals Service, $1,195,000,000, of which not to exceed $6,000 shall be available for official reception and representation expenses, and not to exceed $15,000,000 shall remain available until expended."

This language specifies purpose limitations: about $1.2 billion is available for the "necessary expenses" of the Marshals Service, while no more than $6,000 of that amount is available "for official reception and representation expenses." This language places limits upon the permissible objects for which these funds may be used: the money is available only for the necessary expenses of the Marshals Service and not for, say, the Internal Revenue Service.

The language explicitly provides that $15 million is "available until expended," which is a time limitation—or, in this case, the expression of an indefinite time limitation, as the $15 million is available for an unlimited period. Most appropriations, unlike the $15 million described here, are available only for limited periods of time. Indeed, though $15 million of this amount is available without time limitation, the balance of the $1.2 billion appropriation is available for only one fiscal year. We will also discuss various facets of a time analysis, such as the fancifully named, but conceptually simple, principle known as the bona fide needs rule.

The U.S. Marshals appropriation contains several limitations as to amount: for example, it appropriates a total of about $1.2 billion, but no more than $6,000 for the particular purpose of official reception and representation expenses.

D. Statutory Interpretation: Determining Congressional Intent

"[T]his is a case for applying the canon of construction of the wag who said, when the legislative history is doubtful, go to the statute."

Greenwood v. United States, 350 U.S. 366, 374 (1956) (Frankfurter, J.).

1. The Goal of Statutory Construction

As we have noted elsewhere, an appropriation can be made only by means of a statute. In addition to providing funds, the typical appropriation act includes a variety of general provisions. Anyone who works with appropriations matters will also have frequent need to consult authorizing and program legislation. It should thus be apparent that the interpretation of statutes is of critical importance to appropriations law.

The objective of this section is to provide a brief overview, designed primarily for those who do not work extensively with legislative materials. The cases we cite are but a sampling, selected for illustrative purposes or for a particularly good judicial statement of a point. The literature in the area is voluminous, and readers who need more than we provide here are encouraged to consult one of the established treatises such as Sutherland Statutes and Statutory Construction (hereafter "Sutherland").

The goal of statutory construction is simply stated: to determine and give effect to the intent of the enacting legislature. Philbrook v. Glodgett, 421 U.S. 707, 713 (1975); United States v. American Trucking Ass'ns, Inc., 310 U.S. 534, 542 (1940); 55 Comp. Gen. 307, 317 (1975); 38 Comp. Gen. 229 (1958). While the goal may be simple, the means of achieving it are complex and often controversial. The primary vehicle for determining legislative intent is the language of the statute itself. There is an established body of principles, known as "canons" of construction, that are designed to aid in arriving at the best interpretation of statutory language. The statute's legislative history also is usually consulted to aid in the effort.

At this point, it is important to recognize that the concept of "legislative intent" is in many cases a fiction. Where not clear from the statutory language itself, it is often impossible to ascribe an intent to Congress as a whole. As we will note later, a committee report represents the views of that committee. Statements by an individual legislator represent the views of that individual. Either may, but do not necessarily or inherently, reflect a broader congressional perception.

Even interpretive aids that rely on the statutory language itself do not provide hard and fast rules that can pinpoint congressional intent with scientific precision. One problem is that, more often than not, a statute has no obvious meaning that precisely answers a particular issue in dispute before the courts, the Comptroller General, or another decision maker. If the answers were that obvious, most of the cases discussed in this section would never have arisen.

The reality is that there probably is (and was) no actual "congressional intent" with respect to most specific issues that find their way to the courts, GAO, or other forums. In all likelihood, Congress did not affirmatively consider these specific issues for purposes of forming an intent about them. Necessarily, Congress writes laws in fairly general terms that convey broad concepts, principles, and policies. It leaves administering agencies and courts to fill in the gaps.

Indeed, Congress sometimes deliberately leaves issues ambiguous because it lacks a sufficient consensus to resolve them in the law.

To point out the challenges in statutory interpretation, however, is by no means to denigrate the process. Applying the complex maze of interpretive aids, imperfect as they may be, serves the essential purpose of providing a common basis for problem solving and determining what the law is.

This in turn is important for two reasons. First, everyone has surely heard the familiar statement that our government is a government of laws and not of men. This means that you have a right to have your conduct governed and judged in accordance with identifiable principles and standards, not by the whim of the decision maker. The law should be reasonably predictable. A lawyer's advice that a proposed action is or is not permissible amounts to a reasoned and informed judgment as to what a court is likely to do if the action is challenged. While this can never be an absolute guarantee, it once again must be based on identifiable principles and standards. Conceding its weaknesses, the law of statutory construction represents an organized approach for doing this.

Second, predictability is important in the enactment of statutes as well. Congress legislates against the background of the rules and principles that make up the law of statutory construction, and it must be able to anticipate how the courts will apply them in interpreting the statutes it enacts.

2. The "Plain Meaning" Rule

"The Court's task is to construe not English but congressional English."

Commissioner of Internal Revenue v. Acker, 361 U.S. 87, 95 (1959) (Frankfurter, J., dissenting).

By far the most important rule of statutory construction is this: You start with the language of the statute. Countless Supreme Court decisions reiterate this rule. E.g., Sebelius v. Cloer, ___ U.S. ___, 133 S. Ct. 1886, 1893 (2013); Carcieri v. Salazar, 555 U.S. 379 (2009); BedRoc Limited, LLC v. United States, 541 U.S. 176 (2004); Lamie v. United States Trustee, 540 U.S. 526 (2004); Hartford Underwriters Insurance Co. v. Union Planters Bank, N.A., 530 U.S. 1 (2000); Robinson v. Shell Oil Co., 519 U.S. 337 (1997); Connecticut National Bank v. Germain, 503 U.S. 249 (1992); and Mallard v. United States District Court for the Southern District of Iowa, 490 U.S. 296, 300 (1989). The primary vehicle for Congress to express its intent is the words it enacts into law. As stated in an early Supreme Court decision:

> "The law as it passed is the will of the majority of both houses, and the only mode in which that will is spoken is in the act itself; and we must gather their intention from the language there used . . . ."

Aldridge v. Williams, 44 U.S. (3 How.) 9, 24 (1845). A somewhat better known statement is from United States v. American Trucking Ass'ns, 310 U.S. 534, 543 (1940):

> "There is, of course, no more persuasive evidence of the purpose of a statute than the words by which the legislature undertook to give expression to its wishes."

If the meaning is clear from the language of the statute, there is no need to resort to legislative history or any other extraneous source. As the Supreme Court observed in Connecticut National Bank v. Germain:

> "[I]n interpreting a statute a court should always turn first to one, cardinal canon before all others. We have stated time and again that courts must presume that a legislature says in a statute what it means and means in a statute what it says there. . . . When the words of a statute are unambiguous, then, this first canon is also the last: judicial inquiry is complete."

503 U.S. at 253–254. See also Hartford Underwriters Insurance Co., 530 U.S. 1; Robinson v. Shell Oil Co., 519 U.S. 337 (1997); Mallard, 490 U.S. 296; United States v. Ron Pair Enterprises, Inc., 489 U.S. 235, 241 (1989); Tennessee Valley Authority v. Hill, 437 U.S. 153, 184 n.29 (1978); B-287158, Oct. 10, 2002; B-290021, July 15, 2002; B-288173, June 13, 2002; B-288658, Nov. 30, 2001; 56 Comp. Gen. 943 (1977).

This is the so-called "plain meaning" rule. If the meaning is "plain," that's the end of the inquiry and you apply that meaning. The unanimous opinion in Robinson v. Shell Oil Co. stated the rule as follows:

> "Our first step in interpreting a statute is to determine whether the language at issue has a plain and unambiguous meaning with regard to the particular dispute in the case. Our inquiry must cease if the statutory language and 'the statutory scheme is coherent and consistent.'. . .
>
> "The plainness or ambiguity of statutory language is determined by reference to the language itself, the specific context in which that language is used, and the broader context of the statute as a whole."

519 U.S. at 340–34.

The plain meaning rule thus embodies the universal view that interpretations of a statute should be anchored in, and flow from, the statute's text. Its application to a particular statutory provision turns on subjective judgments over which reasonable and intelligent people will differ.

An example of this is Smith v. United States, 508 U.S. 223 (1993), in which the Justices agreed that the case should be resolved on the basis of the statute's plain meaning, but reached sharply divergent conclusions as to what that plain meaning was. In Smith, the defendant had traded his gun for illegal drugs. He was convicted under a statute that provided enhanced penalties for the "use" of a firearm "during and in relation to . . . [a] drug trafficking crime." The majority affirmed his conviction, reasoning that exchanging a firearm for drugs constituted a "use" of the firearm within the plain meaning of the statute—that is, use in the sense of employ. Three Justices dissented, contending vehemently that the plain meaning of the statute covered only the use of a firearm for its intended purpose as a weapon.

3. The Limits of Literalism: Errors in Statutes and "Absurd Consequences"

"There is no surer way to misread any document than to read it literally."

Even the strictest adherence to the plain meaning rule does not justify application of the literal terms of a statute in all cases. There are two well-established exceptions. The first is that statutory language will not be enforced literally when that language is the product of an obvious drafting error. In such cases, courts (and other decision makers) will, in effect, conform the statute to the obvious intent.

The second exception is the frequently cited canon of construction that statutory language will not be interpreted literally if doing so would produce an "absurd consequence" or "absurd result," that is, one that the legislature, presumably, could not have intended.

a. Errors in Statutes

(1) Drafting errors

A statute may occasionally contain what is clearly a technical or typographical error which, if read literally, could alter the meaning of the statute or render execution effectively impossible. In such a case, if the legislative intent is clear, the intent will be given effect over the erroneous language. For example, one ruling turned on the effect of a parenthetical reference to the Tax Code that had been included in the Indian Gaming Regulatory Act. Chickasaw Nation v. United States, 534 U.S. 84 (2001). After examining the structure and language of the Indian Gaming Regulatory Act as a whole, as well as its legislative history, the Court concluded that the parenthetical reference was "simply a drafting mistake"—specifically, the failure to delete a cross-reference from an earlier version of the bill—and declined to give it any effect. Chickasaw Nation, 534 U.S. at 91.

In a number of other cases, courts have followed the same approach by correcting obvious printing or typographical errors. See United States National Bank of Oregon v. Independent Insurance Agents of America, Inc., 508 U.S. 439 (1993); Ronson Patents Corp. v. Sparklets Devices, Inc., 102 F. Supp. 123 (E.D. Mo. 1951).

Comptroller General decisions have likewise repaired obvious drafting errors. In one situation, a supplemental appropriation act provided funds to pay certain claims and judgments as set forth in Senate Document 94-163. Examination of the documents made it clear that the reference should have been to Senate Document 94-164, as Senate Document 94-163 concerned a wholly unrelated subject. The manifest congressional intent was held controlling, and the appropriation was available to pay the items specified in Senate Document 94-164. B-158642-O.M., June 8, 1976. The same principle had been applied in a very early decision in which an 1894 appropriation provided funds for certain payments in connection with an election held on "November fifth," 1890. The election had in fact been held on November 4. Recognizing the "evident intention of Congress," the decision held that the appropriation was available to make the specified payments. 1 Comp. Dec. 1 (1894). See also 11 Comp. Dec. 719 (1905); 8 Comp. Dec. 205 (1901); 1 Comp. Dec. 316 (1895).

The Justice Department's Office of Legal Counsel applied Comptroller General decisions in an opinion dated May 21, 1996, that addressed an obvious problem with the application of an appropriations act. The act required the United States Information Agency to move an office to south Florida "not later than April 1, 1996," and made funds available for that purpose. However, the act was not signed into law until April 26, 1996. Recognizing that the act could not be implemented as written, the opinion concluded that the funds remained available to finance the move after April 1.

One Supreme Court decision discussed drafting errors and what to do about them. Lamie v. United States Trustee, 540 U.S. 526 (2004). The Court found an "apparent legislative drafting error" in a 1994 statute. Id. at 530. Nevertheless, the Court held that the amended language must be applied according to its plain terms. While the Court acknowledged that the amended statute was awkward and ungrammatical, and that a literal reading rendered some words superfluous and could produce harsh results, none of these defects made the language ambiguous. Id. at 534–36. The Court determined that these flaws did not "lead to absurd results requiring us to treat the text as if it were ambiguous." Id. at 536. The Court also drew a distinction between construing a statute in a way that, in effect, added missing words as opposed to ignoring words that might have been included by mistake. Id. at 538.

(2) Error in amount appropriated

In one case the Comptroller General did not repair an apparent drafting error. A 1979 appropriation act contained an appropriation of $36 million for the Inspector General of the Department of Health, Education, and Welfare. The bills, as passed by both Houses, and the various committee reports specified an appropriation of only $35 million. While it seemed apparent that the $36 million was the result of a typographical error, it was held that the language of the enrolled act signed by the President must control and that the full $36 million had been appropriated. The Comptroller General did, however, inform the Appropriations Committees. 58 Comp. Gen. 358 (1979). See also 2 Comp. Dec. 629 (1896); 1 Bowler, First Comp. Dec. 114 (1894).

However, if the amount appropriated is a total derived from adding up specific sums enumerated in the appropriation act, then the amount appropriated will be the amount obtained by the correct addition, notwithstanding the specification of an erroneous total in the appropriation act. 31 U.S.C. § 1302; 2 Comp. Gen. 592 (1923).

b. Avoiding "Absurd Consequences"

Departures from strict adherence to the statutory text go beyond cases involving drafting and typographical errors. In fact, it is more common to find cases in which the courts do not question that Congress meant to choose the words it did, but conclude that it could not have meant them to apply literally in a particular context. The generally accepted principle here is that the literal language of a statute will not be followed if it would produce a result demonstrably inconsistent with clearly expressed congressional intent.

A case frequently cited for this proposition is Church of the Holy Trinity v. United States, 143 U.S. 457 (1892), which gives several interesting examples. In one of those examples, the Court held that a statute making it a criminal offense to knowingly and willfully obstruct or retard a driver or carrier of the mails did not apply to a sheriff arresting a mail carrier who had been indicted for murder. United States v. Kirby, 74 U.S. (7 Wall.) 482 (1868). Another is an old English ruling that a statute making it a felony to break out of jail did not apply to a prisoner who broke out because the jail was on fire. Holy Trinity, 143 U.S. at 460–61. An example from early administrative decisions is 24 Comp. Dec. 775 (1918), holding that an appropriation for "messenger boys" was available to hire "messenger girls."

In cases decided after Holy Trinity, the Court has emphasized that departures from the plain meaning rule are justified only in "rare and exceptional circumstances," such as the illustrations used in Holy Trinity. Crooks v. Harrelson, 282 U.S. 55, 60 (1930). See also United States v. Ron Pair Enterprises, Inc., 489 U.S. 235, 242 (1989); Griffin v. Oceanic Contractors, Inc., 458 U.S. 564, 571 (1982); Tennessee Valley Authority v. Hill, 437 U.S. 153, 187 n.33 (1978) (citing Crooks v. Harrelson with approval; hereafter TVA v. Hill).

This exception to the plain meaning rule is also sometimes phrased in terms of avoiding absurd consequences. E.g., United States v. Ryan, 284 U.S. 167, 175 (1931). As the dissenting opinion in TVA v. Hill points out (437 U.S. at 204 n.14), there is a bit of confusion in this respect in that Crooks—again, cited with approval by the majority in TVA v. Hill—explicitly states that avoiding absurd consequences is not enough, although the Court has used the absurd consequence formulation in post-Crooks cases such as Ryan. In any event, as a comparison of the majority and dissenting opinions in TVA v. Hill will demonstrate, the absurd consequences test is not always easy to apply in that what strikes one person as absurd may be good law to another.

The case of United States v. Singleton, 144 F.3d 1343 (10th Cir. 1998), vacated on reh'g en banc, 165 F.3d 1297, cert. denied, 527 U.S. 1024 (1999), provides another illustration of this point. Ms. Singleton was convicted of various crimes following testimony against her by a witness who had received a plea bargain in exchange for his testimony. She maintained that her conviction was tainted because the plea bargain constituted a violation of 18 U.S.C. § 201(c)(2), which provides in part:

> "Whoever . . . directly or indirectly . . . promises anything of value to any person, . . . because of the testimony under oath or affirmation given or to be given by such person as a witness upon trial . . . before any court . . . shall be fined under this title or imprisoned for not more than two years, or both."

A three judge panel of the Tenth Circuit agreed and reversed her conviction. They held that the word "whoever" by its plain terms applied to the federal prosecutor and, just as plainly, the plea bargain promised something of value because of testimony to be given as a witness upon trial.

The full Tenth Circuit vacated the panel's ruling and reinstated the conviction. The majority held that the panel's construction of the statute was "patently absurd" and contradicted long-standing prosecutorial practice. 165 F.3d at 1300. The three original panel members remained unconvinced and dissented. Far from being "absurd," they viewed their construction as a "straight-forward interpretation" of the statute that honored important constitutional values. One such value, they said, was "the proper role of the judiciary as the law-interpreting, rather than lawmaking, branch of the federal government." Id. at 1309.

Recent Supreme Court decisions likewise reinforce the need for caution when it comes to departing from statutory language on the basis of its apparent "absurd consequences." See Baker Botts L.L.P. v. ASARCO LLC, ___ U.S. ___, 135 S. Ct. 2158, 2169 (2015) and Lamie v. United States Trustee, 540 U.S. 526, 537–38 (2004) ("harsh" consequences are not the equivalent of absurd consequences); Barnhart v. Thomas, 540 U.S. 20, 28–29 (2003) ("undesirable" consequences are not the equivalent of absurd consequences).

While the absurd consequences rule must be invoked with care, it does have useful applications. The Comptroller General invoked this rule in holding that an appropriation act proviso requiring competition in the award of certain grants did not apply to community development block grants, which were allocated by a statutory formula. B-285794, Dec. 5, 2000 ("Without an affirmative expression of such intent, we are unwilling to read the language of the questioned proviso in a way that would clearly produce unreasonable and impractical consequences."). See also B-260759, May 2, 1995 (rejecting a literal reading of a statutory provision that would defeat its purpose and produce anomalous results).

4. Statutory Aids to Construction

The remainder of this section discusses various sources to assist in determining the meaning of statutory language, plain or otherwise. We start with sources that are contained in the statute being construed or in other statutes that provide interpretive guidance for general application. The main advantage of these statutory aids is that, as laws themselves, they carry authoritative weight. Their main disadvantage is that, while useful on occasion, they have limited scope and address relatively few issues of interpretation.

a. Definitions, Effective Dates, and Severability Clauses

Statutes frequently contain their own set of definitions for terms that they use. These definitions take precedence over other sources to the extent that they apply.

A statute may also contain an effective date provision that sets forth a date (or dates) when it will become operative. These provisions are most frequently used when Congress intends to delay or phase in the effectiveness of a statute in whole or in part. The general rule, even absent an effective date provision, is that statutes take effect on the date of their enactment and apply prospectively. See, e.g., B-300866, May 30, 2003, and authorities cited. Therefore, effective date provisions are unnecessary if the normal rule is intended. (Later we will discuss more complicated issues concerning the retroactive application of statutes.)

Another provision sometimes included is a so-called "severability" clause. The purpose of this provision is to set forth congressional intent in the unhappy event that part of a statute is held to be unconstitutional. The clause states whether or not the remainder of the statute should be "severed" from the unconstitutional part and continue to be operative. Again, the general rule is that statutes will be considered severable absent a provision to the contrary or some other clear indication of congressional intent that the whole statute should fall if part of it is declared unconstitutional. Thus, the clause is unnecessary in the usual case. However, the absence of a severability clause will not create a presumption against severability. See, e.g., New York v. United States, 505 U.S. 144, 186–187 (1992).

b. The Dictionary Act

Chapter 1 of title 1 of the United States Code, §§ 1–8, commonly known as the "Dictionary Act," provides certain rules of construction and definitions that apply generally to federal statutes. For example, section 1 provides in part:

> "In determining the meaning of any Act of Congress, unless the context indicates otherwise—

* * * * *

"the words 'person' and 'whoever' include corporations, companies, associations, firms, partnerships, societies, and joint stock companies, as well as individuals . . . ."

Occasionally, the courts use the Dictionary Act to assist in resolving questions of interpretation. E.g., Burwell v. Hobby Lobby, ___ U.S. ___, 134 S. Ct. 2751, 2768 (2014) (absent a specific statutory provision to the contrary, the Dictionary Act definition of "persons" includes a corporation); Carr v. United States, 560 U.S. 438, 448 (2010) (Dictionary Act's provision that statutory "words used in the present tense include the future as well as the present," 1 U.S.C. § 1, interpreted to mean that the present tense generally does not include the past tense). Courts also hold on occasion that the Dictionary Act does not apply. See Rowland v. California Men's Colony, 506 U.S. 194 (1993) (context refutes application of the title 1, United States Code, definition of "person").

c. Effect of Codification

Positive law codification is the process of Congress enacting, one title at a time, a revision and restatement of the general laws of the United States. 2 U.S.C. § 285b(1); B-324857, Aug. 6, 2015. Positive law codification is meant to "remove ambiguities, contradictions, and other imperfections both of substance and of form," while "conform[ing] to the understood policy, intent, and purpose of the Congress in the original enactments." 2 U.S.C. § 285(b)(1). Codification acts typically delete obsolete provisions and make other technical and clarifying changes to the statutes they codify. Codification acts usually include language stating that they should not be construed as making substantive changes in the laws they replace. See, e.g., Pub. L. No. 97-258, § 4(a), 96 Stat. 877, 1067 (1982) (codifying title 31 of the United States Code). See also Scheidler v. National Organization for Women, 547 U.S. 9 (2006); 69 Comp. Gen. 691 (1990).

A title of the United States Code that has been enacted into positive law is itself legal evidence of the law. 1 U.S.C. § 204(a). In contrast, language appearing in a non-positive law title in the United States Code is only prima facie evidence of the wording of the law, and may be rebutted by a showing that the text of the underlying provision differs. B-324857; B-323357, July 11, 2012.

5. Canons of Statutory Construction

As discussed previously, under the plain meaning rule—the overriding principle of statutory construction—the meaning of a statute must be anchored in its text. Over the years, courts have developed a host of conventions or guidelines for ascertaining the meaning of statutory text that are usually referred to as canons of construction. They range from broad principles that apply in virtually every case (such as the canon that statutes are construed as a whole) to narrow rules that apply in limited contexts.

Like all other aids to construing statutes, the canons represent rules of thumb that are often useful but do not lend themselves to mechanistic application or slavish adherence. As the Supreme Court observed:

"[C]anons are not mandatory rules. They are guides that need not be conclusive. . . . They are designed to help judges determine the Legislature's intent as embodied in particular statutory language. And other circumstances evidencing congressional intent can overcome their force."

Chickasaw Nation v. United States, 534 U.S. 84, 94 (2001).

One problem with the canons is that they often appear to contradict each other. In a frequently cited law review article, Professor Karl Llewellyn presented an analysis demonstrating that for many canons, there was an offsetting canon to the opposite effect.

Recognizing their limitations, this section will briefly describe some of the more frequently invoked canons.

a. Construe the Statute as a Whole

We start with one canon that virtually always applies and is rarely if ever contradicted. As Sutherland puts it:

"A statute is passed as a whole and not in parts or sections and is animated by one general purpose and intent. Consequently, each part or section should be construed in connection with every other part or section so as to produce a harmonious whole."

2A Sutherland, Statutes and Statutory Construction § 45:5 at 204 (7th ed. 2014)

Like all other courts, the Supreme Court follows this venerable canon. E.g., King v. Burwell, ___ U.S. ___, 135 S. Ct. 2480, 2493 (2015) (a "provision that may seem ambiguous in isolation is often clarified by the remainder of the statutory scheme") (internal quotation marks omitted). See also Hibbs v. Winn, 542 U.S. 88, 101 (2004) (courts should construe a statute so that "effect is given to all its provisions, so that no part will be inoperative or superfluous, void or insignificant"); General Dynamics Land Systems, Inc. v. Cline, 540 U.S. 581, 598 (2004) (courts should not ignore "the cardinal rule that statutory language must be read in context since a phrase gathers meaning from the words around it"); B-321685, Mar. 14, 2011, at 4 ("[t]he Supreme Court has indicated that the meaning of a statute is to be determined not just 'by reference to the language itself', but also by reference to 'the specific context in which that language is used and the broader context of the statute as a whole'").

The Court once elaborated on this canon, noting as well that the "holistic" approach may embrace more than a single statute:

"[A] reviewing court should not confine itself to examining a particular statutory provision in isolation. The meaning—or ambiguity—of certain words or phrases may only become evident when placed in context. . . . It is a fundamental canon of statutory construction that the words of a statute must be read in their context and with a view to their place in the overall statutory scheme. . . . A court must therefore interpret the statute as a symmetrical and coherent regulatory scheme, . . . and fit, if possible, all parts into an harmonious whole. . . . Similarly, the meaning of one statute may be affected by other Acts, particularly where Congress has spoken subsequently and more specifically to the topic at hand."

FDA v. Brown & Williamson Tobacco, 529 U.S. 120,132–133 (2000).

Comptroller General decisions also follow this canon:

> "In interpreting provisions of a statute, we follow the settled rule of statutory construction that provisions with unambiguous language and specific directions may not be construed in any manner that will alter or extend their plain meaning. . . . However, if giving effect to the plain meaning of words in a statute leads to an absurd result which is clearly unintended and at variance with the policy of the legislation as a whole, the purpose of the statute rather than its literal words will be followed. . . . Consequently, statutory phrases and individual words cannot be viewed in isolation."

B-287158, Oct. 10, 2002. See also B-318897, Mar. 18, 2010.

The following decisions illustrate applications of the "whole statute" rule:

- Reading the context and purpose of the fiscal year 2013 continuing resolution as a whole, GAO determined that a provision in a fiscal year 2012 appropriation act that required the U.S. Postal Service to continue six-day delivery and rural delivery of mail carried forward into fiscal year 2013. Although the provision was an operational directive, GAO saw no language in the fiscal year 2013 continuing resolution to indicate that Congress did not expect the provision to continue to apply during the continuing resolution. B-324481, Mar. 21, 2013.

- Reading the Homeland Security Act as a whole, GAO construed particular reorganization and congressional notification provisions as a limitation on any general or inherent authority of the Secretary to reorganize the Department of Homeland Security that may otherwise be inferred from other sections of the Act. B-316533, July 31, 2008.

- Despite use of the phrase "notwithstanding any other provision of law" in a provision of an appropriation act, nothing in the statute read as a whole or its legislative history suggested an intended waiver of the Antideficiency Act. B-303961, Dec. 6, 2004; see also B-290125.2, B-290125.3, Dec. 18, 2002 (redacted) (viewed in isolation, the phrase "notwithstanding any other provision of law" might be read as exempting a procurement from GAO's bid protest jurisdiction under the Competition in Contracting Act; however, when the statute is read as a whole, as it must be, it does not exempt the procurement from the Act).

- When read as a whole, the Emergency Steel Loan Guarantee Act of 1999 clearly appropriated loan guarantee programs funds to the Loan Guarantee Board and not the Department of Commerce. B-302335, Jan. 15, 2004.

b. Give Effect to All the Language: No "Surplusage"

Closely related to the "whole statute" canon is the canon that all words of a statute should be given effect, if possible. The theory is that all of the words have meaning since Congress does not include unnecessary language, or "surplusage."

"hereafter"
long term restriction.

The courts and the Comptroller General regularly invoke the "no surplusage" canon. Some examples follow:

- "The rule against superfluities complements the principle that courts are to interpret the words of a statute in context." Hibbs v. Winn, 542 U.S. 88, 101 (2004); see also Corley v. United States, 556 U.S. 303, 314 (2009).

- A statute should be construed so that, "if it can be prevented, no clause, sentence, or word shall be superfluous, void, or insignificant." Alaska Department of Environmental Conservation v. EPA, 540 U.S. 461, 489 n.13 (2004).

- Words in a statute will not be treated as "utterly without effect" even if the consequence of giving them effect is to render the statute unconstitutional. Plaut v. Spendthrift Farm, Inc., 514 U.S. 211, 216 (1995).

- The Social Security Act requires the Social Security Administration to calculate employee wage data "in accordance with such reports" of wages filed by employers with the Internal Revenue Service (IRS). The "such reports" language cannot be read as referring only to a particular report that the IRS no longer requires since this would render the language meaningless, contrary to established maxims of statutory construction. B-261522, Sept. 29, 1995.

- The no surplusage canon applies with even greater weight when the arguably surplus words are part of the elements of a crime. In this case, the Court declined to treat as surplusage the word "willfully" in a statute that subjected to criminal penalties anyone willfully violating certain prohibitions. Ratzlaf v. United States, 510 U.S. 135, 140–141 (1994).

- Appropriation act language stating that none of the funds provided in this or any other act shall hereafter be used for certain purposes constitutes permanent legislation. The argument that the word hereafter should be construed only to mean that the provision took effect on the date of its enactment is unpersuasive. Since statutes generally take effect on their date of enactment, this construction would inappropriately render the word hereafter superfluous. 70 Comp. Gen. 351 (1991).

Although frequently invoked, the no surplusage canon is less absolute than the "whole statute" canon. One important caveat, previously discussed, is that words in a statute will be treated as surplus and disregarded if they were included in error:

"The canon requiring a court to give effect to each word 'if possible' is sometimes offset by the canon that permits a court to reject words 'as surplusage' if 'inadvertently inserted or if repugnant to the rest of the statute . . . .'"

Chickasaw Nation v. United States, 534 U.S. 84, 94 (2001).

The Court also observed that the canon of avoiding surplusage will not be invoked to create ambiguity in a statute that has a plain meaning if the language in question is disregarded. Lamie

v. United States Trustee, 540 U.S. 526, 536 (2004). The rule "applies only if verbosity and prolixity can be eliminated by giving the offending passage, or the remainder of the text, a competing interpretation." Bruesewitz v. Wyeth LLC, 562 U.S. 223 (2011).

c. Apply the Common Meaning of Words

When words used in a statute are not specifically defined, they are generally given their plain or ordinary meaning rather than some obscure usage. E.g., Sebelius v. Cloer, ___ U.S. ___, 133 S. Ct. 1886, 1893 (2013); Carcieri v. Salazar, 555 U.S. 379 (2009); Engine Manufacturers Ass'n v. South Coast Air Quality Management District, 541 U.S. 246 (2004); BedRoc Limited, LLC v. United States, 541 U.S. 176 (2004); 70 Comp. Gen. 705 (1991); B-261193, Aug. 25, 1995; 38 Comp. Gen. 812 (1959).

One commonsense way to determine the plain meaning of a word is to consult a dictionary. E.g., Arizona State Legislature v. Arizona Independent Redistricting Commission, ___ U.S. ___, 135 S. Ct. 2652, 2671 (2015); Carcieri, 555 U.S. at 387–88; Mallard v. United States, 490 U.S. 296, 301 (1989); Arizona v. Inter Tribal Council of Arizona, Inc., ___ U.S. ___, 133 S. Ct. 2247, 2254 (2013). Thus, the Comptroller General relied on the dictionary in B-251189, Apr. 8, 1993, to hold that business suits did not constitute "uniforms," which would have permitted the use of appropriated funds for their purchase. See also B-302973, Oct. 6, 2004; B-261522, Sept. 29, 1995.

Also, if a word has a specific legal meaning, courts tend to apply that meaning when interpreting a statute. United States v. Nason, 269 F.3d 10, 16 (1st Cir. 2001) (stating that "we presume, absent evidence to the contrary, that Congress knew and adopted the widely accepted legal definition of meanings associated with the specific words enshrined in the statute," and referring to Black's Law Dictionary for the "most widely accepted legal meaning" of a term). GAO used this rule of statutory construction to construe a prohibition in a fiscal year 2010 appropriations act, which prohibited the distribution of federal funds to "affiliates," "subsidiaries," and "allied organizations" of the Association of Community Organizations for Reform Now. NeighborWorks, a federally chartered entity, asked if one of its grantees, Affordable Housing Centers of America, fell within the scope of this provision. As the First Circuit Court of Appeals did when interpreting federal statutes, GAO used Black's Law Dictionary, federal statutes, and federal regulations to find the plain legal meaning of these terms. B-320329, Sept. 29, 2010.

As a perusal of any dictionary will show, words often have more than one meaning. The plain meaning will be the ordinary, everyday meaning. E.g., Mallard, 490 U.S. at 301; 38 Comp. Gen. 812 (1959). If a word has more than one ordinary meaning and the context of the statute does not make it clear which is being used, there may well be no plain meaning for purposes of that statute. See Smith v. United States, 508 U.S. 223 (1993), discussed previously.

d. Give a Common Construction to the Same or Similar Words

When Congress uses the same term in more than one place in the same statute, it is presumed that Congress intends for the same meaning to apply absent evidence to the contrary. E.g., United States v. Cleveland Indians Baseball Club, 532 U.S. 200, 213 (2001); Ratzlaf v. United States, 510 U.S. 135 (1994). The Comptroller General stated the principle as follows in 29 Comp. Gen. 143, 145 (1949), a case involving the term "pay and allowances":

"[I]t is a settled rule of statutory construction that it is reasonable to assume that words used in one place in a legislative enactment have the same meaning in every other place in the statute and that consequently other sections in which the same phrase is used may be resorted to as an aid in determining the meaning thereof; and, if the meaning of the phrase is clear in one part of the statute and in others doubtful or obscure, it is in the latter case given the same construction as in the former."

Conversely, when Congress uses a different term, it intends a different meaning. E.g., 56 Comp. Gen. 655, 658 (1977) (term "taking line" presumed to have different meaning than "taking area," which had been used in several other sections in the same statute).

Several different canons of construction revolve around these seemingly straightforward notions. Before discussing some of them, it is important to note once more that these canons, like most others, may or may not make sense to apply in particular settings. Indeed, the basic canon that the same words have the same meaning in a statute is itself subject to exceptions. In Cleveland Indians Baseball Club, the Court cautioned:

"Although we generally presume that identical words used in different parts of the same act are intended to have the same meaning, . . . the presumption is not rigid, and the meaning [of the same words] well may vary with the purposes of the law."

Cleveland Indians Baseball Club, 532 U.S. at 213. To drive the point home, the Court quoted the following admonition from a law review article:

"The tendency to assume that a word which appears in two or more legal rules, and so in connection with more than one purpose, has and should have precisely the same scope in all of them . . . has all the tenacity of original sin and must constantly be guarded against."

Id. See also General Dynamics Land Systems, Inc. v. Cline, 540 U.S. 581, fn. 8 (2004) (quoting the same law review passage, which it notes "has become a staple of our opinions"). In 2007, the Court applied the exception described in the Cleveland Indians Baseball Club case in Environmental Defense v. Duke Energy Corp., 549 U.S. 561 (2007) (upholding differing regulatory definitions of the same statutory term contained in two sections of the Clean Air Act). Rejecting the lower court's holding that there is an "effectively irrebuttable" presumption that the same defined term in different provisions of the same statute must be "interpreted identically," the Court pointed out simply that "[c]ontext counts." Environmental Defense, 549 U.S. at 575–76.

Of course, all bets are off if the statute clearly uses the same word differently in different places. See Robinson v. Shell Oil Co., 519 U.S. 337, 343 (1997) ("[o]nce it is established that the term 'employees' includes former employees in some sections, but not in others, the term standing alone is necessarily ambiguous...").

Two canons are frequently applied to the use of similar—but not identical—words in a statute when they are part of the same phrase. These canons are known as ejusdem generis or "of the same kind," and noscitur a sociis, loosely meaning that words are known by the company they keep. See, e.g., B-320329, Sept. 29, 2010 (applying the principle of ejusdem generis to construe the term "allied organization" to be in the same class as "affiliates" and "subsidiaries" in an appropriations act provision).

One case concerned whether a state's retention of Social Security Act benefits to cover some of its costs for providing foster care violated a provision of the Act that shielded benefits from "execution, levy, attachment, garnishment, or other legal process." Washington State Department of Social and Health Services v. Guardianship Estate of Keffeler, 537 U.S. 371 (2003). The Court noted that, under the two canons—

> "'[W]here general words follow specific words in a statutory enumeration, the general words are construed to embrace only objects similar in nature to those objects enumerated by the preceding specific words.'"

537 U.S. at 379, quoting Circuit City Stores, Inc. v. Adams, 532 U.S. 105, 114–115 (2001). Applying the canons, the Court held that the state's receipt of the Social Security benefits as a "representative payee" did not constitute "other legal process" within the Act's meaning. It reasoned that, based on the accompanying terms, "other legal process" required at a minimum the use of some judicial or quasi-judicial process. See 537 U.S. at 385-86; see also Gustafson v. Alloyd Co., 513 U.S. 561, 573–74 (1995) (concerning the scope of statute that defined the term "prospectus"); Gutierrez v. Ada, 528 U.S. 250, 254–255 (2000) (construing the term "any election" within the statute).

The Court has cautioned, however, that a canon of construction like noscitur a sociis cannot modify the meaning of a term that is specifically defined in a statute. See Schwab v. Reilly, 506 U.S. 770 (2010) ("Although we may look to dictionaries and the Bankruptcy Rules to determine the meaning of words the [United States] Code does not define, . . . the Code's definition of the 'property claimed as exempt' in this case is clear.").

Another familiar canon dealing with word patterns in statutes is expressio unius est exclusio alterius, meaning that the expression of one thing is the exclusion of another. Sutherland describes this canon as simply embodying the commonsense notion that when people say one thing, they generally do not mean something else. 2A Sutherland, § 45:14, at 139-141 (7th ed. 2014). As usual, care must be used in applying this canon. See POM Wonderful LLC v. Coca-Cola Co., ___ U.S. ___, 134 S. Ct. 2228, 2238 (2014); United States v. Vonn, 535 U.S. 55 (2002). The Court observed in Vonn:

> "At best, as we have said before, the canon that expressing one item of a commonly associated group or series excludes another left unmentioned is only a guide, whose fallibility can be shown by contrary indications that adopting a particular rule or statute was probably not meant to signal any exclusion of its common relatives."

537 U.S. at 65.

e. Punctuation, Grammar, Titles, and Preambles Are Relevant but Not Controlling

Punctuation, grammar, titles, and preambles are part of the statutory text. As such, they are fair game for consideration in construing statutes. However, as discussed below, they carry less weight than the substantive terms of the statute. The common principle that applies to these sources is that they can be consulted to help resolve ambiguities in the substantive text, but they cannot be used to introduce ambiguity that does not otherwise exist.

Punctuation and Grammar. Punctuation may be taken into consideration when no better evidence exists. For example, whether an "except" clause is or is not set off by a comma may help determine whether the exception applies to the entire provision or just to the portion immediately preceding the "except" clause. E.g., B-218812, Jan. 23, 1987. Punctuation was a relevant factor in the majority opinion in United States v. Ron Pair Enterprises, Inc., 489 U.S. 235, 241–42 (1989).

On the other hand, punctuation or the lack of it should never be the controlling factor. As the Supreme Court stated in United States National Bank of Oregon v. Independent Insurance Agents of America, Inc., 508 U.S. 439, 454 (1993), "a purported plain-meaning analysis based only on punctuation is necessarily incomplete and runs the risk of distorting a statute's true meaning." In that case, the Court disregarded an interpretation based on the placement of quotation marks in a statute, finding that all other evidence in the statute pointed to a different interpretation.

Likewise, a statute's grammatical structure is useful but not conclusive. Lamie v. United States Trustee, 540 U.S. 526, 534–35 (2004) (the mere fact that a statute is awkwardly worded or even ungrammatical does not make it ambiguous). Nevertheless, the Court sometimes gives significant weight to the grammatical structure of a statute. For example, in Barnhart v. Thomas, 540 U.S. 20, 26 (2003), the Court rejected the lower court's construction of a statute in part because it violated the grammatical "rule of the last antecedent." Also, in Arcadia, Ohio v. Ohio Power Co., 498 U.S. 73 (1991), the Court devoted considerable attention to the placement of the word "or" in a series of clauses. It questioned the interpretation proffered by one of the parties that would have given the language an awkward effect, noting:

> "In casual conversation, perhaps, such absentminded duplication and omission are possible, but Congress is not presumed to draft its laws that way."

Arcadia, Ohio, 498 U.S. at 79.

By contrast, in Nobelman v. American Savings Bank, 508 U.S. 324, 330 (1993), the Court rejected an interpretation, noting:

> "We acknowledge that this reading of the clause is quite sensible as a matter of grammar. But it is not compelled."

Titles and Headings. The title of a statute is relevant in determining its scope and purpose. By "title" in this context we mean the line on the slip law immediately following the words "An Act," as distinguished from the statute's "popular name," if any. For example, Public Law 97-177, 96 Stat. 85 (May 21, 1982), is "An Act [t]o require the Federal Government to pay interest on overdue payments, and for other purposes" (title); section 1 says that the act may be cited as the "Prompt Payment Act" (popular name). A public law may or may not have a popular name; it always has a title. The heading of a particular section of a statute may also be relevant. See, e.g., B-321823, Dec. 6, 2011, at 4 (the heading of a particular statutory provision among the factors considered in construing that provision).

The title of an act may not be used to change the plain meaning of the enacting clauses. It is evidence of the act's scope and purpose, however, and may legitimately be taken into consideration to resolve ambiguities. E.g., Lapina v. Williams, 232 U.S. 78, 92 (1914); White v. United States, 191 U.S. 545, 550 (1903); Church of the Holy Trinity v. United States, 143 U.S. 457, 462–63 (1892); United States v. Fisher, 6 U.S. (2 Cranch) 358, 386 (1805); 36 Comp. Gen. 389 (1956); 19 Comp. Gen. 739, 742 (1940). To illustrate, in Church of the Holy Trinity, the Court used the title of the statute in question, "An act to prohibit the importation and migration of foreigners and aliens under contract or agreement to perform labor in the United States," as support for its conclusion that the statute was not intended to apply to professional persons, specifically in that case, ministers and pastors.

The same considerations apply to a statute's popular name and to the headings, or titles, of particular sections of the statute. See Intel Corp. v. Advanced Micro Devices, Inc., 542 U.S. 241, 256 (2004). See also Immigration & Naturalization Service v. St. Cyr, 533 U.S. 289, 308–309 (2001); Pennsylvania Department of Corrections v. Yeskey, 524 U.S. 206, 212 (1998). In St. Cyr, the Supreme Court concluded that a section entitled "Elimination of Custody Review by Habeas Corpus" did not, in fact, eliminate habeas corpus jurisdiction. It found that the substantive terms of the section were less definitive than the title.

Federal statutes often include an introductory "preamble" or "purpose" section before the substantive provisions in which Congress sets forth findings, purposes, or policies that prompted it to adopt the legislation. Such preambles have no legally binding effect. However, they may provide indications of congressional intent underlying the law. Sutherland states with respect to preambles:

> "Courts have long settled the principle that 'The preamble cannot control the enacting part of the statute, in cases where the enacting part is expressed in clear, unambiguous terms; but in case any doubt arises on the enacting part, the preamble may be resorted to to explain it, and show the intention of the law maker.'"

2A Sutherland, Statutes and Statutory Construction, § 47:4 at 299-300 (7th ed. 2014). For an example in which the Court used statutory findings to inform its interpretation of congressional intent, see General Dynamics Land Systems, Inc. v. Cline, 540 U.S. 581, 589–91 (2004). See also B-285066, May 19, 2000.

f. Avoid Constructions that Pose Constitutional Problems

It is well settled that courts will attempt to avoid a construction of a statute that would render the statute unconstitutional. For example, in Edward J. DeBartolo Corp. v. Florida Gulf Coast Building & Construction Trades Council, 485 U.S. 568, 575 (1988), the Court, while citing numerous precedents, observed:

> "[W]here an otherwise acceptable construction of a statute would raise serious constitutional problems, the Court will construe the statute to avoid such problems unless such construction is plainly contrary to the intent of Congress. . . . This cardinal principle . . . has for so long been applied by this Court that it is beyond debate. . . . [T]he elementary rule is that every reasonable construction must be resorted to, in order to save a statute from unconstitutionality. This approach not only reflects the prudential concern that constitutional

issues not be needlessly confronted, but also recognizes that Congress, like this Court, is bound by and swears an oath to uphold the Constitution. The courts will therefore not lightly assume that Congress intended to infringe constitutionally protected liberties or usurp power constitutionally forbidden it."

As the Court put it in Immigration & Naturalization Service v. St. Cyr, 533 U.S. 289, 300 (2001), where an alternative to a constitutionally problematic interpretation "is fairly possible, . . . we are obligated to construe the statute to avoid such problems."

Two cases arising under the Federal Advisory Committee Act (known as "FACA"), 5 U.S.C. App. §§ 1 et seq., illustrate the lengths to which courts will go to avoid constitutional problems. In one case, the Court held that the Justice Department did not "utilize" within the meaning of FACA an American Bar Association committee that reported to the Department on federal judicial nominees and rated their qualifications. Public Citizen v. United States Department of Justice, 491 U.S. 440 (1989). A later ruling from an appellate court held that the First Lady was a full-time officer or employee of the federal government within the meaning of the Act. Association of American Physicians & Surgeons, Inc. v. Clinton, 997 F.2d 898 (D.C. Cir. 1993). Therefore, a task force she chaired was exempt from FACA under a provision of the Act that excluded "any committee which is composed wholly of full-time officers or employees of the Federal Government." The constitutional issue in both cases was whether application of FACA to the advisory committees involved in those cases would violate separation of powers by infringing upon the President's ability to obtain advice in the performance of his constitutional responsibilities.

However, there are outer limits to interpretations designed to avoid constitutional problems. See Pennsylvania Department of Corrections v. Yeskey, 524 U.S. 206, 212 (1998) ("[t]hat doctrine [of constitutional avoidance] enters in only 'where a statute is susceptible of two constructions'"); Plaut v. Spendthrift Farm, Inc., 514 U.S. 211, 216 (1995) ("[t]o avoid a constitutional question by holding that Congress enacted, and the President approved, a blank sheet of paper would indeed constitute 'disingenuous evasion'").

6. Legislative History

"Where the mind labours to discover the design of the legislature, it seizes every thing from which aid can be derived . . . ."

United States v. Fisher, 6 U.S. (2 Cranch) 358, 386 (1805).

a. Uses and Limitations

The term "legislative history" refers to the body of congressionally generated written documents relating to a bill from the time of introduction to the time of enactment. As we will discuss, there are at least two basic ways to use legislative history. One is to examine the documents that make up the legislative history in order to determine what they say about the meaning and intent of the legislation, and the other is to examine the evolution of the bill's language through the legislative process. Changes made to a bill during its consideration are often instructive in determining its final meaning.

The converse of the plain meaning rule is that it is legitimate and proper to resort to legislative history when the meaning of the statutory language is not plain on its face. United States v. Fisher, 6 U.S. (2 Cranch) 358, 386 (1805); see also United States v. Donruss Co., 393 U.S. 297, 302-03 (1969); Caminetti v. United States, 242 U.S. 470, 490 (1917) (legislative history "may aid the courts in reaching the true meaning of the legislature in cases of doubtful interpretation"). A classic example of the use of legislative history to resolve statutory ambiguity involved a statute using the words "science" or "scientific." Either term, without more, does not inform whether the statute applies to the social sciences as well as the physical sciences. E.g., American Kennel Club, Inc. v. Hoey, 148 F.2d 920, 921 (2nd Cir. 1945); B-181142, Aug. 5, 1974 (GAO recommended that the term "science and technology" in a bill be defined to avoid this ambiguity).

Although one may use legislative history to resolve ambiguities that are not clear in the statutory language, one should not use legislative history to rewrite the statute. For instance, an appropriations provision barred the Air Force from using funds to lease certain aircraft "under any contract entered into under any procurement procedures other than pursuant to" the Competition in Contracting Act. In a floor statement on the bill, the provision's sponsor said that the language would require "full and open competition" for the aircraft and preclude a "sole source" award. However, CICA clearly does not require full and open competition or prohibit sole-source awards. Therefore, the Comptroller General upheld the Air Force's award of a sole-source contract. B-291805, Mar. 26, 2003. As the Comptroller General stated in an earlier case:

> "[A]s a general proposition, there is a distinction to be made between utilizing legislative history for the purpose of illuminating the intent underlying language used in a statute and resorting to that history for the purpose of writing into the law that which is not there."

55 Comp. Gen. 307, 325 (1975).

In many instances courts will consult legislative history even if a statute's meaning appears clear on its face. As the Supreme Court once stated:

> "When aid to construction of the meaning of words, as used in the statute, is available, there certainly can be no 'rule of law' which forbids its use, however clear the words may appear on 'superficial examination.'"

United States v. American Trucking Ass'ns, Inc., 310 U.S. 534, 543-44 (1940). In one case, the Court found the relevant statute to be "unambiguous, unequivocal, and unlimited." Conroy v. Aniskoff, 507 U.S. 511, 514 (1993). Nevertheless, the Court examined the legislative history in detail to confirm that its literal reading of the statute was not absurd, illogical, or contrary to congressional intent.

b. Components and Their Relative Weight

In discussing legislative history, we will first consider use of the explanatory documents that go into it. These documents fall generally into three categories: committee reports, floor debates, and hearings. For probative purposes, they bear an established relationship to one another. Let us emphasize before proceeding, however, that listing items of legislative history in an "order of persuasiveness" is merely a guideline. The evidentiary value of any piece of legislative history depends on its relationship to other available legislative history and, most importantly, to the language of the statute.

(1) Committee reports

Committee reports are reports generated by the legislative committees during an investigation or during consideration of a bill. One such report is the joint explanatory statement, which is often called the statement of managers. This document describes the elements of the conference committee's agreement, as they relate to the House and Senate positions on the bill. See House Rule XXII, cl. 7(e); Senate Rule XXVIII, para. 6; B-142011, Apr. 30, 1971. A joint explanatory statement can be a particularly useful legislative history document because it describes the final bill text to which both chambers ultimately agreed. While joint explanatory statements have some value in determining congressional intent, they do not have "the force of law." Roeder v. Islamic Republic of Iran, 333 F.3d 228, 237 (D.C. Cir. 2003).

Next in the sequence of precedence are the reports of the legislative committees that considered the bill and then reported the bill out to their respective houses. The Supreme Court has been willing to refer to committee reports when appropriate. E.g., Dart Cherokee Basin Operating Co. v. Owens, ___ U.S. ___, 135 S. Ct. 547 (2014); Demore v. Hyung Joon Kim, 538 U.S. 510, 517–20 (2003); Lorillard Tobacco Co. v. Reilly, 533 U.S. 525, 543–544 (2001); Duplex Printing Press Co. v. Deering, 254 U.S. 443, 474 (1921); United States v. St. Paul, Minneapolis & Manitoba Railway Co., 247 U.S. 310, 318 (1918); Lapina v. Williams, 232 U.S. 78, 90 (1914).

However, material in committee reports or a joint explanatory statement will not be used to controvert clear statutory language. Squillacote, 739 F.2d at 1218; Hart v. United States, 585 F.2d 1025 (Ct. Cl. 1978); B-278121, Nov. 7, 1997; B-33911, B-62187, July 15, 1948. Also, such material will not be used to add requirements that Congress did not include in the statute itself. For example, where Congress appropriates lump sum amounts without statutorily restricting the use of those funds, "a clear inference arises that it does not intend to impose legally binding restrictions, and indicia in committee reports and other legislative history as to how the funds should or are expected to be spent do not establish any legal requirements" on the agency. 55 Comp. Gen 307, 319 (1975); see also Hein v. Freedom From Religion Foundation, Inc., 551 U.S. 587, 608 n.7 (2007); Lincoln v. Vigil, 508 U.S. 182, 192 (1993). Also, such material is not entitled to any weight as legislative history if the statement in the report is different from or unrelated to any language in the act itself. Abrego Abrego v. Dow Chemical Co., 443 F.3d 676, 692 (9th Cir. 2006); Brill v. Countrywide Home Loans, Inc., 427 F.3d 446 (7th Cir. 2005); B-320091, July 23, 2010, at n.4.

The following excerpt from a colloquy between Senators Armstrong and Dole demonstrates why committee reports must be used with caution:

"Mr. ARMSTRONG. Mr. President, did members of the Finance Committee vote on the committee report?

"Mr. DOLE. No.

"Mr. ARMSTRONG. Mr. President, the reason I raise the issue is not perhaps apparent on the surface . . . . The report itself is not considered by the Committee on Finance. It was not subject to amendment by the Committee on Finance. It is not subject to amendment now by the Senate…

"I only wish the record to reflect that this is not statutory language. It is not before us. If there were matter within this report which was disagreed to by the Senator from Colorado or even by a majority of all Senators, there would be no way for us to change the report. I could not offer an amendment tonight to amend the committee report.

". . . [F]or any jurist, administrator, bureaucrat, tax practitioner, or others who might chance upon the written record of this proceeding, let me just make the point that this is not the law, it was not voted on, it is not subject to amendment, and we should discipline ourselves to the task of expressing congressional intent in the statute."

Notwithstanding the imperfections of the system, in those cases where there is a need to resort to legislative history, committee reports remain generally recognized as the best source. In this regard, Sutherland observes:

"During the Twentieth Century, courts increasingly have turned to reports of standing committees for aid in interpretation. This movement has coincided with an improvement in the preparation of reports by standing committees and their counsel."

2A Sutherland, § 48:6, at 590 (7th ed. 2014).

(2) Floor debates

Proceeding downward in the order of precedence, after committee reports come floor debates. Statements made in the course of floor debates have traditionally been regarded as suspect, in that they are only "expressive of the views and motives of individual members." Duplex Printing Press Co. v. Deering, 254 U.S. 443, 474 (1921). In addition:

"[I]t is impossible to determine with certainty what construction was put upon an act by the members of a legislative body that passed it by resorting to the speeches of individual members thereof. Those who did not speak may not have agreed with those who did, and those who spoke might differ from each other… "

United States v. Trans-Missouri Freight Ass'n, 166 U.S. 290, 318 (1897). Some older cases, such as Trans-Missouri Freight, indicate that floor debates should never be taken into consideration. Under the more modern view, however, they may be considered in appropriate circumstances, with the real question being the weight the debates should receive in various circumstances.

Floor debates are less authoritative than committee reports. Garcia v. United States, 469 U.S. 70, 76 (1984); Zuber v. Allen, 396 U.S. 168, 186 (1969); United States v. O'Brien, 391 U.S. 367, 385 (1968); United States v. United Automobile Workers, 352 U.S. 567, 585 (1957). It follows that they will not be regarded if they conflict with explicit statements in more authoritative portions of legislative history, such as committee reports. United States v. Wrightwood Dairy Co., 315 U.S. 110, 125 (1942); B-114829, June 27, 1975. Conversely, they will carry more weight if they are mutually reenforcing. National Data Corp. & Subsidiaries v. United States, 50 Fed. Cl. 24, 32, n.14 (2001), aff'd, 291 F.3d 1381 (Fed. Cir.), cert. denied, 537 U.S. 1045 (2002).

Debates will carry considerably more weight when they are the only available legislative history as, for example, in the case of a post-report floor amendment. Northeast Bancorp, Inc. v. Board of Governors of the Federal Reserve System, 472 U.S. 159, 169–70 (1985); Preterm, Inc. v. Dukakis, 591 F.2d 121, 128 (1st Cir.), cert. denied, 441 U.S. 952 (1979). Indeed, the Preterm court suggested that "heated and lengthy debates" in which "the views expressed were those of a wide spectrum" of Members might be more valuable in discerning congressional intent than committee reports, "which represent merely the views of [the committee's] members and may never have come to the attention of Congress as a whole." Preterm, 591 F.2d at 133.

The weight to be given statements made in floor debates varies with the identity of the speaker. Thus, statements by legislators in charge of a bill, such as the pertinent committee chairperson, have been regarded as "in the nature of a supplementary report" and receive somewhat more weight. United States v. St. Paul, Minneapolis & Manitoba Railway Co., 247 U.S. 310, 318 (1918). See also McCaughn v. Hershey Chocolate Co., 283 U.S. 488, 493–94 (1931) (statements by Members "who were not in charge of the bill" were "without weight"); Duplex v. Deering, 254 U.S. at 474–75; NLRB v. Thompson Products, Inc., 141 F.2d 794, 798 (9th Cir. 1944). The Supreme Court's statement in St. Paul Railway Co. gave rise to the practice of "making" legislative history by preparing questions and answers in advance, to be presented on the floor and answered by the Member in charge of the bill.

Statements by the sponsor of a bill are also entitled to somewhat more weight. E.g., Schwegmann Brothers v. Calvert Distillers Corp., 341 U.S. 384, 394–95 (1951); Ex Parte Kawato, 317 U.S. 69, 77 (1942); Bedroc Limited v. United States, 50 F. Supp.2d 1001, 1006 (D. Nev. 1999), aff'd, 314 F.3d 1080 (9th Cir. 2002). However, they are not controlling. General Dynamics Land Systems, Inc. v. Cline, 540 U.S. 581, 597–99 (2004); Chrysler Corp. v. Brown, 441 U.S. 281, 311 (1979).

Statements by the opponents of a bill expressing their "fears and doubts" generally receive little, if any, weight. Shell Oil Co. v. Iowa Department of Revenue, 488 U.S. 19, 29 (1988); Schwegmann, 341 U.S. at 394. However, even the statements of opponents may be "relevant and useful," although not authoritative, in certain circumstances, such as where the supporters of a bill make no response to opponents' criticisms. Arizona v. California, 373 U.S. 546, 583 n.85 (1963); Parlane Sportswear Co. v. Weinberger, 513 F.2d 835, 837 (1st Cir. 1975); Bentley v. Arlee Home Fashions, Inc., 861 F. Supp. 65, 67 (E.D. Ark. 1994).

Where Senate and House floor debates suggest conflicting interpretations and there is no more authoritative source of legislative history available, it is legitimate to give weight to such factors as which house originated the provision in question and which house has the more detailed and "clear cut" history. Steiner v. Mitchell, 350 U.S. 247, 254 (1956); 49 Comp. Gen. 411 (1970).

(3) Hearings

Hearings are the least persuasive form of legislative history. They reflect only the personal opinion and motives of the witness. It is more often than not impossible to attribute these opinions and motives to anyone in Congress, let alone Congress as a whole, unless more authoritative forms of legislative history expressly adopt them. As one court has stated, an isolated excerpt from the statement of a witness at hearings "is not entitled to consideration in determining legislative intent." Pacific Insurance Co. v. United States, 188 F.2d 571, 572 (9th

Cir. 1951). "It would indeed be absurd," said another court, "to suppose that the testimony of a witness by itself could be used to interpret an act of Congress." SEC v. Collier, 76 F.2d 939, 941 (2nd Cir. 1935).

There is one significant exception. Testimony by the government agency that recommended the bill or amendment in question, and which often helped draft it, is entitled to special weight. Shapiro v. United States, 335 U.S. 1, 12 n.13 (1948); SEC v. Collier, 76 F.2d at 941.

Also, testimony at hearings can be more valuable as legislative history if it can be demonstrated that the language of a bill was revised in direct response to that testimony. Relevant factors include the presence or absence of statements in more authoritative history linking the change to the testimony, the proximity in time of the change to the testimony, and the precise language of the change as compared to what was offered in the testimony. See Premachandra v. Mitts, 753 F.2d 635, 640–41 (8th Cir. 1985). See also Allen v. State Board of Elections, 393 U.S. 544, 566–68 (1969); SEC v. Collier, 76 F.2d at 940, 941.

c. Post-enactment Statements

Observers of the often difficult task of discerning congressional intent occasionally ask, "Is there an easier way to do this? Can I just call the sponsor or the committee and ask what they had in mind?" The answer is that post-enactment statements have virtually no weight in determining prior congressional intent. The objective of statutory construction is to ascertain a collective intent, not an individual's intent or, worse yet, an individual's characterization of the collective intent. It is impossible to demonstrate that the substance of a post hoc statement reflects the intent of the pre-enactment Congress, unless it can be corroborated by pre-enactment statements, in which event it would be unnecessary. Or, as the Court has said:

> "Since such statements cannot possibly have informed the vote of the legislators who earlier enacted the law, there is no more basis for considering them than there is to conduct post-enactment polls of the original legislators."

Pittston Coal Group v. Sebben, 488 U.S. 105, 118–19 (1988). See also Bruesewitz v. Wyeth LLC, 562 U.S. 223 (2011) (asserting that post-enactment legislative history is not a legitimate tool of statutory interpretation); Gustafson v. Alloyd Co., 513 U.S. 561, 580 (1995) ("If legislative history is to be considered, it is preferable to consult the documents prepared by Congress when deliberating."); 2A Sutherland, § 48:4, at 573-579 (7th ed. 2014) (to be considered legislative history, material should be generally available to legislators and relied on by them in passing the bill).

In expressing their unwillingness to consider post-enactment statements, courts have not viewed the identity of the speaker (sponsor, committee, committee chairman, etc.) or the form of the statement (report, floor statement, letter, affidavit, etc.) to be relevant. There are numerous cases in which the courts, and particularly the Supreme Court, have expressed the unwillingness to give weight to post-enactment statements. See, e.g., Bread Political Action Committee v. Federal Election Commission, 455 U.S. 577, 582 n.3 (1982); Quern v. Mandley, 436 U.S. 725, 736 n.10 (1978); Regional Rail Reorganization Act Cases, 419 U.S. 102, 132 (1974); United States v. Southwestern Cable Co., 392 U.S. 157, 170 (1968); Haynes v. United States, 390 U.S. 85, 87 n.4 (1968). See also General Instrument Corp. v. FCC, 213 F.3d 724, 733 (D.C. Cir.

2000) (referring to post-enactment statements as "legislative future" rather than legislative history); Cavallo v. Utica-Watertown Health Insurance Co., 3 F. Supp. 2d 223, 230 (N.D. N.Y. 1998).

Courts have not found expressions of intent concerning previously enacted legislation that are made in committee reports, or floor statements during the consideration of subsequent legislation, to be relevant either. E.g., O'Gilvie v. United States, 519 U.S. 79, 90 (1996) ("the view of a later Congress cannot control the interpretation of an earlier enacted statute"); Huffman v. Office of Personnel Management, 263 F.3d 1341, 1354 (Fed. Cir. 2001) (post-enactment statements made in the legislative history of the 1994 amendments have no bearing in determining the legislative intent of the drafters of the 1978 and 1989 legislation).

GAO follows the principle that post-enactment statements shed no useful light on legislative intent. E.g., 72 Comp. Gen. 317 (1993); 54 Comp. Gen. 819, 822 (1975). One type of post-enactment statement is a presidential "signing statement", which usually takes the form of a presidential statement or press release issued in connection with the President's signing of a bill. The Office of Legal Counsel has virtually conceded that presidential signing statements fall within the realm of post-enactment statements that carry no weight as legislative history. See 17 Op. Off. Legal Counsel 131 (1993). In 2007, GAO examined how the federal courts have treated signing statements in their published decisions. A search of all federal case law since 1945 found fewer than 140 cases that cited presidential signing statements. In most instances the signing statements were used to supplement legislative history such as committee reports. Courts also have cited signing statements to establish the date of signing, provide a short summary of the statute, explain the purpose of the statute, or describe the underlying policy behind the statute. GAO concluded that, overall, federal courts infrequently cite or refer to signing statements in their published opinions. When cited or referred to, these signing statements appear to have little impact on judicial decision-making. B-308603, June 18, 2007, Enclosure IV, at 37. See also B-309928, Dec. 20, 2007, and GAO, Presidential Signing Statements: Agency Implementation of Selected Provisions of Law, GAO-08-553T (Washington, D.C.: Mar. 2008) for additional discussion on signing statements.

As with all other principles relating to statutory interpretation, the rule against consideration of post-enactment statements is not absolute. Even post-enactment material may be taken into consideration, despite its very limited value, when there is absolutely nothing else. See B-169491, June 16, 1980.

d. Development of the Statutory Language

As previously noted, examination of legislative history includes not only what the drafters of a bill said about it, but also what they did to it as the bill progressed through the enactment process. Changes made to a bill may provide insight into what the final language means. For example, the deletion from the final version of language that was in the original bill may suggest an intent to reject what was covered by that language. See generally 2A Sutherland, § 48:4, at 573-579 (7th ed. 2014). The same is true of language offered in an amendment that was defeated. Id., § 48:8, at 634-635.

The courts consider the evolution of legislative language in different contexts. See, for example:

- Doe v. Chao, 540 U.S. 614, 621–23 (2004): Congress deleted from the bill language that would have provided for the type of damage award sought by the petitioner.

- Chickasaw Nation v. United States, 534 U.S. 84, 91 (2001): The original Senate bill applied both to taxation and to reporting and withholding. The final version applied only to reporting and withholding, thereby suggesting that a cross-reference to another law dealing with taxation was left in by error.

- Landgraf v. USI Film Products, 511 U.S. 244, 255–256 (1994): The President vetoed a 1990 version of a civil rights bill in part because he objected to the bill's broad retroactivity provisions. This indicates that the absence of comparable retroactivity provisions in the version of the bill enacted in 1991 was not an oversight, but rather part of a political compromise.

See also Resolution Trust Corp. v. Gallagher, 10 F.3d 416, 423 (7th Cir. 1993); Davis v. United States, 46 Fed. Cl. 421 (2000).

As always, care must be exercised when interpreting language changes in a bill, particularly when the accompanying documents do not discuss them. Unless the legislative history explains the reason for the omission or deletion or the reason is clear from the context, drawing conclusions is inherently speculative. Perhaps Congress did not want that particular provision; perhaps Congress felt it was already covered in the same or other legislation. Absent an explanation, the effect of such an omission or deletion is inconclusive. See Fox v. Standard Oil Co., 294 U.S. 87, 96 (1935); Southern Packaging & Storage Co. v. United States, 588 F. Supp. 532, 549 (D.S.C. 1984); 63 Comp. Gen. 498, 501–02 (1984); 63 Comp. Gen. 470, 472 (1984).

7. Presumptions and "Clear Statement" Rules

In a perhaps growing number of specific areas, courts apply extra scrutiny in construing statutes that they regard as departing from traditional norms of legislation. In these areas, the courts require a greater than usual showing that Congress did, in fact, mean to depart from the norm. Typically, the courts will raise the bar by imposing a "presumption" that must be overcome in order to establish that Congress intended the departure. Alternatively but to the same effect, courts sometimes require a "clear statement" by Congress that it intended the departure.

Such presumptions and clear statement rules have been described as "substantive canons" as opposed to "linguistic canons" since, rather than aiding in the interpretation of statutory language per se, they are designed to protect "substantive values drawn from the common law, federal statutes, or the United States Constitution." A few examples are given below.

a. Presumption in Favor of Judicial Review

There is a "strong presumption" in favor of judicial review of administrative actions. E.g., Demore v. Hyung Joon Kim, 538 U.S. 510 (2003); Immigration & Naturalization Service v. St. Cyr, 533 U.S. 289 (2001); McNary v. Haitian Refugee Center, Inc., 498 U.S. 479 (1991); Bowen

v. Michigan Academy of Family Physicians, 476 U.S. 667 (1986). In Bowen, the Court stated the presumption as follows:

"We begin with the strong presumption that Congress intends judicial review of administrative action. From the beginning, 'our cases [have established] that judicial review of a final agency action by an aggrieved person will not be cut off unless there is persuasive reason to believe that such was the purpose of Congress.'"

476 U.S. at 670, quoting Abbott Laboratories v. Gardner, 387 U.S. 136, 140 (1967).

The Court in Bowen went on to note that the presumption of reviewability can be rebutted:

"Subject to constitutional constraints, Congress can, of course, make exceptions to the historic practice whereby courts review agency action. The presumption of judicial review is, after all, a presumption, and like all presumptions used in interpreting statutes, may be overcome by, inter alia, specific language or specific legislative history that is a reliable indicator of congressional intent or a specific congressional intent to preclude judicial review that is fairly discernable in the detail of the legislative scheme."

Id. at 672–73.

Later decisions indicate that a particularly strong showing is required to establish a congressional intent to preclude judicial review of constitutional claims through habeas corpus petitions. See Demore, 538 U.S. 510; St. Cyr, 533 U.S. 289. Thus, the Court observed in St. Cyr, 533 U.S. at 299:

"Implications from statutory text or legislative history are not sufficient to repeal habeas jurisdiction; instead, Congress must articulate specific and unambiguous statutory directives to effect repeal."

Finally, it is important to note one area in which the usual presumption in favor of judicial review becomes a presumption against judicial review: exercises of discretion by the President. In Franklin v. Massachusetts, 505 U.S. 788 (1992), the Supreme Court held that the President is not an "agency" for purposes of the Administrative Procedure Act (APA); therefore, presidential actions are not subject to judicial review under the APA. The Court recognized that the general definition of "agency" in the APA (5 U.S.C. § 551(1)) covered "each authority of the Government of the United States" and that the President was not explicitly excluded from this definition. However, the Court held:

"Out of respect for the separation of powers and the unique constitutional position of the President, we find that textual silence is not enough to subject the President to the provisions of the APA. We would require an express statement by Congress before assuming it intended the President's performance of his statutory duties to be reviewed for abuse of discretion."

505 U.S. at 800–801.

Several subsequent cases have followed and extended Franklin. See Dalton v. Specter, 511 U.S. 462 (1994); Tulare County v. Bush, 185 F. Supp.2d 18 (D.D.C. 2001), aff'd, 306 F.3d 1138

(D.C. Cir. 2002), reh'g en banc denied, 317 F.3d 227 (D.C. Cir.), cert. denied, 540 U.S. 813 (2003).

b. Presumption against Retroactivity

As noted previously, statutes and amendments to statutes generally are construed to apply prospectively only (that is, from their date of enactment or other effective date if one is specified). However, while Congress generally has the power to enact retroactive statutes, the Supreme Court has held:

> "Retroactivity is not favored in the law. Thus, congressional enactments . . . will not be construed to have retroactive effect unless their language requires this result."

Bowen v. Georgetown University Hospital, 488 U.S. 204, 208 (1988).

The Court reaffirmed the presumption against retroactivity of statutes in several recent decisions. E.g., AT&T Corp. v. Hulteen, 556 U.S. 701 (2009); Immigration & Naturalization Service v. St. Cyr, 533 U.S. 289 (2001); Martin v. Hadix, 527 U.S. 343 (1999); Lindh v. Murphy, 521 U.S. 320 (1997); Landgraf v. USI Film Products, 511 U.S. 244 (1994). In Landgraf, the Court elaborated on the policies supporting the presumption against retroactivity:

> "Because it accords with widely held intuitions about how statutes ordinarily operate, a presumption against retroactivity will generally coincide with legislative and public expectations. Requiring clear intent assures that Congress itself has affirmatively considered the potential unfairness of retroactive application and determined that it is an acceptable price to pay for the countervailing benefits. Such a requirement allocates to Congress responsibility for fundamental policy judgments concerning the proper temporal reach of statutes, and has the additional virtue of giving legislators a predictable background rule against which to legislate."

Landgraf, 511 U.S. at 272–73.

In Landgraf, the Court also resolved the "apparent tension" between the presumption against retroactivity in its Bowen line of decisions and another decision, Bradley v. Richmond School Board, 416 U.S. 696 (1974). Bradley held that when a law changes subsequent to the judgment of a lower court, an appellate court must apply the new law, that is, the law in effect when it renders its decision, unless applying the new law would produce "manifest injustice" or there is statutory direction or legislative history to the contrary. The Court affirmed that the presumption embraces statutes that have "genuinely" retroactive effect, by which it meant statutes that apply new standards "affecting substantive rights, liabilities, or duties" to conduct that occurred prior to their enactment. Landgraf, 511 U.S. at 277–78.

By way of summary, the Court in Landgraf set forth the following test for determining whether the presumption against retroactivity applies:

> "When a case implicates a federal statute enacted after the events in suit, the court's first task is to determine whether Congress has expressly prescribed the statute's proper reach. If Congress has done so, of course, there is no need to resort to judicial default rules. When, however, the statute contains no such express command, the court must determine whether

the new statute would have retroactive effect, i.e., whether it would impair rights a party possessed when he acted, increase a party's liability for past conduct, or impose new duties with respect to transactions already completed. If the statute would operate retroactively, our traditional presumption teaches that it does not govern absent clear congressional intent favoring such a result."

Id. at 280.

The Comptroller General also applies the traditional rule that statutes are not construed to apply retroactively unless a retroactive construction is required by their express language or by necessary implication or unless it is demonstrated that this is what Congress clearly intended. See, e.g., 64 Comp. Gen. 493 (1985).

This rule was recently applied to a statute that authorized the United States Court of Appeals for Veterans Claims to reimburse its employees for a portion of their professional liability insurance payments. Since nothing in the statute or its legislative history indicated that the statute was to have retroactive effect, the Comptroller General held that the statute did not authorize reimbursement for insurance payments made prior to December 27, 2001. B-300866, May 30, 2003.

Another line of cases has dealt with a different aspect of retroactivity. GAO is reluctant to construe a statute to retroactively abolish or diminish rights that had accrued before its enactment unless this was clearly the legislative intent. For example, the Tax Reduction Act of 1975 authorized $50 "special payments" to certain taxpayers. Legislation in 1977 abolished the special payments as of its date of enactment. GAO concluded that payments could be made where payment vouchers were validly issued before the cutoff date but lost in the mail. B-190751, Apr. 11, 1978. Similarly, payments could be made to eligible claimants whose claims had been erroneously denied before the cutoff but were later found valid. B-190751, Sept. 26, 1980.

c. Federalism Presumptions

Under the Constitution's Supremacy Clause (U.S. Const. art. VI, cl. 2), Congress, when acting within the scope of its own assigned constitutional authority, can preempt state and local laws. As the Court noted in Wisconsin Public Intervenor v. Mortier, 501 U.S. 597, 604 (1991), "[t]he ways in which federal law may pre-empt state law are well established and in the first instance turn on congressional intent." Specifically, Congress may preempt either by an explicit statutory provision or by establishing a federal statutory scheme that is so pervasive as to leave no room for supplementation by the states. In either event, however, the Court stated:

"When considering pre-emption, 'we start with the assumption that the historic police powers of the States were not to be superseded by the Federal Act unless that was the clear and manifest purpose of Congress.'"

Mortier, 501 U.S. at 605, quoting Rice v. Santa Fe Elevator Corp., 331 U.S. 218, 230 (1947).

The Court continues to apply the "clear and manifest purpose" test to preemption cases. See City of Columbus v. Ours Garage and Wrecker Service, Inc., 536 U.S. 424 (2002). In Ours Garage, the Court construed a statute that included an explicit preemption provision; the issue concerned its scope. Acknowledging that the language could be read to preempt safety regulation by local governments, the Court refused to find preemption:

> "[R]eading [the statute's] set of exceptions in combination, and with a view to the basic tenets of our federal system pivotal in Mortier, we conclude that the statute does not provide the requisite 'clear and manifest indication that Congress sought to supplant local authority.'"

Ours Garage, 536 U.S. at 434.

There also is a presumption against construing federal statutes to abrogate the immunity from suit that states enjoy under the Eleventh Amendment to the United States Constitution. Congress must make its intent to abrogate such immunity "unmistakably clear in the language of the statute." See Nevada Department of Human Resources v. Hibbs, 538 U.S. 721, 726 (2003); Hoffman v. Connecticut Department of Income Maintenance, 492 U.S. 96, 101 (1989) and cases cited. The necessary unmistakable intent to preempt was supplied by the express language of the statute in Hibbs, but such intent was found lacking in Hoffman.

d. Presumption against Waiver of Sovereign Immunity

There is a strong presumption against waiver of the federal government's immunity from suit. GAO and the courts have repeatedly held that waivers of sovereign immunity must be "unequivocally expressed." E.g., United States v. Nordic Village, Inc., 503 U.S. 30 (1992); B-320998, May 4, 2011. Legislative history does not help for this purpose. The relevant statutory language in Nordic Village was ambiguous and could have been read, evidently with the support of the legislative history, to impose monetary liability on the United States. The Court rejected such a reading, applying instead the same approach as described above in its federalism jurisprudence:

> "[L]egislative history has no bearing on the ambiguity point. As in the Eleventh Amendment context, see Hoffman, supra, . . . the 'unequivocal expression' of elimination of sovereign immunity that we insist upon is an expression in statutory text. If clarity does not exist there, it cannot be supplied by a committee report."

Nordic Village, 503 U.S. at 37.

8. Resolving Conflicts between Statutes

Though legislatures enact statutes one at a time, each enactment occurs within a wider context of laws. Often, this wider context of enactments significantly impacts the interpretation of a single statute. To give a simple example, suppose a town council enacts a statute providing that all dogs in the downtown park must be leashed. If this statute were the only one the council enacted on this subject, interpreting it will, in many circumstances, be simple. However, suppose the town council has also enacted a different statute, which provides that all poodles in the town are permitted to roam free. Though each of these two statutes standing alone is simple enough, interpreting and applying them together can be tricky if, for example, one confronts a poodle in the downtown park. Fortunately, there is a set of principles guiding the interpretation of statutes in such situations.

a. Harmonize different statutes

First, we assume that the legislature intended to enact a consistent body of law, and so we try to harmonize conflicting statutes to give full force to each of them. We do not presume that the legislature intended that a later statute repeal an existing one unless there is clear intent to do so. Another way to express this principle is that repeals by implication are disfavored. For example, Congress in 1934 enacted a statute according an employment preference for qualified Indians in the Bureau of Indian Affairs. Morton v. Mancari, 417 U.S. 535, 537 (1974). In 1972, Congress enacted another statute proscribing discrimination in most federal employment on the basis of race. Id. at 540. The appellate court held that the 1972 law implicitly repealed the 1934 law and, therefore, that the Bureau of Indian Affairs was barred from granting an employment preference to Indians. The Supreme Court reversed the lower court, holding that the 1934 law remained in full force. The Court noted that "[i]n the absence of some affirmative showing of an intention to repeal, the only permissible justification for a repeal by implication is when the earlier and later statutes are irreconcilable." Id. at 550. The Court stated that the 1934 and 1972 statutes "can readily co-exist" and that multiple factors indicated that Congress had no intention to repeal the 1934 statute when it acted in 1972. Id. at 551. See also Hawaii v. Office of Hawaiian Affairs, 556 U.S. 163, 175 (2009).

b. More specific enactments control over more general enactments

If harmonizing different statutes and giving full force to all of them solves the issue at hand, the analysis ends there. Only when harmonization does not resolve an issue do we turn to the second principle, which is that more specific enactments control over more general ones. This is true whether the more specific provision is enacted before or after the more general one. For example, Congress enacted a statute providing that national banks could be sued only in the district in which they were established. Radzanower v. Touche Ross & Co., 426 U.S. 148, 150 (1976). Several years later, a different enactment provided that a plaintiff seeking redress under the Securities Exchange Act of 1934 could file suit in any district in which the defendant transacts business. Id. In this case a plaintiff asserted that his suit against a national bank for alleged securities violations could proceed in any district in which the bank transacted business. Id. The Supreme Court disagreed, concluding that the provision pertaining specifically to national banks was more specific and, therefore, that a suit alleging that a national bank violated the Securities Exchange Act could be brought only in the district in which the bank was established. Id. at 158. "Where there is no clear intention otherwise, a specific statute will not be controlled or nullified by a general one, regardless of the priority of enactment." Id. at 153 (internal quotation marks omitted). See also Traynor v. Turnage, 485 U.S. 535, 548 (1988).

c. Enactments later in time supersede earlier ones

If two statutes may not be harmonized and one statute is not more specific than another, there is a final principle to which we may turn, which is that a later enactment supersedes an earlier one. This is often called the "last-in-time" rule. Recall the first principle from this section, which is that we must harmonize different statutes if we can and that repeals by implication are disfavored. If we conclude that a later enactment supersedes an earlier one, then we have, in effect, concluded that the later statute implicitly repealed the earlier one. Because repeals by implication are heavily disfavored, we turn to this principle only when two statutes cannot be reconciled in any reasonable manner, and then only to the extent of the conflict. For example, a statute provided that students who lived outside of the District of Columbia could, under certain circumstances, be "taught free of charge" in District schools. Eisenberg v. Corning, 179 F.2d 275, 276 (1949). A later enactment provided that no appropriations "shall be used for the free instruction of pupils who dwell outside the District of Columbia." Id. The later statute made no mention of the earlier one, so there was no explicit repeal of the earlier law. However, the court held that the statutes conflicted, with "the earlier permitting and the later prohibiting," and therefore that the later statute superseded the earlier one. Id. at 277.

E. Agency Administrative Interpretations

"I was gratified to be able to answer promptly, and I did. I said I didn't know."

Mark Twain, Life on the Mississippi.

This section discusses issues that arise concerning agency interpretations of statutes and of their own regulations. This area of law has produced an enormous volume of court decisions and legal scholarship: one of the foundational cases in this area, Chevron U.S.A. v. Natural Resources Defense Council, 467 U.S. 837 (1984), has been cited over 14,000 times in other court decisions. Clearly, a thorough treatment of this subject would overwhelm our tome on appropriations law. Here we offer only a fleeting introduction to this rich and always evolving area of law. For further information we encourage the reader to consult one of the many excellent treatises that discuss both the foundations of and the most recent developments in administrative law. See, e.g., Kristin E. Hickman and Richard J. Pierce, Jr., Administrative Law Treatise (5th ed., last updated October 2015).

1. Interpretation of Statutes

When Congress vests an agency with responsibility to administer a particular statute, the agency's interpretation of that statute, by regulation or otherwise, is entitled to considerable weight. This principle is really a matter of common sense. An agency that works with a program from day to day develops an expertise that should not be lightly disregarded. Even when dealing with a new law, Congress does not entrust administration to a particular agency without reason, and this decision merits respect.

In the often-cited case of Udall v. Tallman, 380 U.S. 1, 16 (1965), the Supreme Court stated the principle this way:

> "When faced with a problem of statutory construction, this Court shows great deference to the interpretation given the statute by the officers or agency charged with its administration."

In what is now recognized as one of the key cases in determining how much "deference" is due an agency interpretation, Chevron, Inc. v. Natural Resources Defense Council, 467 U.S. 837 (1984), the Court formulated its approach to deference in terms of two questions. The first question is "whether Congress has directly spoken to the precise question at issue." Id. at 842. If it has, the agency must of course comply with clear congressional intent, and regulations to the contrary will be invalidated. Thus, before you ever get to questions of deference, it must first be determined that the regulation is not contrary to the statute, a question of delegated authority rather than deference. "If a court, employing traditional tools of statutory construction, ascertains that Congress had an intention on the precise question at issue, that intention is the law and must be given effect." Id. at 843 n.9. For example, the Court declined to give Chevron deference, or any lesser degree of deference, to an agency interpretation that it found to be "clearly wrong" as a matter of statutory construction, since the agency interpretation was contrary to the act's text, structure, purpose, history, and relationship to other federal statutes. General Dynamics Land Systems, Inc. v. Cline, 540 U.S. 581, 600 (2004).

Once you cross this threshold, that is, once you determine that "the statute is silent or ambiguous with respect to the specific issue," the question becomes "whether the agency's answer is based on a permissible construction of the statute." Chevron at 843. The Court in Chevron went on to say:

> "If Congress has explicitly left a gap for the agency to fill, there is an express delegation of authority to the agency to elucidate a specific provision of the statute by regulation. Such legislative regulations are given controlling weight unless they are arbitrary, capricious, or manifestly contrary to the statute. Sometimes the legislative delegation to an agency on a particular question is implicit rather than explicit. In such a case, a court may not substitute its own construction of a statutory provision for a reasonable interpretation made by the administrator of an agency."

Id. at 843–44.

Reiterating the traditional deference concept, the Court then said that the proper standard of review is not whether the agency's construction is "inappropriate," but merely whether it is "a reasonable one." Id. at 844-45.

When the agency's interpretation is in the form of a regulation with the force and effect of law, the deference, as we have seen, is at its highest. The agency's position is entitled to Chevron deference and must be upheld unless it is arbitrary or capricious. See also Michigan v. EPA, ___ U.S. ___,135 S.Ct. 2699, 2707 (2015) ("[e]ven under this deferential standard, however, agencies must operate within the bounds of reasonable interpretation") (internal citations and quotations omitted). There should be no question of substitution of judgment. If the agency position can be said to be reasonable or to have a rational basis within the statutory grant of authority, it must stand, even if the reviewing body finds some other position preferable. See, e.g., Household Credit Services, Inc. v. Pfennig, 541 U.S. 232 (2004). But see King v. Burwell, ___ U.S. ___, 135 S.Ct. 2480, 2488-89 (2015) (noting that there may be reason to hesitate in "extraordinary cases" before concluding that Congress intended an implicit delegation from Congress to the agency to fill in the statutory gaps; declining to defer to agency interpretation under Chevron because the question presented was "of deep economic and political significance that is central to this statutory scheme" and because it was unlikely that Congress would have delegated the decision at issue to the agency, "which has no expertise in crafting health insurance policy of this sort") (internal citations and quotations omitted). Chevron deference is also given to authoritative agency positions in formal adjudication. See Immigration & Naturalization Service v. Aguirre-Aguirre, 526 U.S. 415 (1999) (holding that a Board of Immigration Appeals statutory interpretation developed in case-by-case formal adjudication should be accorded Chevron deference). But see Mellouli v. Lynch, ___ U.S. ___, 135 S. Ct. 1980, 1989 (2015) (declining to give deference to interpretation devised by Board of Immigration Appeals "[b]ecause it makes scant sense"). For an extensive list of Supreme Court cases giving Chevron deference to agency statutory interpretations found in rulemaking or formal adjudication, see United States v. Mead Corp., 533 U.S. 218, 231 at n.12 (2001).

When the agency's interpretation anything short of a regulation with the force and effect of law or formal adjudication, such as an interpretive regulation, manual, or handbook, the standard of review has traditionally been somewhat lessened. In the past, deference in this context has not been a fixed concept, but has been variable, depending on the interplay of several factors. The Supreme Court explained the approach as follows in Skidmore v. Swift & Co., 323 U.S. 134, 140 (1944):

> "We consider that the rulings, interpretations and opinions of the Administrator under this Act, while not controlling upon the courts by reason of their authority [i.e., the statements in question were not regulations with the force and effect of law], do constitute a body of experience and informed judgment to which courts and litigants may properly resort for guidance. The weight of such a judgment in a particular case will depend upon the thoroughness evident in its consideration, the validity of its reasoning, its consistency with earlier and later pronouncements, and all those factors which give it power to persuade, if lacking power to control."

See also Young v. UPS, ___ U.S. ___, 135 S.Ct. 1338, 1352 (2015) (declining to defer to agency interpretation that conflicted with its prior litigation positions and was issued in guidance document after Supreme Court had granted certiorari). Courts have found that the degree of weight to be given an agency administrative interpretation varies with several factors:

- The nature and degree of expertise possessed by the agency. Barnhart v. Walton, 535 U.S. 212, 222, 225 (2002).

- The duration and consistency of the interpretation. Good Samaritan Hospital v. Shalala, 508 U.S. 402, 417 (1993).

- The soundness and thoroughness of reasoning underlying the position. Skidmore, 323 U.S. at 140; Arriaga v. Florida Pacific Farms, L.L.C., 305 F.3d 1228, 1239 (11th Cir. 2002);

- Evidence (or lack thereof) of congressional awareness of, and acquiescence in, the administrative position. United States v. American Trucking Ass'n, 310 U.S. 534, 549–50 (1940).

"[I]ncreasingly muddled" Supreme Court decisions on the scope of Chevron have left unclear the amount of deference due less formal pronouncements like interpretive rules and informal adjudications. In 2000, the Supreme Court appeared to resolve the issue of how much deference was due these less formal pronouncements. The Court held that interpretations that "lack the force of law" (such as those in "policy statements, agency manuals, and enforcement guidelines") are only entitled to respect under Skidmore to the extent that those interpretations have the "power to persuade." Christensen v. Harris County, 529 U.S. 576, 586-87 (2000).

However, the Supreme Court later clarified this position in Mead Corp., 533 U.S. 218, holding that Chevron deference may extend to statutory interpretations beyond those contained in legislative rules and adjudications where there is "some other indication of a comparable congressional intent" to give such interpretations the force of law.

More recent decisions further indicate that Chevron deference may extend beyond legislative rules and formal adjudications. Most notably, the Court observed in dicta in Barnhart v. Walton, 535 U.S. at 221-22 that Mead Corp. "denied [any] suggestion" in Christensen that Chevron deference was limited to interpretations adopted through formal rulemaking. Rather, the Court noted that while Mead Corp. indicated that "whether a court should give such deference depends in significant part upon the interpretive method used and the nature of the question at issue," the presence or absence of notice-and-comment rulemaking was not dispositive. The Barnhart opinion went on to say that:

> "In this case, the interstitial nature of the legal question, the related expertise of the Agency, the importance of the question to the administration of the statute, the complexity of that administration, and the careful consideration the Agency has given the question over a long period of time all indicate that Chevron provides the appropriate legal lens through which to view the legality of the Agency interpretation here at issue."

Id. at 222. See also General Dynamics Land Systems, Inc. v. Cline, 540 U.S. 581 (2004); Edelman v. Lynchburg College, 535 U.S. 106, 114 (2002). Two additional decisions are instructive in terms of the limits of Chevron. In both cases the Court found that the issuances containing agency statutory interpretations were entitled to some weight, but not Chevron deference. Raymond B. Yates, M.D., P.C. Profit Sharing Plan v. Hendon, 541 U.S. 1 (2004) (agency advisory opinion); Alaska Department of Environmental Conservation v. EPA, 540 U.S. 461 (2004) (internal agency guidance memoranda). As two legal scholars note:

> "After Mead, it is possible to know only that legislative rules and formal adjudications are always entitled to Chevron deference, while less formal pronouncements like interpretative rules and informal adjudications may or may not be entitled to Chevron deference. The deference due a less formal pronouncement seems to depend on the results of judicial application of an apparently open-ended list of factors that arguably qualify as 'other indication[s] of a comparable congressional intent' to give a particular type of agency pronouncement the force of law."

Hickman and Pierce, Administrative Law Treatise, at § 3.5.

For illustrations of how GAO has applied the deference principle in decisions, see:

- 69 Comp. Gen. 274 (1990) (denying an offeror's protest, as the Defense Personnel Support Center's long-standing interpretation of a statutory provision pertaining to Department of Defense food procurements is entitled to deference).

- B-286800, Feb. 21, 2001 (denying an offeror's protest, as the Department of Defense's interpretation of its own regulation was entitled to great weight).

The deference principle does not apply to an agency's interpretation of a statute that is not part of its program or enabling legislation, where the statute is of general applicability, or when an agency resolves a conflict between its statute and another statute. See Adams v. SEC, 287 F.3d 183 (D.C. Cir. 2002); Contractor's Sand & Gravel, Inc. v. Federal Mine Safety & Health Review Commission, 199 F.3d 1335 (D.C. Cir. 2000); Association of Civilian Technicians v. Federal Labor Relations Authority, 200 F.3d 590 (9th Cir. 2000). In at least one "split-jurisdiction" situation, where multiple agencies shared specific statutory responsibility, the Supreme Court held that Chevron deference is due to the primary executive branch enforcer and the agency accountable for overall administration of the statutory scheme. Martin v. Occupational Safety and Health Review Commission, 499 U.S. 144 (1991). However, the Court was careful to limit its holding to that particular case and stated that "we take no position on the division of enforcement and interpretive powers within other regulatory schemes that conform to the split-enforcement structure." Id. at 158. See also Collins v. National Transportation Safety Board, 351 F.3d 1246 (D.C. Cir. 2003) (extending the holding in Martin).

As noted above, a regulation with the force and effect of law merits Chevron deference. In this connection, it is necessary to elaborate somewhat on one of the tests in Chrysler Corp. v. Brown, 441 U.S. 281 (1979)—that the regulation be issued pursuant to a statutory grant of 'legislative' (i.e., rulemaking) authority. Congress may, of course, specifically authorize an agency to promulgate a rule on a specific subject; this constitutes a statutory grant of legislative authority. See Chrysler, 441 U.S. at 302-03 (explicit delegation to SEC under 15 U.S.C. § 78n to issue proxy rules). However, the statutory grant of legislative authority need not be so specific. The Court stated that "what is important is that the reviewing court reasonably be able to conclude that the grant of authority contemplates the regulations issued." Chrysler, 441 U.S. at 308. For example, the Secretary of the Treasury has general authority to "prescribe all needful rules and regulations" to administer the Internal Revenue Code. 26 U.S.C. § 7805. The Court has given Chevron deference to IRS regulations issued through notice and comment rulemaking under the general authority of section 7805. Atlantic Mutual Insurance Co. v. Commissioner of Internal Revenue, 523 U.S. 382 (1998).

We began by noting the increasing role of agency regulations in the overall scheme of federal law. We conclude this discussion with the observation that this enhanced role makes continued litigation on the issues we have outlined inevitable. The proliferation and complexity of case law perhaps lends credence to Professor Davis's mild cynicism:

> "Unquestionably one of the most important factors in each decision on what weight to give an interpretative rule is the degree of judicial agreement or disagreement with the rule."

2 Administrative Law Treatise § 7:13 (2d ed. 1979).

2. Interpretation of Agency's Own Regulations

The principle of giving considerable deference to the administering agency's interpretation of a statute applies at least with equal force to an agency's interpretation of its own regulations. The Supreme Court has stated that "[w]hen the construction of an administrative regulation rather than a statute is in issue, deference is even more clearly in order." Udall v. Tallman, 380 U.S. 1, 16 (1965).

Perhaps the strongest statement is found in a 1945 Supreme Court decision, Bowles v. Seminole Rock & Sand Co., 325 U.S. 410, 413–14 (1945):

> "Since this involves an interpretation of an administrative regulation a court must necessarily look to the administrative construction of the regulation if the meaning of the words used is in doubt. The intention of Congress or the principles of the Constitution in some situations may be relevant in the first instance in choosing between various constructions. But the ultimate criterion is the administrative interpretation, which becomes of controlling weight unless it is plainly erroneous or inconsistent with the regulation."

The Court reaffirmed this principle in Auer v. Robbins, 519 U.S. 452 (1997). See also 72 Comp. Gen. 241 (1993); 57 Comp. Gen. 347 (1978); 56 Comp. Gen. 160 (1976); B-279250 (May 26, 1998). Although Auer calls for deference to an agency's interpretation of its own ambiguous regulation, this general rule does not apply in all cases. For example, deference may be unwarranted where an agency's interpretation does not reflect the agency's fair and considered judgment on the matter in question, such as when it conflicts with a prior interpretation or appears to be nothing more than a "convenient litigating position" or post hoc rationalization advanced by an agency seeking to defend past action against attack. Christopher v. SmithKline Beecham Corp, ___ U.S. ___, 132 S. Ct. 2156, 2166-67 (2012). Furthermore, "[e]ven in cases where an agency's interpretation receives Auer deference, however, it is the court that ultimately decides whether a given regulation means what the agency says" and "[m]orever, Auer deference is not an inexorable command in all cases". Perez v. Mortgage Bankers Association, ___ U.S. ___, 135 S. Ct. 1199, 1208 n.4 (2015).

A good illustration of how all of this can work is found in B-222666, Jan. 11, 1988. The Defense Security Assistance Agency (DSAA) was responsible for issuing instructions and procedures for Foreign Military Sales (FMS) transactions. These appear in the Security Assistance Management Manual. A disagreement arose between DSAA and an Army operating command as to whether certain "reports of discrepancy," representing charges for nonreceipt by customers, should be charged to the FMS trust fund (which would effectively pass the losses on to all FMS customers) or to Army appropriated funds. DSAA took the latter position. GAO reviewed the regulation in question, and found it far from clear on this point. The decision noted that "both of the conflicting interpretations in this case appear to have merit, and both derive support from portions of the regulation." However, while the regulation may have been complex, the solution to the problem was fairly simple. DSAA wrote the regulation and GAO, citing the standard from the Bowles case, could not conclude that DSAA's position was plainly erroneous or inconsistent with the regulation. Therefore, DSAA's interpretation must prevail.

Just as with the interpretation of statutes, inconsistency in the application of a regulation will significantly diminish the deference courts are likely to give the agency's position. E.g., Western States Petroleum Ass'n v. EPA, 87 F.3d 280 (9th Cir. 1996); Murphy v. United States, 22 Cl. Ct. 147, 154 (1990). In addition, the text of a regulation must fairly support the agency's interpretation. See Christensen v. Harris County, 529 U.S. 576, 588 (2000). No Seminole Rock-Auer deference is warranted if the plain and unambiguous language of the regulation is at odds with the agency's interpretation. Id. In such a case, the agency's "interpretation" really amounts to a de facto amendment of the regulation.

An agency's interpretation of its own regulation is entitled to deference only when the regulation interpreted is itself a product of the agency's expertise and authority in a given area. For example, the Attorney General issued an interpretive rule stating that assisting suicide was not a "legitimate medical purpose" for which doctors could prescribe drugs, and doctors doing so would violate the Controlled Substance Act (CSA). Gonzales v. Oregon, 546 U.S. 243 (2006). The Court concluded that the interpretive rule was not a product of the Attorney General's experience or expertise. To the contrary, the rule did "little more than restate the terms of the statute itself." Id. at 257. Accordingly, the rule merited no judicial deference.

Chapter 2: The Legal Framework

A. Appropriations and Related Terminology

This section discusses basic appropriations law terms that appear throughout this publication. Some of our discussion draws upon statutory definitions that apply in various budgetary contexts. We draw other definitions from administrative and judicial decisions, as well as from custom and usage in the budget and appropriations process.

The Comptroller General, in cooperation with the Treasury Department, Office of Management and Budget, and Congressional Budget Office, must maintain and publish standard terms and classifications for "fiscal, budget, and program information," giving particular consideration to the needs of the congressional budget, appropriations, and revenue committees. 31 U.S.C. § 1112(c). Federal agencies must use this standard terminology when they provide information to Congress. 31 U.S.C. § 1112(d).

GAO publishes the terminology developed pursuant to this authority in A Glossary of Terms Used in the Federal Budget Process, GAO-05-734SP (Washington, D.C.: Sept. 2005) [hereinafter Glossary]. Unless otherwise noted, the terminology used throughout this publication is based on the Glossary. The following sections present some of the more important terminology in the budget and appropriations process.

1. Budget Authority: Authority to Obligate

Congress finances federal programs and activities by providing "budget authority," which grants agencies authority to enter into financial obligations that will result in immediate or future outlays of government funds. As defined by the Congressional Budget Act, "budget authority" includes:

> "(i) provisions of law that make funds available for obligation and expenditure (other than borrowing authority), including the authority to obligate and expend the proceeds of offsetting receipts and collections;

> "(ii) borrowing authority, which means authority granted to a Federal entity to borrow and obligate and expend the borrowed funds, including through the issuance of promissory notes or other monetary credits;

> "(iii) contract authority, which means the making of funds available for obligation but not for expenditure; and (iv) offsetting receipts and collections as negative budget authority, and the reduction thereof as positive budget authority."

Only Congress may grant budget authority. Therefore, agency regulations cannot confer budget authority. A regulation may create a liability on the part of the government only if Congress has enacted the necessary budget authority and if the obligation is consistent with all applicable statutes. Without the necessary statutory authority, a regulation purporting to create a liability on the part of the government is invalid and not binding on the government. For example, a claimant asserted that the War Department had a practice of paying for the transportation of officers' privately-owned horses. Atchison, Topeka & Santa Fe Railroad Co. v. United States, 55 Ct. Cl. 339 (1920). However, because Congress had not enacted any statute permitting the War Department to pay these personal expenses, the War Department could not pay them, despite any contrary practice or regulation. Id.

Further illustrations may be found in the following decisions of the Comptroller General:

- Where the program statute provided that federal grants "shall be" a specified percentage of project construction costs, the grantor agency could not issue regulations providing a mechanism for reducing the grants below the specified percentage. 53 Comp. Gen. 547 (1974).

- Where a statute provided that administrative costs could not exceed a specified percentage of funds distributed to states under an allotment formula, the administering agency could not amend its regulations to relieve states of liability for over expenditures or to raise the ceiling. B-178564, July 19, 1977, aff'd 57 Comp. Gen. 163 (1977).

- Absent a clear statutory basis, an agency may not issue regulations establishing procedures to accept government liability or to forgive indebtedness based on what it deems to be fair or equitable. B-201054, Apr. 27, 1981. See also B-118653, July 15, 1969.

- Agencies should not incur obligations for food and light refreshments in reliance on a General Services Administration (GSA) travel regulation for which GSA has no authority. B-288266, Jan. 27, 2003.

See also 62 Comp. Gen. 116 (1983); 56 Comp. Gen. 943 (1977); B-201706, Mar. 17, 1981.

2. Appropriations: Authority to Draw Money from the Treasury

As we have seen in our discussion of the congressional "power of the purse," the Constitution permits the withdrawal of money from the Treasury only where Congress enacts an appropriation authorizing the payment. Therefore, an appropriation is a law authorizing the payment of funds from the Treasury. In addition, most appropriations also authorize agencies to incur obligations and to ultimately draw money from the Treasury to satisfy those obligations. Stated differently, most appropriations provide both budget authority and the authority to make payments from the Treasury. Such appropriations do not represent cash actually set aside in the

Treasury. They represent legal authority granted by Congress to incur obligations and to make disbursements for the purposes, during the time periods, and up to the amount limitations specified in the appropriation acts. See *United States ex rel. Becker v. Westinghouse Savannah River Co.*, 305 F.3d 284 (4th Cir. 2002).

While other forms of budget authority may authorize agencies to incur obligations, the authority to incur obligations by itself is not sufficient to authorize payments from the Treasury. See, e.g., *National Ass'n of Regional Councils v. Costle*, 564 F.2d 583, 586 (D.C. Cir. 1977); *New York Airways, Inc. v. United States*, 369 F.2d 743 (Ct. Cl. 1966). Thus, at some point if obligations are paid, they are paid by and from an appropriation.

Congress may make an appropriation that grants authority to draw money from the Treasury but does not grant budget authority. Such an appropriation is known by a more specific term. For example, a "liquidating appropriation" provides authority to draw money from the Treasury to satisfy obligations incurred pursuant to contract authority (discussed in the next sub-section). A "deficiency appropriation" provides authority to satisfy obligations that exceeded an agency's available budget authority. The word "appropriation" appearing alone nearly always refers to a provision of law that grants both budget authority and authority to make payments from the Treasury.

Appropriations are identified on financial documents by means of "account symbols," which are assigned by the Treasury Department, based on the number and types of appropriations an agency receives and other types of funds it may control. An appropriation account symbol is a group of numbers, or a combination of numbers and letters, which identifies the agency responsible for the account, the period of availability of the appropriation, and the specific fund classification. Detailed information on reading and identifying account symbols is contained in the Treasury Financial Manual (I TFM 2-1500). Specific accounts for each agency are listed in a publication entitled Federal Account Symbols and Titles, issued quarterly as a supplement to the TFM.

3. Contract Authority: Obligations in Advance of Appropriations

Contract authority is a form of budget authority that permits agencies to incur obligations in advance of appropriations. Glossary at 22. It is to be distinguished from every government agency's inherent authority to use budget authority to enter into contracts necessary to carry out its statutory functions.

Contract authority itself is not an appropriation; it grants authority to enter into binding contracts but not the funds to make payments under them. Congress must provide funds to satisfy the contractual obligations, either by making a subsequent appropriation called a "liquidating appropriation" or by granting authority to use receipts or offsetting collections for this purpose. See *PCL Construction Service, Inc. v. United States*, 41 Fed. Cl. 242 (1998); *National Ass'n of*

Regional Councils v. Costle, 564 F.2d 583, 586 (D.C. Cir. 1977); B-300167, Nov. 15, 2002; B-228732, Feb. 18, 1988. Contract authority constitutes budget authority. The subsequent liquidating appropriation does not grant authority to incur obligations and, therefore, is not budget authority. B-171630, Aug. 14, 1975.

Congress may provide contract authority in appropriation acts (for example, B-174839, Mar. 20, 1984) or, more commonly, in other types of legislation (for example, B-228732, Feb. 18, 1988). Either way, the authority must be specific. 31 U.S.C. § 1301(d).

Contract authority has a "period of availability" analogous to that for an appropriation. Unless otherwise specified, if it appears in an appropriation act in connection with a particular appropriation, its period of availability will be the same as that for the appropriation. If it appears in an appropriation act without reference to a particular appropriation, its period of availability, again unless otherwise specified, will be the fiscal year covered by the appropriation act. 32 Comp. Gen. 29, 31 (1952); B-76061, May 14, 1948. See Cray Research, Inc. v. United States, 44 Fed. Cl. 327, 331 n.4 (1999); Costle, 564 F.2d at 587–88. This period of availability refers to the time period during which the contracts must be entered into.

Since the contracts entered into pursuant to contract authority constitute obligations binding on the United States, Congress has little practical choice but to make the necessary liquidating appropriations. B-228732, Feb. 18, 1988; B-226887, Sept. 17, 1987. As the Supreme Court has put it:

> "The expectation is that appropriations will be automatically forthcoming to meet these contractual commitments. This mechanism considerably reduces whatever discretion Congress might have exercised in the course of making annual appropriations."

Train v. City of New York, 420 U.S. 35, 39 n.2 (1975). A failure or refusal by Congress to make the necessary appropriation would not defeat the obligation, and the party entitled to payment would most likely be able to recover in a lawsuit. E.g., B-211190, Apr. 5, 1983.

4. Offsetting Collections: Authority to Obligate Funds Collected

The federal government receives money from numerous sources and in numerous contexts. Our interest from an appropriations law perspective is whether funds received by an agency are available for obligation without further congressional action.

For our purposes, we discuss two types of collections that may be received by the government: offsetting collections and offsetting receipts. Offsetting collections are collections authorized by law to be credited to appropriation or fund expenditure accounts. Generally, offsetting collections are collections resulting from business-type or market-oriented activities, such as the sale of goods or services to the public, and intragovernmental transactions. For example, the Secretary of the Interior is authorized to collect recreation fees from visitors to national parks.

These fees are available for expenditure without further appropriation by Congress. 16 U.S.C. § 6806.

Laws authorizing offsetting collections make them available for obligation to meet the account's purpose without further congressional action. Accordingly, because the receiving agency has the authority to obligate and expend offsetting collections, offsetting collections constitute budget authority. An appropriation is authority to incur obligations and to make payments from the Treasury for specified purposes. Thus, offsetting collections are an appropriation and are subject to the fiscal laws governing appropriated funds. B-230110, Apr. 11, 1988; 63 Comp. Gen. 285 (1984).

In contrast, offsetting receipts are collections that cannot be obligated and expended without further congressional action. Offsetting receipts are not available to an agency unless Congress appropriates them. Offsetting receipts are not available to the receiving agency for obligation; accordingly, offsetting receipts do not constitute budget authority. An example of offsetting receipts is the motor vehicle and engine compliance program fee collected by EPA. These fees are deposited into the Environmental Services Special Fund but are not available to EPA without further appropriation. 42 U.S.C. § 7552.

5. Borrowing Authority: Incurring Obligations Against Borrowed Amounts

"Borrowing authority" is authority that permits agencies to incur obligations and make payments to liquidate the obligations out of borrowed moneys. Borrowing authority may consist of (a) authority to borrow from the Treasury; (b) authority to sell agency debt securities and, therefore, to borrow directly from the public; (c) authority to borrow from the Federal Financing Bank, or (d) some combination of the above.

Borrowing from the Treasury is the most common form and is also known as "public debt financing." Generally, GAO has expressed a preference for financing through direct appropriations rather than through borrowing authority on the grounds that the appropriations process provides enhanced congressional control. E.g., B-301397, Sept. 4, 2003; B-141869, July 26, 1961. The Congressional Budget Act met this concern to an extent by requiring generally that new borrowing authority, as with new contract authority, be limited to the extent or amounts provided in appropriation acts. 2 U.S.C. § 651(a). GAO has recommended that borrowing authority be provided only to those accounts that can generate enough revenue in the form of collections from nonfederal sources to repay their debt. GAO, Budget Issues: Budgeting for Federal Capital, GAO/AIMD-97-5 (Washington, D.C.: Nov. 12, 1996); Budget Issues: Agency Authority to Borrow Should Be Granted More Selectively, GAO/AFMD-89-4 (Washington, D.C.: Sept. 15, 1989). On occasion, however, GAO has recommended borrowing authority when supplemental appropriations might otherwise be necessary. See GAO, Aviation Insurance: Federal Insurance Program Needs Improvements to Ensure Success, GAO/RCED-94-151 (Washington, D.C.: July 15, 1994).

A type of borrowing authority specified in the expanded definition of budget authority contained in the Omnibus Budget Reconciliation Act of 1990 is monetary credits. The monetary credit is a relatively uncommon concept in government transactions. At the present time, it exists mostly in a handful of statutes authorizing the government to use monetary credits to acquire property such as land or mineral rights. Examples are the Rattlesnake National Recreation Area and Wilderness Act of 1980, discussed in 62 Comp. Gen. 102 (1982), and the Cranberry Wilderness Act, discussed in B-211306, Apr. 9, 1984.

Under the monetary credit procedure, the government does not issue a check in payment for the acquired property. Instead, it gives the seller "credits" in dollar amounts reflecting the purchase price. The holder may then use these credits to offset or reduce amounts it owes the government in other transactions that may, depending on the terms of the governing legislation, be related or unrelated to the original transaction. The statute may use the term "monetary credit" (as in the Cranberry legislation) or some other designation such as "bidding rights" (as in the Rattlesnake Act). Where this procedure is authorized, the acquiring agency does not need to have appropriations or other funds available to cover the purchase price because no cash disbursement is made. An analogous device authorized for use by the Commodity Credit Corporation is "commodity certificates."

6. Loan and Loan Guarantee Authority

A loan guarantee is any guarantee, insurance, or other pledge with respect to the payment of all or a part of the principal or interest on any debt obligation of a nonfederal borrower to a nonfederal lender. The government does not know whether or to what extent it may be required to honor the guarantee until there has been a default.

In the past, loan guarantees were expressly excluded from the definition of budget authority. Budget authority was created only when an appropriation to liquidate loan guarantee authority was made. This changed with the enactment of the Federal Credit Reform Act of 1990, effective starting with fiscal year 1992. Under this legislation, the "cost" of both loan and loan guarantee programs is budget authority. Cost means the estimated long-term cost to the government of a loan or loan guarantee (defaults, delinquencies, interest subsidies, etc.), calculated on a net present value basis, excluding administrative costs. Except for entitlement programs (the statute notes the guaranteed student loan program and the veterans' home loan guaranty program as examples) and certain Commodity Credit Corporation programs, new loan guarantee commitments may be made only to the extent budget authority to cover their costs is provided in advance or other treatment is specified in appropriation acts. Appropriations of budget authority are to be made to "credit program accounts," and the programs administered from revolving nonbudgetary "financing accounts."

The Federal Credit Reform Act reflects the thrust of proposals by GAO, the Office of Management and Budget, the Congressional Budget Office, and the Senate Budget Committee.

See GAO, Credit Reform: U.S. Needs Better Method for Estimating Cost of Foreign Loans and Guarantees, GAO/NSIAD/GGD-95-31 (Washington, D.C.: Dec. 19, 1994); Credit Reform: Case-by-Case Assessment Advisable in Evaluating Coverage and Compliance, GAO/AIMD-94-57 (Washington, D.C.: July 28, 1994). See also GAO, Budget Issues: Budgetary Treatment of Federal Credit Programs, GAO/AFMD-89-42 (Washington, D.C.: Apr. 10, 1989) (discussion of the "net present value" approach to calculating costs).

7. Reappropriation

The term "reappropriation" means congressional action to continue the availability, whether for the same or different purposes, of all or part of the unobligated portion of budget authority that has expired or would otherwise expire. Reappropriations are counted as budget authority in the first year for which the availability is extended.

8. Classifications of Budget Authority

Appropriations are classified in different ways for different purposes. Some are discussed elsewhere in this publication. The following classifications, although phrased in terms of appropriations, apply equally to the broader concept of budget authority.

a. Classification Based on Duration

(1) One-year appropriation: An appropriation that is available for obligation only during a specific fiscal year. This is the most common type of appropriation. It is also known as a "fiscal year" or "annual" appropriation. *Oct 1 – Sep 30th, 1 yr expiration (default)*

(2) Multiple year appropriation: An appropriation that is available for obligation for a definite period of time in excess of one fiscal year. *yr to yr expiration/renewal.*

(3) No-year appropriation: An appropriation that is available for obligation for an indefinite period. A no-year appropriation is usually identified by appropriation language such as "to remain available until expended." *X*

b. Classification Based on Presence or Absence of Monetary Limit

(1) Definite appropriation: An appropriation of a specific amount of money

(2) Indefinite appropriation: An appropriation of an unspecified amount of money. An indefinite appropriation may appropriate all or part of the receipts from certain sources, the specific amount of which is determinable only at some future date, or it may appropriate "such sums as may be necessary" for a given purpose.

CDC has something like multi yr. – where base yr + then follow with optional yr to yr extension.

c. Classification Based on Permanency (yr to yr)

(1) Current appropriation: An appropriation made by Congress in, or immediately prior to, the fiscal year or years during which it is available for obligation.

(2) Permanent appropriation: A "standing" appropriation which, once made, is always available for specified purposes and does not require repeated action by Congress to authorize its use. Legislation authorizing an agency to retain and use receipts tends to be permanent; if so, it is a form of permanent appropriation.

d. Classification Based on Availability for New Obligations

(1) Current or unexpired appropriation: An appropriation that is available for incurring new obligations.

(2) Expired appropriation: An appropriation that is no longer available to incur new obligations, although it may still be available for the recording and/or payment (liquidation) of obligations properly incurred before the period of availability expired.

(3) Canceled appropriation: An appropriation whose account is closed, and is no longer available for obligation or expenditure for any purpose.

An appropriation may combine characteristics from more than one of the above groupings. For example, a "permanent indefinite" appropriation is open ended as to both period of availability and amount. Examples are 31 U.S.C. § 1304 (payment of certain judgments against the United States) and 31 U.S.C. § 1322(b)(2) (refunding amounts erroneously collected and deposited in the Treasury).

B. The Budget and Appropriations Process

An appropriate subtitle for this section might be "Life Cycle of an Appropriation." An appropriation has a conception, birth, death, and even an afterlife. The various phases in an appropriation's "life cycle" may be identified as follows:

- executive budget formulation and transmittal,
- congressional action,
- budget execution and control,
- audit and review, and
- account closing.

1. Historical Perspective

The first general appropriation act, passed by Congress on September 29, 1789, appropriated a total of $639,000 and illustrates what was once a relatively uncomplicated process:

> "Be it enacted by the Senate and House of Representatives of the United States of America in Congress assembled, That there be appropriated for the service of the present year, to be paid out of the monies which arise, either from the requisitions heretofore made upon the several states, or from the duties on impost and tonnage, the following sums, viz. A sum not exceeding two hundred and sixteen thousand dollars for defraying the expenses of the civil list, under the late and present government; a sum not exceeding one hundred and thirty-seven thousand dollars for defraying the expenses of the department of war; a sum not exceeding one hundred and ninety thousand dollars for discharging the warrants issued by the late board of treasury, and remaining unsatisfied; and a sum not exceeding ninety-six thousand dollars for paying the pensions to invalids."

1 Stat. 95. As the size and scope of the federal government have grown, so has the complexity of the appropriations and of the appropriations process.

In 1789, the House established the Ways and Means Committee to report on revenues and spending, only to disband it that same year following the creation of the Treasury Department. The House Ways and Means Committee was re-established to function permanently in 1795 and was recognized as a standing committee in 1802.

On the Senate side, the Finance Committee was established as a standing committee in 1816. Up until that time, the Senate had referred appropriation measures to temporary select committees. By 1834, jurisdiction over all Senate appropriation bills was consolidated in the Senate Finance Committee.

In the mid-nineteenth century, a move was begun to restrict appropriation acts to only those expenditures that had been previously authorized by law. The purpose was to avoid the delays caused when legislative items or "riders" were attached to appropriation bills. Rules were eventually passed by both houses of Congress to require, in general, prior legislative authorizations for the enactment of appropriations.

Fiscal years allow financial transactions to be classified into particular time periods. The need for such temporal classification has been termed an "absolute necessity." Sweet v. United States, 34 Ct. Cl. 377, 386 (1899). See also Bachelor v. United States, 8 Ct. Cl. 235, 238 (1872) (reasons for classifying transactions into fiscal years are "so obvious . . . that no one can fail to see their importance"). Prior to 1842, the government did not distinguish between fiscal year and calendar year. The practical needs of government led Congress to establish a fiscal year that does not run concurrently with the calendar year: one case explained that a different fiscal year arose for the sake of the "convenience of the public service in the administration of the expense, accounts, and estimates of the Government." Sweet v. United States, 34 Ct. Cl. at 386-87.

Under the financial strains caused by the Civil War, appropriations committees first appeared in both the House and the Senate, diminishing the jurisdiction of the Ways and Means and Finance Committees, respectively. Years later, the need for major reforms was again accentuated by the burdens of another war. Following World War I, Congress passed the Budget and Accounting Act, 1921, Pub. L. No. 67-13, 42 Stat. 20 (June 10, 1921).

Before 1921, departments and agencies generally made individual requests for appropriations. These submissions were compiled for congressional review in an uncoordinated "Book of Estimates." The Budget and Accounting Act enhanced budgetary efficiency and aided in the performance of constitutional checks and balances through the budget process. It required the President to submit a national budget each year and restricted the authority of the agencies to present their own proposals. See 31 U.S.C. §§ 1104, 1105. With this centralization of authority for the formulation of the executive branch budget in the President and the newly established Bureau of the Budget (now Office of Management and Budget), Congress also took steps to strengthen its oversight capability over fiscal matters by establishing what was then called the General Accounting Office.

The decades immediately following World War II saw growth in both the size and the complexity of the federal budget. It became apparent that the congressional role in the "budget and appropriations" process centered heavily on the appropriations phase and placed too little emphasis on the budgetary phase. In other words, Congress responded to the President's spending and revenue proposals only through the cumulative result of individual pieces of legislation reached through an agglomeration of separate actions. Congress did not look at the budget as a whole, nor did it examine or vote on overall spending or revenues. There was no process by which Congress could establish its own spending priorities. Thus, the impetus for a congressional budget process began in the early 1970s. It was not created in a single step; rather, it was created in stages—and for the most part new pieces did not replace but were added to existing processes. As William G. Dauster, former Chief Counsel on the Committee on the Budget, put it: "[t]he law governing the budget process resembles nothing so much as sediment. It has accumulated in several statutes, each layered upon the prior one . . . [t]his incremental growth has created something of a legal nettle." Budget Process Law Annotated, S. Print No. 103-49, at xxxv (1993).

Among the several statutes on the budget process is the Congressional Budget Act and Impoundment Control Act of 1974. It established a process for Congress to systematically consider the total federal budget and determine priorities for allocating budget resources. The design of programs and the allocation of spending within each mission area is left to the authorizing and appropriations committees. The focus is on overall fiscal policy and an allocation across priorities.

The statute made several major changes to the existing budget and appropriations process. For example:

It established a detailed calendar governing the various stages of the congressional budget and appropriations process. 2 U.S.C. § 631.

It provided for congressional review of the President's budget, the establishment of target ceilings for federal expenditures through one or more concurrent resolutions, and the evaluation of spending bills against these targets. 2 U.S.C. §§ 632–642. Prior to this time, Congress had considered the President's budget only in the context of individual appropriation bills. To implement the new process, the law created Budget Committees in both the Senate and the House, and a Congressional Budget Office (CBO). 2 U.S.C. § 601. The law requires the CBO to prepare estimates of new budget authority, outlays, or revenue provided by bills or resolutions reported from committees of either house, or estimates of the costs that the government would incur in carrying out the provisions of the proposed legislation. 2 U.S.C. § 602.

Prompted by the growth of "backdoor spending," it enhanced the role of the Appropriations Committees in reviewing proposals for contract authority, borrowing authority, and mandatory entitlements. 2 U.S.C. § 651.

The 1974 legislation also imposed limitations on the impounding of appropriated funds by the executive branch. 2 U.S.C. §§ 681–688.

2. Executive Budgeting: the Budget and Accounting Act, 1921

With this as an historical backdrop, the first step in the life cycle of an appropriation is the long and exhaustive administrative process of budget preparation and review, a process that may well take place several years before the budget for a particular fiscal year is ready to be submitted to Congress. The primary participants in the process at this stage are the agencies and individual organizational units, which review current operations, program objectives, and future plans, and the Office of Management and Budget (OMB), which coordinates and formulates a consolidated budget submission.

Throughout this preparation period, there is a continuous exchange of information among the various federal agencies, OMB, and the President, including revenue estimates and economic outlook projections from the Treasury Department, the Council of Economic Advisers, the Congressional Budget Office, and the Departments of Commerce and Labor.

The President must submit his budget request to Congress on or before the first Monday in February of each year, for use during the following fiscal year. 2 U.S.C. § 631.17 Numerous statutory provisions, the most important of which are 31 U.S.C. §§ 1104–1109, prescribe the content and nature of the materials and justifications that must be submitted with the President's

Federal Appropriations Law

budget request. Specific instructions and policy guidance are contained in OMB Circular No. A-11.

3. Congressional Budgeting: the Congressional Budget Act of 1974

The next phase in the life cycle of an appropriation is sometimes referred to as "congressional budgeting." Under the Congressional Budget Act, Congress must agree on governmentwide budget totals. A timetable for congressional budget action is set forth in 2 U.S.C. § 631, with further detail in sections 632–656. Key steps in that timetable are summarized below.

February 15. The Congressional Budget Office submits to the House and Senate Budget Committees its annual report required by 2 U.S.C. § 602(e). The report contains the Congressional Budget Office's analysis of fiscal policy and budget priorities.

Within 6 weeks after President submits a budget request, or at such time as may be requested by the Committee on the Budget. Each congressional committee with legislative jurisdiction submits to the appropriate Budget Committee its views and estimates on spending and revenue levels for the following fiscal year on matters within its jurisdiction. 2 U.S.C. § 632(d). The House and Senate Budget Committees then hold hearings and prepare their respective versions of a concurrent resolution, which is intended to be the overall budget plan against which individual appropriation bills are to be evaluated.

April 15. Congress completes action on the concurrent resolution, which includes a breakdown of estimated new budget authority and outlays for each major budget function. 2 U.S.C. § 632(a). The conference report on the concurrent resolution allocates the totals among individual committees. 2 U.S.C. § 633(a). The resolution may also include "reconciliation directives"—directives to individual committees to recommend legislative changes in revenues or spending to meet the goals of the budget plan. 2 U.S.C. § 641(a).

4. Appropriations: the Enactment of Budget Authority

a. The Legislative Process

After completing work on its budget totals, Congress begins considering annual appropriations bills. In exercising the broad discretion granted by the Constitution, Congress can approve funding levels contained in the President's budget request, increase or decrease those levels, eliminate proposals, or add programs not requested by the administration.

In simpler times, Congress often made appropriations in the form of a single, consolidated appropriation act. The most recent regular consolidated appropriation act was the General Appropriation Act of 1951, Pub. L. No. 759, 64 Stat. 595 (Sept. 6, 1950). Since that time, Congress has generally made appropriations in a series of regular appropriation acts plus one or more supplemental appropriation acts. Most regular appropriation acts are organized based on

Page 60

one or more major departments and a number of smaller agencies (corresponding to the jurisdiction of appropriations subcommittees), although a few are based solely on function. An agency may receive funds under more than one appropriation act. The individual structures are of course subject to change over time. At the present time, there are 12 regular appropriation acts, as follows:

[handwritten: 12 diff committees]

- Agriculture, Rural Development, Food and Drug Administration, and related agencies

- Commerce, Justice, Science, and related agencies

- Department of Defense

- Energy and Water Development and related agencies

[handwritten: www. cdc. gov./budget/.]

- Financial Services and General Government

- Department of Homeland Security

- Department of the Interior, Environment, and related agencies

- Departments of Labor, Health and Human Services, and Education, and related agencies

- Legislative Branch

- Military Construction and Veteran Affairs, and related agencies

- Department of State, Foreign Operations, and related programs

- Departments of Transportation, Housing and Urban Development, and related agencies

House consideration of the individual appropriation bills begins as each subcommittee of the House Appropriations Committee studies appropriation requests and evaluates the performance of the agencies within its jurisdiction. Typically, each subcommittee will conduct hearings at which federal officials give testimony concerning both the costs and achievements of the various programs administered by their agencies and provide detailed justifications for their funding requests. Eventually, each subcommittee reports a single appropriation bill for consideration by the entire committee. In turn, the House Appropriations Committee reports annual appropriations bills to the whole House. Under the Congressional Budget Act, the House Appropriations Committee should report the last annual appropriation bill by June 10, and the House should complete all action on appropriation bills by June 30. 2 U.S.C. § 631.

As the House passes individual appropriation bills, it sends them to the Senate. As in the House, the Senate considers each appropriation measure first in subcommittee, which then reports the bill the full Appropriations Committee, which then reports it to the full Senate. In the event of variations in the Senate and House versions of a particular appropriation bill, a conference committee, including representatives of both houses of Congress, is formed. The conference committee's role is to resolve all differences, but the full House and Senate must also vote to approve the conference report.

Following either the Senate's passage of the House version of an appropriation measure, or the approval of a conference report by both bodies, the enrolled bill is then sent to the President for signature or veto. The Congressional Budget Act envisions completion of the process by October 1, the beginning of the new fiscal year.

b. Points of Order   *Objection raised in House & Sen.*

The rules of the Senate and House of Representatives contain a number of requirements relevant to an understanding of appropriations law and the legislative process. For example, House Rule XXI(2) prohibits appropriations for objects not previously authorized by law. Senate Rule XVI contains a similar but more limited prohibition. Other examples are the prohibition against including general legislation in appropriation acts (Senate Rule XVI, House Rule XXI), and the prohibition against consideration by a conference committee of matters not committed to it by either House (Senate Rule XXVIII, House Rule XXII). The applicability of Senate and House rules is exclusively within the province of the particular House.

In addition, rather than expressly prohibiting a given item, legislation may provide that it shall not be in order for the Senate or House to consider a bill or resolution containing that item. An important example is from the Congressional Budget Act of 1974, which defines "spending authority" as authority provided in laws other than appropriation acts to obligate the United States to make payments. 2 U.S.C. § 651(c)(2). It is not in order for either house to consider any bill, resolution, or amendment containing certain types of new spending authority, such as contract authority, unless that bill, resolution, or amendment also provides that the new authority is to be effective for any fiscal year only to the extent provided in appropriation acts. 2 U.S.C. § 651(a). There are similar provisions pertaining to entitlement authority, which is statutory authority, whether temporary or permanent—

> "to make payments (including loans and grants), the budget authority for which is not provided for in advance by appropriation Acts, to any person or government if, under the provisions of the law containing that authority, the United States is obligated to make such payments to persons or governments who meet the requirements established by that law."

Entitlement authority is treated as spending authority during congressional consideration of the budget. In order to make entitlements subject to the reconciliation process, the Congressional

Budget Act provides that proposed legislation providing new entitlement authority to become effective prior to the start of the next fiscal year will be subject to a point of order. 2 U.S.C. § 651(b)(1). Entitlement legislation, which would require new budget authority in excess of the allocation made pursuant to the most recent budget resolution, must be referred to the appropriations committees. Id. § 651(b)(2).

In addition, the Balanced Budget and Emergency Deficit Control Act of 1985 added a definition of "credit authority" to the Congressional Budget Act, specifically, "authority to incur direct loan obligations or to incur primary loan guarantee commitments." 2 U.S.C. § 622(10). Any bill, resolution, or conference report providing new credit authority will be subject to a point of order unless the new authority is limited to the extent or amounts provided in advance in appropriation acts. 2 U.S.C. § 651(a).

The effect of these rules and of statutes like 2 U.S.C. § 651(a) is to subject the noncomplying bill to a "point of order." A point of order is a procedural objection raised on the House or Senate floor or in committees by a Member alleging a departure from a rule or statute governing the conduct of business. See GAO, A Glossary of Terms Used in the Federal Budget Process , GAO-05-734SP (Washington, D.C.: Sept. 2005). It differs from an absolute prohibition in that (a) it is always possible that no one will raise a point of order and (b) if raised, it may or may not be sustained. Also, some laws, like the Congressional Budget Act, authorize points of order to be raised, and some measures may be considered under special resolutions waiving points of order. If a point of order is raised and sustained, the offending provision is effectively killed and may be revived only if it is amended to cure the noncompliance.

The potential effect of a rule or statute subjecting a provision to a point of order is limited to the pre-enactment stage. If a point of order is not raised, or is raised and not sustained, the provision, if enacted, is no less valid. To restate, a rule or statute subjecting a given provision to a point of order has no effect or application once the legislation or appropriation has been enacted. 65 Comp. Gen. 524, 527 (1986); 57 Comp. Gen. 34 (1977); 34 Comp. Gen. 278 (1954); B-173832, Aug. 1, 1975; B-123469, Apr. 14, 1955; B-87612, July 26, 1949.

c. Incorporation by Reference

Sometimes a statutory provision expressly refers to an outside source. This is known as incorporation by reference, and is the use of legislative language to make extra-statutory material part of the legislation by indicating that the extra-statutory material should be treated as if it were written out in full in the legislation. See generally Black's Law Dictionary 834 (9th ed. 2010). Incorporation by reference differs from the use of legislative history to construe statutes: a key characteristic of incorporation by reference is the express statutory reference to an outside source. No such express statutory reference exists when GAO or the courts make other uses of legislative history.

Incorporation by reference is a well-accepted legislative tool. Indeed, there are numerous instances in which the Supreme Court, for more than 100 years, has accepted incorporation by reference without objection. See, e.g., Tennessee v. Lane, 541 U.S. 509, 517 (2004); United States v. Sharpnack, 355 U.S. 286, 293 (1958); In re Heath, 144 U.S. 92, 94 (1892); see also Hershey Foods Corp. v. Department of Agriculture, 158 F. Supp. 2d 37 (D.D.C. 2001), aff'd, 293 F.3d 520 (D.C. Cir. 2002). In these cases, the language of the statute evidenced a clear congressional intent to incorporate by reference, and the referenced material was specifically ascertainable from the face of the legislative language, so all would know with certainty the duties, terms, conditions, and constraints enacted into law.

In a 2008 decision, GAO considered the legal effect of seven appropriations provisions in the Consolidated Appropriations Act, 2008, that incorporated by reference specified passages of an explanatory statement of the House Committee on Appropriations that was printed in the Congressional Record on December 17, 2007. B-316010, Feb. 25, 2008. This explanatory statement contained more specific allocations for the agencies affected. After reviewing the language of the seven provisions, GAO determined that:

> "Because the language of the seven provisions clearly and unambiguously expresses an intent to appropriate amounts as allocated in the explanatory statement and because reference to the explanatory statement permits the agencies and others to ascertain with certainty the amounts and purposes for which these appropriations are available, these provisions establish the referenced allocations contained in the explanatory statement as legally binding restrictions on the agencies' appropriations."

Id. at 8. GAO thus concluded that the affected agencies were required to obligate and expend amounts appropriated in the seven provisions in accordance with the referenced allocations in the explanatory statement. See also B-319009, Apr. 27, 2010 (incorporation by reference for purposes of reprogramming requirement).

d. What Constitutes an Appropriation

> "Any time the Congress specifies the manner in which a Federal entity shall be funded and makes such funds available for obligation and expenditure, that constitutes an appropriation, whether the language is found in an appropriation act or in other legislation."

B-193573, Dec. 19, 1979.

Some agency activities, such as those arising from permanent provisions permitting the obligation and expenditure of amounts collected from user fees, are not financed by annual appropriations because Congress need not enact annual legislation authorizing the obligations and expenditures. Nonetheless, such activities are financed by appropriations and, absent any statute stating otherwise, such activities are subject to the limitations imposed by law upon the use of all appropriated amounts.

Occasionally, however, questions arise regarding whether a particular statute does indeed make amounts available for obligation and expenditure—that is, whether the statute makes an appropriation. The starting point for any analysis to answer such a question is 31 U.S.C. § 1301(d), which provides:

> "A law may be construed to make an appropriation out of the Treasury or to authorize making a contract for the payment of money in excess of an appropriation only if the law specifically states that an appropriation is made or that such a contract may be made."

Thus, the rule is that the making of an appropriation must be expressly stated. An appropriation cannot be inferred or made by implication. E.g., 50 Comp. Gen. 863 (1971).

Regular annual and supplemental appropriation acts present no problems in this respect as they will be apparent on their face. They, as required by 1 U.S.C. § 105, bear the title "An Act making appropriations . . . ." Other statutes that are not regular annual or supplemental appropriations acts may also explicitly state that they make an appropriation. See, e.g., 31 U.S.C. § 1304(a) ("necessary amounts are appropriated to pay final judgments, awards, compromise settlements"); 31 U.S.C. § 1324 ("necessary amounts are appropriated to the Secretary of Treasury for refunding internal revenue collections"); B-321823, Dec. 6, 2011.

Though the making of an appropriation must be expressly stated, a statute need not use the word "appropriation." If the statute contains a specific direction to pay and a designation of the funds to be used, such as a direction to make a specified payment or class of payments "out of any money in the Treasury not otherwise appropriated," then this amounts to an appropriation. 63 Comp. Gen. 331 (1984); 13 Comp. Gen. 77 (1933). See also 34 Comp. Gen. 590 (1955).

For example, a private relief act that directs the Secretary of the Treasury to pay, out of any money in the Treasury not otherwise appropriated, a specified sum of money to a named individual constitutes an appropriation. 23 Comp. Dec. 167, 170 (1916). Another example involved a statute that authorized the Secretary of the Treasury to reimburse local fire departments or districts for costs incurred in fighting fires on federal property. B-160998, Apr. 13, 1978. Since the statute directed the Secretary to make payments "from any moneys in the Treasury not otherwise appropriated" (i.e., it contained both the specific direction to pay and a designation of the funds to be used), the Comptroller General concluded that section 11 constituted a permanent indefinite appropriation.

Both elements of the test—that is, a specific direction to pay and a designation of funds to be used—must be present. Thus, a direction to pay without a designation of the source of funds is not an appropriation. For example, a private relief act that contains merely an authorization and direction to pay but no designation of the funds to be used does not make an appropriation. 21 Comp. Dec. 867 (1915); B-26414, Jan. 7, 1944. Similarly, public legislation enacted in 1978 authorized the U.S. Treasury to make an annual prepayment to Guam and the Virgin Islands of the amount estimated to be collected over the course of the year for certain taxes, duties, and fees. While it was apparent that the prepayment at least for the first year would have to come from the general fund of the Treasury, the legislation was silent as to the source of the funds for the prepayments, both for the first year and for subsequent years. While the statute may have established a permanent authorization, it was not sufficient under 31 U.S.C. § 1301(d) to constitute an actual appropriation. B-114808, Aug. 7, 1979. (Congress subsequently made the necessary appropriation in Pub. L. No. 96-126, 93 Stat. 954, 966 (Nov. 27, 1979).)

The designation of a source of funds without a specific direction to pay is also not an appropriation. 67 Comp. Gen. 332 (1988).

Thus far, we have been talking about the authority to incur obligations and make payments that are not associated with any fee collections. In addition, a statute makes an appropriation if it (1) authorizes the collection of fees, and (2) makes the fees available for expenditure for a specified purpose. Such statutes constitute continuing or permanent appropriations; that is, the money is available for obligation or expenditure without further action by Congress. For example, Congress authorized the Commission on the Bicentennial to charge fees for the licensing of its logo, with the statute specifying that "[a]mounts charged . . . shall be available to the Commission." B-228777, Aug. 26, 1988. GAO concluded that the Commission "is authorized by its statute to retain and expend proceeds from the commercial licensing of its logo for authorized Commission purposes, subject to the same restrictions and limitations applicable to the use of all appropriated funds." Id.

Similarly, Congress may create a "revolving fund"—that is, a fund that finances a cycle of business-like activities through amounts the fund receives. Legislation creating a revolving fund establishes a continuing appropriation which, unless restricted by the terms of the legislation, is available for obligation without further legislative action to carry out the fund's authorized purposes. B-204078.2, May 6, 1988. Often, a statute will specify a fund in the Treasury to which the collections are to be deposited. This is not essential, however. A statute that clearly makes receipts available for obligation or expenditure without further congressional action will be construed as authorizing the establishment of such a fund as a necessary implementation procedure. 59 Comp. Gen. 215 (1980) (42 U.S.C. § 5419); B-226520, Apr. 3, 1987 (nondecision letter) (26 U.S.C. § 7475). See also 13 Comp. Dec. 700 (1907).

Even if a statute does indeed grant an agency authority to obligate and expend funds, sometimes a related question arises, which is whether such obligations and expenditures are subject to restrictions that generally govern the availability of appropriated funds. First, "any time the Congress specifies the manner in which a Federal entity shall be funded and makes such funds available for obligation and expenditure, that constitutes an appropriation." B-193573, Dec. 19, 1979. However, as is the case with nearly any general principle, Congress may make an exception and provide in particular circumstances that an agency does not operate with appropriated funds even though it is an arm of the United States government. Such entities operate without the restrictions that apply to the use of appropriated funds, though these entities must operate consistently with their authorizing legislation.

However, non-appropriated fund instrumentalities and government corporations are rare exceptions to a vast general rule, which is that funds obligated and expended by federal entities are appropriated funds that are subject to the legal provisions that govern the availability of appropriated funds. For example, because a revolving fund is a continuing appropriation, funds obligated and expended from revolving funds are, as a general matter, subject to the legal provisions that govern the availability of appropriated funds. This is true even if the revolving fund is not financed by annual appropriations. One case applying this rule involved the Tobacco User Fee Fund, which contained amounts collected from tobacco companies and was used to pay the salaries of tobacco inspectors in the Department of Agriculture. 63 Comp. Gen. 285 (1984). GAO concluded that amounts in the fund were appropriated and, therefore, that amounts in the fund were subject to restrictions on the payment of employee health benefits. Id.

Another case concerning whether particular funds are appropriated involved donated funds. The American Battle Monuments Commission had statutory authority to receive donations to fund construction of a memorial. B-275669.2, July 30, 1997. Some other entities, such as the Holocaust Memorial Council, had funds that by law were not considered appropriated; thus, they could obligate funds without regard for procurement requirements in the Federal Property and Administrative Services Act. Though the American Battle Monuments Commission argued that it should also be free of such requirements, GAO noted that Congress had not provided that the Commission's funds were not to be considered appropriated. Thus, GAO concluded that the donations were considered appropriated funds and, therefore, that the Commission was required to comply with the Federal Property and Administrative Services Act. Many other cases through the years have applied the principle that, unless Congress provides otherwise, funds obligated and expended by federal agencies are considered appropriated and are subject to the statutes governing the proper use of federal funds.

5. Budget Execution: the Obligation and Expenditure of Budget Authority

The body of enacted appropriation acts for a fiscal year, as amplified by legislative history and the relevant budget submissions, becomes the government's financial plan for that fiscal year. The "execution and control" phase refers generally to the period of time during which the budget authority made available by the appropriation acts remains available for obligation. An agency's task during this phase is to spend the money Congress has given it to carry out the objectives of its program legislation.

a. Making Amounts Available for Obligation: Apportionment and Allotment

The Office of Management and Budget apportions or distributes budgeted amounts to the executive branch agencies, thereby making funds in appropriation accounts (administered by the

Treasury Department) available for obligation. 31 U.S.C. §§ 1511–1516. The apportionment system through which budget authority is distributed by time periods (usually quarterly) or by activities is intended to achieve an effective and orderly use of available budget authority, and to reduce the need for supplemental or deficiency appropriations. Each agency then makes allotments pursuant to the OMB apportionments or other statutory authority. 31 U.S.C. §§ 1513(d), 1514. An allotment is a delegation of authority to agency officials that allows them to incur obligations within the scope and terms of the delegation. Further detail on the budget execution phase may also be found in GAO, A Glossary of Terms Used in the Federal Budget Process, GAO-05-734SP (Washington, D.C.: Sept. 2005), and OMB Circular No. A-11, Preparation, Submission and Execution of the Budget, pt. 4, Instructions on Budget Execution (July 25, 2014).

b. Audits and Financial Management

Every federal department or agency has the fundamental responsibility to ensure that its application of public funds adheres to the terms of the pertinent authorization and appropriation acts, as well as any other relevant statutory provisions. Ensuring the legality of proposed payments is one of the basic responsibilities of agency certifying officers. Executive agency management has the responsibility of establishing and maintaining appropriate accounting and internal controls. 31 U.S.C. § 3512(b). The Federal Managers' Financial Integrity Act of 198233 increased government-wide emphasis on internal accounting and administrative controls. Agencies must establish internal accounting and administrative control systems to provide reasonable assurance that obligations and costs apply with applicable law, that assets are safeguarded against waste, loss, unauthorized use, or misappropriation, and that revenues and expenditures are accounted for properly. These systems must be in accordance with standards prescribed by the Comptroller General (see GAO, Standards for Internal Control in the Federal Government, GAO-14-704G (Washington, D.C.: Sept.2014)), and agencies must conduct annual reviews of their systems in accordance with Office of Management and Budget (OMB) guidelines and report the results of these reviews to the President and to Congress. OMB Circular No. A-123, Management Accountability and Control (Dec. 21, 2004).

The Chief Financial Officers Act of 1990 established a Chief Financial Officer (CFO) in the cabinet departments and several other executive branch agencies (commonly known as the "CFO Act agencies"), and created the Office of Federal Financial Management within OMB to oversee federal financial management policy. Pub. L. No. 101-576, 104 Stat. 2838 (Nov. 15, 1990). CFOs must work with OMB to develop and oversee financial management plans, programs, and activities within the agency. 31 U.S.C. §§ 901–903. The CFO Act, as amended, also provides for the preparation and audit of annual agency financial statements for executive branch agencies. 35 U.S.C. § 3535. In addition, the Secretary of the Treasury, in coordination with the Director of the Office of Management and Budget, is required to annually prepare and submit to the President and the Congress a financial statement for the executive branch of the government that has been audited by GAO. 31 U.S.C. § 331(e). GAO also regularly audits federal programs.

Many agencies also have an internal audit function performed by an Office of the Inspector General established under the Inspector General Act of 1978, or other law. Inspectors General are charged with conducting and supervising audits and investigations, promoting economy, efficiency, and effectiveness, preventing and detecting fraud and abuse, and providing a means of keeping the head of the agency and Congress informed about problems and deficiencies relating to the agency's programs.

c. Account Closing

In the final phase of our "life cycle" analogy, an appropriation "dies" in a sense at the end of its period of obligational availability. There is, however, an afterlife to the extent of any unexpended balances. Unexpended balances, both obligated and unobligated, retain a limited availability for five fiscal years following expiration of the period for which the source appropriation was made. At midnight on the last day of an appropriation's period of availability, the appropriation account expires and is no longer available for incurring new obligations. The expired appropriation remains available for 5 years for the purpose of paying obligations incurred prior to the account's expiration and adjusting obligations that were previously unrecorded or under recorded. 31 U.S.C. § 1553(a). After 5 years, the expired account is closed and the balances remaining are canceled. 31 U.S.C. § 1552(a).

6. Administrative Discretion

"[S]ome play must be allowed to the joints if the machine is to work."

Tyson & Brother v. Banton, 273 U.S. 418, 446 (1927) (Justice Holmes, dissenting).

Throughout this publication, the reader will encounter frequent references to administrative discretion. The concept of discretion implies choice or freedom of judgment, and appears in a variety of contexts. There are many things an agency does every day that involve making choices and exercising discretion. There is often more than one way to do something, and reasonable minds may differ as to which way is the best. If a given choice is within the actor's legitimate range of discretion, then it is not illegal.

One type of discretion commonly occurs in the context of purpose availability. A decision may conclude that an appropriation is legally available for a particular expenditure if the agency, in its discretion, determines that the expenditure is a suitable means of accomplishing an authorized end. An agency has discretionary authority to provide refreshments at award ceremonies under the Government Employees Incentive Awards Act, 31 U.S.C. §§ 4501–4507. Agency A may choose to do so while agency B chooses not to. As a matter of law, both agencies are correct, even though they chose differently.

Under the Administrative Procedure Act (APA), action that is "committed to agency discretion by law" is not subject to judicial review. 5 U.S.C. § 701(a)(2). One particularly important example is an agency's decision to allocate funds within a lump-sum appropriation. Such decisions are committed to agency discretion by law and, therefore, are not subject to judicial review. Lincoln v. Vigil, 508 U.S. 182 (1993). The Court noted that "the very point of a lump-sum appropriation is to give an agency the capacity to adapt to changing circumstances and meet its statutory responsibilities in what it sees as the most effective or desirable way." Id. at 191. See also Hein v. Freedom From Religion Foundation, Inc., 551 U.S. 587 (2007); 55 Comp. Gen. 307 (1975); B-278121, Nov. 7, 1997.

To say that an agency has freedom of choice in a given matter does not mean that there are no limits to that freedom. Discretion is not unbridled license. The decisions have frequently pointed out that discretion means legal discretion, not unlimited discretion. The point was stated as follows in 18 Comp. Gen. 285, 292 (1938):

> "Generally, the Congress in making appropriations leaves largely to administrative discretion the choice of ways and means to accomplish the objects of the appropriation, but, of course, administrative discretion may not transcend the statutes, nor be exercised in conflict with law, nor for the accomplishment of purposes unauthorized by the appropriation . . . ."

See also 72 Comp. Gen. 310, 311 (1993); 35 Comp. Gen. 615, 618 (1956); 4 Comp. Gen. 19, 20 (1924); 7 Comp. Dec. 31 (1900); 5 Comp. Dec. 151 (1898); B-253338, Nov. 23, 1993; B-130288, Feb. 27, 1957; B-49169, May 5, 1945; A-24916, Nov. 5, 1928.

One way to illustrate the concept of "legal discretion" is to visualize a person standing in the center of a circle. The circumference of the circle represents the limits of discretion, imposed either by law or by the difficult to define but nonetheless real concept of "public policy." The person is free to move in any direction, to stay near the center or to venture close to the perimeter, even to brush against it, but must stay within the circle. If our actor crosses the line of the circumference, he has exceeded or, to use the legal term, "abused" his discretion.

When GAO is performing its audit function, it may criticize a particular exercise of discretion as ill-conceived, inefficient, or perhaps wasteful. From the legal standpoint, however, there is no illegal expenditure as long as the actor remains within the circle. For example, a Coast Guard employee used his government purchase card to purchase beer brewing equipment and ingredients. GAO, Purchase Cards: Control Weaknesses Leave DHS Highly Vulnerable to Fraudulent, Improper, and Abusive Activity, GAO-06-957T (Washington, D.C.: July 2006), at 30. While on duty he brewed alcohol for consumption at social functions for the Coast Guard Academy. Coast Guard personnel stated that the ingredients were purchased using funds from a private foundation, and GAO did not reach any conclusions about the legality of the purchases. Nonetheless, GAO pointed out that the brewing activities fell "short of prudent use of taxpayer dollars" and that the private funds "could have been spent for other purposes, for example educational grants, had they not been used to brew beer."

In addition, the size of the circle may vary. Government corporations frequently have a broader range of discretion than noncorporate agencies.

a. Failure or Refusal to Exercise Discretion

Where a particular action or decision is committed to agency discretion by law, the agency is under a legal duty to actually exercise that discretion. The failure or refusal to exercise discretion committed by law to the agency can be an abuse of discretion. As the following cases demonstrate, the fact of exercising discretion and the particular results of that exercise are two very different things.

We start with a Supreme Court decision, Work v. United States ex rel. Rives, 267 U.S. 175 (1925). That case involved section 5 of the Dent Act, ch. 94, 40 Stat. 1272, 1274 (Mar. 2, 1919), under which Congress authorized the Secretary of the Interior to compensate a class of people who incurred losses in furnishing supplies or services to the government during World War I. The Secretary's determinations on particular claims were to be final and conclusive. The statute "was a gratuity based on equitable and moral considerations" (id. at 181), vesting the Secretary with the ultimate power to determine which losses should be compensated.

The plaintiff in Rives had sought mandamus to compel the Secretary to consider and allow a claim for a specific loss incurred as a result of the plaintiff's obtaining a release from a contract to buy land. The Secretary had previously denied the claim because he had interpreted the statute as not embracing money spent on real estate. In holding that the Secretary had done all that was required by law, the Court cited and distinguished a line of cases—

> "in which a relator in mandamus has successfully sought to compel action by an officer who has discretion concededly conferred on him by law. The relator [plaintiff] in such cases does not ask for a decision any particular way but only that it be made one way or the other."

Id. at 184.

The Secretary had made a decision on the claim, had articulated reasons for it, and had not exceeded the bounds of his statutory authority. That was enough. A court could compel the Secretary to actually exercise his discretion, that is, to act on a claim one way or the other, but could not compel him to exercise that discretion to achieve a particular result.

In Simpkins v. Davidson, 302 F. Supp. 456 (S.D. N.Y. 1969), the plaintiff sued to compel the Small Business Administration (SBA) to make a loan to him. The court found that the plaintiff was entitled to submit an application, and to have the SBA consider that application and reach a decision on whether or not to grant the loan. However, he had no right to the loan itself, and the court could not compel the SBA to exercise its discretion to achieve a specific result. A very similar case on this point is Dubrow v. Small Business Administration, 345 F. Supp. 4 (C.D. Cal. 1972). See also B-226121-O.M., Feb. 9, 1988, citing and applying these cases.

Another case involved a provision of the Farm and Rural Development Act that authorized the Secretary of Agriculture to forgo foreclosure on certain delinquent loans. The plaintiffs were a group of farmers who alleged that the Secretary had refused to consider their requests. The Court of Appeals for the Tenth Circuit held that the Secretary was required to consider the requests:

"The word 'may,' the Secretary 'may' permit deferral, is, in our view, a reference to the discretion of the Secretary to grant the deferral upon a showing by a borrower. It does not mean as the Secretary argues that he has the discretion whether or not to implement the Act at all and not to consider any 'requests' under the statutory standards."

Matzke v. Block, 732 F.2d 799, 801 (10th Cir. 1984).

The Comptroller General applied these principles in a case concerning a statute that gave agencies discretionary authority to consider and settle certain employee personal property claims. 62 Comp. Gen. 641 (1983). GAO concluded that an agency could not adopt a policy of refusing all claims. While GAO would not purport to tell another agency which claims it should or should not consider—that part was discretionary—the decision noted that "a blanket refusal to consider all claims is, in our opinion, not the exercise of discretion" (id. at 643), and held "that an agency has the duty to actually exercise its discretion and that this duty is not satisfied by a policy of refusing to consider all claims" (id. at 645). Thus, for example, an agency would be within its discretion to make and announce a policy decision not to consider claims of certain types, such as claims for stolen cash, or to impose monetary ceilings on certain types of property, or to establish a minimum amount for the filing of claims. What it cannot do is disregard the statute in its entirety.

b. Regulations May Limit Discretion

By issuing regulations, an agency may voluntarily (and perhaps even inadvertently) limit its own discretion. A number of cases have held that an agency must comply with its own regulations, even if the action is discretionary by statute.

The leading case is United States ex rel. Accardi v. Shaughnessy, 347 U.S. 260 (1954). The Attorney General had been given statutory discretion to suspend the deportation of aliens under certain circumstances, and had, by regulation, given this discretion to the Board of Immigration Appeals. The Supreme Court held that, regardless of what the situation would have been if the regulations did not exist, the Board was required under the regulations to exercise its own judgment, and it was improper for the Attorney General to attempt to influence that judgment, in this case, by issuing a list of "unsavory characters" he wanted to have deported. "In short, as long as the regulations remain operative, the Attorney General denies himself the right to sidestep the Board or dictate its decision in any manner." Id. at 267. Of course, the Attorney General could always amend his regulations, but an amendment could operate prospectively only.

Awards under the Government Employees Incentive Awards Act, 5 U.S.C. §§ 4501–4507 are wholly discretionary. GAO reviewed Army regulations that provided that "awards will be granted" if certain specified criteria were met, and noted that the Army had circumscribed its own discretion by committing itself to make an award if those conditions were met. B-202039, May 7, 1982. Reviewing Air Force regulations under similar legislation applicable to military personnel, the Court of Claims noted in Griffin v. United States, 215 Ct. Cl. 710, 714 (1978):

> "Thus, we think that the Secretary may have originally had uncontrolled and unreviewable discretion . . . but as he published procedures and guidelines, as he received responsive suggestions, as he implemented them and through his subordinates passed upon compensation claims, we think by his choices he surrendered some of his discretion, and the legal possibility of abuse of discretion came into the picture."

For additional authority on the proposition that an agency can, by regulation, restrict otherwise discretionary action, see United States v. Nixon, 418 U.S. 683 (1974); Vitarelli v. Seaton, 359 U.S. 535 (1959); Service v. Dulles, 354 U.S. 363 (1957); United States v. Morgan, 193 F.3d 252 (4th Cir. 1999); Clarry v. United States, 85 F.3d 1041 (2nd Cir. 1996); Waldron v. Immigration & Naturalization Service, 17 F.3d 511, 519 (2nd Cir. 1994); Montilla v. Immigration & Naturalization Service, 926 F.2d 162 (2nd Cir. 1991). See also B-316381, July 18, 2008; 67 Comp. Gen. 471 (1988).

Recent case law has recognized a number of limits, caveats, and nuances to the Accardi doctrine. While there are occasional exceptions, the doctrine generally will not be applied to bind an agency by its informal rules, policies, or other issuances that the court concludes are intended to provide internal guidance rather than to confer rights or benefits on the public. See Farrell v. Department of the Interior, 314 F.3d 584, 591 (Fed. Cir. 2002) (holding that agency statement that was not formally promulgated is not binding on the agency unless the agency intended to be bound by it). Even if a court concludes that a rule, or policy document, is binding on the agency under Accardi, the court may not invalidate the agency action if it concludes that the departure from the rule was nonprejudicial or "harmless error." See Wilkinson v. Legal Services Corp., 27 F. Supp. 2d 32 (D.D.C. 1998). In addition, the courts are very reluctant to apply Accardi to criminal proceedings or exercises of prosecutorial-type discretion, such as an agency decision not to initiate an enforcement action. See Carranza v. Immigration & Naturalization Service, 277 F.3d 65, 68 (1st Cir. 2002); United States v. Lee, 274 F.3d 485 (8th Cir. 2001); United States v. Shakir, 113 F. Supp. 2d 1182 (M.D. Tenn. 2000); United States v. Briscoe, 69 F. Supp. 2d 738, 747 (D.V.I. 1999), aff'd, 234 F.3d 1266 (3rd Cir. 2000); Nichols v. Reno, 931 F. Supp. 748 (D. Colo. 1996); Walker v. Reno, 925 F. Supp. 124 (N.D. N.Y. 1995).

c. Insufficient Funds

Sometimes the actual funding Congress appropriates for a program may fall short of original expectations. What is an agency to do when it finds that it does not have enough money to accommodate an entire class of beneficiaries? Obviously, it can ask Congress for more. However, as any program administrator knows, asking and getting are two different things. If the agency cannot get additional funding and the program legislation fails to provide guidance, the agency may, within its discretion, establish reasonable classifications, priorities, and/or eligibility requirements, as long as it does so on a rational and consistent basis.

As the Supreme Court explained in a case involving an assistance program administered by the Bureau of Indian Affairs (BIA):

> "[I]t does not necessarily follow that the Secretary is without power to create reasonable classifications and eligibility requirements in order to allocate the limited funds available to him for this purpose. [Citations omitted.] Thus, if there were only enough funds appropriated to provide meaningfully for 10,000 needy Indian beneficiaries and the entire class of eligible beneficiaries numbered 20,000, it would be incumbent upon the BIA to develop an eligibility standard to deal with this problem, and the standard, if rational and proper, might leave some of the class otherwise encompassed by the appropriation without benefits. But in such a case the agency must, at a minimum, let the standard be generally known so as to assure that it is being applied consistently and so as to avoid both the reality and the appearance of arbitrary denial of benefits to potential beneficiaries."

Morton v. Ruiz, 415 U.S. 199, 230–31 (1974).

In one case, the plaintiff sued for construction differential subsidy payments under the Merchant Marine Act, administered by the Maritime Administration (MarAd). Suwannee River Finance, Inc. v. United States, 7 Cl. Ct. 556 (1985). In response to a sudden and severe budget reduction, MarAd had cut off all subsidies for nonessential changes after a specified date, and had notified the plaintiff to that effect. Noting that "[a]fter this budget cut, MarAd obviously could no longer be as generous in paying subsidies as it had been before," the court held MarAd's approach to be "a logical, effective and time-honored method for allocating the burdens of shrinking resources" and well within its administrative discretion. Id. at 561.

In another example, due to a severe drought in the summer of 1980, the Small Business Administration (SBA) found that its appropriation was not sufficient to meet demand under its disaster loan program. B-202568, Sept. 11, 1981. Rather than treating applicants on a "first come, first served" basis, SBA amended its regulations to impose several new restrictions, including a ceiling of 60 percent of actual physical loss. GAO reviewed SBA's actions and found them completely within the agency's administrative discretion.

A conceptually related situation is a funding shortfall in an appropriation used to fund a number of programs. Again, the agency must allocate its available funds in some reasonable fashion. Mandatory programs take precedence over discretionary ones. Within the group of mandatory programs, more specific requirements should be funded first, such as those with specific time schedules, with remaining funds then applied to the more general requirements. B-159993, Sept. 1, 1977; B-177806, Feb. 24, 1978 (nondecision letter). These principles apply equally, of course, to the allocation of funds between mandatory and nonmandatory expenditures within a single-program appropriation. E.g., 61 Comp. Gen. 661, 664 (1982).

Other cases recognizing an agency's discretion in coping with funding shortfalls are City of Los Angeles v. Adams, 556 F.2d 40, 49–50 (D.C. Cir. 1977), and McCarey v. McNamara, 390 F.2d 601 (3rd Cir. 1968).

7. Transfer and Reprogramming

For a variety of reasons, agencies have a legitimate need for a certain amount of flexibility to deviate from their budget estimates. Two ways to shift money are transfer and reprogramming. While the two concepts are related in this broad sense, they are nevertheless different.

a. Transfer

Transfer is the shifting of funds between appropriations. For example, if an agency receives one appropriation for Operations and Maintenance and another for Capital Expenditures, a shifting of funds from either one to the other is a transfer.

(1) Transfers are Prohibited without Statutory Authority

Agencies may transfer funds only when expressly authorized by law:

> "An amount available under law may be withdrawn from one appropriation account and credited to another or to a working fund only when authorized by law."

31 U.S.C. § 1532. In addition to this express prohibition, an unauthorized transfer would violate 31 U.S.C. § 1301(a) (which prohibits the use of appropriations for other than their intended purpose), would constitute an unauthorized augmentation of the receiving appropriation, and could, if the transfer led to overobligating the receiving appropriation, result in an Antideficiency Act (31 U.S.C. § 1341) violation as well. E.g., B-286929, Apr. 25, 2001; B-248284.2, Sept. 1, 1992; B-222009-O.M., Mar. 3, 1986; 15 Op. Off. Legal Counsel 74 (1991).

Transfers without statutory authority are equally forbidden whether they are (1) transfers from one agency to another, (2) transfers from one account to another within the same agency, or (3) transfers to an interagency or intra-agency working fund. In each instance, statutory authority is required. An agency's erroneous characterization of a proposed transfer as a "reprogramming" is irrelevant. See B-202362, Mar. 24, 1981. Moreover, informal congressional approval of an unauthorized transfer of funds between appropriation accounts does not have the force and effect of law. B-248284.2, Sept. 1, 1992.

The prohibition applies even if the transfer is intended as a temporary expedient (for example, to alleviate a temporary exhaustion of funds) and the agency contemplates reimbursement. Thus, without statutory authority, an agency cannot "borrow" from another account or another agency. 36 Comp. Gen. 386 (1956); 13 Comp. Gen. 344 (1934); B-290011, Mar. 25, 2002.

The prohibition against transfer would not apply to "transfers" of an agency's administrative allocations within a lump-sum appropriation since the allocations are not legally binding. This is a reprogramming, which we discuss below. Thus, where the then Department of Health, Education, and Welfare received a lump-sum appropriation covering several grant programs, it could set aside a portion of each program's allocation for a single fund to be used for "cross-cutting" grants intended to serve more than one target population, as long as the grants were for projects within the scope or purpose of the lump-sum appropriation. B-157356, Aug. 17, 1978.

(2) Transfers Authorized By Law

Statutory transfer authority does not require any particular "magic words." Of course the word "transfer" will help, but it is not necessary as long as the words that are used make it clear that transfer is being authorized. B-213345, Sept. 26, 1986; B-217093, Jan. 9, 1985; B-182398, Mar. 29, 1976 (letter to Senator Laxalt), modified on other grounds by 64 Comp. Gen. 370 (1985).

Some agencies have limited transfer authority either in permanent legislation or in appropriation act provisions. Such authority will commonly set a percentage limit on the amount that may be transferred from a given appropriation and/or the amount by which the receiving appropriation may be augmented. B-290659, Oct. 31, 2002; B-167637, Oct. 11, 1973. For example, the Department of Agriculture may make transfers between its appropriations. 7 U.S.C. § 2257. The amount of such transfers may not exceed seven percent of the "donor" appropriation and the receiving appropriation may not be augmented by more than seven percent except in extraordinary emergencies. See also B-279886, Apr. 28, 1998 (noting five percent limit on transfer in Department of Justice appropriation).

If an agency has transfer authority of this type, its exercise is not precluded by the fact that the amount of the receiving appropriation had been reduced from the agency's budget request. B-151157, June 27, 1963. Also, the transfer statute is an independent grant of authority and, unless expressly provided otherwise, the percentage limitations do not apply to transfers under any separate transfer authority the agency may have. B-239031, June 22, 1990.

As mentioned above, Congress may also authorize one agency to transfer funds to another agency. For example, the Federal Transit Administration (FTA) must make a designated amount of funds appropriated to its capital investment grant program available to the Denali Commission. 49 U.S.C. § 5309(m)(6). Because FTA has specific direction to transfer the funds, it should make the transfers using the Department of Treasury's nonexpenditure transfer procedures, not the Economy Act or other interagency agreements. B-319189, Nov. 12, 2010.

The prohibition against transfer applies not only to interagency funds, but to the consolidation of all or parts of different appropriations of the same agency into a single fund as well. In a few instances, an agency may "pool" portions of agency unit appropriations to implement a particular statute. For example, an agency could transfer portions of unit appropriations to an agencywide pool to fund the Merit Pay System established by the Civil Service Reform Act of 1978. B-195775, Sept. 10, 1979. The transfers, while not explicitly authorized in the statute, were necessary to implement the law and carry out the legislative purpose. Similarly, the Treasury Department could pool portions of appropriations made to several separate bureaus to fund an Executive Development Program also authorized by the Civil Service Reform Act. 60 Comp. Gen. 686 (1981). However, pooling that would alter the purposes for which funds were appropriated is an impermissible transfer unless authorized by statute. E.g., B-209790-O.M., Mar. 12, 1985. It is also impermissible to transfer more than the cost of the goods or services provided to an ordering agency. 70 Comp. Gen. 592, 595 (1991).

Congress may reappropriate an unexpended balance for a different purpose. Such funds cease to be available for the purposes of the original appropriation. 18 Comp. Gen. 564 (1938); A-79180, July 30, 1936. Cf. 31 U.S.C. § 1301(b) (reappropriation for different purpose to be accounted for as a new appropriation). If the reappropriation is of an amount "not to exceed" a specified sum, and the full amount is not needed for the new purpose, the balance not needed reverts to the source appropriation. 18 Comp. Gen. at 565.

(3) Transfer Authority of General Applicability, Including the Account Adjustment Statute

Under the account adjustment statute, an agency may temporarily charge one appropriation for an expenditure benefiting another appropriation of the same agency, as long as amounts are available in both appropriations and the accounts are adjusted to reimburse the appropriation initially charged during or as of the close of the same fiscal year. 31 U.S.C. § 1534. This statute facilitates "common service" activities. See generally S. Rep. No. 89-1284 (1966). For example, an agency procuring equipment to be used jointly by several bureaus or offices within the agency funded under separate appropriations may initially charge the entire cost to a single appropriation and later apportion the cost among the appropriations of the benefiting components.

Under the account adjustment statute, the Department of Homeland Security's Preparedness Directorate had authority to fund shared services that benefited the directorate as a whole by initially obligating the services against one appropriation within the directorate and then allocating the costs to the benefiting appropriations. B-308762, Sept. 17, 2007. However, the

Directorate did not appear to properly allocate the costs. To the extent it did not properly record its obligations prior to the end of the fiscal year against each benefiting appropriation for the estimated value of the services each appropriation received, as required by the account adjustment statute, the Directorate improperly augmented its appropriations.

Another type of transfer authority is illustrated by 31 U.S.C. § 1531, which authorizes the transfer of unexpended balances incident to executive branch reorganizations, but only for purposes for which the appropriation was originally available. Cases discussing this authority include 31 Comp. Gen. 342 (1952) and B-92288 et al., Aug. 13, 1971.

(4) Restrictions Applicable to Transferred Amounts

The precise parameters of transfer authority will, of course, depend on the terms of the statute which grants it. As an initial matter, an amount transferred from one appropriation to another is available "for the same purpose and subject to the same limitations provided by the law appropriating the amount." 31 U.S.C. § 1532.

For example, funds withdrawn from other agencies' appropriations and credited to the Library of Congress FEDLINK revolving fund retained their time character and did not assume the time character of the FEDLINK revolving fund. B-288142, Sept. 6, 2001. The Library of Congress proposed retaining in the fund amounts of fiscal year money advanced by other agencies in earlier fiscal years when orders were placed and, to the extent the advances were not needed to cover the costs of the orders, applying the excess amounts to new orders placed in subsequent fiscal years. The Library pointed out that the law establishing the revolving fund made amounts in the fund available without fiscal year limitation. The Comptroller General concluded that "amounts withdrawn from a fiscal year appropriation and credited to a no year revolving fund, such as the FEDLINK revolving fund, are available for obligation only during the fiscal year of availability of the appropriation from which the amount was withdrawn." Id. Section 1532 is a significant control feature protecting Congress's constitutional prerogatives of the purse. Placing time limits on the availability of appropriations is a fundamental means of congressional control because it permits Congress to periodically review a given agency's programs and activities. Given the significance of time restrictions in preserving congressional powers of the purse, GAO looks for clear legislative expressions of congressional intent before interpreting legislation to override time limitations that Congress, through the appropriations process, has imposed on an agency's use of funds. The Comptroller General rejected the Library's view that the language in the FEDLINK statute overrode the time limitation imposed on funds transferred into FEDLINK because, until the Library had earned those amounts by performing the services ordered from the Library, these transferred amounts were not a part of the corpus of FEDLINK. Id.

Restrictions applicable to the receiving account but not to the donor account may or may not apply. Where transfers are intended to accomplish a purpose of the source appropriation (Economy Act transactions, for example), transferred funds have been held not subject to such restrictions. E.g., 21 Comp. Gen. 254 (1941); 18 Comp. Gen. 489 (1938); B-35677, July 27, 1943; B-131580-O.M., June 4, 1957. However, for transfers intended to permit a limited augmentation of the receiving account (7 U.S.C. § 2257, for example), this principle is arguably inapplicable in view of the fundamentally different purpose of the transfer.

Some transfer statutes have included requirements for approval by one or more congressional committees. In light of the Supreme Court's decision in Immigration & Naturalization Service v. Chadha, 462 U.S. 919 (1983), such "legislative veto" provisions are no longer valid. Whether the transfer authority to which the veto provision is attached remains valid depends on whether it can be regarded as severable from the approval requirement. This in turn depends on an evaluation, in light of legislative history and other surrounding circumstances, of whether Congress would have enacted the substantive authority without the veto provision. See, e.g., 15 Op. Off. Legal Counsel 49 (1991) (the Justice Department's Office of Legal Counsel (OLC) concluded that an unconstitutional legislative veto provision of the Selective Service Act was severable from the statute's grant of authority to the President to obtain expedited delivery of military contracts); 6 Op. Off. Legal Counsel 520 (1982) (OLC concluded that a Treasury Department transfer provision was severable and therefore survived a legislative veto provision).

b. Reprogramming

In 1985, the Deputy Secretary of Defense made the following statement:

> "The defense budget does not exist in a vacuum. There are forces at work to play havoc with even the best of budget estimates. The economy may vary in erms of inflation; political realities may bring external forces to bear; fact-of-life or programmatic changes may occur. The very nature of the lengthy and overlapping cycles of the budget process poses continual threats to the integrity of budget estimates. Reprogramming procedures permit us to respond to these unforeseen changes and still meet our defense requirements."

The thrust of this statement, while made from the perspective of the Defense Department, applies at least to some extent to all agencies.

Reprogramming is the shifting of funds within an appropriation to purposes other than those contemplated at the time of appropriation. GAO, A Glossary of Terms Used in the Federal Budget Process, GAO-05-734SP (Washington, D.C.: Sept. 2005), at 85. More specifically, it is the application of appropriations within a particular account to purposes, or in amounts, other than those justified in the budget submissions or otherwise considered or indicated by congressional committees in connection with the enactment of appropriation legislation. B-323792, Jan. 23, 2012; B-164912-O.M., Dec. 21, 1977. The term "reprogramming" appears to have come into use in the mid-1950s although the practice, under different names, predates that time.

Reprogramming is best understood in comparison to the transfer. A transfer shifts budget authority from one appropriation to another. In contrast, a reprogramming shifts funds within a single appropriation. Agencies generally may transfer funds only with explicit statutory authority. 31 U.S.C. § 1532; 70 Comp. Gen. 592 (1991). In contrast, agencies generally are free to reprogram, even if doing so is inconsistent with the budget estimates presented to the Congress, as long as the resulting obligations and expenditures are consistent with the purpose restrictions applicable to the appropriation. See Lincoln v. Vigil, 508 U.S. 182, 192 (1993) ("After all, the very point of a lump-sum appropriation is to give an agency the capacity to adapt to changing circumstances and meet its statutory responsibilities in what it sees as the most effective or desirable way"); B-323792, Jan. 23, 2013; B-279338, Jan. 4, 1999; B-215002, Aug. 3, 1987; B-196854.3, Mar. 19, 1984 (Congress is "implicitly conferring the authority to reprogram" by enacting lump-sum appropriations); 55 Comp. Gen. 307 (1975); B-123469, May 9, 1955; 4B Op. Off. Legal Counsel 701 (1980) (discussing the Attorney General's authority to reprogram to avoid deficiencies). This is true even though the agency may already have administratively allotted the funds to a particular object. 20 Comp. Gen. 631 (1941). In some situations, an agency may be required to reprogram funds to satisfy other obligations. E.g., Cherokee Nation of Oklahoma v. Leavitt, 543 U.S. 631, 641–43 (2005) (government must reprogram unrestricted funds to cover contractual obligations); Blackhawk Heating & Plumbing Co. v. United States, 622 F.2d 539, 552 n.9 (satisfaction of obligations under a settlement agreement).

For example, the United States Information Agency (USIA) received two appropriations: one for salaries and expenses and another for radio construction. B-248284.2, Sept. 1, 1992. USIA wished to obligate $4.6 million for an exhibition. Though its salaries and expenses appropriation was available for this purpose, the agency had insufficient funds remaining in that appropriation. Instead, USIA used its radio construction appropriation for the exhibition. Though the agency characterized its use of funds from the radio construction appropriation as a "reprogramming," the characterization was improper because the radio construction appropriation was not available for the purpose of funding an exhibition. Id. If USIA had the requisite statutory authority, it could have transferred the amount from its radio construction appropriation to its salaries and expenses appropriation. However, USIA lacked such transfer authority.

Though agencies generally have authority to reprogram funds, Congress may limit this authority. For example, Congress required the Commodity Futures Trading Commission to notify the Senate and House Committees on Appropriations prior to obligating or expending funds through a reprogramming to undertake certain enumerated activities. B-323792, Jan. 23, 2013. In the face of such restrictions, a key question is whether a particular shifting of funds is, in fact, a reprogramming. A comparison to transfers is useful. Agencies may transfer amounts only if they have statutory authority. It is comparatively easy to assess a transfer: each appropriation is well-defined and delineated with specific language in an appropriations act. The shifting of funds from one of these appropriations to another is a transfer. In contrast, a reprogramming is a shifting of funds from one purpose to another within a single appropriation. The appropriations act does not set forth the subdivisions that are relevant to determine whether an agency has reprogrammed funds. Therefore, reference to the language of the relevant appropriations act sheds little light on whether a particular shifting of funds is indeed a reprogramming.

Nevertheless, it is imperative to define the necessary subdivisions to give meaning and force to statutory provisions that restrict an agency's authority to reprogram. Typically, the itemizations and categorizations in the agency's budget documents as well as statements in committee reports and the President's budget submission, contain the subdivisions within an agency's appropriation that are relevant to determine whether an agency has reprogrammed funds. B 323792, Jan. 23, 2013. For instance, for FY 2012, the Commodity Futures Trading Commission (CFTC) received a single lump-sum appropriation. Id. CFTC's FY 2012 budget request included an item within that lump sum to fund an Office of Proceedings. A reprogramming would occur if CFTC shifted amounts that it had previously designated to carry out the functions of the Office of Proceedings to carry out different functions.

Some statutory reprogramming restrictions also provide for committee approval. As in the case of transfer, under the Supreme Court's decision in Immigration & Naturalization Service v. Chadha, 462 U.S. 919 (1983), statutory committee approval or veto provisions are no longer permissible. However, an agency may continue to observe committee approval procedures as part of its informal arrangements, although they would not be legally binding. B-196854.3, Mar. 19, 1984.

In addition to various statutory reprogramming restrictions, many non-statutory reprogramming arrangements exist between various agencies and their congressional oversight committees. These arrangements often include procedures for notification. These non-statutory arrangements do not have the force and effect of law. Lincoln v. Vigil, 508 U.S. 182, 192 (1993); TVA v. Hill, 437 U.S. 153, 191 (1978); 55 Comp. Gen. 307, 319 (1975). However, "we hardly need to note that an agency's decision to ignore congressional expectations may expose it to grave political consequences." Lincoln, 508 U.S. at 193. There are, at present, no reprogramming guidelines applicable to all agencies. As one might expect, reprogramming policies, procedures, and practices vary considerably among agencies. For example, in view of the nature of its activities and appropriation structure, the Defense Department has detailed and sophisticated procedures.

8. Impoundment Precluding the Obligation or Expenditure of Budget Authority

While an agency's basic mission is to carry out its programs with the funds Congress has appropriated, there is also the possibility that, for a variety of reasons, the full amount appropriated by Congress will not be expended or obligated by the administration. Under the Impoundment Control Act of 1974, an impoundment is an action or inaction by an officer or employee of the United States that delays or precludes the obligation or expenditure of budget authority provided by Congress. 2 U.S.C. §§ 682(1), 683. The act applies to "Salaries and

Expenses" appropriations as well as program appropriations. See, e.g., B-320091, July 23, 2010; 64 Comp. Gen. 370, 375–76 (1985).

There are two types of impoundment actions: deferrals and rescission proposals. In a deferral, an agency temporarily withholds or delays funds from obligation or expenditure. The President is required to submit a special message to Congress reporting any deferral of budget authority. Deferrals are authorized only to provide for contingencies, to achieve savings made possible by changes in requirements or greater efficiency of operations, or as otherwise specifically provided by law. A deferral may not be proposed for a period beyond the end of the fiscal year in which the special message reporting it is transmitted, although, for multiple year funds, nothing prevents a new deferral message covering the same funds in the following fiscal year. 2 U.S.C. §§ 682(1), 684.

A rescission involves the cancellation of budget authority previously provided by Congress (before that authority would otherwise expire), and can be accomplished only through legislation. See, e.g., B-322906, July 19, 2012 (update of statistical data concerning rescissions proposed and enacted since the passage of the Impoundment Control Act of 1974 through fiscal year 2011); GAO, Impoundment Control Act: Use and Impact of Rescission Procedures, GAO-10-320T (Washington, D.C.: Dec. 16, 2009) (testimony containing useful charts and reflections on the use of rescissions as a budget tool). The President must advise Congress of any proposed rescissions, again in a special message. The President is authorized to withhold budget authority that is the subject of a rescission proposal for a period of 45 days of continuous session following receipt of the proposal. Unless Congress acts to approve the proposed rescission within that time, the budget authority must be made available for obligation. 2 U.S.C. §§ 682(3), 683, 688.

The Impoundment Control Act requires the Comptroller General to monitor the performance of the executive branch in reporting proposed impoundments to Congress. A copy of each special message reporting a proposed deferral or rescission must be delivered to the Comptroller General, who then must review each such message and present his views to the Senate and House of Representatives. 2 U.S.C. § 685(b). If the Comptroller General finds that the executive branch has established a reserve or deferred budget authority and failed to transmit the required special message to Congress, the Comptroller General so reports to Congress. 2 U.S.C. § 686(a); GAO, Impoundment Control: Deferrals of Budget Authority in GSA, GAO/OGC-94-17 (Washington, D.C.: Nov. 5, 1993) (unreported impoundment of General Service Administration funds); Impoundment Control: Comments on Unreported Impoundment of DOD Budget Authority, GAO/OGC-92-11 (Washington, D.C.: June 3, 1992) (unreported impoundment of V-22 Osprey funds). The Comptroller General also reports to Congress on any special message transmitted by the executive branch that has incorrectly classified a deferral or a rescission. 2 U.S.C. § 686(b). GAO will construe a deferral as a de facto rescission if the timing of the proposed deferral is such that "funds could be expected with reasonable certainty to lapse before they could be obligated, or would have to be obligated imprudently to avoid that consequence." 54 Comp. Gen. 453, 462 (1974). Upon request, GAO will also assess whether executive branch agencies have withheld funds proposed for cancellation in the President's budget.

If, under the Impoundment Control Act, the executive branch is required to make budget authority available for obligation (if, for example, Congress does not pass a rescission bill) and fails to do so, the Comptroller General is authorized to bring a civil action in the U.S. District Court for the District of Columbia to require that the budget authority be made available. 2 U.S.C. § 687.

The expiration of budget authority or delays in obligating it resulting from ineffective or unwise program administration are not regarded as impoundments unless accompanied by or derived from an intention to withhold the budget authority. B-229326, Aug. 29, 1989. Similarly, an improper obligation, although it may violate several other statutes, is generally not an impoundment. 64 Comp. Gen. 359 (1985).

There is also a distinction between deferrals, which must be reported, and "programmatic" delays, which are not impoundments and are not reportable under the Impoundment Control Act. A programmatic delay is one in which operational factors unavoidably impede the obligation of budget authority, notwithstanding the agency's reasonable and good faith efforts to implement the program. B-290659, July 24, 2002; GAO, Impoundment Control: Deferral of DOD Budget Authority Not Reported, GAO/OGC-91-8 (Washington, D.C.: May 7, 1991); Impoundment Control: Deferrals of Budget Authority for Military Construction Not Reported, GAO/OGC-91-3 (Washington, D.C.: Feb. 5, 1991). Since intent is a relevant factor, the determination requires a case-by-case evaluation of the agency's justification ·in light of all of the surrounding circumstances. A programmatic delay may become a reportable deferral if the programmatic basis ceases to exist.

Delays resulting from the following factors may be programmatic, depending on the facts and circumstances involved:

- conditions on availability for using funds not met (B-290659, July 24, 2002);

- contract delays due to shipbuilding design modification, verification, or changes in scope (GAO/OGC-90-4);

- uncertainty as to the amount of budget authority that will ultimately be available for the program (B-203057, Sept. 15, 1981; B-207374, July 20, 1982, noting that the uncertainty is particularly relevant when it "arises in the context of continuing resolution funding, where Congress has not yet spoken definitively");

- time required to set up the program or to comply with statutory conditions on obligating the funds (B-96983, B-225110, Sept. 3, 1987);

- compliance with congressional committee directives (B-221412, Feb. 12, 1986);

- delay in receiving a contract proposal requested from contemplated sole source awardee (B-115398, Feb. 6, 1978);

- historically low loan application level (B-115398, Sept. 28, 1976);

- late receipt of complete loan applications (B-195437.3, Feb. 5, 1988);

- delay in awarding grants pending issuance of necessary regulations (B-171630, May 10, 1976); and

- administrative determination of allowability and accuracy of claims for grant payments (B-115398, Oct. 16, 1975).

GAO did find an impoundment, as opposed to a programmatic delay, in a 1991 case. The Department of Defense withheld military construction funds to improve program efficiency, not because of an unavoidable delay. Because the Department did not take the necessary steps to implement the program while funds were temporarily unobligated, the withholding constituted an impoundment. B-241514.2, Feb. 5, 1991.

9. Deficit Reduction: the Balanced Budget and Emergency Deficit Control Act

The Balanced Budget and Emergency Deficit Control Act of 1985 (BBEDCA) established a process known as "sequestration" to enforce certain deficit reduction goals. It was enacted to deal with a growing budget deficit (excess of total outlays over total receipts for a given fiscal year). 2 U.S.C. § 622(6). BBEDCA established "maximum deficit amounts" for fiscal years 1985 to 1990. Pub. L. No. 99-177, § 201(a)(1). If the deficit exceeded these statutory limits, the President was required to issue a sequestration order (a cancellation of budgetary resources) that would reduce all nonexempt spending by a uniform percentage. Id. § 252. In the spring of 1990, it became clear that the deficit was going to exceed BBEDCA maximum deficit limits by a considerable amount. To respond to these large deficits, President George H.W. Bush and congressional leadership convened negotiations on the budget in May 1990. The result was the Omnibus Budget Reconciliation Act of 1990. Pub. L. No. 101-508, 104 Stat. 1388 (Nov. 5, 1990).

The Omnibus Budget Reconciliation Act of 1990 included the Budget Enforcement Act (1990 BEA), which provided a major overhaul of the BBEDCA procedures. The 1990 BEA effectively replaced BBEDCA's system of deficit limits with two enforcement mechanisms: limits on discretionary spending and a pay-as-you-go-requirement (PAYGO) for direct spending and revenue legislation. If discretionary appropriations enacted exceeded the annual limits, then the law provided for a sequestration of budget authority. If Congress failed to achieve budget neutrality on direct spending, then there would be an offsetting sequestration of nonexempt mandatory accounts. The 1990 BEA required OMB and CBO to estimate new budget authority and outlays provided by any new legislation through a process that came to be called "scorekeeping." CBO would transmit its estimates to OMB, which would report any discrepancies to Congress. The 1990 BEA required that OMB's estimates be used to determine whether a sequestration was necessary.

In 1993, the discretionary spending limits and the PAYGO rules were extended through fiscal year 1998. Pub. L. No. 103-66, 107 Stat. 683 (Aug. 10, 1993). The 1997 Budget Enforcement Act (1997 BEA) again extended the discretionary spending caps and the PAYGO rules through fiscal year 2002. Pub. L. No. 105-33, title X, §§ 10203, 10205, 111 Stat. 251, 701–03 (Aug. 5, 1997). Although the overall discretionary spending caps expired in 2002, additional caps on Highway and Mass Transit spending established under the Transportation Equity Act for the 21st Century (TEA-21)63 continued through fiscal year 2003, and another set of caps on conservation spending, established as part of the fiscal year 2001 Interior Appropriations Act, were set through fiscal year 2006. In addition, the sequestration procedures were to apply through fiscal year 2006 to the conservation category. However, Public Law 107-312 eliminated the PAYGO sequestration requirement. Pub. L. No. 107-312, 116 Stat. 2456 (Dec. 2, 2002).

In addition to the statutory spending caps, Congress in fiscal year 1994 began including overall limits on discretionary spending in the concurrent budget resolution that have become known as congressional caps. H.R. Con. Res. 64, 103rd Cong. § 12(b) (1993). Congress established these caps to manage its internal budget process, while the BEA statutory caps continued to govern for sequestration purposes. The congressional caps were enforceable in the Senate by a point of order that prohibited the consideration of a budget resolution that exceeded the limits for that fiscal year (the point of order could be waived or suspended by a three-fifths vote). Although the statutory 1997 BEA limits expired at the end of fiscal year 2002, Congress continues to use the concurrent resolution on the budget to establish and enforce congressional budgetary limits. H.R. Con. Res. 95, 108th Cong. § 504 (2003).

In February 2010, the Statutory Pay-As-You-Go Act of 2010 (Statutory PAYGO) revived a version of the PAYGO requirement for direct spending and revenue legislation. Pub. L. No. 113-139, title I, 124 Stat. 8 (Feb. 12, 2010). Statutory PAYGO provides that if the net effect of direct spending and revenue legislation enacted in a year increases the deficit, then there will be a sequestration of nonexempt direct spending to eliminate the increase. 2 U.S.C. §§ 931–939.

In August 2011, the Budget Control Act of 2011 restored a sequestration process to enforce newly-enacted discretionary spending limits for fiscal years 2012 to 2021. Pub. L. No. 112-25,

125 Stat. 240 (Aug. 2, 2011). These discretionary spending limits reduced projected spending by about $1 trillion. 2 U.S.C. § 901(c); B-324723, July 31, 2013. If new budget authority exceeds the discretionary spending limits in those fiscal years, then the law provides for a sequestration to eliminate the breach. 2 U.S.C. §§ 901, 901a.

The Budget Control Act also aimed to achieve additional deficit reduction by fiscal year 2021. The Act created the Joint Select Committee on Deficit Reduction, which was tasked with proposing legislation by December 2, 2011, to reduce the deficit by at least $1.2 trillion through fiscal year 2021. The Joint Committee failed to propose a bill by its statutory deadline, and Congress and the President subsequently failed to enact legislation. This failure triggered a new sequestration process, the so-called "Joint Committee sequestration," to otherwise achieve the $1.2 trillion reduction. 2 U.S.C. § 901a. The law currently provides for annual reductions of discretionary spending through fiscal year 2021 and of direct spending through fiscal year 2025.

C. Authorizations versus Appropriations

1. Distinction between Authorization and Appropriation

Appropriation acts must be distinguished from two other types of legislation: "enabling" or "organic" legislation and "appropriation authorization" legislation. Enabling or organic legislation is legislation that creates an agency, establishes a program, or prescribes a function, such as the Department of Education Organization Act or the Federal Water Pollution Control Act. While the organic legislation may provide the necessary authority to conduct the program or activity, it usually does not provide budget authority. Nor does organic legislation typically provide any form of an appropriation.

Appropriation authorization legislation, as the name implies, is legislation that authorizes the appropriation of funds to implement the organic legislation. It may be included as part of the organic legislation or it may be separate. As with organic legislation, appropriation authorization legislation typically does not provide budget authority or an appropriation:

> "The mere authorization of an appropriation does not authorize expenditures on the faith thereof or the making of contracts obligating the money authorized to be appropriated."

16 Comp. Gen. 1007, 1008 (1937). See also 27 Comp. Dec. 923 (1921) ("The expression 'authorized to be appropriated' . . . clearly indicates that no appropriation is made or intended to be made, but the bill when enacted becomes the authority of law for an expected appropriation in the future"); 67 Comp. Gen. 332 (1988); 37 Comp. Gen. 732 (1958); 35 Comp. Gen. 306 (1955); 26 Comp. Gen. 452 (1947); 15 Comp. Gen. 802 (1936); 4 Comp. Gen. 219 (1924); A 27765, July 8, 1929.

Agencies may incur obligations only after Congress grants budget authority. Congress may confer budget authority in any law. However, provisions conferring budget authority and authority to make payments to liquidate obligations nearly always appear in appropriations acts, not in organic legislation or in appropriation authorization legislation.

Like organic legislation, authorization legislation is considered and reported by the committees with legislative jurisdiction over the particular subject matter, whereas appropriation bills are exclusively within the jurisdiction of the appropriations committees.

There is no general requirement, either constitutional or statutory, that an appropriation act be preceded by a specific authorization act. E.g., 71 Comp. Gen. 378, 380 (1992). The existence of a statute (organic legislation) imposing substantive functions upon an agency is itself sufficient authorization for the necessary appropriations. B-173832, July 16, 1976; B-173832, Aug. 1, 1975; B-111810, Mar. 8, 1974. Moreover, expiration of an authorization of appropriations does not prohibit an agency from using available appropriations to carry out a program required or permitted by existing enabling legislation. B-323433, Aug. 14, 2012 (Social Security Administration has adequate authority under organic legislation to continue mandatory and discretionary grant programs upon the expiration of an authorization of appropriations).

However, statutory requirements for authorizations do exist in a number of specific situations: for example, one provision states that "[a]ppropriations to carry out the provisions of this chapter shall be subject to annual authorization." Department of Energy Organization Act, § 660, 42 U.S.C. § 7270. Another provides that no funds may be appropriated for military construction, military procurement, and certain related research and development "unless funds therefor have been specifically authorized by law." 10 U.S.C. § 114(a). In addition, rules of the House of Representatives generally prohibit the reporting of an appropriation in a general appropriation bill for expenditures not previously authorized by law. See Rule XXI(2)(a)(1), Rules of the House of Representatives. The effect of this Rule is to subject the "offending" appropriation to a point of order. A more limited provision exists in Rule XVI, Standing Rules of the Senate.

An authorization act is basically a directive to Congress itself, which Congress is free to follow or alter (up or down) in the subsequent appropriation act. B-323433, Aug. 14, 2012. A statutory requirement for prior authorization is also essentially a congressional mandate to itself. Thus, for example, if Congress appropriates money to the Defense Department in violation of 10 U.S.C. § 114, there are no practical consequences. The appropriation is just as valid, and just as available for obligation, as if section 114 had been satisfied or did not exist.

Authorizations take many different forms, depending in part on whether they are contained in the organic legislation or are separate legislation. Authorizations contained in organic legislation may be "definite" (setting dollar limits either in the aggregate or for specific fiscal years) or "indefinite" (authorizing "such sums as may be necessary to carry out the provisions of this act"). An indefinite authorization serves little purpose other than to comply with House Rule XXI. Appropriation authorizations enacted as separate legislation resemble appropriation acts in structure, for example, the annual Department of Defense Authorization Acts.

In sum, the typical sequence is: (1) organic legislation; (2) authorization of appropriations, if not contained in the organic legislation; and (3) the appropriation act. While this may be the "normal" sequence, there are deviations and variations, and it is not always possible to neatly label a given piece of legislation. Consider, for example, the following:

> "The Secretary of the Treasury is authorized and directed to pay to the Secretary of the Interior . . . for the benefit of the Coushatta Tribe of Louisiana . . . out of any money in the Treasury not otherwise appropriated, the sum of $1,300,000."

Pub. L. No. 100-411, § 1(a)(1), 102 Stat. 1097 (Aug. 22, 1988). This is the first section of a law enacted to settle land claims by the Coushatta Tribe against the United States and to prescribe the use and distribution of the settlement funds. Applying the test described above in section B.4, it is certainly an appropriation—it contains a specific direction to pay and designates the funds to be used—but, in a technical sense, it is not an appropriation act. Also, it contains its own authorization. Thus, we have an authorization and an appropriation combined in a statute that is neither an authorization act (in the sense described above) nor an appropriation act.

2. Specific Problem Areas and the Resolution of Conflicts

a. Introduction

Appropriation acts, as we have seen, do not exist in a vacuum. They are enacted against the backdrop of program legislation and, in many cases, specific authorization acts. This section deals with two broad but closely related issues. First, what precisely can Congress do in an appropriation act? Is it limited to essentially "rubber stamping" what has previously been authorized? Second, what does an agency do when faced with what it perceives to be an inconsistency between an appropriation act and some other statute?

The remaining portions of this section raise these issues in a number of specific contexts. In this introduction, we present four important principles. The resolution of problems in the relationship of appropriation acts to other statutes will almost invariably lie in the application of one or more of these principles.

First, Congress intends to achieve a consistent body of law. Therefore, multiple statutes should be construed harmoniously so as to give maximum effect to all of them wherever possible. E.g., Posadas v. National City Bank of New York, 296 U.S. at 503; Strawser v. Atkins, 290 F.3d 720 (4th Cir.), cert. denied, 537 U.S. 1045 (2002); B-290011, Mar. 25, 2002; 53 Comp. Gen. 853, 856 (1974); B-208593.6, Dec. 22, 1988. One particularly important consequence of this principle is that except as specified in the appropriation act, appropriations to carry out enabling or authorizing laws must be expended in accordance with the original authorization both as to the amount of funds to be expended and the nature of the work authorized. B-307720, Sept 27, 2007; B-258000, Aug. 31, 1994; B-220682, Feb. 21, 1986; B-204874, July 28, 1982; B-151157, June 27, 1963; 36 Comp. Gen. 240, 242 (1956); B-151157, June 27, 1963; B-125404, Aug. 31,

1956. While it is true that one Congress cannot bind a future Congress, nor can it bind subsequent action by the same Congress, an authorization act is more than an academic exercise and its requirements must be followed unless changed by subsequent legislation.

Congress is free to amend or repeal prior legislation. This leads to an important corollary to the principle that Congress intends to achieve a consistent body of law, which is that "repeals by implication" are disfavored, and statutes will be construed to avoid this result whenever reasonably possible. That is, courts generally will find that a statute repeals an earlier one only if the repeal is explicit. E.g., Tennessee Valley Authority v. Hill, 437 U.S. 153, 189–90 (1978); Morton v. Mancari, 417 U.S. 535, 549 (1974); Posadas v. National City Bank of New York, 296 U.S. 497, 503 (1936); B-307720, Sept. 27, 2007; B-290011, Mar. 25, 2002; B-261589, Mar. 6, 1996; 72 Comp. Gen. 295, 297 (1993); 64 Comp. Gen. 142, 145 (1984); 58 Comp. Gen. 687, 691–92 (1979); B-258163, Sept. 29, 1994; B-236057, May 9, 1990. Repeals by implication are particularly disfavored in the appropriations context. Robertson v. Seattle Audubon Society, 503 U.S. 429, 440 (1992).

A repeal by implication will be found only where "the intention of the legislature to repeal [is] clear and manifest." Posadas, 296 U.S. at 503. See also B-236057, May 9, 1990. The principle that implied repeals are disfavored applies with special weight when it is asserted that a general statute repeals a more specific statute. 72 Comp. Gen. at 297.

Second, if two statutes are in irreconcilable conflict, the more recent statute, as the latest expression of Congress, governs. As one court concluded in a statement illustrating the eloquence of simplicity, "[t]he statutes are thus in conflict, the earlier permitting and the later prohibiting," so the later statute supersedes the earlier. Eisenberg v. Corning, 179 F.2d 275, 277 (D.C. Cir. 1949). In a sense, the "last in time" rule is yet another way of expressing the repeal by implication principle. We state it separately to highlight its narrowness: it applies only when the two statutes cannot be reconciled in any reasonable manner, and then only to the extent of the conflict. E.g., B-323157, May 21, 2012 ("[W]hen two, equally specific provisions are in irreconcilable conflict, the Supreme Court views the later act as an implied repeal of the earlier one to the extent of the conflict . . . . This is because the more recent enactment is the latest expression of Congress."); B-308715, Apr. 20, 2007 ("It is well established that a later enacted, specific statute will typically supersede a conflicting previously enacted, general statute to the extent of the inconsistency."). See also Posadas, 296 U.S. at 503; B-255979, Oct. 30, 1995; B-203900, Feb. 2, 1989; B-226389, Nov. 14, 1988; B-214172, July 10, 1984, aff'd upon reconsideration, 64 Comp. Gen. 282 (1985). We will see later in this section that while the last in time rule can be stated with eloquent simplicity, its application is not always so simple.

Third, despite the occasional comment to the contrary in judicial decisions (a few of which we will note later), Congress can and does "legislate" in appropriation acts. E.g., Strawser v. Atkins, 290 F.3d 720, 734 (4th Cir. 2002) ("Where Congress chooses to amend substantive law in an appropriations rider, we are bound to follow Congress's last word on the matter even in an appropriations law."); Preterm, Inc. v. Dukakis, 591 F.2d 121 (1st Cir.), cert. denied, 441 U.S. 952 (1979); Friends of the Earth v. Armstrong, 485 F.2d 1 (10th Cir. 1973), cert. denied, 414 U.S. 1171 (1974); Eisenberg, 179 F.2d 275; Tayloe v. Kjaer, 171 F.2d 343 (D.C. Cir. 1948). It may well be that the device is "unusual and frowned upon." Preterm, 591 F.2d at 131. See also Building & Construction Trades Department, AFL-CIO v. Martin, 961 F.2d 269, 273 (D.C. Cir. 1992), cert. denied, 506 U.S. 915 (1992) ("While appropriations are 'Acts of Congress' which can substantively change existing law, there is a very strong presumption that they do not . . . and that when they do, the change is only intended for one fiscal year."). It also may well be that the appropriation act will be narrowly construed when it is in apparent conflict with authorizing legislation. Calloway v. District of Columbia, 216 F.3d 1, 9 (D.C. Cir. 2000); Donovan v. Carolina Stalite Co., 734 F.2d 1547, 1558 (D.C. Cir. 1984). Nevertheless, appropriation acts are, like any other statute, passed by both Houses of Congress and either signed by the President or enacted over a presidential veto. As such, and subject of course to constitutional strictures, they are "just as effective a way to legislate as are ordinary bills relating to a particular subject." Friends of the Earth, 485 F.2d at 9; Envirocare of Utah Inc. v. United States, 44 Fed. Cl. 474, 482 (1999).

Fourth, legislative history is not legislation. As useful and important as legislative history may be in resolving ambiguities and determining congressional intent, it is the language of the appropriation act, and not the language of its legislative history, that is enacted into law. E.g., Shannon v. United States, 512 U.S. 573, 583 (1994) (declining to give effect to "legislative history that is in no way anchored in the text of the statute."). As the Supreme Court stated in a case previously cited, which we will discuss in more detail later:

> "Expressions of committees dealing with requests for appropriations cannot be equated with statutes enacted by Congress . . . ."

Tennessee Valley Authority v. Hill, 437 U.S. at 191; see also Lincoln v. Vigil, 508 U.S. 182, 192 (1993); Thompson v. Cherokee Nation of Oklahoma, 334 F.3d 1075 (Fed. Cir. 2003).

These, then, are the "guiding principles" that will be applied in various combinations and configurations to analyze and resolve the problem areas identified in the remainder of this section. Many situations will require the application of multiple principles. For example, the Small Business Administration (SBA) believed there was a conflict between the spending levels established for certain programs in its authorizing legislation and the levels provided for the same programs in SBA's FY 1984 appropriations act, as fleshed out by an accompanying conference report. 64 Comp. Gen. 282 (1985). GAO concluded that the two statutes were not in conflict, that the appropriation did not implicitly repeal or amend the authorizations, and that the spending levels in the authorization were controlling. GAO explained that "an existing statutory limitation [here, the levels in the authorization act] cannot be superseded or repealed by statements, explanations, recommendations, or tables contained only in committee reports or in other legislative history." This case applied both the principle that Congress intends to achieve a consistent body of law and the principle that legislative history is not legislation.

A useful supplemental reference on many of the topics we discuss is Louis Fisher, The Authorization-Appropriation Process in Congress: Formal Rules and Informal Practices, 29 Cath. U.L. Rev. 51 (1979).

b. Variations in Amount

(1) Appropriation exceeds authorization

Generally speaking, Congress is free to appropriate more money for a given object than the amount previously authorized:

> "While legislation providing for an appropriation of funds in excess of the amount contained in a related authorization act apparently would be subject to a point of order under rule 21 of the Rules of the House of Representatives, there would be no basis on which we could question otherwise proper expenditures of funds actually appropriated."

B-123469, Apr. 14, 1955.

The governing principle was stated as follows:

> "It is fundamental . . . that one Congress cannot bind a future Congress and that the Congress has full power to make an appropriation in excess of a cost limitation contained in the original authorization act. This authority is exercised as an incident to the power of the Congress to appropriate and regulate expenditures of the public money."

36 Comp. Gen. 240, 242 (1956). For example, the National Park Service could obligate its lump-sum construction appropriation for projects in various parks, even though such obligations would exceed the amounts authorized to be appropriated by an earlier law. B-148736, Sept. 15, 1977.

(2) Appropriation less than authorization

Congress is free to appropriate less than an amount authorized either in an authorization act or in program legislation, again, as in the case of exceeding an authorization, at least where it does so directly. E.g., 53 Comp. Gen. 695 (1974). This includes the failure to fund a program at all, that is, not to appropriate any funds. United States v. Dickerson, 310 U.S. 554 (1940).

A case in point is City of Los Angeles v. Adams, 556 F.2d 40 (D.C. Cir. 1977). The Airport and Airway Development Act of 1970 authorized airport development grants "in aggregate amounts not less than" specified dollar amounts for specified fiscal years, and provided an apportionment formula. Pub. L. No. 91-258, title I, 84 Stat. 219 (May 21, 1970). Subsequent appropriation acts included specific limitations on the aggregate amounts to be available for the grants, less than the amounts authorized. The court concluded that both laws could be given effect by limiting the amounts available to those specified in the appropriation acts, but requiring that they be distributed in accordance with the formula of the authorizing legislation. In holding the appropriation limits controlling, the court said:

> "According to its own rules, Congress is not supposed to use appropriations measures as vehicles for the amendment of general laws, including revision of expenditure authorization. . . . Where Congress chooses to do so, however, we are bound to follow Congress's last word on the matter even in an appropriations law."

Id. at 48–49.

Another relevant case is Highland Falls-Fort Montgomery Central School District v. United States, 48 F.3d 1166 (1995). The Impact Aid Act entitles school districts financially impacted as the result of a substantial federal presence in the school district to financial assistance to mitigate the impact. The Act entitled school districts to amounts as determined by the Department of Education that are attributable to each of three separate categories of impact: (1) federal ownership of property within a school district, (2) increases in school enrollments attributable to children of persons who reside or work on federal property, and (3) sudden and substantial increases in attendance by school children. The Act provides an allocation formula to be used by the Secretary if annual appropriations are inadequate to fully fund each of the three aid categories.

The annual appropriations acts for 1989 through 1993 did not provide enough money to fully fund each of the three categories of impact aid. However, in those years, Congress earmarked specific amounts for each category of impact aid in the appropriation act. The Department of Education followed the funding directives contained in the appropriations acts rather than the allocation formula contained in the Impact Aid Act for those fiscal years. One school district sued arguing that the Department should have applied the allocation formula and fully funded the first category (which would have resulted in the school district receiving more aid overall). The court found in favor of the Department of Education, which was relying on the most recent expression of congressional intent (here, the appropriations acts) to resolve the irreconcilable conflict between the impact aid formula and the appropriation earmarks.

Occasionally Congress enacts permanent legislation stating that particular payments will be made in the future. Congress may enact a subsequent appropriation that makes a smaller payment than was contemplated in the permanent legislation. Such a reduction is permissible and binding as long as the intent to reduce the amount of the payment is clear. For example, permanent legislation set the salaries of certain territorial judges. United States v. Fisher, 109 U.S. 143 (1883). Congress subsequently appropriated a lesser amount, "in full compensation" for that particular year. The Court held that Congress had the power to reduce the salaries, and had effectively done so. "It is impossible that both acts should stand. No ingenuity can reconcile them. The later act must therefore prevail . . . ." Id. at 146. See also United States v. Mitchell, 109 U.S. 146 (1883). In another case, the Court found a mandatory authorization effectively suspended by a provision in an appropriation act prohibiting the use of funds for the payment in question "notwithstanding the applicable portions of" the authorizing legislation. United States v. Dickerson, 310 U.S. 554 (1940).

In these cases, the "reduction by appropriation" was effective because the intent of the congressional action was unmistakable. The mere failure to appropriate sufficient funds is not enough. For example, the Court refused to find a repeal by implication in "subsequent enactments which merely appropriated a less amount . . . and which contained no words that expressly, or by clear implication, modified or repealed the previous law." United States v. Langston, 118 U.S. 389, 394 (1886); see also In re Aiken County, 725 F.3d 255, 260 (D.C. Cir. 2013); United States v. Vulte, 233 U.S. 509 (1914). A failure to appropriate in this type of situation will prevent administrative agencies from making payment, but, as in Langston and Vulte, is unlikely to prevent recovery by way of a lawsuit. See also Wetsel-Oviatt Lumber Co., Inc. v. United States, 38 Fed. Cl. 563, 570–571 (1997); New York Airways, Inc. v. United States, 369 F.2d 743 (Ct. Cl. 1966); Gibney v. United States, 114 Ct. Cl. 38 (1949).

Constitutional questions may arise if Congress attempts to repeal an entitlement that has already vested. The Supreme Court made the distinction between vested and non-vested entitlements clear:

"No one disputes that Congress may prospectively reduce the pay of members of the Armed Forces, even if that reduction deprived members of benefits they had expected to be able to earn. . . . It is quite a different matter, however, for Congress to deprive a service member of pay due for services already performed, but still owing. In that case, the congressional action would appear in a different constitutional light."

United States v. Larionoff, 431 U.S. 864, 879 (1977).

(3) Earmarks in authorization act

A number of cases have considered the question of whether there is a conflict when an authorization establishes a minimum earmark ("not less than," "shall be available only"), and the related appropriation is a lump-sum appropriation which does not expressly mention the earmark. Is the agency in this situation required to observe the earmark? Applying the principle that an appropriation must be expended in accordance with the related authorization unless the appropriation act provides otherwise, GAO has concluded that the agency must observe the earmark. 64 Comp. Gen. 388 (1985); B-220682, Feb. 21, 1986 ("an earmark in an authorization act must be followed where a lump sum is appropriated pursuant to the authorization"); B-207343, Aug. 18, 1982; B-193282, Dec. 21, 1978 (concluding that INS was required to make $2 million of its lump-sum appropriation available to investigate and prosecute alleged Nazi war criminals based on a $2 million earmark in its related authorization act). See also B-131935, Mar. 17, 1986. This result applies even though following the earmark will drastically reduce the amount of funds available for non-earmarked programs funded under the same appropriation. 64 Comp. Gen. at 391. (These cases can also be viewed as another application of the rule against repeal by implication.)

If Congress expressly appropriates an amount at variance with a previously enacted authorization earmark, the appropriation will control under the last in time rule. For example, an authorization act had expressly earmarked $18 million for the United Nations International Children's Emergency Fund (UNICEF) for specific fiscal years. 53 Comp. Gen. 695 (1974). A subsequent appropriation act provided a lump sum, out of which only $15 million was earmarked for UNICEF. The Comptroller General concluded that the $15 million specified in the appropriation act was controlling and represented the maximum available for UNICEF for that fiscal year.

c. Variations in Purpose

As noted previously, it is only the appropriation, not the authorization by itself, that permits the incurring of obligations and the making of expenditures. It follows that an authorization does not, as a general proposition, expand the scope of availability of appropriations beyond what is permissible under the terms of the appropriation act. The authorized purpose must be implemented either by a specific appropriation or by inclusion in a broader lump-sum appropriation. Thus, an appropriation made for specific purposes is not available for related but more extended purposes contained in the authorization act but not included in the appropriation. 19 Comp. Gen. 961 (1940). See also 37 Comp. Gen. 732 (1958); 35 Comp. Gen. 306 (1955); 26 Comp. Gen. 452 (1947).

In addition to simply electing not to appropriate funds for an authorized purpose, Congress can expressly restrict the use of an appropriation for a purpose or purposes included in the authorization. E.g., B-24341, Apr. 1, 1942 ("[W]hatever may have been the intention of the original enabling act it must give way to the express provisions of the later act which appropriated funds but limited their use").

Similarly, by express provision in an appropriation act, Congress can expand authorized purposes. For example, an appropriation expressly included two mandatory earmarks for projects beyond the scope of the related authorization. 67 Comp. Gen. 401 (1988). Noting that "the appropriation language provides its own expanded authorization for these programs," GAO concluded that the agency was required to reserve funds for the two mandatory earmarks before committing the balance of the appropriation for discretionary expenditures.

Except to the extent Congress expressly expands or limits authorized purposes in the appropriation act, the appropriation must be used in accordance with the authorization act in terms of purpose. Thus, GAO concluded that an appropriation to construct a bridge across the Potomac River pursuant to a statute authorizing construction of the bridge and prescribing its location was not available to construct the bridge at a slightly different location even though the planners favored the alternate location. B-125404, Aug. 31, 1956. Similarly, the Flood Control Act of 1970 authorized construction of a dam and reservoir for the Ellicott Creek project in New York. Subsequently, legislation was proposed to authorize channel construction instead of the dam and reservoir, but was not enacted. A continuing resolution made a lump-sum appropriation for flood control projects "authorized by law." The Comptroller General concluded that the appropriation did not repeal the prior authorization, and that therefore, the funds could not properly be used for the alternative channel construction. B-193307, Feb. 6, 1979.

d. Period of Availability

An authorization of appropriations, like an appropriation itself, may authorize appropriations to be made on a multiple year or no-year, as well as fiscal year, basis. The question we address here is the extent to which the period of availability specified in an authorization or enabling act is controlling. Congress can, in an appropriation act, enact a different period of availability than that specified in the authorization. Generally, the period of availability in the appropriations act controls. For instance, an appropriation of funds "to remain available until expended" (no-year) was found controlling over a provision in the authorizing legislation that authorized appropriations on a 2-year basis. B-182101, Oct. 16, 1974. See also B-149372, B-158195, Apr. 29, 1969 (two-year appropriation of presidential transition funds held controlling notwithstanding provision in Presidential Transition Act of 1963, which authorized services and facilities to former President and Vice President only for 6 months after expiration of term of office).

Until 1971, GAO considered whether appropriation language specifically referred to the authorization. If it did, then GAO considered the provisions of the authorization act—including any multiple year or no-year authorizations—to be incorporated by reference into the provisions of the appropriation act. This was regarded as sufficient to overcome 31 U.S.C. § 1301(c), which presumes that an appropriation is for one fiscal year unless the appropriation states otherwise, and to overcome the presumption of fiscal year availability derived from the enacting clause of the appropriation act. If the appropriation language did not specifically refer to the authorization act, the appropriation was held to be available only for the fiscal year covered by the appropriation act. 45 Comp. Gen. 508 (1966); 45 Comp. Gen. 236 (1965); B-147196, Apr. 5, 1965; B-127518, May 10, 1956; B-37398, Oct. 26, 1943. The reference had to be specific; the phrase "as authorized by law" was not enough. B-127518, May 10, 1956.

By 1971, however, Congress was enacting (and continues to enact) a general provision in all appropriation acts: "[n]o part of any appropriation contained in this Act shall remain available for obligation beyond the current fiscal year unless expressly so provided herein." Now, if an appropriation act contains the provision quoted in the preceding paragraph, it will not be sufficient for an appropriation contained in that act to merely incorporate a multiple year or no-year authorization by reference. The effect of this general provision is to require the appropriation language to expressly provide for availability beyond one year in order to overcome the enacting clause. B-319734, July 26, 2010; 50 Comp. Gen. 857 (1971).

The general provision resulted from the efforts of the House Committee on Appropriations in connection with the 1964 foreign aid appropriations bill. In its report on that bill, the Committee first described then-existing practice:

> "The custom and practice of the Committee on Appropriations has been to recommend appropriations on an annual basis unless there is some valid reason to make the item available for longer than a one-year period. The most common technique in the latter instances is to add the words 'to remain available until expended' to the appropriation paragraph. "

> "In numerous instances, . . . the Congress has in the underlying enabling legislation authorized appropriations therefor to be made on an 'available until expended' basis. When he submits the budget, the President generally includes the phrase 'to remain available until expended' in the proposed appropriation language if that is what the Executive wishes to propose. The Committee either concurs or drops the phrase from the appropriation language."

H.R. Rep. No. 88-1040, at 55 (1963). The Committee then noted a situation in the 1963 appropriation that had apparently generated some disagreement. The President had requested certain refugee assistance funds to remain available until expended. The report goes on to state:

> "The Committee thought the funds should be on a 1-year basis, thus the phrase 'to remain available until expended' was not in the bill as reported. The final law also failed to include the phrase or any other express language of similar import. Thus Congress took affirmative action to limit the availability to the fiscal year 1963 only."

Id. at 56. The Committee then quoted what is now 31 U.S.C. § 1301(c), and stated:

> "The above quoted 31 U.S.C. [§ 1301(c)] seems clearly to govern and, in respect to the instant class of appropriation, to require the act making the appropriation to expressly provide for availability longer than 1 year if the enacting clause limiting the appropriations in the law to a given fiscal year is to be overcome as to any specific appropriation therein made. And it accords with the rule of reason and ancient practice to retain control of such an elementary matter wholly within the terms of the law making the appropriation. The two hang together. But in view of the question in the present case and the possibility of similar questions in a number of others, consideration may have to be given to revising the provisions of 31 U.S.C. [§ 1301(c)] to make its scope and meaning crystal clear and perhaps update it as may otherwise appear desirable."

Section 1301(c) was not amended, but soon after the above discussion appeared, appropriation acts started including the general provision stating that "[n]o part of any appropriation contained in this Act shall remain available for obligation beyond the current fiscal year unless expressly so provided herein." This added another ingredient to the recipe that had not been present in the earlier decisions, although it took several years before the new general provision began appearing in almost all appropriation acts.

When the issue arose again in a 1971 case, GAO considered the new appropriation act provision and the 1963 comments of the House Appropriations Committee. In that decision, GAO noted that "it seems evident that the purpose [of the new general provision] is to overcome the effect of our decisions . . . regarding the requirements of 31 U.S.C. [§ 1301(c)]," and further noted the apparent link between the discussion in House Report 1040 and the appearance of the new provision. 50 Comp. Gen. at 859. See also 58 Comp. Gen. 321 (1979); B-207792, Aug. 24, 1982. Thus, the appropriation act will have to expressly repeat the multiple year or no-year language of the authorization, or at least expressly refer to the specific section of the authorizing statute in which it appears.

Changes in the law from year to year may produce additional complications. For example, an authorization act provided that funds appropriated and apportioned to states would remain available for obligation for three fiscal years, after which time any unobligated balances would be reapportioned. This amounted to a no-year authorization. For several years, appropriations to fund the program were made on a no-year basis, thus permitting implementation of the authorization provision. Starting with fiscal year 1978, however, the appropriation act was changed and the funds were made available for two fiscal years. This raised the question of whether the appropriation act had the effect of overriding the apparently conflicting authorizing language, or if it meant merely that reapportionment could occur after two fiscal years instead of three, thus effectively remaining a no-year appropriation.

GAO concluded that the literal language and plain meaning of the appropriation act must govern. In addition to the explicit appropriation language, the appropriation acts contained the general provision restricting availability to the current fiscal year unless expressly provided otherwise therein. Therefore, any funds not obligated by the end of the 2-year period would expire and could not be reapportioned. B-151087, Feb. 17, 1982; B-151087, Sept. 15, 1981.

e. Authorization Enacted After Appropriation

Our discussion thus far has, for the most part, been in the context of the typical sequence—that is, the authorization act is passed before the appropriation act. Sometimes, however, consideration of the authorization act is delayed and is enacted after the appropriation act. Determining the relationship between the two acts involves application of the same general principles we have been applying when the acts are enacted in the normal sequence.

The first step in the analysis is to attempt to construe the statutes together in some reasonable fashion. To the extent this can be done, there is no real conflict, and the reversed sequence of enactment will, in many cases, make no difference. Earlier, for example, we discussed the rule that a specific earmark in an authorization act must be followed when the related appropriation is an unspecified lump sum. In two of the cases cited for that proposition—B-220682, Feb. 21, 1986 and B-193282, Dec. 21, 1978—the appropriation act had been enacted prior to the authorization, a factor that did not affect the outcome.

For example, the 1979 Justice Department authorization act authorized a lump-sum appropriation to the Immigration and Naturalization Service (INS) and provided that $2 million "shall be available" for the investigation and prosecution of certain cases involving alleged Nazi war criminals. The 1979 appropriation act made a lump-sum appropriation to the INS but contained no specific mention of the Nazi war criminal item. The appropriation act was enacted on October 10, 1978, but the authorization act was not enacted until November. In response to a question as to the effect of the authorization provision on the appropriation, the Comptroller General advised that the two statutes could be construed harmoniously, and that the $2 million earmarked in the authorization act could be spent only for the purpose specified. It was further noted that the $2 million represented a minimum, but not a maximum. B-193282, Dec. 21, 1978, amplified by B-193282, Jan. 25, 1979. This is the same result that would have been reached if the normal sequence of enactment had been followed.

Similarly, a provision in the 1987 Defense Appropriation Act prohibited the Navy from including certain provisions in ship maintenance contracts. The 1987 authorization act, enacted after the appropriation, amended a provision in title 10 of the United States Code to require the prohibited provisions. Application of the last in time rule would have negated the appropriation act provision. However, it was possible to give effect to both provisions by construing the appropriation restriction as a temporary exemption from the permanent legislation in the authorization act. B-226389, Nov. 14, 1988. Again, this is the same result that would have been reached if the authorization act were enacted first.

If the authorization and appropriation cannot be reasonably reconciled, the last-in-time rule will apply as it would under the typical sequence, except here, the result will differ because the authorization is the later enacted of the two. For example, the 1989 Treasury Department appropriation act contained a provision prohibiting placing certain components of the Department under the oversight of the Treasury Inspector General. A month later, Congress enacted legislation placing those components under the Inspector General's jurisdiction and transferring their internal audit staffs to the Inspector General "notwithstanding any other provision of law." But for the "notwithstanding" clause, it might have been possible to use the same approach as in B-226389 and find the appropriation restriction a temporary exemption from the new permanent legislation. In view of the "notwithstanding" clause, however, GAO found that the two provisions could not be reconciled, and concluded that the Inspector General legislation, as the later enactment, superseded the appropriation act provision. B-203900, Feb. 2, 1989.

Two other examples invoking the last in time rule can be found in dueling Defense Department authorization and appropriation act provisions. In one case, the Defense appropriations act for 1992 directed the Defense Department to extend a contract relating to the Civilian Heath and Medical Program for Uniformed Services (CHAMPUS) program for another year. However, the defense authorization act for 1992 countermanded that mandate and permitted the Defense Department to award a new contract. The Comptroller General had little difficulty concluding that the two provisions were irreconcilably in conflict. B-247119, Mar. 2, 1992. Indeed, the legislative history demonstrated that the drafters of the appropriation and authorization acts sought to trump each other on this point as their two bills proceeded through Congress. The more difficult issue was how to apply the last in time rule to the case. The complication was that, while Congress had completed action on the authorization bill first (one day before the appropriation bill), the President acted in the opposite order—signing the appropriation bill into law nine days before he signed the authorization bill. Noting that the date on which the President signs a bill is clearly the date it becomes law, the Comptroller General held that the authorization act was the later in time, and thus, its provisions controlled.

Just as with any other application of the last in time rule, the later enactment prevails only to the extent of the irreconcilable conflict. B-61178, Oct. 21, 1946 (specific limitations in appropriation act not superseded by after-enacted authorization absent indication that authorization was intended to alter provisions of prior appropriation).

f. Two Statutes Enacted on Same Day

The Supreme Court has said that the doctrine against repeal by implication is even more forceful "where the one act follows close upon the other, at the same session of the Legislature." Morf v. Bingaman, 298 U.S. 407, 414 (1936); see also Auburn Housing Authority v. Martinez, 277 F.3d 138, 145 (2nd Cir. 2002); B-277905, Mar. 17, 1998. Accordingly, the doctrine against repeal by implication reaches perhaps its strongest point (and the "last in time" rule is correspondingly at its weakest) when both statutes are enacted on the same day. Except in the very rare case in which the intent of one statute to affect the other is particularly manifest, it makes little sense to apply a last in time concept where the time involved is a matter of hours, or as in one case (B-79243, Sept. 28, 1948), 7 minutes. Thus, the starting point is the presumption—applicable in all cases but even stronger in this situation—that Congress intended both statutes to stand together. 67 Comp. Gen. 332, 335 (1988); B-204078.2, May 6, 1988.

When there is an apparent conflict between an appropriation act and another statute enacted on the same day, the approach is to make every effort to reconcile the statutes so as to give maximum effect to both. In some cases, it will be found that there is no real conflict. For example, one statute authorized certain Commodity Credit Corporation appropriations to be made in the form of current, indefinite appropriations, while the appropriation act, enacted on the same day, made line-item appropriations. There was no conflict because the authorization provision was a directive to Congress itself that Congress was free to disregard, subject to a possible point of order, when making the actual appropriation. 67 Comp. Gen. 332 (1988). Similarly, there was no inconsistency between an appropriation act provision, which required that Panama Canal Commission appropriations be spent only in conformance with the Panama Canal Treaty of 1977 and its implementing legislation, and an authorization act provision, enacted on the same day, requiring prior specific authorizations. B-204078.2, May 6, 1988.

In other cases, applying traditional rules of statutory construction will produce reconciliation. For example, if one statute can be said to be more specific than the other, they can be reconciled by applying the more specific provision first, with the broader statute then applying to any residual issues. See B-231662, Sept. 1, 1988; B-79243, Sept. 28, 1948.

Legislative history may also help. For example, authorizing legislation extended the life of the Solar Energy and Energy Conservation Bank to March 15, 1988. The 1988 appropriation, enacted on the same day, made a two-year appropriation for the Bank. Not only were there no indications of any intent for the appropriation to have the effect of extending the Bank's life, there were specific indications to the contrary. Thus, GAO regarded the appropriation as available, in theory for the full two-year period, except that the authority for anyone to obligate the appropriation would cease when the Bank went out of existence. B-207186, Feb. 10, 1989.

The most extreme situation, and one in which the last in time rule by definition cannot possibly apply, is two conflicting provisions in the same statute. Even here, the approaches outlined above will usually prove successful. See, e.g., B-211306, June 6, 1983. We have found only one case in which two provisions in the same act were found irreconcilable. One provision in an appropriation act appropriated funds to the Army for the purchase of land; another provision a few pages later in the same act expressly prohibited the use of Army appropriations for the purchase of land. The Comptroller of the Treasury concluded, in a very brief decision, that the prohibition nullified the appropriation. 26 Comp. Dec. 534 (1920). The advantage of this result, although not stated this way in the decision, is that Congress would ultimately have to resolve the conflict and it is easier to make expenditures that have been deferred than to recoup money after it has been spent.

In one case, the fact that two allegedly conflicting provisions were contained in the same statute influenced the court to reconcile them. Auburn Housing Authority v. Martinez, 277 F.3d 138 (2nd Cir. 2002). The funding restriction provision used the word "hereafter," which, as the court acknowledged, ordinarily connotes permanence. However, the court nonetheless held that this provision applied only for the duration of the fiscal year and did not constitute an implied repeal of the other provision. The opinion observed in this regard:

"Given the unique circumstances of this case, the court is not convinced that the mere presence of the word 'hereafter' in section 226 clearly demonstrates Congress's intent to repeal section 519(n). This could be a different case if sections 226 and 519(n) appeared in separate statutes, but that is not the question we consider in the instant appeal."

Auburn Housing Authority, 277 F.3d at 146.

g. Ratification by Appropriation

"Ratification by appropriation" is the doctrine by which Congress can, by the appropriation of funds, confer legitimacy on an agency action that was questionable when it was taken. Clearly Congress may ratify that which it could have authorized. Swayne & Hoyt, Ltd. v. United States, 300 U.S. 297, 301–02 (1937). It is also settled that Congress may manifest its ratification by the appropriation of funds. Ex Parte Endo, 323 U.S. 283, 303 n.24 (1944); Brooks v. Dewar, 313 U.S. 354, 360–61 (1941).

We must also emphasize that "ratification by appropriation is not favored and will not be accepted where prior knowledge of the specific disputed action cannot be demonstrated clearly." District of Columbia Federation of Civic Ass'ns v. Airis, 391 F.2d 478, 482 (D.C. Cir. 1968); Associated Electric Cooperative, Inc. v. Morton, 507 F.2d 1167, 1174 (D.C. Cir. 1974), cert. denied, 423 U.S. 830 (1975).

Thus, a simple lump-sum appropriation, without more, will generally not afford sufficient basis to find a ratification by appropriation. Endo, 323 U.S. at 303 n.24; Airis, 391 F.2d at 481–82; Wade v. Lewis, 561 F. Supp. 913, 944 (N.D. Ill. 1983); B-213771, July 10, 1984. The appropriation "must plainly show a purpose to bestow the precise authority which is claimed." Endo, 323 U.S. at 303 n.24. Accord: Schism v. United States, 316 F.3d 1259, 1289–1290 (Fed. Cir. 2002), cert. denied, 539 U.S. 910 (2003), 123 S. Ct. 2246 (2003) ("ratification ordinarily cannot occur in the appropriations context unless the appropriations bill itself expressly allocates funds for a specific agency or activity"); A-1 Cigarette Vending, Inc. v. United States, 49 Fed. Cl. 345, 354 (2001), aff'd sub nom. 304 F.3d 1349 (Fed. Cir. 2002), cert. denied sub nom. 538 U.S. 921 (2003) ("[S]imply because the lack of an appropriation demonstrates a lack of authority does not mean that an appropriation by itself will create such authority. . . . [A] general appropriation of funds for an overall program is not sufficient to bestow authority upon a particular aspect of an agency's program.").

Some courts have used language which, when taken out of context, implies that appropriations cannot serve to ratify prior agency action. E.g., University of the District of Columbia Faculty Ass'n v. Board of Trustees of the University of the District of Columbia, 994 F. Supp. 1, 10 (D.D.C. 1998), aff'd, 163 F.3d 616 (D.C. Cir. 1998). Nevertheless, while the doctrine may not be favored, it does exist. The courts demonstrate their reluctance to apply this doctrine by giving extra scrutiny to alleged ratifications by appropriation. Their reluctance to find such ratifications probably stems from a more general judicial aversion to interpreting appropriation acts as changing substantive law. Thus, one court observed:

> "[I]t is well recognized that Congress does not normally perform legislative functions—such as ratification—through appropriations bills. . . . This does not mean that Congress cannot effect a ratification through an appropriations bill, but it does mean that Congress must be especially clear about its intention to do so."

Thomas v. Network Solutions, Inc., 2 F. Supp. 2d 22, 32 at n.12 (D.D.C. 1998), aff'd, 176 F.3d 500 (D.C. Cir. 1999), cert. denied, 528 U.S. 1115 (2000) (citations omitted).

We turn now to some specific situations in which the doctrine of ratification by appropriation has been accepted or rejected.

Presidential reorganizations have generated a large number of cases. Generally, when the President has created a new agency or has transferred a function from one agency to another, and Congress subsequently appropriates funds to the new agency or to the old agency for the new function, the courts have found that the appropriation ratified the presidential action. Fleming v. Mohawk Wrecking & Lumber Co., 331 U.S. 111, 116 (1947); Isbrandtsen-Moller Co. v. United States, 300 U.S. 139, 147 (1937).

The transfer to the Equal Employment Opportunity Commission (EEOC) in 1978 of enforcement responsibility for the Age Discrimination in Employment Act and the Equal Pay Act produced a minor flood of litigation. Although the courts were not uniform, a clear majority found that the subsequent appropriation of funds to the EEOC ratified the transfer. EEOC v. Dayton Power & Light Co., 605 F. Supp. 13 (S.D. Ohio 1984); EEOC v. Delaware Dept. of Health & Social Services, 595 F. Supp. 568 (D. Del. 1984); EEOC v. New York, 590 F. Supp. 37 (N.D. N.Y. 1984); EEOC v. Radio Montgomery, Inc., 588 F. Supp. 567 (W.D. Va. 1984); EEOC v. City of Memphis, 581 F. Supp. 179 (W.D. Tenn. 1983); Muller Optical Co. v. EEOC, 574 F. Supp. 946 (W.D. Tenn. 1983), aff'd on other grounds, 743 F.2d 380 (6th Cir. 1984). Contra EEOC v. Martin Industries, 581 F. Supp. 1029 (N.D. Ala.), appeal dismissed, 469 U.S. 806 (1984); EEOC v. Allstate Ins. Co., 570 F. Supp. 1224 (S.D. Miss. 1983), appeal dismissed, 467 U.S. 1232 (1984). Congress resolved any doubt by enacting legislation in 1984 to expressly ratify all prior reorganization plans implemented pursuant to any reorganization statute.

On the other hand, a class of cases where ratification by appropriation was not found concern proposed construction projects funded under lump-sum appropriations where the effect would be either to expand the scope of a prior congressional authorization or to supply an authorization required by statute but not obtained. Libby Rod & Gun Club v. Poteat, 594 F.2d 742 (9th Cir. 1979); National Wildlife Federation v. Andrus, 440 F. Supp. 1245 (D.D.C. 1977); Atchison, Topeka & Santa Fe Railway Co. v. Callaway, 382 F. Supp. 610 (D.D.C. 1974); B-223725, June 9, 1987.

A few additional cases in which ratification by appropriation was found are summarized below:

- The Tennessee Valley Authority (TVA) had asserted the authority to construct power plants. TVA's position was based on an interpretation of its enabling legislation that the court found consistent with the purpose of the legislation although the legislation itself was ambiguous. The appropriation of funds to TVA for power plant construction ratified TVA's position. Young v. Tennessee Valley Authority, 606 F.2d 143 (6th Cir. 1979), cert. denied, 445 U.S. 942 (1980).

- The authority of the Postmaster General to conduct a mail transportation experiment was ratified by the appropriation of funds to the former Post Office Department under circumstances showing that Congress was fully aware of the experiment. The court noted that existing statutory authority was broad enough to encompass the experiment and that nothing prohibited it. Atchison, Topeka & Santa Fe Railway Co. v. Summerfield, 229 F.2d 777 (D.C. Cir. 1955), cert. denied, 351 U.S. 926 (1956).

- The authority of the Department of Justice to retain private counsel to defend federal officials in limited circumstances, while not explicitly provided by statute, is regarded as ratified by the specific appropriation of funds for that purpose. 2 Op. Off. Legal Counsel 66 (1978).

- Another Office of Legal Counsel opinion described instances in which Congress has ratified by appropriation the use of United States combat forces. The opinion concludes on this point:

  "In sum, basic principles of constitutional law—and, in particular, the fact that Congress may express approval through the appropriations process—and historical practice in the war powers area, as well as the bulk of the case law and a substantial body of scholarly opinion, support the conclusion that Congress can authorize hostilities through its use of the appropriations power. Although it might be the case that general funding statutes do not necessarily constitute congressional approval for conducting hostilities, this objection loses its force when the appropriations measure is directly and conspicuously focused on specific military action."

Note that in all of the cases in which ratification by appropriation was approved, the agency had at least an arguable legal basis for its action. See Airis, 391 F.2d at 481 n.20; B-232482, June 4, 1990. The doctrine has not been used to excuse violations of law. Also, when an agency action is constitutionally suspect, the courts will require that congressional action be particularly explicit. Greene v. McElroy, 360 U.S. at 506–07; Martin Industries, 581 F. Supp. at 1033–37; Muller Optical Co., 574 F. Supp. at 954.

The Comptroller General condensed the foregoing principles into this test for ratification by appropriation:

> "To conclude that Congress through the appropriations process has ratified agency action, three factors generally must be present. First, the agency takes the action pursuant to at least arguable authority; second, the Congress has specific knowledge of the facts; and third, the appropriation of funds clearly bestows the claimed authority."

B-285725, Sept. 29, 2000. In this case GAO rejected the District of Columbia government's assertion that Congress had ratified certain funding practices that otherwise violated the Antideficiency Act, 31 U.S.C. § 1341. Specifically, GAO concluded that information contained in the District's budget justifications did not constitute notice to Congress because it (1) lacked clarity and precision, (2) did not create any awareness that could be imputed to Congress as a whole, and (3) was not reflected in any legislative language that could reasonably be viewed as authorizing the practices in question.

h. Repeal by Implication

We have on several occasions referred to the rule against repeal by implication. The leading case in the appropriations context is Tennessee Valley Authority v. Hill, 437 U.S. 153 (1978) (hereafter TVA v. Hill). In that case, Congress had authorized construction of the Tellico Dam and Reservoir Project on the Little Tennessee River, and had appropriated initial funds for that purpose. Subsequently, Congress passed the Endangered Species Act of 1973, 16 U.S.C. §§ 1531 et seq. Under the provisions of that Act, the Secretary of the Interior declared the "snail darter," a 3-inch fish, to be an endangered species. It was eventually determined that the Little Tennessee River was the snail darter's critical habitat and that completion of the dam would result in extinction of the species. Consequently, environmental groups and others brought an action to halt further construction of the Tellico Project. In its decision, the Supreme Court held in favor of the plaintiffs, notwithstanding the fact that construction was well under way and that, even after the Secretary of the Interior's actions regarding the snail darter, Congress had continued to make yearly appropriations for the completion of the dam project.

The appropriation involved was a lump-sum appropriation that included funds for the Tellico Dam but made no specific reference to it. However, passages in the reports of the appropriations committees indicated that those committees intended the funds to be available notwithstanding the Endangered Species Act. The Court held that this was not enough. The doctrine against repeal by implication, the Court said, applies with even greater force when the claimed repeal rests solely on an appropriation act:

> "When voting on appropriations measures, legislators are entitled to operate under the assumption that the funds will be devoted to purposes which are lawful and not for any purpose forbidden."

Id. at 190. Noting that "[e]xpressions of committees dealing with requests for appropriations cannot be equated with statutes enacted by Congress" (id. at 191), the Court held that the unspecified inclusion of the Tellico Dam funds in a lump-sum appropriation was not sufficient to constitute a repeal by implication of the Endangered Species Act insofar as it related to that project. In other words, the doctrine of ratification by appropriation we discussed in the preceding section does not apply, at least when the appropriation is an otherwise unspecified lump sum, where the effect would be to change an existing statutory requirement.

Some subsequent cases applying the concept of TVA v. Hill (although not all citing that case) include Miccosukee Tribe of Indians of Florida v. U.S. Army Corps of Engineers, 619 F.3d 1289 (11th Cir. 2010); Donovan v. Carolina Stalite Co., 734 F.2d 1547 (D.C. Cir. 1984); 64 Comp. Gen. 282 (1985); B-208593.6, Dec. 22, 1988; B-213771, July 10, 1984; B-204874, July 28, 1982; and B-193307, Feb. 6, 1979. For example, the otherwise unrestricted appropriation of coal trespass receipts to the Bureau of Land Management did not implicitly amend or repeal the provisions of the Federal Land Policy and Management Act prescribing the use of such funds. B-204874, July 28, 1982.

Thus, if Congress wants to use an appropriation act as the vehicle for suspending, modifying, or repealing a provision of existing law, it must do so advisedly, speaking directly and explicitly to the issue. The Last Best Beef, LLC v. Dudas, 506 F.3d 333 (4th Cir. 2007); Miccosukee Tribe of Indians of Florida v. U.S., 650 F. Supp. 2d 1235 (S.D. Fla., 2009).

The Supreme Court conveyed this message succinctly:

> "[A]lthough repeals by implication are especially disfavored in the appropriations context, Congress nonetheless may amend substantive law in an appropriations statute, as long as it does so clearly."

Robertson v. Seattle Audubon Society, 503 U.S. 429, 440 (1992) (citations omitted). In this case, the Court found an implied repeal by appropriation act to be clear and explicit.

Determining whether an appropriation implicitly repeals another statute requires an analysis of the particular statutory language involved. For example, in one case the court held that an annual appropriation restriction enacted for many years stating that "[n]one of the funds appropriated herein shall be available to investigate or act upon applications for relief from Federal firearms disabilities under 18 U.S.C. § 925(c)" clearly superseded the provision in title 18 of the United States Code. This case cited many other decisions that reached the same conclusion with respect to this particular appropriation language. Pontarelli v. United States Department of the Treasury, 285 F.3d 216 (3rd Cir. 2002). Another case finding a clear implied repeal by appropriation is Bald Eagle Ridge Protection Ass'n, Inc. v. Mallory, 119 F. Supp. 2d 473 (M.D. Pa. 2000), aff'd, 275 F.3d 33 (3rd Cir. 2001).

Examples of cases that reconciled the appropriation and other statutory provisions, and thus found no implied repeal include: Strawser v. Atkins, 290 F.3d 720 (4th Cir.), cert. denied, 537 U.S. 1045 (2002); Auburn Housing Authority v. Martinez, 277 F.3d 138 (2nd Cir. 2002); Firebaugh Canal Co. v. United States, 203 F.3d 568 (9th Cir. 2000); Ramey v. Stevedoring Services of America, 134 F.3d 954 (9th Cir. 1998); Environmental Defense Center v. Babbitt, 73 F.3d 867 (9th Cir. 1995).

Still other cases hold that appropriation restrictions alleged to be permanent in superseding other laws were effective only for a fiscal year. E.g., Auburn Housing Authority, 277 F.3d 138; Building & Construction Trades Department, AFL-CIO v. Martin, 961 F.2d 269, 273 (D.C. Cir.), cert. denied, 506 U.S. 915 (1992). In a related context, the court in Williams v. United States, 240 F.3d 1019 (Fed. Cir. 2001), cert. denied, 535 U.S. 911 (2002), disagreed with a series of Comptroller General decisions and held that appropriation language enacted in 1982 that required specific congressional authorization for pay raises for judges was not permanent legislation but expired at the end of fiscal year 1982.

In 2004, the Seventh Circuit interpreted appropriation restrictions to avoid repeal by implication. City of Chicago v. Department of the Treasury, 384 F.3d 429 (7th Cir. 2004). The City of Chicago had sued the former Bureau of Alcohol, Tobacco, and Firearms under the Freedom of Information Act (FOIA) to obtain access to certain information from the agency's firearms databases. The Court of Appeals for the Seventh Circuit held that the information was not exempt from disclosure under FOIA, and the agency appealed to the Supreme Court. While the appeal was pending, Congress enacted appropriations language for fiscal years 2003 and 2004 providing that no funds shall be available or used to take any action under FOIA or otherwise that would publicly disclose the information. On remand from the Supreme Court, the Seventh Circuit decided that the appropriations language had essentially no impact on the case. Citing a number of cases on the rule disfavoring implied repeals (particularly by appropriations act), the court held that the appropriations rider did not repeal FOIA or otherwise affect the agency's legal obligation to release the information in question. The court concluded that "FOIA deals only peripherally with the allocation of funds—its main focus is to ensure agency information is made available to the public." City of Chicago, 384 F.3d at 435. After the 2004 decision, the agency filed a request for rehearing. Before the rehearing, Congress passed the Consolidated Appropriations Act of 2005 specifying that no funds be used to provide the data sought by the City, and further provided that the data be "immune from judicial process." The court determined that this statutory language showed that Congress's "obvious intention . . . was to cut off all access to the databases for any reason." City of Chicago v. Department of the Treasury, 423 F.3d 777, 780 (7th Cir. 2005).

i. Lack of Authorization

As we have previously noted, there is no general statutory requirement that appropriations be preceded by specific authorizations, although they may be required in some instances. Where authorizations are not required by law, Congress may, subject to a possible point of order, appropriate funds for a program or object that has not been previously authorized or which exceeds the scope of a prior authorization. If so, the enacted appropriation, in effect, carries its own authorization and is available to the agency for obligation and expenditure. E.g., 67 Comp. Gen. 401 (1988); B-219727, July 30, 1985; B-173832, Aug. 1, 1975.

It has also been held that, as a general proposition, the appropriation of funds for a program whose funding authorization has expired, or is due to expire during the period of availability of the appropriation, provides sufficient legal basis to continue the program during that period of availability, absent indication of contrary congressional intent. 65 Comp. Gen. 524 (1986); 65 Comp. Gen. 318, 320–21 (1986); 55 Comp. Gen. 289 (1975); B-131935, Mar. 17, 1986; B-137063, Mar. 21, 1966. For example, the Social Security Administration (SSA) should continue mandatory and discretionary grant programs, even when faced with expired authorizations of appropriations, where the relevant enabling legislation had not expired and the agency had an appropriation available to cover the costs of the programs. B-323433, Aug. 14, 2012. Following the enactment of legislation establishing the Work Incentives Planning and Assistance Program and the Protection and Advocacy for Beneficiaries of Social Security Program, Congress passed authorizations of appropriations to carry out the functions. SSA asserted that it could not continue the programs upon the expiration of the authorization of appropriations. Reminding SSA that there is no general requirement that an authorization of appropriations precede an appropriation, GAO held that enabling legislation provided the requisite authority to obligate agency appropriations in those situations where authorizations expire. The result in these cases follows in part from the fact that the total absence of appropriations authorization legislation would not have precluded the making of valid appropriations for the programs. E.g., B-202992, May 15, 1981. In addition, as noted, the result is premised on the conclusion, derived either from legislative history or at least the absence of legislative history to the contrary, that Congress did not intend for the programs to terminate.

There are limits on how far this principle can be taken, depending on the particular circumstances. For example, a 1988 continuing resolution provided funds for the Solar Bank, to remain available until September 30, 1989. Legislation enacted on the same day provided for the Bank to terminate on March 15, 1988. Based in part on legislative history indicating the intent to terminate the Bank on the specified sunset date, GAO distinguished prior decisions in which appropriations were found to authorize program continuation and concluded that the appropriation did not authorize continuation of the Solar Bank beyond March 15, 1988. B-207186, Feb. 10, 1989.

In another example, section 8 of the Civil Rights Commission's authorizing act stated that "the provisions of this Act shall terminate on September 30, 1991." While Congress was actively working on reauthorization legislation for the Commission toward the end of fiscal year 1991, this legislation was not enacted until after September 30, 1991. Nevertheless, Congress had enacted a continuing resolution for the early part of fiscal year 1992 that specifically included funding for the Commission. The Comptroller General first observed that the line of cases discussed above permitting programs to continue after expiration of their authorization did not apply. Unlike the mere authorization lapse in those cases, the statute here provided that the Commission would "terminate" on September 30 of that fiscal year. The Comptroller General also distinguished the Solar Bank case, discussed above, since the provision for termination of the Commission was enacted long before the continuing resolution that provided for the Commission's funding after September 30. Ultimately, the funding provision for the Commission was irreconcilable with the section 8 termination provision and effectively suspended the operation of section 8. 71 Comp. Gen. 378 (1992). The decision noted the clear intent of Congress that the Commission continue to operate without interruption after September 30, 1991.

A device Congress has used on occasion to avoid this type of problem is an "automatic extension" provision under which funding authorization is automatically extended for a specified time period if Congress has not enacted new authorizing legislation before it expires. An example is discussed in B-214456, May 14, 1984.

Questions concerning the effect of appropriations on expired or about-to-expire authorizations have tended to arise more frequently in the context of continuing resolutions.

Where specific authorization is statutorily required, the case may become more difficult. In Libby Rod & Gun Club v. Poteat, 594 F.2d 742 (9th Cir. 1979), the court held that a lump-sum appropriation available for dam construction was not, by itself, sufficient to authorize a construction project for which specific authorization had not been obtained as required by 33 U.S.C. § 401. The court suggested that TVA v. Hill and similar cases do not "mandate the conclusion that courts can never construe appropriations as congressional authorization," although it was not necessary to further address that issue in view of the specific requirement in that case. Poteat, 594 F.2d at 745–46. The result would presumably have been different if Congress had made a specific appropriation "notwithstanding the provisions of 33 U.S.C. § 401." It should be apparent that the doctrines of repeal by implication and ratification by appropriation are relevant in analyzing issues of this type.

D. Constitutional Limitations upon the Power of the Purse

The Supreme Court recognized the breadth of the power of the purse, but also its limitations, in South Dakota v. Dole, 483 U.S. 203 (1987) (noting that"[Congress's] spending power is of course not unlimited."). In Dole, the Supreme Court listed what it referred to as four "general restrictions" on the spending power: (1) the exercise of the spending power must be in pursuit of the general welfare; (2) conditions imposed on the use of federal funds must be reasonably related to the articulated goals; (3) the intent of Congress to impose conditions must be authoritative and unambiguous; and (4) the action in question must not be prohibited by an independent constitutional bar. Id. at 207–08. See also, e.g., Nevada v. Skinner, 884 F.2d 445, 447–48 (9th Cir. 1989).

With respect to the fourth restriction, the courts have struck down several funding conditions as unconstitutional. For example:

- An appropriation act provision that prohibited the payment of salary to certain named individuals was an unconstitutional bill of attainder. United States v. Lovett, 328 U.S. 303 (1946).

- A court invalidated a provision in the 1989 District of Columbia appropriation act prohibiting the use of funds unless the District adopted legislation spelled out in the rider. The provision was struck down on First Amendment grounds. Clarke v. United States, 705 F. Supp. 605 (D.D.C. 1988), aff'd, 886 F.2d 404 (D.C. Cir. 1989), vacated en banc as moot, 915 F.2d 699 (D.C. Cir. 1990).

- The Supreme Court struck down a provision that prohibited grantees from representing clients in efforts to amend or otherwise challenge existing welfare law. Legal Services Corp. v. Velazquez, 531 U.S. 533 (2001). The provision interfered with the First Amendment rights of clients represented by LSC-funded attorneys.

- A court declared unconstitutional an appropriation provision forbidding the use of federal mass transit grant funds for any activity that promoted the legalization or medical use of marijuana, for example, posting an advertisement on a bus. American Civil Liberties Union (ACLU) v. Mineta, 319 F. Supp. 2d 69 (D.D.C. 2004). Relying on Legal Services Corp., the court held that the provision constituted "viewpoint discrimination" in violation of the First Amendment. ACLU, 319 F. Supp. 2d The Supreme Court overturned a funding condition in the United States Leadership Against HIV/AIDS, Tuberculosis, and Malaria Act of 2003. AID v. Alliance for Open Society International, Inc., ___ U.S. ___, 133 S. Ct. 2321 (2013). The condition required, among other things, that funding recipients agree that they oppose prostitution and sex trafficking in their award documents. This requirement violated the First Amendment. The Court said that the requirement "goes beyond preventing recipients from using funds in a way that would undermine the federal program. It requires them to pledge allegiance to the Government's policy of eradicating prostitution." 133 S. Ct. at 2332. at 83–87.

The Dole Court added that funding conditions would also exceed the Spending Clause if "the financial inducement offered by Congress might be so coercive as to pass the point at which 'pressure turns into compulsion.'" 483 U.S. at 211. Courts have been reluctant to find funding conditions as unduly coercive, though, with an important recent exception by the Supreme Court, discussed below.

Examples of courts' reluctance include:

- In Dole itself, the Supreme Court found that a law conditioning states' receipt of federal highway funds on the adoption of a minimum drinking age of 21 was a valid use of Congress's spending power. 483 U.S. 203.

- The Supreme Court upheld the so-called Solomon Amendment, which denied federal grants to institutions of higher education that prohibit or prevent military recruitment on campus. Rumsfeld v. Forum for Academic and Institutional Rights, Inc., 547 U.S. 47, (2006). An association of law schools and faculty members challenged the constitutionality of the Solomon Amendment, arguing that it violated their First Amendment rights to oppose federal policies that prohibited homosexuals from serving openly in the military. The Supreme Court rejected these arguments, nothing that under the Spending Clause, "Congress is free to attach reasonable and unambiguous conditions to federal financial assistance that educational institutions are not obliged to accept." 547 U.S. at 59.

- A court upheld a statutory provision known as the "Civil Rights Remedies Equalization Act," 42 U.S.C. § 2000d 7, which clearly conditioned a state's acceptance of federal funds on its waiver of its Eleventh Amendment immunity to suits under various federal antidiscrimination laws. Barbour v. Washington Metropolitan Transit Authority, 374 F.3d 1161 (D.C. Cir. 2004), cert. denied, 544 U.S. 904 (2005).

- The Supreme Court upheld a condition in the Children's Internet Protection Act (CIPA) as a legitimate exercise of congressional spending power. United States v. American Library Ass'n, Inc., 539 U.S. 194 (2003). CIPA barred public libraries from receiving federal assistance to provide computer access to the Internet unless they installed software to block obscenity and child pornography and prevent minors from obtaining access to material harmful to them. Pub. L. No. 106-554, § 1711. The Court rejected the claim that CIPA constituted an impermissible coercion, explaining that CIPA did not penalize libraries that chose not to install the software. Rather, it simply precluded the use of taxpayer funds to subsidize those libraries that chose not to install such software. Id. at 2307–08.

- Several courts have rejected challenges to section 3 of the Religious Land Use and Institutionalized Persons Act of 2000 (RLUIPA), 42 U.S.C. § 2000cc-1, which limits restrictions on the exercise of religion by persons institutionalized in a program or activity that receives federal financial assistance. Cutter v. Wilkinson, 544 U.S. 709 (2005); Charles v. Verhagen, 348 F.3d 601 (7th Cir. 2003); Williams v. Bitner, 285 F.

Supp. 2d 593 (M.D. Pa. 2003), aff'd in part, remanded in part 455 F.3d 186 (3rd Cir. 2006).

The Supreme Court recently found that one federal funding condition went too far. The Court considered the constitutionality of a number of provisions in the Patient Protection and Affordable Care Act (PPACA). National Federation of Independent Business v. Sebelius, 567 U.S. ___, 132 S. Ct. 2566 (2012). One PPACA provision withheld all Medicaid funding from states that declined to participate in a Medicaid extension program. The Supreme Court held that this provision was not a valid exercise of Congress's spending power, as it coerced states to either accept the Medicaid expansion or risk losing all Medicaid funding. The Court explained that this would have an excessive impact on a state's budget. Accordingly, the Court severed this unconstitutional provision from the rest of the act.

E. General Provisions: When Construed as Permanent Legislation

Appropriation acts, in addition to making appropriations, frequently contain a variety of provisions either restricting the availability of the appropriations or making them available for some particular use. Such provisions come in two forms: (a) "provisos" attached directly to the appropriating language and (b) general provisions. A general provision may apply solely to the act in which it is contained ("No part of any appropriation contained in this Act shall be used . . ."), or it may have general applicability ("No part of any appropriation contained in this or any other Act shall be used . . ."). General provisions may be phrased in the form of restrictions or positive authority.

Provisions of this type are no less effective merely because they are contained in appropriation acts. Congress may repeal, amend, or suspend a statute by means of an appropriation bill, so long as its intention to do so is clear. Robertson v. Seattle Audubon Society, 503 U.S. 429, 440 (1992); McHugh v. Rubin, 220 F.3d 53, 57 (2d Cir. 2000); see also United States v. Dickerson, 310 U.S. 554 (1940); Cella v. United States, 208 F.2d 783, 790 (7th Cir. 1953), cert. denied, 347 U.S. 1016 (1954); NLRB v. Thompson Products, Inc., 141 F.2d 794, 797 (9th Cir. 1944); B-300009, July 1, 2003; 41 Op. Att'y Gen. 274, 276 (1956).

Congress likewise can enact general or permanent legislation in appropriation acts, but again its intent to do so must be clear:

> While appropriations are 'Acts of Congress' which can substantively change existing law, there is a very strong presumption that they do not . . . and that when they do, the change is only intended for one fiscal year."

Building & Construction Trades Department, AFL-CIO v. Martin, 961 F.2d 269, 273 (D.C. Cir.), cert. denied, 506 U.S. 915 (1992).

As another court put it:

> "Congress may create permanent, substantive law through an appropriations bill only if it is clear about its intentions. Put another way, Congress cannot rebut the presumption against permanence by sounding an uncertain trumpet."

Atlantic Fish Spotters Ass'n v. Evans, 321 F.3d 220, 224 (1st Cir. 2003).

Rules of both the Senate and the House of Representatives prohibit the inclusion of general legislation in appropriation acts. Senate Rule XVI; House Rule XXI. However, this merely subjects the provision to a point of order and does not affect the validity of the legislation if the point of order is not raised, or is raised and not sustained. Thus, once a given provision has been enacted into law, the question of whether it is "general legislation" or merely a restriction on the use of an appropriation, that is, whether it might have been subject to a point of order, is academic.

This section deals with the question of when provisos or general provisions appearing in appropriation acts can be construed as permanent legislation.

Since an appropriation act is made for a particular fiscal year, the starting presumption is that everything contained in the act is effective only for the fiscal year covered. Thus, the rule is: A provision contained in an annual appropriation act is not to be construed to be permanent legislation unless the language used therein or the nature of the provision makes it clear that Congress intended it to be permanent. The presumption can be overcome if the provision uses language indicating futurity or if the provision is of a general character bearing no relation to the object of the appropriation. B-319414, June 9, 2010; 65 Comp. Gen. 588 (1986); 62 Comp. Gen. 54 (1982); 36 Comp. Gen. 434 (1956); 32 Comp. Gen. 11 (1952); 24 Comp. Gen. 436 (1944); 10 Comp. Gen. 120 (1930); 5 Comp. Gen. 810 (1926); 7 Comp. Dec. 838 (1901).

1. Words of Futurity

In analyzing a particular provision, the starting point in ascertaining Congress's intent is, as it must be, the language of the statute. The question to ask is whether the provision uses "words of futurity." The most common word of futurity is "hereafter" and provisions using this term have often been construed as permanent. For specific examples, see Cella v. United States, 208 F.2d at 790; 70 Comp. Gen. 351 (1991); 26 Comp. Gen. 354, 357 (1946); 2 Comp. Gen. 535 (1923); 11 Comp. Dec. 800 (1905); B-108245, Mar. 19, 1952; B-100983, Feb. 8, 1951; B-76782, June 10, 1948. However, use of the word "hereafter" may not guarantee that an appropriation act provision will be found to constitute permanent law. Thus, in Auburn Housing Authority v. Martinez, 277 F.3d 138 (2nd Cir. 2002), the court declined to give permanent effect to a provision that included the word "hereafter". The court acknowledged that "hereafter" generally denoted futurity, but held that this was not sufficient to establish permanence in the circumstances of that case. To read "hereafter" as giving permanence to one provision would have resulted in repealing another provision enacted in the same act. The court concluded that this result was not what Congress had intended.

As Auburn Housing Authority indicates, mere use of the word "hereafter" may not be adequate as an indication of future effect to establish permanence. Other facts such as the precise location of the word "hereafter" and the sense in which it is used are also important. Moreover, the use of the word "hereafter" may not be sufficient, for example, if it appears only in an exception clause and not in the operative portion of the provision, B-228838, Sept. 16, 1987, or if it is used in a way that does not necessarily connote futurity beyond the end of the fiscal year. Williams v. United States, 240 F.3d 1019, 1063 (Fed. Cir. 2001).

Words of futurity other than "hereafter" have also been deemed sufficient. Thus, there is no significant difference in meaning between "hereafter" and "after the date of approval of this act." 65 Comp. Gen. at 589; 36 Comp. Gen. at 436; B-209583, Jan. 18, 1983. Similarly, an appropriations provision requiring an agency action "not later than one year" after enactment of the appropriations act, which would occur after the end of the fiscal year, is permanent because that prospective language indicates an intention that the provision survive past the end of the fiscal year. B-319414, June 9, 2010. Using a specific date rather than a general reference to the date of enactment produces the same result. B-287488, June 19, 2001; B-57539, May 3, 1946. "Henceforth" may also do the job. B-209583. So may specific references to future fiscal years. B-208354, Aug. 10, 1982. On the other hand, the word "hereinafter" was not considered synonymous with hereafter by the First Circuit Court of Appeals and was not deemed to establish a permanent provision. Atlantic Fish Spotters Ass'n, 321 F.3d 220. Rather, the court held that hereinafter is universally understood to refer only to what follows in the same writing (i.e., statute). Id. at 225–26.

One decision concluded that the words "at any time" were words of futurity in a provision which authorized reduced transportation rates to military personnel who were "given furloughs at any time." 24 Comp. Gen. 436, Dec. 7, 1944. In that decision, however, the conclusion of permanence was further supported by the fact that Congress appropriated funds to carry out the provision in the following year as well and did not repeat the provision but merely referred to it.

The words "or any other act" in a provision addressing funds appropriated in or made available by "this or any other act" are not words of futurity. They merely refer to any other appropriation act for the same fiscal year. Williams v. United States, 240 F.3d at 1063; 65 Comp. Gen. 588; B-230110, Apr. 11, 1988; B-228838, Sept. 16, 1987; B-145492, Sept. 21, 1976. See also A-88073, Aug. 19, 1937 ("this or any other appropriation"). Similarly, the words "notwithstanding any other provision of law" are not words of futurity and, standing alone, offer no indication as to the duration of the provision. B-271412, June 13, 1996; B-208705, Sept. 14, 1982.

The words "this or any other act" may be used in conjunction with other language that makes the result, one way or the other, indisputable. The provision is clearly not permanent if the phrase "during the current fiscal year" is added. Norcross v. United States, 142 Ct. Cl. 763 (1958). Addition of the phrase "with respect to any fiscal year" would indicate, all other potential considerations aside, that Congress intended the provision to be permanent. B-230110, Apr. 11, 1988. For example, in the 2006 Department of Justice Appropriations Act, as part of the language of ATF's Salaries and Expenses appropriation, Congress included a proviso stating that "no funds appropriated under this or any other Act with respect to any fiscal year may be used to disclose part or all of the contents of the Firearms Trace System database" to anyone other than a law enforcement agency or a prosecutor in connection with a criminal investigation or prosecution. GAO determined that the proviso constituted permanent legislation because the forward-looking effect of the phrase "this or any other Act" coupled with the phrase "with respect to any fiscal year" indicates Congress's intention that the provision be permanent. B-309704, Aug. 28, 2007; see also B-316510, July 15, 2008 (a similar proviso in ATF's 2008 appropriation, using the phrase "beginning in fiscal year 2008 and thereafter," is also permanent law).

If words of futurity indicate permanence, it follows that a proviso or general provision that does not contain words of futurity will generally not be construed as permanent. 65 Comp. Gen. 588; 32 Comp. Gen. 11; 20 Comp. Gen. 322 (1940); 10 Comp. Gen. 120; 5 Comp. Gen. 810; 3 Comp. Gen. 319 (1923); B-209583, Jan. 18, 1983; B-208705, Sept. 14, 1982; B-66513, May 26, 1947; A-18614, May 25, 1927. The courts have applied the same analysis. See United States v. Vulte, 233 U.S. 509, 514 (1914); Minis v. United States, 40 U.S. (15 Pet.) 423 (1841); Bristol-Myers Squibb Company v. Royce Laboratories, Inc., 69 F.3d 1130, 1136 (Fed. Cir. 1995); United States v. International Business Machines Corp., 892 F.2d 1006, 1009 (Fed. Cir. 1989); National Labor Relations Board v. Thompson Products, Inc., 141 F.2d 794 (9th Cir. 1944); City of Hialeah v. United States Housing Authority, 340 F. Supp. 885 (S.D. Fla. 1971).

In particular, the absence of the word "hereafter" is viewed as telling evidence that Congress did not intend a provision to be permanent. E.g., Building & Construction Trades Department, 961 F.2d at 273; International Business Machines Corp., 892 F.2d at 1009; Department of Justice, Office of Legal Counsel, Memorandum for James S. Gilliland, General Counsel, Department of Agriculture, Severability and Duration of Appropriations Rider Concerning Frozen Poultry Regulations, June 4, 1996. For example, the court in Building & Construction Trades Department concluded that the absence of the word hereafter in an appropriation provision was more significant than the inclusion of other language that might have indicated permanence.

2. Other Indicia of Permanence

As the preceding paragraphs indicate, the language of the statute is the crucial determinant of whether a provision is permanent. However, other factors may also be taken into consideration. Thus, the repeated inclusion of a provision in annual appropriation acts indicates that it is not considered or intended by Congress to be permanent. 32 Comp. Gen. 11; 10 Comp. Gen. 120; B-270723, Apr. 15, 1996; A-89279, Oct. 26, 1937; 41 Op. Att'y Gen. at 279–80. However, where adequate words of futurity exist, the repetition of a provision in the following year's appropriation act has been viewed simply as an "excess of caution." 36 Comp. Gen. at 436. This factor is of limited usefulness, since the failure to repeat in subsequent appropriation acts a provision that does not contain words of futurity can also be viewed as an indication that Congress did not consider it to be permanent and simply did not want it to continue. See 18 Comp. Gen. 37 (1938); A-88073, Aug. 19, 1937. Thus, if the provision does not contain words of futurity, then repetition or non-repetition lead to the same result—that the provision is not permanent. If the provision does contain words of futurity, then non-repetition indicates permanence but repetition, although it suggests non-permanence, is inconclusive.

The inclusion of a provision in the United States Code is relevant as an indication of permanence but is not controlling. B-319414, June 9, 2010; 36 Comp. Gen. 434; 24 Comp. Gen. 436. Failure to include a provision in the Code would appear to be of no significance. A reference by the codifiers to the failure to reenact a provision suggests non-permanence. 41 Op. Att'y Gen. at 280–81.

Legislative history is also relevant, but has been used for the most part to support a conclusion based on the presence or absence of words of futurity. See Cella v. United States, 208 F.2d at 790 n.1; NLRB v. Thompson Products, 141 F.2d at 798; 65 Comp. Gen. 588; B-277719, Aug. 20, 1997; B-209583, Jan. 18, 1983; B-208705, Sept. 14, 1982; B- 108245, Mar. 19, 1952; B-57539, May 3, 1946. In one case, a general provision requiring the submission of a report "annually to the Congress" was held not permanent in view of conflicting expressions of congressional intent. B-192973, Oct. 11, 1978. Legislative history by itself has not been used to find futurity where it is missing in the statutory language. See Building & Construction Trades Department, 961 F.2d at 274.

The degree of relationship between a given provision and the object of the appropriation act in which it appears or the appropriating language to which it is appended is a factor to be considered. If the provision bears no direct relationship to the appropriation act in which it appears, this is an indication of permanence. For example, a provision prohibiting the retroactive application of an energy tax credit provision in the Internal Revenue Code was found sufficiently unrelated to the rest of the act in which it appeared, a supplemental appropriations act, to support a conclusion of permanence. B-214058, Feb. 1, 1984. See also B-319414, June 9, 2010; 62 Comp. Gen. at 56; 32 Comp. Gen. 11; 26 Comp. Gen. at 357; B-37032, Oct. 5, 1943; A-88073, Aug. 19, 1937. The closer the relationship, the less likely it is that the provision will be viewed as permanent. A determination under rules of the Senate that a proviso is germane to the subject matter of the appropriation bill will negate an argument that the proviso is sufficiently unrelated as to suggest permanence. B-208705, Sept. 14, 1982.

The phrasing of a provision as positive authorization rather than a restriction on the use of an appropriation is an indication of permanence, but usually has been considered in conjunction with a finding of adequate words of futurity. B-319414, June 9, 2010; 36 Comp. Gen. 434; 24 Comp. Gen. 436.

Finally, a provision may be construed as permanent if construing it as temporary would render the provision meaningless or produce an absurd result. 65 Comp. Gen. 352 (1986); 62 Comp. Gen. 54; B-200923, Oct. 1, 1982. These decisions dealt with a general provision designed to prohibit cost-of-living pay increases for federal judges "except as may be specifically authorized by Act of Congress hereafter enacted." Pub. L. No. 97-92, § 140, 95 Stat. 1183, 1200 (Dec. 15, 1981). The provision appeared in a fiscal year 1982 continuing resolution, which expired on September 30, 1982. The next applicable pay increase would have been effective October 1, 1982. Thus, if the provision were not construed as permanent, it would have been meaningless "since it would have been enacted to prevent increases during a period when no increases were authorized to be made." 62 Comp. Gen. at 56–57. Similarly, GAO concluded that a provision with no words of futurity was permanent, because it was to become effective on the last day of the fiscal year. 9 Comp. Gen. 248 (1929). An alternative construction would have rendered the provision effective for only 1 day, which was clearly inconsistent with legislative intent. See also B-319414, June 9, 2010; B-270723, Apr. 15, 1996; 65 Comp. Gen. at 590; B-214058, Feb. 1, 1984.

In sum, the six additional factors mentioned above are all relevant indicia of whether a given provision should be construed as permanent.

However, the presence or absence of words of futurity remains the crucial factor, and the additional factors have been used for the most part to support a conclusion based primarily on this presence or absence. Four of the factors—occurrence or nonoccurrence in subsequent appropriation acts, inclusion in United States Code, legislative history, and phrasing as positive authorization—have never been used as the sole basis for finding permanence in a provision without words of futurity. The two remaining factors—relationship to rest of statute and meaningless or absurd result—can be used to find permanence in the absence of words of futurity, but the conclusion is almost invariably supported by at least one of the other factors, such as legislative history.

Chapter 4: Availability of Appropriations: Purpose

A. General Principles

1. Introduction: 31 U.S.C. § 1301(a)

This chapter introduces the concept of the "availability" of appropriations. The decisions are often stated in terms of whether appropriated funds are or are not "legally available" for a given obligation or expenditure. This is simply another way of saying that a given item is or is not a legal expenditure. Whether appropriated funds are legally available for something depends on three things:

Major restrictions

1. the purpose of the obligation or expenditure must be authorized;

2. the obligation must occur within the time limits applicable to the appropriation; and

3. the obligation and expenditure must be within the amounts Congress has established.

Thus, there are three elements to the concept of availability: purpose, time, and amount. All three must be observed for the obligation or expenditure to be legal. This chapter discusses availability as to purpose.

One of the fundamental statutes dealing with the use of appropriated funds is 31 U.S.C. § 1301(a):

> "Appropriations shall be applied only to the objects for which the appropriations were made except as otherwise provided by law."

Simple, concise, and direct, this statute was originally enacted in 1809 (ch. 28, § 1, 2 Stat. 535, (Mar. 3, 1809)) and is one of the cornerstones of congressional control over the federal purse. Because money cannot be paid from the Treasury except under an appropriation (U.S. Const. art. I, § 9, cl. 7), and because an appropriation must be derived from an act of Congress, it is for Congress to determine the purposes for which an appropriation may be used. Simply stated, 31 U.S.C. § 1301(a) says that public funds may be used only for the purpose or purposes for which they were appropriated. It prohibits charging authorized items to the wrong appropriation, and unauthorized items to any appropriation. See, e.g., B-302973, Oct. 6, 2004 (agency could not charge authorized activities such as cost comparison studies to an appropriation that specifically prohibits its use for such studies). Anything less would render congressional control largely meaningless. An earlier Treasury Comptroller was of the opinion that the statute did not make any new law, but merely codified what was already required under the Appropriations Clause of the Constitution. 4 Lawrence, First Comp. Dec. 137, 142 (1883).

Administrative applications of the purpose statute can be traced back almost to the time the statute was enacted. See, for example, 36 Comp. Gen. 621, 622 (1957), which quotes part of a decision dated February 21, 1821. In an 1898 decision captioned "Misapplication of Appropriations," the Comptroller of the Treasury talked about 31 U.S.C. § 1301(a) in these terms:

> "It is difficult to see how a legislative prohibition could be expressed in stronger terms. The law is plain, and any disbursing officer disregards it at his peril."

4 Comp. Dec. 569, 570 (1898).

The starting point in applying 31 U.S.C. § 1301(a) is that, absent a clear indication to the contrary, the common meaning of the words in the appropriation act and the program legislation it funds governs the purposes to which the appropriation may be applied. To illustrate, the Comptroller General held in 41 Comp. Gen. 255 (1961) that an appropriation available for the "replacement" of state roads damaged by nearby federal dam construction could be used only to restore those roads to their former condition, not for improvements such as widening. Similarly, funds provided for the modification of existing dams for safety purposes could not be used to construct a new dam, even as part of an overall safety strategy. B-215782, Apr. 7, 1986.

If a proposed use of funds is inconsistent with the statutory language, the expenditure is improper, even if it would result in substantial savings or other benefits to the government. Thus, while the Federal Aviation Administration (FAA) could construct its own roads needed for access to FAA facilities, it could not contribute a share for the improvement of county-owned roads, even though the latter undertaking would have been much less expensive. B-143536, Aug. 15, 1960. See also 39 Comp. Gen. 388 (1959).

The limitation in 31 U.S.C. § 1301(a) applies to revolving funds. GAO has held that revolving funds are appropriations, and, accordingly, that the legal principles governing appropriations also apply to revolving funds. See B-247348, June 22, 1992; B-240914, Aug. 14, 1991. See also 63 Comp. Gen. 110, 112 (1983), and decisions cited therein.

The concept of purpose permeates much of this publication. For example:

- A specific appropriation must be used to the exclusion of a more general appropriation that might otherwise have been viewed as available for the particular item.

- Transfer between appropriations is prohibited without specific statutory authority, even where reimbursement is contemplated.

It follows that deliberately charging the wrong appropriation for purposes of expediency or administrative convenience, with the expectation of rectifying the situation by a subsequent transfer from the right appropriation, violates 31 U.S.C. § 1301(a). 36 Comp. Gen. 386 (1956);

26 Comp. Gen. 902, 906 (1947); 19 Comp. Gen. 395 (1939); 14 Comp. Gen. 103 (1934); B-248284.2, Sept. 1, 1992; B-104135, Aug. 2, 1951; B-97772, May 18, 1951. The fact that the expenditure would be authorized under some other appropriation is irrelevant. Charging the "wrong" appropriation, unless authorized by some statute such as 31 U.S.C. § 1534, violates the purpose statute. For several examples, see U.S. General Accounting Office, Improper Accounting for Costs of Architect of the Capitol Projects, PLrd-81-4 (Washington, D.C.: Apr. 13, 1981).

The transfer rule illustrates the close relationship between 31 U.S.C. § 1301(a) and statutes relating to amount such as the Antideficiency Act, 31 U.S.C. § 1341. An unauthorized transfer violates 31 U.S.C. § 1301(a) because the transferred funds would be used for a purpose other than that for which they were originally appropriated. B-279886, Apr. 28, 1998; B-278121, Nov. 7, 1997; B-248284.2, Sept. 1, 1992. If the receiving appropriation is exceeded, the Antideficiency Act is also violated. Further, informal congressional approval of an unauthorized transfer of funds between appropriation accounts does not have the force and effect of law. B-278121 and B-248284.2, supra.

Although every violation of 31 U.S.C. § 1301(a) is not automatically a violation of the Antideficiency Act, and every violation of the Antideficiency Act is not automatically a violation of 31 U.S.C. § 1301(a), cases frequently involve elements of both. Thus, an expenditure in excess of an available appropriation violates both statutes. The reason the purpose statute is violated is that, unless the disbursing officer used personal funds, he or she must necessarily have used money appropriated for other purposes. 4 Comp. Dec. 314, 317 (1897). The relationship between purpose violations and the Antideficiency Act wil be explored further.

Brief mention should also be made of the axiom that an agency cannot do indirectly what it is not permitted to do directly. Thus, an agency cannot use the device of a contract, grant, or agreement to accomplish a purpose it could not do by direct expenditure. See 18 Comp. Gen. 285 (1938) (contract stipulation to pay wages in excess of Davis-Bacon Act rates held unauthorized). See also B-259499, Aug. 22, 1995 (agreement to provide personal services to agency that is not authorized to contract for personal services is not authorized under the Economy Act).

Similarly, a grant of funds for unspecified purposes would be improper. 55 Comp. Gen. 1059, 1062 (1976). Settlements cannot include benefits that the agency does not have authority to provide. See B-247348, June 22, 1992 (broad authority to provide remedies for claims arising under Title VII of the Civil Rights Act does not permit an agency to provide unauthorized benefits). See also B-239592, Aug. 23, 1991.

2. Determining Authorized Purposes

a. Statement of Purpose

Where does one look to find the authorized purposes of an appropriation? The first place, of course, is the appropriation act itself and its legislative history. If the appropriation is general, it may also be necessary to consult the legislation authorizing the appropriation, if any, and the underlying program or organic legislation, together with their legislative histories.

The actual language of the appropriation act is always of paramount importance in determining the purpose of an appropriation. Every appropriation has one or more purposes in the sense that Congress does not provide money for an agency to do with as it pleases, although purposes are stated with varying degrees of specificity. One end of the spectrum is illustrated by this old private relief act:

> "[T]he Secretary of the Treasury ...is hereby, authorized and directed to pay to George H. Lott, a citizen of Mississippi, the sum of one hundred forty-eight dollars ...."

Act of March 23, 1896, ch. 71, 29 Stat. 711.

This is one extreme. There is no need to look beyond the language of the appropriation; it was available to pay $148 to George H. Lott, and for absolutely nothing else. Language this specific leaves no room for administrative discretion. For example, the Comptroller General has held that language of this type does not authorize reimbursement to an agency where the agency erroneously paid the individual before the private act had been passed. In this situation, the purpose for which the appropriation was made had ceased to exist. B-151114, Aug. 26, 1964.

At the other extreme, smaller agencies may receive only one appropriation. The purpose of the appropriation will be to enable the agency to carry out all of its various authorized functions. For example, the Consumer Product Safety Commission receives but a single appropriation "for necessary expenses of the Consumer Product Safety Commission." To determine permissible expenditures under this type of appropriation, it would be necessary to examine all of the agency's substantive legislation, in conjunction with the "necessary expense" doctrine.

Between the two extremes are many variations. A common form of appropriation funds a single program. For example, the Interior Department receives a separate appropriation to carry out the Payments in Lieu of Taxes Act (PILT), 31 U.S.C. § 6901-6904. While the appropriation is specific in the sense that it is limited to PILT payments and associated administrative expenses, it is nevertheless necessary to look beyond the appropriation language and examine the PILT statute to determine authorized expenditures.

Once the purposes have been determined by examining the various pieces of legislation, 31 U.S.C. § 1301(a) comes into play to restrict the use of the appropriation to these purposes only, together with one final generic category of payments--payments authorized under general legislation applicable to all or a defined group of agencies and not requiring specific appropriations. For example, legislation enacted in 1982 amended 12 U.S.C. § 1770 to authorize federal agencies to provide various services, including telephone service, to employee credit unions. Pub. L. No. 97-320, § 515, 96 Stat. 1469, 1530 (Oct. 15, 1982). Prior to this legislation, an agency would have violated 31 U.S.C. § 1301(a) by providing telephone service to a credit union, even on a reimbursable basis, because this was not an authorized purpose under any agency appropriation. 60 Comp. Gen. 653 (1981). The 1982 amendment made the providing of special services to credit unions an authorized agency function, and hence an authorized purpose, which it could fund from unrestricted general operating appropriations. 66 Comp. Gen. 356 (1987). Similarly, a recently enacted statute gives agencies the discretion to use appropriated funds to pay the expenses their employees incur for obtaining professional credentials. 5 U.S.C. § 5757(a). See also B-289219, Oct. 29, 2002. See also B-302548, Aug. 20, 2004 (section 5757(a) does not authorize the agency to pay for an employee's membership in a professional association unless membership is a prerequisite to obtaining the professional license or certification). Prior to this legislation, agencies could not use appropriated funds to pay fees incurred by their employees in obtaining professional credentials. See, e.g., 47 Comp. Gen. 116 (1967). Other examples are interest payments under the Prompt Payment Act (31 U.S.C. §§ 3901-3907) and administrative settlements less than $2,500 under the Federal Tort Claims Act (28 U.S.C. §§ 2671 et seq.).

b. Specific Purpose Stated in Appropriation Act

Where an appropriation specifies the purpose for which the funds are to be used, 31 U.S.C. § 1301(a) applies in its purest form to restrict the use of the funds to the specified purpose. For example, an appropriation for topographical surveys in the United States was not available for topographical surveys in Puerto Rico. 5 Comp. Dec. 493 (1899). Similarly, an appropriation to install an electrical generating plant in the customhouse building in Baltimore could not be used to install the plant in a nearby post office building, even though the plant would serve both buildings and thereby reduce operating expenses. 11 Comp. Dec. 724 (1905). An appropriation for the extension and remodeling of the State Department building was not available to construct a pneumatic tube delivery system between the State Department and the White House. 42 Comp. Gen. 226 (1962). In another example involving a line-item appropriation for a grant project, because the funds were made available for a specific grantee in a specific amount to accomplish a specific purpose, the agency could not grant less than Congress has directed by using some of the appropriation to pay its administrative costs. 72 Comp. Gen. 317 (1993); 69 Comp. Gen. 660, 662 (1990). An appropriation to the Department of Labor for payment to the New York Workers' Compensation Board for the processing of claims related to the September 11, 2001, terrorist attack on the World Trade Center was not available to make payments to other New York State entities. B-303927, June 7, 2005. And, as noted previously, an appropriation for the "replacement" of state roads could not be used to make improvements on them. 41 Comp. Gen. 255 (1961).

It is well settled, but warrants repeating, that even an expenditure that may be reasonably related to a general appropriation may not be paid out of that appropriation where the expenditure falls specifically within the scope of another appropriation. 63 Comp. Gen. 422 (1984); B-300325, Dec. 13, 2002; B-290005, July 1, 2002. It is also well settled that when two appropriations are available for the same purpose, the agency must select which to use, and that once it has made an election, the agency must continue to use the same appropriation for that purpose unless the agency, at the beginning of the fiscal year, informs Congress of its intent to change for the next fiscal year. B-307382, Sept. 5, 2006; B-272191, Nov. 4, 1997. See also 68 Comp. Gen 337 (1989); 59 Comp. Gen 518 (1980). An exception to this requirement is when Congress specifically authorizes the use of two appropriation accounts. B-272191, supra (statutory language makes clear that Congress intended that the "funds appropriated to the Secretary [of the Army] for operation and maintenance" in the fiscal year 1993 Defense Appropriations Act are "[i]n addition to …the funds specifically appropriated for real property maintenance under the heading [RPM,D]" in that appropriation act).

The following cases will further illustrate the interpretation and application of appropriation acts denoting a specific purpose to which the funds are to be dedicated. In each of the examples, the appropriation in question was the U.S. Forest Service's appropriation for the construction and maintenance of "Forest Roads and Trails."

In 37 Comp. Gen. 472 (1958), the Forest Service sought to construct airstrips on land in or adjacent to national forests. The issue was the extent to which the costs could be charged to the Roads and Trails appropriation as opposed to other Forest Service appropriations such as "Forest Protection and Utilization." At hearings before the appropriations committees, Forest Service officials had announced their intent to charge most of the landing fields to the Roads and Trails appropriation. The appropriation act in question provided that "appropriations available to the Forest Service for the current fiscal year shall be available for" construction of the landing fields up to a specified dollar amount, but the item was not mentioned in any of the individual appropriations. GAO concluded that the proposal to indiscriminately charge the landing fields to Roads and Trails would violate 31 U.S.C. § 1301(a). The Roads and Trails appropriation could be used for only those landing fields that were directly connected with and necessary to accomplishing the purposes of that appropriation. Landing fields not directly connected with the purposes of the Roads and Trails appropriation, for example, airstrips needed to assist in firefighting in remote areas, had to be charged to the appropriation to which they were related, such as Forest Protection and Utilization. The mere mention of intent at the hearings was not sufficient to alter the availability of the appropriations. Later, in 53 Comp Gen. 328 (1973), the Comptroller General held that the Forest Roads and Trails appropriation could not be charged with the expense of closing roads or trails and returning them to their natural state, such activity being neither "construction" nor "maintenance."

Again, in B-164497(3), Feb. 6, 1979, GAO decided that the Forest Service could not use the Roads and Trails appropriation to maintain a part of a federally constructed scenic highway on Forest Service land in West Virginia, although the state was prevented from maintaining it because the scenic highway was closed to commercial traffic. The Roads and Trails account was improper to charge with the maintenance because the term "forest road" was statutorily defined as a service or access road "necessary for the protection, administration, and utilization of the [national forest] system and the use and development of its resources." The highway, a scenic parkway reserved exclusively for recreational and passenger travel through a national forest, was not the type of forest road the appropriation was available to maintain. The decision further noted, however, that the Forest Protection and Utilization appropriation was somewhat broader and could be used for the contemplated maintenance.

A 1955 case illustrates a type of expenditure that could properly be charged to the Roads and Trails account. Construction of a timber access road on a national forest uncovered a site of old Indian ruins. Since the road construction itself was properly chargeable to the Roads and Trails appropriation, the Forest Service could use the same appropriation to pay the cost of archaeological and exploratory work necessary to obtain and preserve historical data from the ruins before they were destroyed by the construction. (Rerouting was apparently not possible.) B-125309, Dec. 6, 1955.

In any case, an appropriation serves as a limitation, or more accurately, a series of limitations relating to time and amount in addition to purpose. In some situations, an appropriation is simultaneously a grant of authority. For example, 5 U.S.C. § 3109 authorizes agencies to procure the services of experts and consultants, but only "[w]hen authorized by an appropriation or other statute." In contrast with the statute authorizing services for credit unions noted earlier, 5 U.S.C. § 3109 by itself does not authorize an agency to spend general operating appropriations to hire consultants. Unless an agency has received this authority somewhere in its permanent legislation, the hiring of consultants under section 3109 is an authorized purpose only if it is specified in the agency's appropriation act.

3. New or Additional Duties

Appropriation acts tend to be bunched at certain times of the year while substantive legislation may be enacted any time. A frequently recurring situation is where a statute is passed imposing new duties on an agency but not providing any additional appropriations. The question is whether implementation of the new statute must wait until additional funds are appropriated, or whether the agency can use its existing appropriations to carry out the new function, either pending receipt of further funding through the normal budget process or in the absence of additional appropriations (assuming in either case the absence of contrary congressional intent).

The rule is that existing agency appropriations that generally cover the type of expenditures involved are available to defray the expenses of new or additional duties imposed by proper legal authority. The test for availability is whether the duties imposed by the new law bear a sufficient relationship to the purposes for which the previously enacted appropriation was made so as to justify the use of that appropriation for the new duties.

For example, in the earliest published decision cited for the rule, the Comptroller General held that the Securities and Exchange Commission could use its general operating appropriation for fiscal year 1936 to perform additional duties imposed on it by the later enacted Public Utility Holding Company Act of 1935 (49 Stat. 803 (Aug. 26, 1935)). 15 Comp. Gen. 167 (1935).

Similarly, the Interior Department could use its 1979 "Departmental Management" appropriation to begin performing duties imposed by the Public Utilities Regulatory Policies Act of 1978, and to provide reimbursable support costs for the Endangered Species Committee and Review Board created by the Endangered Species Act Amendments of 1978. Both statutes were enacted after the Interior Department's 1979 appropriation. B-195007, July 15, 1980. In another case, a statute directing the Department of Health and Human Services (HHS) to make payments to qualified health plans did not, by its terms, enact an appropriation to make those payments. However, as the Secretary of HHS had delegated authority for administration of the statute to an HHS component, the Centers for Medicare and Medicaid Services (CMS), a CMS program appropriation would have been available for the payments, as were user fees collected under program authority. B-325630, Sept. 30, 2014

The rule has also been applied to additional duties imposed by executive order. 32 Comp. Gen. 347 (1953); 30 Comp. Gen. 258 (1951). Additional cases are 30 Comp. Gen. 205 (1950); B-290011, Mar. 25, 2002; B-211306, June 6, 1983; B-153694, Oct. 23, 1964.

A variation occurred in 54 Comp. Gen. 1093 (1975). The unexpended balance of a Commerce Department appropriation, which had been used to administer a loan guarantee program and to make collateral protection payments under the Trade Expansion Act of 1962, 19 U.S.C. §§ 1901-1920 (1970), was transferred to a similar but new program by the Trade Act of 1974. The 1974 statute repealed the earlier provisions. This meant that the transferred funds could no longer be used for expenses under the 1962 act--including payments on guarantee commitments--even though that was the purpose for which they were originally appropriated, unless the expenditures could also be viewed as relating to the Commerce Department's functions under the 1974 act. Applying the rationale of the later-imposed duty cases, the Comptroller General concluded that the purposes of the two programs were sufficiently related so that the Commerce Department could continue to use the transferred funds to make collateral protection payments and to honor guarantees made under the 1962 act.

A related question is the extent to which an agency may use current appropriations for preliminary administrative expenses in preparation for implementing a new law, prior to the receipt of substantive appropriations for the new program. Again, the appropriation is available provided it is sufficiently broad to embrace expenditures of the type contemplated. Thus, the National Science Foundation could use its fiscal year 1967 appropriations for preliminary expenses of implementing the National Sea Grant College and Program Act of 1966, enacted after the appropriation, since the purposes of the new act were basically similar to the purposes of the appropriation. 46 Comp. Gen. 604 (1967). The preliminary tasks in that case included such things as development of policies and plans, issuance of internal instructions, and the establishment of organizational units to administer the new program.

Similarly, the Bureau of Land Management could use current appropriations to determine fair market value and to initiate negotiations with owners in connection with the acquisition of mineral interests under the Cranberry Wilderness Act, even though actual acquisitions could not be made until funding was provided in appropriation acts. B-211306, June 6, 1983. See also B-153694, Oct. 23, 1964; B-153694, Sept. 2, 1964. Of course, an appropriation is not available if Congress has prohibited the agency from using it. In B-308715, Apr. 20, 2007, the Department of Energy is specifically barred under 42 U.S.C. § 7278 from using funds made available under an Energy and Water Development Appropriations Act to implement or finance any authorized loan guarantee program unless specific provision has been made for that program in an appropriations act. Since no provision was made, Energy could not use the Energy and Water appropriation to begin implementing the loan guarantee program.

Where Congress has not made a specific appropriation available to fund additional or new duties and an existing appropriation is used based upon a determination that the new duties bear a sufficient relationship to the purpose for which the existing appropriation was made, the agency may not reimburse the existing appropriation that was used once the new appropriation is available. 30 Comp. Gen. 258 (1951); B-290011, supra. The shifting of money from one appropriation to another in the absence of statutory authority is prohibited by 31 U.S.C. § 1532. Compare B-300673, July 3, 2003, where GAO concluded that the Chief Administrative Officer (CAO) for the House of Representatives was allowed to use the CAO fiscal year 2003 Salaries and Expenses appropriation to reimburse the House of Representatives Child Care Center revolving fund for certain payments incurred by the Center at the beginning of fiscal year 2003 during a period covered by a continuing resolution, before enactment of the fiscal year 2003 appropriation. In this case, CAO's fiscal year 2003 appropriation expressly directed that it cover the Center director's salary and employees' training costs for fiscal year 2003 and thereafter. Under the plain meaning of the appropriation language, the CAO appropriation was the proper one to charge for all expenses incurred in fiscal year 2003.

4. Termination of Program

a. Termination Desired

If Congress appropriates money to implement a program, can the agency use that money to terminate the program? (Expenses of terminating a program could include such things as contract termination costs and personnel reduction-in-force expenses.) If implementation of the program is mandatory, the answer is no. In 1973, for example, the administration attempted to terminate certain programs funded by the Office of Economic Opportunity (OEO), relying in part on the fact that it had not requested any funds for OEO for 1974. The programs in question were funded under a multiple year authorization that directed that the programs be carried out during the fiscal years covered by the authorization. The U.S. District Court for the District of Columbia held that funds appropriated to carry out the programs could not be used to terminate them. Local 2677, American Federation of Government Employees v. Phillips, 358 F. Supp. 60 (D.D.C. 1973). The court cited 31 U.S.C. § 1301(a) as one basis for its holding. Id. at 76 n.17. See also 63 Comp. Gen. 75, 78 (1983).

Where the program is nonmandatory, the agency has more discretion, but there are still limits. In B-115398, Aug. 1, 1977, the Comptroller General advised that the Air Force could terminate B-1 bomber production, which had been funded under a lump-sum appropriation and was not mandated by any statute. Later cases have stated the rule that an agency may use funds appropriated for a program to terminate that program where (1) the program is nonmandatory and (2) the termination would not result in curtailment of the overall program to such an extent that it would no longer be consistent with the scheme of applicable program legislation. 61 Comp. Gen. 482 (1982) (Department of Energy could use funds appropriated for fossil energy research and development to terminate certain fossil energy programs); B-203074, Aug. 6, 1981. Several years earlier, GAO had held that the closing of all Public Health Service hospitals would exceed the Surgeon General's discretionary authority because a major portion of the Public Health Service Act would effectively be inoperable without the Public Health Service hospital system. B-156510, Feb. 23, 1971; B-156510, June 7, 1965.

The concepts are further illustrated in a series of cases involving the Clinch River Nuclear Breeder Reactor. In 1977, the administration proposed using funds appropriated for the design, development, construction, and operation of the reactor to terminate the project. Construction of a breeder reactor had been authorized, but not explicitly mandated, by statute. As contemplated by the program legislation, the Energy Research and Development Administration, the predecessor of the Department of Energy, had submitted program criteria for congressional approval. GAO reviewed the statutory scheme, found that the approved program criteria were "as much a part of [the authorizing statute] as if they were explicitly stated in the statutory language itself," and concluded that use of program funds for termination was unauthorized. B-115398, June 23, 1977. Two subsequent opinions reached the same conclusion, supported further by a provision in a 1978 supplemental appropriation act that specifically earmarked funds for the reactor. B-164105, Mar. 10, 1978; B-164105, Dec. 5, 1977.

By 1983 the situation had changed. Congressional support for the reactor had eroded considerably, no funds were designated for it for fiscal year 1984, and it became apparent that further funding for the project was unlikely. In light of these circumstances, GAO revisited the termination question and concluded that the Department of Energy now had a legal basis to use 1983 funds to terminate the project in accordance with the project justification data that provided for termination in the event of insufficient funds to permit effective continuation. 63 Comp. Gen. 75 (1983).

b. Reauthorization Pending

Another variation occurs when an entity's enabling legislation is set to expire and Congress shows signs of extending or reauthorizing the entity, but has not yet provided funds or authority to continue. For example, the U.S. Advisory Commission on Intergovernmental Relations (ACIR) was statutorily authorized to give continuing attention to intergovernmental problems. In 1995, ACIR was statutorily terminated effective September 30, 1996. About 2 months before ACIR was to terminate, Congress enacted legislation giving ACIR a new responsibility to provide research and a report under a contract with the National Gambling Impact Study Commission. Although Congress continued ACIR's existence beyond fiscal year 1996 for the limited purpose of providing research for the Gambling Commission, Congress appropriated no funds for fiscal year 1997. ACIR had separate statutory authority, 42 U.S.C. § 4279, to receive and expend unrestricted contributions made to ACIR from state governments. In B-274855, Jan. 23, 1997, GAO held that this statute constituted an appropriation (a permanent, indefinite appropriation) separate from ACIR's annually enacted fiscal year appropriation, and that from October 1, 1996, until such time as ACIR was awarded the research contract, ACIR could use its unconditional state government contributions.

Another situation may occur when an entity's authorizing legislation is set to terminate and Congress provides an appropriation but does not reauthorize the entity until months later. In 71 Comp. Gen. 378 (1992), the U.S. Commission on Civil Rights was set to terminate by operation of law on September 30, 1991. The Commission was not reauthorized until November 26, 1991. However, during the interim and prior to the expiration date, Congress provided the Commission with appropriations for fiscal year 1992. Once a termination or sunset provision for an entity becomes effective, the agency ceases to exist and no new obligations may be incurred after the termination date. However, when Congress desires to extend, amend, suspend, or repeal a statute, it can accomplish its purpose by including the requisite language in an appropriations or other act of Congress. After viewing the legislative actions, in their entirety, on the Commission's reauthorization and appropriation bills, GAO determined that Congress clearly intended for the Commission to continue to operate after September 30, 1991. GAO held that the specific appropriation provided to the Commission served to suspend its termination until the Commission was reauthorized.

B. The "Necessary Expense" Doctrine

1. The Theory

The preceding discussion establishes the primacy of 31 U.S.C. § 1301(a) in any discussion of purpose availability. The next point to emphasize is that 31 U.S.C. § 1301(a) does not require, nor would it be reasonably possible, that every item of expenditure be specified in the appropriation act. While the statute is strict, it is applied with reason.

The spending agency has reasonable discretion in determining how to carry out the objects of the appropriation. This concept, known as the "necessary expense doctrine," has been around almost as long as the statute itself. An early statement of the rule is contained in 6 Comp. Gen. 619, 621 (1927):

"It is a well-settled rule of statutory construction that where an appropriation is made for a particular object, by implication it confers authority to incur expenses which are necessary or proper or incident to the proper execution of the object, unless there is another appropriation which makes more specific provision for such expenditures, or unless they are prohibited by law, or unless it is manifestly evident from various precedent appropriation acts that Congress has specifically legislated for certain expenses of the Government creating the implication that such expenditures should not be incurred except by its express authority."

The necessary expense rule is really a combination of two slightly different but closely related concepts:

1. An appropriation made for a specific object is available for expenses necessarily incident to accomplishing that object unless prohibited by law or otherwise provided for. For example, an appropriation to erect a monument at the birthplace of George Washington could be used to construct an iron fence around the monument where administratively deemed necessary to protect the monument. 2 Comp. Dec. 492 (1896). Likewise, an appropriation to purchase bison for consumption covers the slaughtering and processing of the bison as well as the actual purchase. B-288658, Nov. 30, 2001.

2. Appropriations, even for broad categories such as salaries, frequently use the term "necessary expenses." As used in this context, the term refers to "current or running expenses of a miscellaneous character arising out of and directly related to the agency's work." 38 Comp. Gen. 758, 762 (1959); 4 Comp. Gen. 1063, 1065 (1925).

Although the theory is identical in both situations, the difference is that expenditures in the second category relate to somewhat broader objects.

The Comptroller General has never established a precise formula for determining the application of the necessary expense rule. In view of the vast differences among agencies, any such formula would almost certainly be unworkable. Rather, the determination must be made essentially on a case-by-case basis.

In addition to recognizing the differences among agencies when applying the necessary expense rule, we act to maintain a vigorous body of case law responsive to the changing needs of government. In this regard, our decisions indicate a willingness to consider changes in societal expectations regarding what constitutes a necessary expense. This flexibility is evident, for example, in our analysis of whether an expenditure constitutes a personal or an official expense. As will be discussed more fully, use of appropriations for such an expenditure is determined by continually weighing the benefit to the agency, such as the productivity, safety, recruitment and retention of a dynamic workforce and other considerations enabling efficient, effective, and responsible government. We recognize, however, that these factors can change over time. B-302993, June 25, 2004 (modifying earlier decisions to reflect determination that purchase of kitchen appliances for use by agency employees in an agency facility is reasonably related to the efficient performance of agency activities, provides other benefits such as assurance of a safe workplace, and primarily benefits the agency, even though employees enjoy a collateral benefit); B-286026, June 12, 2001(overruling GAO's earlier decisions based on reassessment of the training opportunities afforded by examination review courses); B-280759, Nov. 5, 1998 (overruling GAO's earlier decisions on the purchase of business cards). See also 71 Comp. Gen 527 (1992) (eldercare is not a typical employee benefit provided to the nonfederal workforce and not one that the federal workforce should expect); B-288266, Jan. 27, 2003 (GAO explained it remained "willing to reexamine our case law" regarding light refreshments if it is shown to frustrate efficient, effective, and responsible government).

When applying the necessary expense rule, an expenditure can be justified after meeting a three-part test:

1. The expenditure must bear a logical relationship to the appropriation sought to be charged. In other words, it must make a direct contribution to carrying out either a specific appropriation or an authorized agency function for which more general appropriations are available.

2. The expenditure must not be prohibited by law.

3. The expenditure must not be otherwise provided for, that is, it must not be an item that falls within the scope of some other appropriation or statutory funding scheme.

E.g., B-303170, Apr. 22, 2005; 63 Comp. Gen. 422, 427-28 (1984); B-240365.2, Mar. 14, 1996; B-230304, Mar. 18, 1988.

a. Relationship to the Appropriation

The first test--the relationship of the expenditure to the appropriation--is the one that generates by far the lion's share of questions. On the one hand, the rule does not require that a given expenditure be "necessary" in the strict sense that the object of the appropriation could not possibly be fulfilled without it. Thus, the expenditure does not have to be the only way to accomplish a given object, nor does it have to reflect GAO's perception of the best way to do it. Yet on the other hand, it has to be more than merely desirable or even important. E.g., 34 Comp. Gen. 599 (1955); B-42439, July 8, 1944. An expenditure cannot be justified merely because some agency official thinks it is a good idea, nor can it be justified simply because it is a practice engaged in by private business. See B-288266, Jan. 27, 2003.

The important thing is not the significance of the proposed expenditure itself or its value to the government or to some social purpose in abstract terms, but the extent to which it will contribute to accomplishing the purposes of the appropriation the agency wishes to charge. For example, the Forest Service can use its appropriation for "Forest Protection and Utilization" to buy plastic litterbags for use in a national forest. 50 Comp. Gen. 534 (1971). See also 72 Comp. Gen. 73 (1992) (the Environmental Protection Agency (EPA) can purchase buttons promoting indoor air quality for its conference since the message conveyed is related to EPA's mission); 71 Comp. Gen. 28 (1991) (the Internal Revenue Service (IRS) can cover cost of its employees filing electronic tax returns because it trains employees); B-257488, Nov. 6, 1995 (the Food and Drug Administration is permitted to purchase "No Red Tape" buttons to promote employee efficiency and effectiveness and thereby the agency's purpose). However, operating appropriations of the Equal Employment Opportunity Commission (EEOC) are not available to pay IRS the taxes due on judgment proceeds recovered by EEOC in an enforcement action. While the payment would further a purpose of the IRS, it would not contribute to fulfilling the purposes of the EEOC appropriation. 65 Comp. Gen. 800 (1986). See also B-323122, Aug. 24, 2012 (Consumer Product Safety Commission may not issue gift cards to Web site subscribers where it does not establish that gift card distribution is essential to achieve a statutory responsibility); 70 Comp. Gen. 248 (1991) (purchasing T-shirts for Combined Federal Campaign (CFC) contributors is not permitted because T-shirts are not essential to achieving the authorized purpose of CFC).

If the basic test is the relationship of the expenditure to the appropriation sought to be charged, it should be apparent that the "necessary expense" concept is a relative one. As stated in 65 Comp. Gen. 738, 740 (1986):

> "We have dealt with the concept of 'necessary expenses' in a vast number of decisions over the decades. If one lesson emerges, it is that the concept is a relative one: it is measured not by reference to an expenditure in a vacuum, but by assessing the relationship of the

expenditure to the specific appropriation to be charged or, in the case of several programs funded by a lump-sum appropriation, to the specific program to be served. It should thus be apparent that an item that can be justified under one program or appropriation might be entirely inappropriate under another, depending on the circumstances and statutory authorities involved."

The evident difficulty in stating a precise rule emphasizes the role and importance of agency discretion. It is in the first instance up to the administrative agency to determine that a given item is reasonably necessary to accomplishing an authorized purpose. Once the agency makes this determination, GAO will normally not substitute its own judgment for that of the agency. In other words, the agency's administrative determination of necessity will be given considerable deference.

Generally, the interpretation of a statute by the agency that Congress has charged with the responsibility for administering it is entitled to considerable weight. This discretion, however, is not without limits. The agency's interpretation must be reasonable and must be based on a permissible construction of the statute. United States v. Mead Corp., 533 U.S. 218, 226-238 (2001); Chevron, Inc. v. Natural Resources Defense Council, 467 U.S. 837 (1984). See also B-286661, Jan. 19, 2001 (expansive definition exceeds the bounds of the Privatization Act and violates the requirement of 31 U.S.C. § 1301(a)).

The standard GAO uses in evaluating purpose availability is summarized in the following passage from B-223608, Dec. 19, 1988:

"When we review an expenditure with reference to its availability for the purpose at issue, the question is not whether we would have exercised that discretion in the same manner. Rather, the question is whether the expenditure falls within the agency's legitimate range of discretion, or whether its relationship to an authorized purpose or function is so attenuated as to take it beyond that range."

A decision on a "necessary expense" question therefore involves (1) analyzing the agency's appropriations and other statutory authority to determine whether the purpose is authorized and (2) evaluating the adequacy of the administrative justification, to decide whether the agency has properly exercised, or exceeded, its discretion.

The role of discretion in purpose availability is further complicated by the fact that not all federal establishments have the same range of discretion. For example, a government corporation with the authority to determine the character and necessity of its expenditures has, by virtue of its legal status, a broader measure of discretion than a "regular" agency. But even this discretion is not unlimited and is bound at least by considerations of sound public policy. See 14 Comp. Gen. 755 (1935), aff'd upon reconsideration, A-60467, June 24, 1936.

Two decisions involving the Bonneville Power Administration (BPA) will illustrate. In 1951, the Interior Department asked whether funds appropriated to BPA could be used to enter into a contract to conduct a survey to determine the feasibility of "artificial nucleation and cloud modification" (artificial rainmaking in English) for a portion of the Columbia River drainage basin. If the amount of rainfall during the dry season could be significantly increased by this method, the amount of marketable power for the region would be enhanced. Naturally, BPA did not have an appropriation specifically available for rainmaking. However, in view of BPA's statutory role in the sale and disposition of electric power in the region, GAO concluded that the expenditure was authorized. B-104463, July 23, 1951.

The Interior Department then asked whether, assuming the survey results were favorable, BPA could contract with the rainmakers. GAO thought this was going too far and questioned whether BPA's statutory authority to encourage the widest possible use of electric energy really contemplated artificial rainmaking. GAO emphasized that the expenditure would be improper for a department or agency with the "ordinary authority usually granted" to federal agencies. However, the legislative history of BPA's enabling statute indicated that Congress intended that it have a degree of freedom similar to public corporations and that it be largely free from "the requirements and restrictions ordinarily applicable to the conduct of Government business." Therefore, while the Comptroller General expressly refused to "approve" the rainmaking contract, he felt compelled to hold that BPA's funds were legally available for it. B-105397, Sept. 21, 1951.

For the typical federal department or agency, the range of discretion will be essentially the same, with variations in the kinds of things justifiable under the necessary expense umbrella stemming from program differences. For example, necessary expenses for an agency with law enforcement responsibilities may include items directly related to that authority, which would be inappropriate for agencies without law enforcement functions. Thus, the Immigration and Naturalization Service could use its Salaries and Expenses appropriation to purchase and install lights, automatic warning devices, and observation towers along the boundary between the United States and Mexico. 29 Comp. Gen. 419 (1950). See also 7 Comp. Dec. 712 (1901). Similarly, in B-204486, Jan. 19, 1982, the Federal Bureau of Investigation could buy insurance on an undercover business not so much to insure the property, but to enhance the credibility of the operation.

The procurement of evidence is also authorized as a necessary expense for an agency with law enforcement responsibilities. For example, Forest Service appropriations could be used to pay towing and storage charges for a truck seized as evidence of criminal activities in a national forest. B-186365, Mar. 8, 1977. See also 27 Comp. Gen. 516 (1948); 26 Comp. Dec. 780, 783 (1920); B-56866, Apr. 22, 1946. Also, the Customs Service could use its operating appropriations to cover the cost of extending its psychological assessment and referral services to its employees' family members adversely affected by work-related incidents arising from law enforcement activities involving death or serious injury to its employee in the line of duty. B-270446, Feb. 11, 1997.

Cases involving fairs and expositions provide further illustration. For the most part, when Congress desires federal participation in fairs or expositions, it has been authorized by specific legislation. See, e.g., B-160493, Jan. 16, 1967 (legislation authorized federal participation in HemisFair 1968 in San Antonio). For another example, United States participation in the 1927 International Exposition in Seville, Spain, was specifically authorized by statute. See 10 Comp. Gen. 563, 564 (1931).

However, specific statutory authority is not essential. If participation is directly connected with and is in furtherance of the purposes for which a particular appropriation has been made, and an appropriate administrative determination is made to that effect, the appropriation is available for the expenditure. B-290900, Mar. 18, 2003 (Bureau of Land Management (BLM) may use its appropriated funds to pay its share of the cost to produce a brochure that educates the public regarding lighthouse preservation because the brochure supports BLM in meeting its responsibility under its lighthouse preservation program); B-286457, Jan. 29, 2001 (demolition of old air traffic control tower that would obstruct the view from the new one is directly connected with and in furtherance of the construction of a new tower such that the demolition expenses are covered by Federal Aviation Administration's appropriation act for tower construction); B-280440, Feb. 26, 1999 (Immigration and Naturalization Service's (INS) Salaries and Expenses appropriation is available to purchase medals to be worn by uniformed employees of the Border Patrol division of INS to commemorate the division's 75th anniversary). See also 16 Comp. Gen. 53 (1936); 10 Comp. Gen. 282 (1930); 7 Comp. Gen. 357 (1927); 4 Comp. Gen. 457 (1924). Authority to disseminate information will generally provide adequate justification. E.g., 7 Comp. Gen. 357; 4 Comp. Gen. 457. In addition, an agency may use appropriated funds to provide prizes to individuals to further the collection of information necessary to accomplish the agency's statutory mandate. See, e.g., B-310981, Jan. 25, 2008; B-304718, Nov. 9, 2005; B-286536, Nov. 17, 2000; 70 Comp. Gen 720 (1991); B-230062, Dec. 22, 1988. But see B-323122, Aug. 24, 2012 (Consumer Product Safety Commission may not use appropriated funds to issue gift cards to individuals subscribing to a safety oriented Web site where it does not establish that gift card distribution is essential to achieve a statutory responsibility)..

In the absence of either statutory authority or an adequate justification under the necessary expense doctrine, the expenditure, like any other expenditure, is illegal. Thus, the Department of Housing and Urban Development (HUD) had no authority to finance participation at a trade exhibition in the Soviet Union where HUD's primary purpose was to enhance business opportunities for American companies. 68 Comp. Gen. 226 (1989); B-229732, Dec. 22, 1988. Regardless of whether it may or may not have been a good idea, commercial trade promotion is not one of the purposes for which Congress appropriates money to HUD.

No discussion would be complete without some mention of the "marauding woodpecker" case. It appears that in 1951, marauding woodpeckers were causing considerable damage to government-owned transmission lines and the Southwestern Power Administration, Interior Department (Interior) wanted to buy guns with which to shoot the woodpeckers. Interior first went to the Army, but the Army advised that the types of guns and ammunition desired were not available, so Interior next came to GAO. The Comptroller General held that, if administratively determined to be necessary to protect the transmission lines, Interior could buy the guns and ammunition from the Southwestern Power Administration's construction appropriation. The views of the woodpeckers were not solicited. B-105977, Dec. 3, 1951. Actually, this was not a totally novel issue. Several years earlier, GAO had approved the use of an Interior Department "maintenance of range improvements" appropriation for the control of coyotes, rodents, and other "predatory animals." A-82570, Dec. 30, 1936. See also A-82570, B-120739, Aug. 21, 1957.

b. Expenditure Otherwise Prohibited

The second test under the necessary expense doctrine is that the expenditure must not be prohibited by law. As a general proposition, neither a necessary expense rationale nor the "necessary expense" language in an appropriation act can be used to overcome a statutory prohibition. E.g., B-277905, Mar. 17, 1998 (expenditure for installation and maintenance of water pipelines to support a military base golf course not permissible because such expenditure is specifically prohibited by 10 U.S.C. § 2246, which prohibit the use of appropriated funds to "equip, operate, or maintain" a golf course); B-247348, June 22, 1992 (detail of Government Printing Office employee to Library of Congress not permissible because 44 U.S.C. § 316 prohibits details for "duties not pertaining to the work of public printing and binding"). In 38 Comp. Gen. 758 (1959) and 4 Comp. Gen. 1063 (1925), the Comptroller General held that the necessary expense language did not overcome the prohibition in 41 U.S.C. § 12 against contracting for public buildings or public improvements in excess of appropriations for the specific purpose. In large measure, this is little more than an application of the rule against repeal by implication.

There are exceptions where applying the rule would make it impossible to carry out a specific appropriation. A very small group of cases stands for the proposition that, where a specific appropriation is made for a specific purpose, an expenditure that is "absolutely essential" to accomplishing the specific object may be incurred even though the expenditure would otherwise be prohibited. In order for this exception to apply, the expenditure must literally be absolutely essential in the sense that the object of the appropriation could not be accomplished without it. Also, the rule would not apply to the use of a more general appropriation.

For example, in 2 Comp. Gen. 133 (1922), modifying 2 Comp. Gen. 14 (1922), an appropriation to provide airmail service between New York, Chicago, and San Francisco was held available to construct hangars and related facilities at a landing field in Chicago notwithstanding the requirement for a specific appropriation in 41 U.S.C. § 12. The reason was that it would have been impossible to provide the service, and hence, to accomplish the purpose of the appropriation, without erecting the facilities. See also 17 Comp. Gen. 636 (1938) and 22 Comp. Dec. 317 (1916). (The 1938 decision cites the rule but the decision itself is an ordinary necessary expense case.)

An 1899 case, 6 Comp. Dec. 75, provides another good illustration of the concept. The building housing the Department of Justice (Justice) had become unsafe and overcrowded. Congress enacted legislation to authorize and fund the construction of a new building. The statute specifically provided that the new building be constructed on the site of the old building, but did not address the question of how Justice would function during the construction period. The obvious solution was to rent another building until the new one was ready, but 40 U.S.C. § 34 prohibited the rental of space in the District of Columbia except under an appropriation specifically available for that purpose, and Justice had no such appropriation. On the grounds that any other result would be absurd, the Comptroller of the Treasury held that Justice could rent interim space notwithstanding the statutory prohibition. While the decision was not couched in terms of the expenditure being "absolutely essential," it said basically the same thing. Since Justice could not cease to function during the construction period, the appropriation for construction of the new building could not be fulfilled without the expenditure for interim space.

c. Expenditure Otherwise Provided For

The third test is that an expenditure cannot be authorized under a necessary expense theory if it is otherwise provided for under a more specific appropriation or statutory funding mechanism. It is well settled that even an expenditure that may be reasonably related to a general appropriation may not be paid out of that appropriation where the expenditure falls specifically within the scope of another appropriation. See, e.g., B-291241, Oct. 8, 2002; B-290005, July 1, 2002; B-289209, May 31, 2002.

The fact that the more specific appropriation may be exhausted is immaterial. Thus, in B-139510, May 13, 1959, the Navy could not use its shipbuilding appropriation to deepen a channel in the Singing River near Pascagoula, Mississippi, to permit submarines then under construction to move to deeper water. The reason was that this was a function for which funds were traditionally appropriated to the Corps of Engineers, not the Navy. The fact that appropriations had not been made in this particular instance was irrelevant.

Similarly, the Navy could not use appropriations made for the construction or procurement of vessels and aircraft to provide housing for civilian employees engaged in defense production activities because funds for that purpose were otherwise available. 20 Comp. Gen. 102 (1940).

In another case, Federal Prison Industries could use its revolving fund to build industrial facilities incident to a federal prison, or to build a residential camp for prisoners employed in federal public works projects, but could not use that fund to construct other prison facilities because such construction was statutorily provided for elsewhere. B-230304, Mar. 18, 1988.

In these cases, the existence of a more specific source of funds, or a more specific statutory mechanism for getting them, is the governing factor and overrides the "necessary expense" considerations.

2. General Operating Expenses

An illustration of how the necessary expense concept works common to all agencies is the range of expenditures permissible under general operating appropriations. All agencies, regardless of program differences, have certain things in common. Specifically, they all have employees, occupy space in buildings, and maintain an office environment. To support these functions, they incur a variety of administrative expenditures. Some are specifically authorized by statute; others flow logically from the requirements of maintaining a workforce.

All agencies receive general operating appropriations for these administrative expenses. Depending largely on the size of the agency, they may be separate lump-sum appropriations or may be combined with program funds. The most common (but not the only) form of general operating appropriation is entitled "Salaries and Expenses (S&E)." Although an S&E appropriation may contain earmarks, for the most part it does not specify the types of "expenses" for which it is available. Employee salaries, together with related items such as agency contributions to health insurance and retirement, of course, comprise the bulk of an S&E appropriation. This section summarizes some of the other items chargeable to S&E funds as necessary expenses of running the agency.

a. Training

Training of government employees is governed by the Government Employees Training Act, 5 U.S.C. chapter 41. The authority of the Government Employees Training Act is broad, but it is not unlimited. For example, tryouts for the U.S. Olympic Shooting Team do not constitute training under the Act. 68 Comp. Gen. 721 (1989). Nor do routine meetings, however formally structured, qualify as training. 68 Comp. Gen. 606 (1989). See also 68 Comp. Gen. 604 (1989); B-272280, May 29, 1997 (examination expenses that substitute for a college course are covered where the skipped course is part of an approved training program for which the agency would otherwise pay).

For an entity not covered by the definition of "agency" in the Act, the authority to conduct training is limited. The particular training program must be (1) necessary to carry out the purpose for which the appropriation is made, (2) for a period of brief duration, and (3) special in nature. 36 Comp. Gen. 621 (1957) (including extensive citations to earlier decisions). See also 68 Comp. Gen. 127 (1988).

Training of nonfederal personnel, where necessary to the implementation of a federal program, is a straightforward "necessary expense" question under the relevant program appropriation. E.g., 18 Comp. Gen. 842 (1939).

In B-148826, July 23, 1962, the Comptroller General held that the Defense Department could pay $1 each to students participating in a civil defense training course as consideration for a release from liability.

b. Travel

Reimbursement for travel expenses incurred on official travel is now authorized by statute. E.g., 5 U.S.C. § 5702. However, even before the legislation was enacted, expenses incurred on authorized official travel were reimbursable as a necessary expense. 4 Comp. Dec. 475 (1898).

Of course there are limits, and expenses are reimbursable only to the extent authorized by statute and implementing regulations. Thus, in an early case, expenses of a groom and valet incurred by an Army officer in Belgium could not be regarded as necessary travel expenses and therefore could not be reimbursed from Army appropriations. 21 Comp. Dec. 627 (1915).

Senior-level officials frequently travel for political purposes. As the Justice Department has pointed out, it is often impossible to neatly categorize travel as either purely business or purely political. To the extent it is possible to distinguish, appropriated funds should not be used for political travel. 6 Op. Off. Legal Counsel 214 (1982). GAO has conducted occasional reviews in this area, and has commented on the lack of legally binding guidelines against which to evaluate particular expenditures. E.g., U.S. General Accounting Office, Review of White House and Executive Agency Expenditures for Selected Travel, Entertainment, and Personnel Costs, AFMD-81-36 (Washington, D.C.: Mar. 6, 1981); Review of the Propriety of White House and Executive Agency Expenditures for Selected Travel, Entertainment, and Personnel Costs, FGMSD-81-13 (Washington, D.C.: Oct. 20, 1980).

Finally, there are situations in which expenses of congressional travel may be charged to the appropriations of other agencies. Under 31 U.S.C. § 1108(g):

> "Amounts available under law are available for field examinations of appropriation estimates. The use of the amounts is subject only to regulations prescribed by the appropriate standing committees of Congress."

Thus, travel expenses of congressional committee members and staff incident to "field examinations" of appropriation requests may be charged to the agency whose programs and budget are being examined. B-214611, Apr. 17, 1984; B-129650, Jan. 2, 1957. Before the above provision was enacted as permanent legislation, similar provisions had appeared for many years in various appropriation acts. See 6 Comp. Gen. 836 (1927); 23 Comp. Dec. 493 (1917).

Travel expenses of congressional spouses (Members and staff) may not be paid from appropriated funds. B-204877, Nov. 27, 1981.

Federal employees may retain promotional travel benefits, including frequent flyer miles or upgrades, when the benefits are earned as a result of official travel and if the promotional item is obtained under the same terms as those offered the general public and at no additional cost to the government. Pub. L. No. 107-107, div. A, title XI, § 1116, 115 Stat. 1012, 1241 (Dec. 28, 2001).

c. Postage Expenses

Agencies are required to reimburse the Postal Service for mail sent by or to them as penalty mail. Reimbursement is to be made "out of any appropriations or funds available to them." 39 U.S.C. § 3206(a). This statute amounts to an exception to the general purpose statute, 31 U.S.C. § 1301(a), in that the expenditure may be charged to any appropriation available to the agency. Penalty mail costs do not have to be charged to the particular bureau or activity that generated the cost. 33 Comp. Gen. 206 (1953). By virtue of this statutory authority, the use of appropriations for one component of an agency to pay penalty mail costs of another component funded under a separate appropriation does not constitute an unauthorized transfer of appropriations. 33 Comp. Gen. 216 (1953). The same principle applies to reimbursement for registry fees. 36 Comp. Gen. 239 (1956).

d. Books and Periodicals

Expenditures for books and periodicals are evaluated under the necessary expense rule. Thus, the American Battle Monuments Commission could use its Salaries and Expenses (S&E) appropriation to buy books on military leaders to help it decide what people and events to memorialize. 27 Comp. Gen. 746 (1948).

The National Science Foundation could subscribe to a publication called "Supervisory Management" to be used as training material in a supervisory training program under the Government Employees Training Act. If determined necessary to the course, the subscription could be paid from the Foundations S&E appropriation. 39 Comp. Gen. 320 (1959). Similarly, the Interior Department's Mining Enforcement and Safety Administration could subscribe to the "Federal Employees News Digest" if determined to be necessary in carrying out the agency's statutory functions. 55 Comp. Gen. 1076 (1976).

Subsequently, when the Federal Employees News Digest came under some criticism, it became necessary to explain that a decision such as 55 Comp. Gen. 1076 is neither an endorsement of a particular publication nor an exhortation for agencies to buy it. It is merely a determination that the purchase is legally authorized. B-185591, Feb. 7, 1985.

In B-171856, Mar. 3, 1971, the Interior Department was permitted to purchase newspapers to send to a number of Inuit families in Alaska. Members of the families had been transported to

Washington state to help in fighting a huge fire, and the newspapers were seen as necessary to keep the families advised of the status of the operation and also as a measure to encourage future volunteerism.

e. Miscellaneous Items Incident to the Federal Workplace

We have viewed certain civic, charitable, and similar community support activities involving limited use of agency resources and employee time as permissible expenses. For instance, agencies may spend their appropriations, within reason, to cooperate with government-sanctioned charitable fund-raising campaigns, including such things as permitting solicitation during working hours, preparing campaign instructions, and distributing campaign materials. 67 Comp. Gen. 254 (1988) (Combined Federal Campaign). See also B-155667, Jan. 21, 1965; B-154456, Aug. 11, 1964; B-119740, July 29, 1954. Similarly, some use of employee time and agency equipment can occur to carry out limited National Guard and Reserve functions or to assist with adopt-a-school programs. 71 Comp. Gen. 469 (1992); B-277678, Jan. 4, 1999. This authority, however, does not extend to giving T-shirts to Combined Federal Campaign contributors. 70 Comp. Gen. 248 (1991). Also, an agency may not use its appropriations to pay for food at a CFC event unless the agency can present compelling empirical evidence demonstrating that food would likely generate or increase contributions to the CFC. B-325023, July 11, 2014.

An agency may use its general operating appropriations to fund limited amounts of promotional material in support of the United States savings bond campaign. B-225006, June 1, 1987.

Support that agencies are authorized by law to provide to federal credit unions may, if administratively determined to be necessary, include automatic teller machines. 66 Comp. Gen. 356 (1987). The justification was adequate in that case because the facility in question operated on three shifts 7 days a week and the credit union could not remain open to accommodate workers on all shifts.

The Salaries and Expenses appropriation of the Internal Revenue Service (IRS) could be used to procure credit bureau reports if administratively determined to be necessary in connection with investigating applicants for employment with IRS. B-117975, Dec. 29, 1953. However, the Customs and Border Protection's (CBP) Salaries and Expenses appropriation was not available to pay for credit monitoring services for its employees in the New Orleans area who, as a result of Hurricane Katrina, were victims of identity theft. Neither government action nor inaction compromised the employees' identities, and in this case the CBP employees individually, not the government, would be the primary beneficiaries of the proposed credit monitoring, which was considered part of the employees' overall management of their personal finances. B-309604, Oct. 10, 2007.

GAO considered different circumstances in B-310865, Apr. 14, 2008, where the proposed purchase of credit monitoring services related to a data breach caused by government action or inaction that compromised employees' or private citizens' identities. The Nuclear Regulatory Commission (NRC) asked whether, in the event of such a breach, payment for credit monitoring services would be permissible as a cost-effective means of addressing the adverse consequences resulting from the government's mistaken disclosure of an employee's or private citizen's personal information. Recognizing that Congress has required agencies to address breaches and mitigate risks when government action or inaction mistakenly compromises personal information, GAO concluded that the purchase of credit monitoring services for affected individuals would constitute a means of mitigating the risks as long as the agency determined that it was necessary under the particular circumstances.

IRS was authorized to undertake employee counseling and referral programs related to eldercare. The expenditure was justified under 5 U.S.C. § 7901, which authorized "preventative programs related to health." 71 Comp. Gen. 527 (1992).

Outplacement assistance to employees may be regarded as a legitimate matter of agency personnel administration if the expenditures are found to benefit the agency and are reasonable in amount. 68 Comp. Gen. 127 (1988); B-272040, Oct. 29, 1997. The Government Employees Training Act authorizes training in preparation for placement in another federal agency under conditions specified in the statute. 5 U.S.C. § 4103(b). Similarly, employee retirement education and retirement counseling, including individual financial planning for retirement, fall within the legitimate range of an agency's discretion to administer its personnel system and therefore are legitimate agency expenses. B-301721, Jan. 16, 2004.

Payment of an honorarium to an invited guest speaker (other than a government employee) is permissible under a necessary expense rationale. See A-69906, Mar. 16, 1936 (payment of an honorarium by an agency of the District of Columbia government was found to be an allowable administrative expense). See also B-20517, Sept. 24, 1941.

Fees for the notarization of documents are properly payable from appropriated funds where no government notary is available. B-33846, Apr. 27, 1943.

An agency's appropriations are not available to reimburse the Civil Service Retirement Fund for losses due to overpayments to a retired employee resulting from the agency's erroneous processing of information. 54 Comp. Gen. 205 (1974).

The Federal Reserve Board could not match employee contributions to an employee savings plan established by the Board. B-174174, Sept. 24, 1971.

C. Specific Purpose Authorities and Limitations

1. Introduction

This section will explore a number of selected specific topics concerning purpose availability. Our topic selection is designed to highlight certain restrictions; our objective is to describe what is authorized as well as what is unauthorized. Most of the topics are a mixture of both…

[Subsections 2, 3 & 4 redacted]

5. Entertainment--Recreation--Morale and Welfare

a. Introduction

The concept to be explored in this section is the rule that appropriated funds may not be used for entertainment except when specifically authorized by statute and also authorized or approved by proper administrative officers. E.g., 69 Comp. Gen. 197 (1990); 43 Comp. Gen. 305 (1963). The basis for the rule is that entertainment is essentially a personal expense even where it occurs in some business-related context. Except where specifically appropriated for, entertainment cannot normally be said to be necessary to carry out the purposes of an appropriation.

The reader will readily note the sharp distinction between government practice and corporate practice in this regard. "Entertainment" as a business-related expense is an established practice in the corporate sector. No one questions that it can be equally business-related for a government agency. The difference--and the policy underlying the rule for the government--is summarized in the following passage from B-223678, June 5, 1989:

"The theory is not so much that these items can never be business-related, because sometimes they clearly are. Rather, what the decisions are really saying is that, because public confidence in the integrity of those who spend the taxpayers' money is essential, certain items which may appear frivolous or wasteful--however legitimate they may in fact be in a specific context-- should, if they are to be charged to public funds, be authorized specifically by the Congress."

Another way of expressing this idea is found in the following passage from B-288266, Jan. 27, 2003:

"[R]eference to 'common business practice' is not in itself an adequate justification for spending public money on food or, for that matter, other objects. An expenditure of public funds must be anchored in existing law, not the practices and conventions of the private sector."

(1) Application of the rule

As a general proposition, the rule applies to all federal departments and agencies operating with appropriated funds. For example, in 1977 it was held applicable to the Alaska Railroad. B-124195-O.M., Aug. 8, 1977.

The question in B-170938, Oct. 30, 1972, was whether the entertainment prohibition applied to the revolving fund of the National Credit Union Administration. The fund is derived from fees collected from federal credit unions and not from direct appropriations from the Treasury. Nevertheless, the authority to retain and use the collections constitutes a continuing appropriation since, but for that authority, the fees would have to be deposited in the Treasury and Congress would have to make annual appropriations for the agency's expenses. Therefore, the revolving fund could not be used for entertainment.

There are three situations in which the rule has not been applied. The first is certain government corporations. For example, the Corporation for Public Broadcasting, since it was established as a private nonprofit corporation and is not an agency or establishment of the U.S. government (notwithstanding that it receives appropriations), could use its funds to hold a reception in the Cannon House Office Building. B-131935, July 16, 1975.

The rule has also been held not to apply to government corporations that are classed as government agencies but which have statutory authority to determine the character and necessity of their expenditures. B-127949, May 18, 1956 (Saint Lawrence Seaway Development Corporation); B-35062, July 28, 1943. There are limits, however. See, e.g., B-45702, Nov. 22, 1944, disallowing the cost of a "luncheon meeting" of government employees.

The second exception is donated funds where the recipient agency has statutory authority to accept and retain the gift.

The third exception, infrequently applied, is for certain commissions with statutory authority to procure supplies, services, or property, and to make contracts, without regard to the laws and procedures applicable to federal agencies, and to exercise those powers that are necessary to enable the commission to carry out the purposes for which it was established efficiently and in the public interest. B-138969, Apr. 16, 1959 (Lincoln Sesquicentennial Commission); B-138925, Apr. 15, 1959 (Civil War Centennial Commission); B-129102, Oct. 2, 1956 (Woodrow Wilson Foundation).

(2) What is entertainment?

The Comptroller General has not attempted a precise definition of the term "entertainment." In one decision, GAO noted that one court had defined the term as "a source or means of amusement, a diverting performance, especially a public performance, as a concert, drama, or the like." Another court said that entertainment "denotes that which serves for amusement and

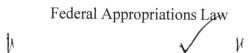

amusement is defined as a pleasurable occupation of the senses, or that which furnishes it, as dancing, sports, or music." 58 Comp. Gen. 202, 205 (1979), overruled on other grounds, 60 Comp. Gen. 303 (1981).

For purposes of this discussion, the term entertainment, as used in decisions of the Comptroller General and Comptroller of the Treasury, is an "umbrella" term that includes: food and drink, either as formal meals or as snacks or refreshments; receptions, banquets, and the like; music, live or recorded; live artistic performances; and recreational facilities. Our treatment includes one other category that, even though not entertainment as such, is closely related to the entertainment cases: facilities for the welfare or morale of employees.

Earlier decisions from time to time had occasion to address the components of entertainment. Can it include liquor? Responding to an inquiry from the Navy, a Comptroller of the Treasury, obviously not a teetotaler, said: "Entertainments ...without wines, liquors or cigars, would be like the play of Hamlet with the melancholy Dane entirely left out of the lines." 14 Comp. Dec. 344, 346 (1907).

In a 1941 decision (B-20085, Sept. 10, 1941), the Coordinator of Inter-American Affairs asked whether authorized entertainment could include such items as cocktail parties, banquets and dinners, theater attendance, and sightseeing parties. The Comptroller General, recognizing that an appropriation for entertainment conferred considerable discretion, replied, in effect, "all of the above."

That's entertainment.

b. Food for Government Employees

It may be stated as a general rule that appropriated funds are not available to pay subsistence or to provide free food to government employees at their official duty stations ("at headquarters") unless specifically authorized by statute. In addition to the obvious reason that food is a personal expense and government salaries are presumed adequate to enable employees to eat regularly, furnishing free food might violate 5 U.S.C. § 5536, which prohibits an employee from receiving compensation in addition to the pay and allowances fixed by law. See, e.g., 68 Comp. Gen. 46, 48 (1988); 42 Comp. Gen. 149, 151 (1962); B-272985, Dec. 30, 1996.

The "free food" rule applies to snacks and refreshments as well as meals. For example, in 47 Comp. Gen. 657 (1968), the Comptroller General held that Internal Revenue Service appropriations were not available to serve coffee to either employees or private individuals at meetings. Similarly prohibited was the purchase of coffeemakers and cups. Although serving coffee or refreshments at meetings may be desirable, it generally is not considered a "necessary expense" in the context of appropriations availability. See also B-233807, Aug. 27, 1990; B-159633, May 20, 1974.

The question of food for government employees arises in many contexts and there are certain well-defined exceptions. For example, the government may pay for the meals of civilian and military personnel in travel status because there is specific statutory authority to do so. The rule and exception are illustrated by 65 Comp. Gen. 16 (1985), in which the question was whether the National Oceanic and Atmospheric Administration could provide in-flight meals, at government expense, to persons on extended flights on government aircraft engaged in weather research. The answer was yes for government personnel in travel status, no for anyone else, including government employees not in official travel status. See also B-256938, Sept. 21, 1995 (because the aircraft and its airbase were determined to be a U.S. Customs aircraft pilot's permanent duty station, the pilot could be reimbursed only for meals purchased incident to duties performed away from the aircraft outside the limits of his official duty station).

While feeding employees may not be regarded as a "necessary expense" as a general proposition, it may qualify when the agency is carrying out some particular statutory function where the necessary relationship can be established. Thus, in B-300826, Mar. 3, 2005, the National Institutes of Health (NIH) could use appropriated funds to provide meals and light refreshments to federal government (as well as nonfederal) attendees and presenters at an NIH-sponsored conference to coordinate and discuss Parkinson's disease research efforts within the scientific community. The conference was held in furtherance of NIH's statutory mission in 42 U.S.C. § 281 to "conduct and support" research with respect to particular diseases, and it was therefore within NIH's authority to pay for all legitimate, reasonable costs of hosting the formal conference. GAO determined that providing meals and refreshments was an allowable conference cost so long as the meals and refreshments were incidental to the conference, attendance at the meals was important to ensure full participation in the conference, and the meals and refreshments were part of a formal conference that included substantial functions occurring separately from when the food is served.

In another case GAO concluded that it was a permissible implementation of a statutory accident prevention program for the Marine Corps to set up rest stations on highways leading to a Marine base to serve coffee and doughnuts to Marines returning from certain holiday weekends. B-201186, Mar. 4, 1982. See also 65 Comp. Gen 738 (1986) (refreshments at awards ceremonies), discussed later in this section. A related example is B-235163.11, Feb. 13, 1996, in which GAO determined that appropriated funds could be used to pay for the dinner of a nonfederal award recipient and her spouse at a National Science Foundation awards ceremony because of the statutory nature of the award. Exceptions of this type illustrate the relativity of the necessary expense doctrine pointed out earlier in our general discussion.

We turn now to a discussion of the rule and its exceptions in several other contexts.

(1) Working at official duty station under unusual conditions

The well-settled rule is that, except in extreme emergencies that are explained below, the government may not furnish free food (the decisions sometimes get technical and use terms like "per diem" or "subsistence") to employees at their official duty station, even when they are working under unusual circumstances.

An early illustration is 16 Comp. Gen. 158 (1936), in which the expense of meals was denied to an Internal Revenue investigator who was required to maintain a 24-hour surveillance. The reason payment was denied is that the investigator would presumably have eaten (and incurred the expense of) three meals a day even if he had not been required to work the 24-hour shift. A similar example is B-272985, Dec. 30, 1996, in which the expense of meals was denied to a Central Intelligence Agency (CIA) security detail while providing 24-hour security to the Director or Deputy Director of the CIA.

Payment was also denied in 42 Comp. Gen. 149 (1962), where a postal official had bought carry-out restaurant food for postal employees conducting an internal election who were required to remain on duty beyond regular working hours.

Similarly, the general rule was applied to deny reimbursement for food in the following situations:

- Federal mediators required to conduct mediation sessions after regular hours. B-169235, Apr. 6, 1970; B-141142, Dec. 15, 1959.

- District of Columbia police officers involved in clean-up work after a fire in a municipal building. B-118638.104, Feb. 5, 1979.

- Geological Survey inspectors at offshore oil rigs who had little alternative than to buy lunch from private caterers at excessive prices. B-194798, Jan. 23, 1980. See also B-202104, July 2, 1981 (Secret Service agents on 24-hour-a-day assignment required to buy meals at high cost hotels).

- Law enforcement personnel retained at staging area for security purposes prior to being dispatched to execute search warrants. B-234813, Nov. 9, 1989.

- Air Force enlisted personnel assigned to a security detail at an off-base social event. B-232112, Mar. 8, 1990.

An exception was permitted in 53 Comp. Gen. 71 (1973). In that case, the unauthorized occupation of a building in which the Bureau of Indian Affairs was located necessitated the assembling of a cadre of General Services Administration special police, who unexpectedly spent the whole night there in alert status until relieved the following morning. Agency officials purchased and brought in sandwiches and coffee for the cadre. GAO concluded that it would not question the agency's determination that the expenditure was incidental to the protection of government property during an extreme emergency involving danger to human life and the destruction of federal property, and approved reimbursement. The decision emphasized, however, that it was an exception and that the rule still stands.

A similar exception was permitted in B-189003, July 5, 1977, where agents of the Federal Bureau of Investigation (FBI) had been forced to remain at their duty stations within the office during a severe blizzard in Buffalo, New York. The area was in a state of emergency and was later declared a national disaster area. GAO agreed with the agency's determination that the situation presented a danger to human life of Buffalo citizens and that it was imperative for FBI employees to maintain the essential functions of the office during the emergency.

The rationale of 53 Comp. Gen. 71 and B-189003 was applied in B-232487, Jan. 26, 1989, for government employees required to work continually for a 24-hour period to evacuate and secure an area threatened by the derailment of a train carrying toxic liquids.

The exception, however, is limited. The requirement to remain on duty for a 24-hour period, standing alone, is not enough. In B-185159, Dec. 10, 1975, for example, the cost of meals was denied to Treasury Department agents required to work over 24 hours investigating a bombing of federal offices. The Comptroller General pointed out that dangerous conditions alone are not enough. Under the exception established in 53 Comp. Gen. 71, it is necessary to find that the situation involves imminent danger to human life or the destruction of federal property. Also, in that case, the agents were only investigating a dangerous situation that had already occurred and there was no suggestion that any further bombings were imminent. A similar case is B-217261, Apr. 1, 1985, involving a Customs Service official required to remain in a motel room for several days on a surveillance assignment. See also 16 Comp. Gen. 158 (1936); B-202104, July 2, 1981.

Short of the emergency situation described in B-189003, July 5, 1977, inclement weather is not enough to support an exception. There are numerous cases in which employees have spent the night in motels rather than returning home in a snowstorm, in order to be able to get to work the following day. Reimbursement for meals has consistently been denied. 68 Comp. Gen. 46 (1988); 64 Comp. Gen. 70 (1984); B-226403, May 19, 1987; B-200779, Aug. 12, 1981; B-188985, Aug. 23, 1977. It makes no difference that the employee was directed by his or her supervisor to rent the room (B-226403 and B-188985), or that the federal government in Washington was shut down (68 Comp. Gen. 46).

Naturally, statutory authority will overcome the prohibition. Thus, where the Veterans Administration (VA) had statutory authority to accept uncompensated services and to contract for related "necessary services," the VA could, upon an administrative determination of necessity, contract with local restaurants for meals to be furnished without charge to uncompensated volunteer workers at VA outpatient clinics when their scheduled assignment extended over a meal period. B-145430, May 9, 1961. Similarly, in B-241708, Sept. 27, 1991, the Comptroller General determined that because the Bureau of Indian Affairs (BIA) hired emergency firefighters under special statutory authority, 43 U.S.C. § 1469, BIA's practice of furnishing hot meals and snack lunches for emergency firefighters was legally permissible. There is also authority to make subsistence payments to law enforcement officials and members of their immediate families when threats to their lives force them to occupy temporary accommodations. 5 U.S.C. § 5706a.

(2) Government Employees Training Act

The Government Employees Training Act (Training Act) authorizes agencies to "pay …for all or a part of the necessary expenses of training," 5 U.S.C. § 4109, and to pay "for expenses of attendance at meetings which are concerned with the functions or activities for which the appropriation is made," 5 U.S.C. § 4110, regardless of whether the event is held within the employees' official duty station. The Comptroller General has interpreted and applied the Training Act to accommodate the day-to-day realities of governmental operations within the limits imposed by the statutes and has determined that the Training Act permits agencies to pay for the costs of meals and refreshments at meetings and training events under specific circumstances, which are outlined below. B-288266, Jan. 27, 2003; B-233807, Aug. 27, 1990.

(a) Attendance at meetings and conferences

This section addresses when the government may pay for meals at meetings and conferences when attendance is authorized under the principles and statutes set forth in section C.2. As the reader will discover from the discussion that follows, there are many authorities available to planners of meetings and conferences for this purpose, and planners should become familiar with them. For day-to-day routine business meetings, our case law has consistently held that the Training Act does not provide authority to use appropriations to supply food items. As our case law demonstrates, agencies appear to struggle with this rule. In this regard, our case law is not static nor inflexible. As recent history demonstrates, GAO is willing to reexamine its case law and to revise, to the extent permitted by law, rules that agency officials believe frustrate efficient, effective, and responsible government. B-288266, Jan. 27, 2003. Any revision, of course, must be founded on sound legal reasoning, and must include appropriate controls to prevent abuses and ensure public confidence in the integrity of those who spend the taxpayers' money.

For meetings sponsored by nongovernment organizations, the attendee will commonly be charged a fee, usually but not necessarily called a registration fee. If a single fee is charged covering both attendance and meals and no separate charge is made for meals, the government may pay the full fee, assuming of course that funds are otherwise available for the cost of attendance. 38 Comp. Gen. 134 (1958); B-249351, May 11, 1993; B-233807, Aug. 27, 1990; B-

66978, Aug. 25, 1947. The same is true for an evening social event where the cost is a mandatory nonseparable element of the registration fee. 66 Comp. Gen. 350 (1987).

If a separate charge is made for meals, the government may pay for the meals if there is a showing that (1) the meals are incidental to the meeting; (2) attendance of the employee at the meals is necessary to full participation in the business of the conference; and (3) the employee is not free to take the meals elsewhere without being absent from essential formal discussions, lectures, or speeches concerning the purpose of the conference. B-233807, Aug. 27, 1990; B-160579, Apr. 26, 1978; B-166560, Feb. 3, 1970. Absent such a showing, the government may not pay for the meals. B-154912, Aug. 26, 1964; B-152924, Dec. 18, 1963; B-95413, June 7, 1950; B-88258, Sept. 19, 1949. As an examination of the cited cases will reveal, these rules apply regardless of whether the conference takes place within the employees duty station area or someplace else.

Where the government is authorized to pay for meals under the above principles, the employee normally cannot be reimbursed for purchasing alternate meals. See B-193504, Aug. 9, 1979; B-186820, Feb. 23, 1978. Personal taste is irrelevant. Thus, an employee who, for example, loathes broccoli will either have to eat it anyway, pay for a substitute meal from his or her own pocket, or go without. For an employee on travel or temporary duty status, which is where this rule usually manifests itself, per diem is reduced by the value of the meals provided. E.g., 60 Comp. Gen. 181, 183-84 (1981). The rule will not apply, however, where the employee is unable to eat the meal provided (and cannot arrange for an acceptable substitute) because of bona fide medical or religious reasons. B-231703, Oct. 31, 1989 (per diem not required to be reduced where employee, an Orthodox Jew who could not obtain kosher meals at conference, purchased substitute meals elsewhere).

The above rules will not apply to day-to-day routine agency-sponsored meetings. GAO has described "day-to-day" business meetings as meetings that involve discussions of the internal procedures or operations of the agency. See 68 Comp. Gen. 604, 605 (1989). Meetings or conferences that are not routine involve topical matters of general interest that might appeal to governmental and nongovernmental participants. Id. Attendance at routine agency-sponsored meetings will generally be subject to the prohibition on furnishing free food to employees at their official duty stations. Thus the cost of meals could not be provided at a conference of field examiners of the National Credit Union Administration. B-180806, Aug. 21, 1974. Use of appropriated funds was prohibited for coffee breaks at a management seminar, B-159633, May 20, 1974; meals served during "working sessions" at Department of Labor business meetings, B-168774, Jan. 23, 1970; and meals at monthly luncheon meetings for officials of law enforcement agencies, B-198882, Mar. 25, 1981. Appropriated funds also could not be used for meals at quarterly managers meetings of the U.S. Army Corps of Engineers, 72 Comp. Gen. 178 (1993), and meals and refreshments served to government employees attending Federal Communication

Commission radio spectrum auctions. B-260692, Jan. 2, 1996. See also 47 Comp. Gen. 657 (1968); B-45702, Nov. 22, 1944.

In B-137999, Dec. 16, 1958, the commissioners of the Outdoor Recreation Resources Review Commission had statutory authority to be reimbursed for actual subsistence expenses. This was held to include the cost of lunches during meetings at a Washington hotel. However, the cost of lunches for staff members of the Commission could not be paid.

Merely calling the cost of meals a "registration fee" will not avoid the prohibition. In a 1975 case, the cost of meals was disallowed for Army employees at an Army-sponsored "Operations and Maintenance Seminar." The charge had been termed a registration fee but covered only luncheons, dinner, and coffee breaks. B-182527, Feb. 12, 1975. See also B-195045, Feb. 8, 1980.

In B-187150, Oct. 14, 1976, grant funds provided to the government of the District of Columbia under the Social Security Act for personnel training and administrative expenses could not be used to pay for a luncheon at a 4-hour conference of officials of the D.C. Department of Human Resources. The conference could not be reasonably characterized as training and did not qualify as an allowable administrative cost under the program regulations.

While 5 U.S.C. § 4110 does not apply to a routine business meeting, in B-281063, Dec. 1, 1999, the Nuclear Regulatory Commission (NRC) could pay an all-inclusive facility rental fee for a meeting to discuss internal matters, even though the fee resulted in food being served to NRC employees at their official duty stations. Because the fee would have remained the same for NRC whether or not it accepted and its employees ate the food, the harm that the general rule is meant to prevent (i.e., expenditure of federal funds on personal items) was not present.

In January 2000, the General Services Administration (GSA) published an amendment to the Federal Travel Regulations to address "conference planning." 41 C.F.R. pts. 301-11 and 301-74, 65 Fed. Reg. 1326 (Jan. 10, 2000). The amendment defined "conference" as "[a] meeting, retreat, seminar, symposium or event that involves attendee travel." The amendment included a provision permitting agencies to pay for light refreshments for agency employees at conferences. 41 C.F.R. § 301-74.11. In agency guidance explaining the regulation, GSA advised agencies that they could use appropriated funds to pay for refreshments for nontravelers at some conferences. In particular, GSA advised that if the majority of the attendees were in travel status, the agency could fund refreshments for all attendees.

In a 2003 decision, GAO explained that GSA's statutory basis for the light refreshment provision is 5 U.S.C. § 5702, which addresses the subsistence expenses of federal employees "when traveling on official business away from the employees designated post of duty"; therefore, while Congress has authorized GSA to prescribe regulations necessary for the administration of travel and subsistence expenses, GSA's authority does not extend to employees who are not in travel status. B-288266, Jan. 27, 2003. Accordingly, GAO held that the light refreshment provision of the travel regulation applies only to federal employees who are in travel status. Id. The decision also clarified that although section 4110 generally applies only to meetings sponsored by nongovernmental organizations, the Comptroller General extended section 4110 to a government-sponsored meeting, regardless of whether an employee is in travel status or not, as long as the meeting satisfies the same conditions as required for nongovernment-sponsored meetings and the government-sponsored meeting is not an internal day-to-day business meeting.

In response to this decision, GSA agreed that its authority extended only to employees in travel status and in its guidance would refer agencies to GAO decisions holding that section 4110 of the Training Act authorizes agencies to provide light refreshments to nontravelers at a government-sponsored meeting as long as the meeting meets the requirements of section 4110 and is not a "day-to-day" or "routine" business meeting. Letter from Raymond J. McNamara, General Counsel, GSA, to Anthony H. Gamboa, General Counsel, GAO, undated, received by GAO June 9, 2003.

In 1980, the President's Committee on Employment of the Handicapped held its annual meeting in the Washington Hilton Hotel. The affair was to last 3 days and included a luncheon and two banquets. There was no registration fee for the meeting but there were charges for the meals. GAO's Equal Employment Opportunity Office planned to send three employees to the meeting and asked whether the agency could pick up the tab for the meals. The three employees were to make a presentation at the meeting and it seemed clear that attendance was authorized under 5 U.S.C. § 4110. Also, if a registration fee were involved, the prior decisions noted above would presumably have answered the question. The Comptroller General reviewed the precedents such as B-160579, Apr. 26, 1978, and B-166560, Feb. 3, 1970, and took the logical step of applying them to the situation at hand. Thus, GAO could pay for the meals if administrative determinations were made that (1) the meals were incidental to the meeting; (2) attendance at the meals was necessary for full participation at the meeting; and (3) the employees would miss essential formal discussions, lectures, or speeches concerning the purpose of the meeting if they took their meals elsewhere. B-198471, May 1, 1980.

This decision, so it seems, became perceived as the loophole through which the lunch wagon could be driven. So apparently compelling is the quest for free food that it became necessary to issue several additional decisions to clarify B-198471 and to explain precisely what the rationale of that decision does and does not authorize.

In 64 Comp. Gen. 406 (1985), the Comptroller General held that the cost of meals could not be reimbursed for employees attending monthly meetings of the Federal Executive Association within their duty station area. The meetings were essentially luncheon meetings at which representatives of various government agencies could discuss matters of mutual interest. The decision stated:

"What distinguishes [B-198471] ...is that the President's annual meeting was a 3-day affair with meals clearly incidental to the overall meeting, while in [the cases in which reimbursement has been denied] the only meetings which took place were the ones which took place during a luncheon meal.... In order to meet the three-part test [of B-198471], a meal must be part of a formal meeting or conference that includes not only functions such as speeches or business carried out during a seating at a meal but also includes substantial functions that take place separate from the meal. [W]e are unwilling to conclude that a meeting which lasts no longer than the meal during which it is conducted qualifies for reimbursement."

Id. at 408 (explanatory information provided).

A similar case the following year, 65 Comp. Gen. 508 (1986), reiterated that the above-quoted test of 64 Comp. Gen. 406 must precede the application of the three-part test of B-198471. The three-part test, and hence the authority to reimburse, relates to a meal that is incident to a meeting, not a meeting that is incident to a meal. 65 Comp. Gen. at 510; 64 Comp. Gen. at 408. See also B-249249, Dec. 17, 1992.

Two 1989 decisions, 68 Comp. Gen. 604 and 68 Comp. Gen. 606, defined the rules further, holding that 5 U.S.C. § 4110 and B-198471 do not apply to purely internal business meetings or conferences sponsored by government agencies. See also 72 Comp. Gen. 178 (1993); B-247563, Dec. 11, 1996; B-270199, Aug. 6, 1996; and B-260692, Jan. 2, 1996. Noting that this result is consistent with the legislative history of 5 U.S.C. § 4110 as summarized in prior decisions, both decisions stated:

"We think ...that there is a clear distinction between the payment of meals incidental to formal conferences or meetings, typically externally organized or sponsored, involving topical matters of general interest to governmental and nongovernmental participants, and internal business or informational meetings primarily involving the day-to-day operations of government. With respect to the latter, 5 U.S.C. § 4110 has little bearing ...."

68 Comp. Gen. at 605 and 608. One of the decisions went a step further and commented that the claim in 65 Comp. Gen. 508 "should have been summarily rejected based on the application of the general rule." 68 Comp. Gen. at 609. Naturally, if the meeting or conference does not have the necessary connection with official agency business, the cost of meals may not be paid regardless of who sponsors the meeting or where it is held. Thus, a registration fee consisting primarily of the cost of a luncheon was disallowed for three Community Services Administration employees attending a Federal Executive Board meeting at which Combined Federal Campaign (CFC) awards were to be presented. B-195045, Feb. 8, 1980. Similarly, an employee of the Department of Housing and Urban Development could not be reimbursed for meals incident to meetings of a local business association. B-166560, May 27, 1969.

In a 1981 case, the Internal Revenue Service bought tickets for several of its agents to attend the Fourth Annual Awards and Scholarship Dinner of the National Association of Black Accountants. The purposes of attending the banquet were to establish contacts for recruitment purposes and to demonstrate the commitment of the IRS to its equal employment opportunity program. However, attendance could not be authorized under either 5 U.S.C. § 4109 or 5 U.S.C. § 4110, and the expenditure was therefore prohibited by 5 U.S.C. § 5946. B-202028, May 14, 1981.

However, in B-249249, Dec. 17, 1992, the Comptroller General held that the Federal Bureau of Investigation (FBI) could reimburse an FBI agent for the cost of a retirement banquet. The agent represented the FBI at the banquet honoring a local police chief and presented him with a plaque and commendation letter from the FBI Director. "The agent's attendance at the function was in furtherance of the agency's functions or activities for which its appropriations were made and the meal was incidental to the retirement ceremony." The Department of Justice, Office of Legal Counsel, applying this decision, stated that "[w]e believe that the Comptroller General's holding was correct and would be applicable to an employee of a United States Attorney's Office attending the same kind of event under like circumstances." 17 Op. Off. Legal Counsel 70 (1993). The Office of Legal Counsel cautioned, however, that the application of the ruling should be carefully limited to where the nature of the ceremonial event "provides good reason to believe that the official or employee's attendance advances the offices authorized functions." Id.

Before we depart the topic of meals at meeting and conferences, two cases involving a different twist--payment for meals not eaten--deserve mention. In B-208729, May 24, 1983, the Army Missile Command sponsored a luncheon to commemorate Dr. Martin Luther King, Jr., that was open to both government employees and members of the local community. Attendees were to be charged a fee for the lunch. In order to secure the necessary services, the Army contracted with a caterer (in this case the local Officers Club), guaranteeing a minimum revenue based on the anticipated number of guests. Bad weather on the day of the luncheon resulted in reduced attendance. Under the circumstances, GAO approved payment of the guaranteed minimum as a program expense.

GAO similarly approved payment of a guaranteed minimum balance in B-230382, Dec. 22, 1989, this time involving the Army's "World-Wide Audio Visual Conference." As in B-208729, attendees were charged for the meal but attendance was less than expected. This case had two additional complications. First, the official who made the arrangements lacked the authority to do so. Payment could therefore be authorized only on a quantum meruit basis. Second, the arrangements also included a buffet, open bar, and several coffee breaks. Payment for these items could not be authorized, even under the quantum meruit concept, since they would not have been authorized had proper procurement procedures been followed.

(b) Training

Under the Government Employees Training Act (Training Act), an agency may pay, or reimburse an employee for, necessary expenses incident to an authorized training program. 5 U.S.C. § 4109. This applies whether the training is held through a nongovernment facility or by the federal government itself. 5 U.S.C. § 4105; B-258442, Apr. 19, 1995; B-244473, Jan. 13, 1992. The event, however, must comply with the Training Act's definition of "training" in 5 U.S.C. § 4101(4). 72 Comp. Gen. 178 (1993). As with meetings, an agency may pay for the costs of meals and refreshments when they are included as an incidental and nonseparable portion of a training registration or attendance fee. 66 Comp. Gen. 350, 1987; B-288266, Jan. 27, 2003. If the cost of the food is not included in a registration or attendance fee, the Comptroller General has held that the government can provide meals or refreshments under this authority if the agency determines that providing meals or refreshments is necessary to achieve the objectives of the training program. 48 Comp. Gen. 185 (1968); 39 Comp. Gen. 119 (1959); B-247966, June 16, 1993; B244473, Jan. 13, 1992; B-193955, Sept. 14, 1979. The government may also furnish meals to nongovernment speakers as an expense of conducting the training. 48 Comp. Gen. 185.

In 50 Comp. Gen. 610 (1971), the Training Act was held to authorize the procurement of catering services for a Department of Agriculture training conference where government facilities were deemed inadequate in view of the nature of the program.

The fact that an agency characterizes its meeting as "training" is not controlling. In other words, for purposes of authorizing the government to feed participants, something does not become training simply because it is called training. In B-168774, Sept. 2, 1970, headquarters employees of the then Department of Health, Education, and Welfare met with consultants in a nearby hotel at what the agency termed a "research training conference." However, the conference consisted of little more than "working sessions" and included no employee training as defined in the Training Act. Therefore, the cost of meals could not be paid. See also 72 Comp. Gen. 178 (1993); 68 Comp. Gen. 606 (1989); B-247563, Dec. 11, 1996; B-208527, Sept. 20, 1983; B-187150, Oct. 14, 1976; B-140912, Nov. 24, 1959.

In 65 Comp. Gen. 143 (1985), GAO held that a Social Security Administration employee who had been invited as a guest speaker at the opening day luncheon of a legitimate agency training conference in the vicinity of her duty station could be reimbursed for the cost of the meal. The decision unfortunately confuses 5 U.S.C. §§ 4109 and 4110 by analyzing the case under section 4110 yet concluding that reimbursement is authorized "as a necessary training expense," which is the standard under section 4109.

(3) Award ceremonies

General operating appropriations may be used to provide refreshments at award ceremonies under the Government Employees' Incentive Awards Act, 5 U.S.C. §§ 4501-4506. 65 Comp.

Gen. 738 (1986); B-271551, Mar. 4, 1997. This Act authorizes an agency to use its operating appropriations to cover the "necessary expense for the honorary recognition of" the employee or employees receiving the awards. 5 U.S.C. § 4503. The Act also directs the Office of Personnel Management to prescribe regulations and instructions to govern agency awards programs. 5 U.S.C. § 4506.

In 65 Comp. Gen. 738, the Social Security Administration asked whether it could use operating appropriations, apart from its limited entertainment appropriation, to provide refreshments at its annual awards ceremony. GAO observed that the Incentive Awards Act (5 U.S.C. § 4503) authorizes agencies to "pay a cash award to, and incur necessary expense for the honorary recognition of" employees. The decision reasoned that the concept of a necessary expense is, within limits, a relative one based on the relationship of the expenditure to the particular appropriation or program involved. Thus, while the necessary relationship does not exist with respect to an agency's day-to-day operations, the agency would be within its legitimate discretion to determine that refreshments would materially enhance the effectiveness of a ceremonial function, specifically in this case an awards ceremony which is a valid component of the agency's statutorily authorized awards program.

The decision essentially followed B-167835, Nov. 18, 1969, which had concluded that the Incentive Awards Act authorized the National Aeronautics and Space Administration to fund part of the cost of a banquet at which the President was to present the Medal of Freedom to the Apollo 11 astronauts. What made the fuller treatment in 65 Comp. Gen. 738 necessary was that a 1974 decision, B-114827, Oct. 2, 1974, had found the cost of refreshments at an awards ceremony under the Incentive Awards Act payable only from specific entertainment appropriations. The 1986 case partially modified B-114827 to the extent it had held that an entertainment appropriation was the only available funding source. Finally, 65 Comp. Gen. 738 distinguished 43 Comp. Gen. 305 (1963), which had disallowed the cost of refreshments at an awards ceremony for persons who were not federal employees (and therefore not authorized under the Incentive Awards Act nor governed by the "necessary expense" language of that statute).

GAO has emphasized that the purpose of awards ceremonies is to foster public recognition of employees' meritorious performance and allow other employees to honor and congratulate their colleagues. 65 Comp. Gen. at 740. In B-247563, Dec. 11, 1996, the Comptroller General determined that the Department of Veterans Affairs Medical Center's use of appropriated funds for a breakfast at which the Medical Center Director presented awards was improper because there was no public recognition of the award recipients. The record indicated that (1) only those employees specifically recognized and the Medical Center Director participated in the event and (2) the employees' contributions were not otherwise publicized within the Medical Center community.

In this same decision, however, the Comptroller General did not find unauthorized the Medical Center's use of its appropriation to purchase light refreshments for an annual picnic and Valentine's Day Dance, at which the agency presented performance award certificates and years of service awards. The Comptroller General found that the Medical Center publicly recognized employees' accomplishments at both events but cautioned that where an agency combines awards receptions with social events, "the expenditures should be subject to greater scrutiny than expenditures made in connection with more traditional awards ceremonies." B-247563, supra.

Recent Comptroller General decisions have permitted appropriated funds to be used to provide meals as well as refreshments at awards ceremonies. For example, in B-270327, Mar. 12, 1997, the Defense Reutilization and Marketing Service (DRMS) was permitted to pay luncheon expenses not to exceed $20 per employee at worldwide DRMS award ceremonies. The Comptroller General explained that Office of Personnel Management (OPM) regulations purposely leave it up to the agencies to design their award programs, and that "we must respect and defer to OPM's regulatory decisions and the implicit delegation of authority to agencies to make implementing decisions vis-à-vis their incentive awards programs so long as such decisions are consistent with the essential requirements of the Act." Id. The Comptroller General found that the $20 per person maximum did not offend any OPM regulatory guidance or express provisions of the Government Employees' Incentive Awards Act. Id. See also B-288536, Nov. 19, 2001 (Bureau of Indian Affairs was permitted to pay for the cost of a buffet luncheon at an incentive awards ceremony).

The Government Employees' Incentive Awards Act does not apply to members of the armed forces. However, the uniformed services have similar authority, including the identical "necessary expense" language, in 10 U.S.C. § 1124. Therefore, 65 Comp. Gen. 738 applies equally to award ceremonies conducted under the authority of 10 U.S.C. § 1124. 65 Comp. Gen. at 739 n.2.

(4) Cafeterias and lunch facilities

The government has no general responsibility to provide luncheon facilities for its employees. 10 Comp. Gen. 140 (1930). However, plans for the construction of a new government building may include provision for a lunch room or cafeteria, in which event the appropriation for construction of the building will be available for the lunch facility. 9 Comp. Gen. 217 (1929).

An agency may subsidize the operation of an employees' cafeteria if the expenditure is administratively determined to be necessary to the efficiency of operations and a significant factor in the hiring and retaining of employees and in promoting employee morale. B-216943, Mar. 21, 1985; B-169141, Nov. 17, 1970; B169141, Mar. 23, 1970. See also B-204214, Jan. 8, 1982 (temporarily providing paper napkins in new government cafeteria); U.S. General Accounting Office, Benefits GSA Provides by Operating Cafeterias in Washington, D.C., Federal Buildings, LCD-78-316 (Washington, D.C.: May 5, 1978).

The purchase of equipment for use in other than an established cafeteria may also be authorized when the agency determines that the primary benefit of its use accrues to the agency by serving a valid operational purpose, such as providing for an efficient working environment or meeting health needs of employees, notwithstanding a collateral benefit to the employees. In B-302993, June 25, 2004, GAO approved the purchase of kitchen appliances, ordinarily considered to be personal in nature, for common use by employees in an agency facility. The appliances included refrigerators, microwaves, and commercial coffee makers. The agency demonstrated that equipping the workplace with these appliances was reasonably related to the efficient performance of agency activities and provided other benefits to the agency, including the assurance of a safe workplace. GAO also advised the agency that it should establish policies for uniform procurement and use of such equipment. In developing a policy, the agency should address the ongoing need for specific equipment throughout the building, the amount of the agency's appropriation budgeted for this purpose, price limitations placed on the equipment purchases, and whether the equipment should be purchased centrally or by individual units within headquarters. It is important that the policy ensure that appropriations are not used to provide any equipment for the sole use of an individual, and that the agency locate refrigerators, microwaves, and coffee makers acquired with appropriated funds only in common areas where they are available for use by all personnel. It should also be clear that appropriated funds will not be used to furnish goods, such as the coffee itself or microwaveable frozen foods, to be used in the kitchen area. These remain costs each employee is expected to bear.

The decision in B-302993, June 25, 2004, represented a departure from earlier cases which permitted such purchases under more restrictive circumstances where the agency could identify a specific need:

- B-180272, July 23, 1974: purchase of a sink and refrigerator to provide lunch facilities for the Occupational Safety and Health Review Commission where there was no government cafeteria on the premises.

- B-210433, Apr. 15, 1983: purchase of microwave oven by Navy facility to replace nonworking stove. Facility was in operation 7 days a week, some employees had to remain at their duty stations for 24-hour shifts, and there were no readily accessible eating facilities in the area during nights and weekends.

- B-276601, June 26, 1997: purchase of a refrigerator for personal food items of Central Intelligence Agency (CIA) employees. CIA headquarters facility was relatively distant from private eating establishments, the CIA did not permit delivery service to enter the facility due to security concerns, and the cafeteria served only breakfast and lunch.

- B-173149, Aug. 10. 1971: purchase of a set of stainless steel cooking utensils for use by air traffic controllers to prepare food at a flight service station where there were no other readily accessible eating facilities and the employees were required to remain at their post of duty for a full 8-hour shift. But see B-326021, Dec. 23, 2014 (appropriations not available to purchase disposable cups, plates, and cutlery for employee use where the agency did not demonstrate that provision of the items directly advanced its statutory mission or that the benefit accruing to the government through the provision of such items outweighed the personal nature of the expense).

c. Entertainment for Government Employees Other Than Food

(1) Miscellaneous cases

There have been relatively few cases in this area, probably because there are few situations in which entertainment for government employees could conceivably be authorized.An early decision held that 10 U.S.C. § 4302, which authorizes training for Army enlisted personnel "to increase their military efficiency and to enable them to return to civilian life better equipped for industrial, commercial, and business occupations," did not include sending faculty members and students of the Army Music School to grand opera and symphony concerts. 4 Comp. Gen. 169 (1924). Another decision found it improper to hire a boat and crew to send federal employees stationed in the Middle East on a recreational trip to the Red Sea. B-126374, Feb. 14, 1956.

A 1970 decision deserves brief mention although its application will be extremely limited. Legislation in 1966 established the Wolf Trap Farm Park in Fairfax County, Virginia, as a park for the performing arts and directed the Interior Department to operate and maintain it. A certifying officer of the National Park Service asked whether he could certify a voucher for symphony, ballet, and theater tickets for Wolf Trap's Artistic Director. The Comptroller General held that such payments could be made if an appropriate Park Service official determined that attendance was necessary for the performance of the Artistic Directors official duties. The justification was that the Artistic Director attended these functions not as personal entertainment but so that he could review the performances to determine which cultural and theatrical events were appropriate for booking at Wolf Trap. B-168149, Feb. 3, 1970. As noted, this case would seem to have little precedent value except for the Artistic Director at Wolf Trap.

(2) Cultural awareness programs

One area that has generated several decisions, and a change in GAO's position, has been equal employment opportunity special emphasis or cultural awareness programs. There are many areas in which the law undergoes refinement from time to time but remains essentially unchanged. There are other areas in which the law has changed to reflect changes in American society. This is one of those latter areas.

The issue first arose in 58 Comp. Gen. 202 (1979). In that case, the Bureau of Mines, Interior Department, in conjunction with the Equal Employment Opportunity Commission, sponsored a

program of live entertainment for National Hispanic Heritage Week. The program consisted of such items as a lecture and demonstration of South American folk music, a concert, a slide presentation, and an exhibit of Hispanic art and ceramics. The decision concluded that, while the Bureau's Spanish-Speaking Program was a legitimate component of the agency's overall Equal Employment Opportunity (EEO) program, appropriated funds could not be used to procure entertainment. This holding was followed in two more cases, B-194433, July 18, 1979, and B-199387, Aug. 22, 1980.

In 1981, however, GAO reconsidered its position. The Internal Revenue Service asked whether it could certify a voucher covering payments for a performance by an African dance troupe and lunches for guest speakers at a ceremony observing National Black History Month. The Comptroller General held the expenditure proper in 60 Comp. Gen. 303 (1981). The decision stated:

"[W]e now take the view that we will consider a live artistic performance as an authorized part of an agency's EEO effort if, as in this case, it is part of a formal program determined by the agency to be intended to advance EEO objectives, and consists of a number of different types of presentations designed to promote EEO training objectives of making the audience aware of the culture or ethnic history being celebrated."

Id. at 306. Further, the lunches for the guest speakers could be paid under 5 U.S.C. § 5703 if they were in fact away from their homes or regular places of business. The prior inconsistent decisions--58 Comp. Gen. 202, B-194433, and B-199387--were overruled.

It should be emphasized that the prior decisions were overruled only to the extent inconsistent with the new holding. Two specific elements of 58 Comp. Gen. 202 were not involved in the 1981 decision and remain valid. First, use of appropriated funds to serve meals or refreshments remains:improper except under specific statutory authority. 58 Comp. Gen. at 206. Second, 58 Comp. Gen. 202 found the purchase of commercial insurance on art objects improper. Id. at 207. This portion also remains valid. The Comptroller General also determined that transportation costs of an employee participating in a cultural program are not authorized unless the employee is participating in the program as a performer or making some other type of direct contribution to the EEO event. B-243862, July 28, 1992.

The decision at 60 Comp. Gen. 303 was expanded in B-199387, Mar. 23, 1982, to include small "samples" of ethnic foods prepared and served during a formal ethnic awareness program as part of the agency's equal employment opportunity program. In the particular program being considered, the attendees were to pay for their own lunches, with the ethnic food samples of minimal proportion provided as a separate event. Thus, the samples could be distinguished from meals or refreshments, which remain unauthorized. (The decision did not specify how many "samples" an individual might consume in order to develop a fuller appreciation.) Compare that situation to the facts in B-301184, Jan. 15, 2004, where GAO found that the U.S. Army Corps of

Engineers' appropriation was not available to pay for the costs of food offered at the Corps' North Atlantic Division's February 2003 Black History Month program. The evidence in the record, including the time of the program, the food items served, and the amounts available, indicated that a meal, not a sampling of food, was offered.

In 1999, the Comptroller General clarified that 60 Comp. Gen. 303 does not require that a program or event have specific advance written approval in a formal agency issuance to be considered a formal Equal Employment Opportunity program for which funds are available. "What is required is that the agency through an authorized official determines that the planned performance advances EEO objectives." B-278805, July 21, 1999.

Although 60 Comp. Gen. 303 was not cast in precisely these terms, it is another example of the "theory of relativity" in purpose availability. Equality in all aspects of federal employment is now a legal mandate. An agency is certainly within its discretion to determine that fostering racial and ethnic awareness is a valid--perhaps indispensable--means of advancing this objective. This being the case, it is not at all far-fetched to conclude that certain expenditures that might be wholly inappropriate in other contexts could reasonably relate to this purpose. Thus, hiring an African dance troupe could not be justified to further an objective of, for example, conducting a financial audit or constructing a building or procuring a tank, but the relationship changes when the objective is promoting cultural awareness.

Once the concept of the preceding paragraph is understood, it should be apparent why, in 64 Comp. Gen. 802 (1985), GAO distinguished the cultural awareness cases and concluded that the Army could not use appropriated funds to provide free meals for handicapped employees attending a luncheon in honor of National Employ the Handicapped Week. This is not to say that an agency's EEO program should not embrace the handicapped--on the contrary, it can, should, and is required to--but merely that "[u]nlike ethnic and cultural minorities, handicapped persons do not possess a common cultural heritage" within the intended scope of the cultural awareness cases. Id. at 804 (quoting from the request for decision).

13. Personal Expenses and Furnishings

a. Introduction

Items that are classified as personal expenses or personal furnishings may not be purchased with appropriated funds without specific statutory authority. Most of the cases tend to involve government employees, the theory being simply that there are certain things an employee is expected to provide for him(her)self. A prime example is food.

The rule on personal expenses and furnishings was stated as follows in 3 Comp. Gen. 433 (1924):

"[P]ersonal furnishings are not authorized to be purchased under appropriations in the absence of specific provision therefor contained in such appropriations or other acts, if such furnishings are for the personal convenience, comfort, or protection of such employees, or are such as to be reasonably required as a part of the usual and necessary equipment for the work on which they are engaged or for which they are employed."

This decision is still cited frequently and the rule is applied in many contexts. Of course, over the years, exceptions have evolved, both statutory and nonstatutory. The remainder of this section explores several categories of personal expenses.

b. Business or Calling Cards

Business cards or calling cards are commonly used in the commercial world. (We use the terms synonymously here even though there may be technical distinctions.) Until 1998, we considered them inherently personal in nature, and therefore, a personal expense that was not payable from appropriated funds, absent specific statutory authority. See B-246616, July 17, 1992. In 1998, however, we agreed that an agency, applying a necessary expense analysis, may reasonably determine that its appropriations are available to obtain business cards for employees who regularly deal with the public or organizations outside their immediate office. B-280759, Nov. 5, 1998.

The previous rule had its origins in decisions of the Comptroller of the Treasury. For example, in 20 Comp. Dec. 248 (1913), the Comptroller of the Treasury considered the argument that was usually presented in every case--that the cards were to be used for official business purposes. Nonetheless, business or calling cards were considered more a matter of personal convenience than necessity. Therefore, the Comptroller advised federal agencies that the cost of business cards is a personal expense and, therefore, is not chargeable to public funds.

In more recent years, the Comptroller General applied the long-standing prohibition of the use of appropriated funds for: reimbursement of an employee of the National Highway Traffic Safety Administration who had purchased business cards at his own expense (B-195036, July 11, 1979); purchase of a Forest Service public affairs officer's "identification cards," since the cards were to be used for the same purposes as traditional business cards (68 Comp. Gen. 467 (1989)); and payment for "cards of introduction" (B-149151, July 20, 1962).

In 1998, GAO re-examined the prohibition. In B-280759, Nov. 5, 1998, GAO did not object to the use of Operation and Maintenance (O&M) funds for the purchase of business cards for use by civilian personnel specialists of the Army Civilian Personnel Advisory Center. The Advisory Center acts as a liaison between Army employing units and their employees, and provides advice and assistance to employers and employees. The specialists would use the business cards to provide the Center's customers with accurate information on how to contact the specialist assigned to a customer's case. Applying a necessary expense analysis, we concluded that business cards would advance the Center's mission, and that use of the Army's O&M appropriation (which funds the Center's activities) to purchase business cards for the specialists was proper. See also Memorandum from Richard L. Shiffrin, Deputy Assistant Attorney General, Office of Legal Counsel, Department of Justice, to Emily C. Hewitt, General Counsel, General Services Administration, Aug. 11, 1997.

We have considered the cost of business or calling cards for Members of Congress and their staff who require them a necessary and justifiable expense, given the nature of Members' constituent responsibilities. See B-198419, Nov. 25, 1980; B-198419, July 8, 1980.

Also, we have considered reception and representation (or comparable forms of "entertainment") appropriations to be available to purchase business cards for employees whose jobs included representation. B-223678, June 5, 1989 (noting that business cards are a "legitimate and accepted" representation device, so the expenditure is subject to the limitation of that appropriation). See also 72 Comp. Gen. 146 (1993); 68 Comp. Gen. 467, 468 n.1 (1989); B-246616, July 17, 1992).

We considered a variation on business cards in B-173239, June 15, 1978. The Board for International Broadcasting wanted to use what it termed "transmittal slips" to accompany the distribution of its annual report. The transmittal slip resembled a business card and contained the words "With the compliments of (name and title), Board for International Broadcasting." It was not necessary to decide whether the "slips" were business cards or not, because 44 U.S.C. § 1106 expressly provides that documents distributed by an executive department or independent establishment may not contain or include a notice that they are being sent with "the compliments" of a government official. Use of the transmittal slips was therefore unauthorized.

Also, "name tags" to be worn on the person were not considered the same as business cards and could be provided from appropriated funds. B-236763, Jan. 10, 1990. A name tag is more closely analogous to a government identification card, which is clearly not a personal expense. 2 Comp. Gen. 429 (1923). See also 11 Comp. Gen. 247 (1931) (identification insignia to be worn on caps).

c. Health, Medical Care and Treatment

(1) Medical care

The rule for medical care is that, except for illness directly resulting from the nature of the employment, medical care and treatment are personal to the employee and payment may not be made from appropriated funds unless provided for in a contract of employment or by statute or valid regulation. 57 Comp. Gen. 62 (1977); 53 Comp. Gen. 230 (1973). The case most frequently cited for this rule is 22 Comp. Gen. 32 (1942), which contains citations to many of the earlier decisions.

Exceptions have been recognized where a particular item could be justified as being primarily for the benefit of the government rather than the employees. The exceptions involve primarily physical examinations and inoculation. For example, appropriated funds were held available in the following cases:

- 41 Comp. Gen. 387 (1961) (desensitization treatment for a Department of Agriculture horticulturist with a known history of severe reaction to bee and wasp stings).

- 23 Comp. Gen. 888 (1944) (purchase of drugs and their administration by private doctor to employees exposed to spinal meningitis in line of duty; otherwise, agency would have risked having to quarantine the employees and close the facility).

- B-108693, Apr. 8, 1952 (X-rays for Weather Bureau personnel being assigned to Alaska, presumably necessitated by a high incidence of tuberculosis among Eskimos).

By virtue of legislation enacted in 1946 and now found at 5 U.S.C. § 7901, each agency is authorized to establish a health service program to promote and maintain the physical and mental fitness of employees under its jurisdiction. The statute expressly limits authorized health service programs to (1) treatment of on-the-job illness and dental conditions requiring emergency attention; (2) pre-employment and other examinations; (3) referral of employees to private physicians and dentists; and (4) preventive programs relating to health.

Under this legislative authority, the Comptroller General advised, for example, that an agency could, upon determining that it will be in the government's interest to do so, provide immunization against specific diseases without charge to employees. 47 Comp. Gen. 54 (1967).

In 57 Comp. Gen. 62 (1977), the Comptroller General held that the Environmental Protection Agency was authorized by 5 U.S.C. § 7901 to procure diagnostic and preventive psychological counseling services for its employees. The service could encompass problem identification, referral for treatment or rehabilitation to an appropriate service or resource, and follow-up to help an employee readjust to the job during and after treatment, but could not include the actual treatment and rehabilitation. Actual treatment and rehabilitation remain the employee's responsibility.

In B-270446, Feb. 11, 1997, provision of psychological assessment and referral services for Customs Service employees' family members was determined to be for the benefit of the government and, therefore, permitted under 5 U.S.C. § 7901. The Service's Employee Assistance Program may render these services for family members adversely affected by work-related activities of, or traumatic incidents involving death or serious injury to, an employee in the line of duty carrying out the agency's law enforcement activities. Cf. 71 Comp. Gen. 527 (1992) (a federal agency may not use appropriated funds to provide space for eldercare facilities for the adult relatives of agency employees, but may provide employee referral and counseling programs).

In B-198804, Dec. 31, 1980, GAO refused to expand the holding in 57 Comp. Gen. 62 to permit an agency to pay the expenses of alcoholism treatment and rehabilitation for one of its employees. Treatment and rehabilitation, as stressed in 57 Comp. Gen. 62, are the employee's responsibility. It made no difference that the employee had been erroneously advised that the expenses would be covered by her health insurance and had already incurred the expenses, since the government cannot be bound by the unauthorized acts or representations of its agents.

Federal agencies are authorized under 5 U.S.C. § 7901 to establish smoking cessation programs for their employees, and may use their operating appropriations to pay the costs. 68 Comp. Gen. 222 (1989). In light of the body of evidence of the health hazards of smoking, the decision reasoned, programs to help employees quit smoking are clearly "preventive programs relating to health" for purposes of the statute.

Physical fitness programs may qualify as preventive health programs under 5 U.S.C. § 7901 to the extent permissible under applicable regulations such as Office of Management and Budget Circulars, the Federal Personnel Manual, and regulations of the General Services Administration. In addition, it may be possible to justify some programs under the necessary expense concept without the need to invoke the statute. For example, in 63 Comp. Gen. 296 (1984), GAO applied the necessary expense doctrine to conclude that Bureau of Reclamation funds were available for physical exercise equipment to be used in a mandatory physical fitness program for firefighters.

In 64 Comp. Gen. 835 (1985), GAO considered the scope of a permissible fitness program under section 7901, concluding that a program could include comprehensive physical fitness evaluations and laboratory blood tests. Based on the statute alone, it could also include physical exercise. However, regulations then in effect precluded use of appropriated funds for physical exercise as part of a health service program. The decision further noted, as 63 Comp. Gen. 296 had held, that physical exercise costs incident to a mandatory program necessitated by the demands of designated positions could be paid as a necessary expense without the need to rely on 5 U.S.C. § 7901. See also B-216852-O.M., Mar. 6, 1985 (discussing GAO's own authority to establish a fitness program); B-216852, Dec. 17, 1984 (nondecision letter).

Subsequent to 64 Comp. Gen. 835, the Office of Personnel Management revised its regulations to include physical fitness programs and facilities as permissible preventive health services. Based on the revised regulations, an agency may now use appropriated funds to provide access to a private fitness center's exercise facilities, although both GAO and OPM caution that expenditures of this type should be carefully monitored and should be undertaken only where all other resources have been considered and rejected. 70 Comp. Gen. 190 (1991). However, appropriated funds are not authorized for payment of: (1) employees' membership fees to a contracted private fitness center in advance of employees' use of facilities (B-288013, Dec. 11,

2001); or (2) registration fees for employee members of an agency's on-site fitness center to participate in local competitive fitness or sports activities. Participation in such events is generally a personal activity, not an essential part of a government-sponsored preventive health program. 73 Comp. Gen. 169 (1994).

Medical treatment not within the scope of 5 U.S.C. § 7901 remains subject to the general rule expressed in cases such as 22 Comp. Gen. 32. Thus, the cost of an ambulance called by an agency medical officer to take an employee to a hospital could not be paid from appropriated funds. B-160272, Nov. 14, 1966. (This is the kind of expense that can be covered by employee health insurance plans.) In another case, GAO rejected the contention that medical expenses are automatically "necessary expenses," and concluded that Internal Revenue Service (IRS) appropriations were not available to reimburse the State Department for medical services provided to IRS overseas employees and their dependents under the Foreign Service Act of 1946. 53 Comp. Gen. 230 (1973). The decision noted that several other agencies had received specific statutory authority to participate in the program.

A review of the decisions involving medical examinations will further illustrate the relationship of 5 U.S.C. § 7901 to the decisional rules. Prior to the enactment of section 7901, a pre-employment physical examination, the purpose of which was to determine an applicant's eligibility for a federal job, was the applicant's responsibility and was not chargeable to appropriated funds. 22 Comp. Gen. 243 (1942).

Applying the "primary benefit of the government" standard, however, the Comptroller General found post-employment examinations permissible in certain situations. Thus, in 22 Comp. Gen. 32 (1942), GAO told the Army that it could use its appropriations to provide periodic physical examinations to detect arsenic poisoning in civilian workers in a chemical warfare laboratory. The decision noted that instances of arsenic poisoning "might have a depressing effect on the morale of fellow workers" and might make it more difficult to find qualified people to do the work. In another case, a civilian employee joined the Army during World War II. He received a medical discharge, and thereafter applied for reinstatement to his former civilian job. GAO advised that the agency could pay for a physical examination which it required prior to reinstatement. 23 Comp. Gen. 746 (1944).

In 1946, 5 U.S.C. § 7901 was enacted. Now, agencies have specific authority to include medical examinations, including pre-employment examinations, without charge to applicants, in the health programs they are authorized to establish. 30 Comp. Gen. 493 (1951). While the statute authorizes establishment of government programs, it does not authorize the reimbursement of privately incurred expenses. Thus, an applicant who declines to use an available government doctor for a pre-employment examination and instead chooses to have it performed by a private doctor may not be reimbursed. 31 Comp. Gen. 465 (1952).

In situations not covered by the statute, the "primary benefit of the government" test continues to apply. Thus, based on the earlier precedents, the cost of medical examinations by private physicians was approved in the following cases:

- 30 Comp. Gen. 387 (1951) (physical examinations of Department of Agriculture employees engaged in testing repellents and insecticides for use by the armed forces; no government medical facilities available).

- 41 Comp. Gen. 531 (1962) (annual physical examinations for Saint Lawrence Seaway Development Corporation employees engaged in strenuous physical work, often under severe weather conditions; no public health facilities in area).

The examinations in both of the above cases could have been included in an authorized health service program. As noted, however, facilities were not available in either case. Thus, since the examinations were for the primary benefit of the government, appropriated funds were available to have them performed by private physicians. See also 73 Comp. Gen. 219 (1994) (National Transportation Safety Board could reimburse air safety investigators for the costs of physical exams required to obtain a Federal Aviation Administration (FAA) medical certificate if the agency's public health facility has no FAA-certified physician); B-286137, Feb. 21, 2001 (U.S. Geological Survey could pay for eye examinations for employees whose work requires visual acuity, but may not pay for their prescription eyeglasses, which are personal and useful to employees who need them inside, as well as outside, the workplace).

In 65 Comp. Gen. 677 (1986), the Navy could pay for a medical examination required for a private individual joining a government research exercise under invitational travel orders. Although government medical facilities were presumably available, there was no need to note this fact in the decision. Since the individual was neither a government employee nor an applicant for a government job, she could not be required to use the government facility and, since the Navy wanted her participation, it could not very well expect her to bear the expense.

Conversely, in B-253159, Nov. 22, 1993, the costs of medical examinations performed by private physicians for two Centers for Disease Control and Prevention employees and their dependents were not reimbursable because the examinations were neither required by the agency nor for the benefit of the government. The two employees and their dependents obtained the examinations in preparation for their relocation to assignments outside the United States. See also A. Carter, Jr., GSBCA No. 15435, 01-1 B.C.A. ¶ 31,404 (Apr. 9, 2001) (Department of Defense should reimburse its civilian employee for dependents' immunizations, and may reimburse him for dependents' physical examinations (both required to obtain return visas to the United States), if the Navy determines that the examinations were primarily for the benefit of the government).

(2) Purchase of health-related items

The purchase of health-related items, while conceptually related to the medical care cases, is also an application of the "personal expense" rule set forth in 3 Comp. Gen. 433, cited at the beginning of this section, that personal equipment needed to qualify an employee to perform the regular duties of his or her position may not be paid from appropriated funds. The rule is illustrated in B-187246, June 15, 1977. There, a Community Services Administration employee's doctor had placed him under certain restrictions because of a back injury. Specifically, he was to use a "sacro-ease positioner" for his office chair and could drive cars only with a minimum 116-inch wheel base, bucket seats, and full power. While the equipment may have been necessary for that particular individual to perform his duties, it was not essential to the transaction of official business from the government's standpoint. Therefore, the items could not be provided from appropriated funds.

In B-166411, Sept. 3, 1975, an employee who, as a result of a back injury, needed a bedboard while traveling could not be reimbursed beyond the normal per diem. The bedboard was a personal expense. Similarly, gratuities for wheelchair services while traveling were held nonreimbursable in B-151701, July 3, 1963.

A different type of situation arose in B-215640, Jan. 14, 1985. An agency asked whether it could purchase a heavy-duty office chair for an employee who needed extra physical support because he weighed over 300 pounds and had broken 15 regular chairs. While the particular type of chair in question was necessitated by the employee's physical condition, it is nevertheless the case that an office chair is not "personal equipment" but is an item the government is normally expected to provide for its employees. The purchase was therefore authorized.

Another exception occurred in 23 Comp. Gen. 831 (1944). There, GAO approved the rental of an amplifying device to be attached to an official telephone for use by an employee with a hearing handicap. The device was seen as a means of obtaining the best results from available personnel. The precedent value of this decision is somewhat speculative. On the one hand, the device would not become the property of the individual. Yet on the other hand, the decision seems to have been based largely on the difficulty of hiring "qualified" employees in view of the wartime draft situation. (Whether consideration was given to hiring women is not mentioned.)

Generally, however, exceptions stem from some statutory basis. Thus, in 56 Comp. Gen. 398 (1977), the Comptroller General approved the purchase of a motorized wheelchair for use by a Social Security Administration employee. The decision emphasized that a wheelchair is normally the employee's personal expense. In this case, however, the employee had his own nonpowered wheelchair and needed a motorized wheelchair only because the agency had not complied with the Architectural Barriers Act of 1968. The wheelchair would, of course, become the property of the government and was approved only as a temporary expedient pending compliance with the statute.

One important statute in this regard is the Rehabilitation Act of 1973, 29 U.S.C. § 791. Pursuant to the Rehabilitation Act, federal agencies are required to make "reasonable accommodations" for the known physical or mental limitations of qualified employees with disabilities. See 29 C.F.R. §§ 1614.203(b), 1630.9(a). We discuss the Rehabilitation Act in the next section.

Health-related items may also be authorized as "special protective equipment" under 5 U.S.C. § 7903. Thus, prescription ground safety glasses may be purchased for employees engaged in hazardous duties. The glasses become and remain the property of the government. The government can also pay the cost of related eye refraction examinations in limited circumstances. 51 Comp. Gen. 775 (1972).

Relying on 3 Comp. Gen. 433 rather than 5 U.S.C. § 7903, GAO, in 45 Comp. Gen. 215 (1965), approved the purchase of special prescription filter spectacles and clinical eye examinations necessary to obtain the proper prescription for employees operating stereoscopic map plotting instruments. Employees who did not use special glasses frequently lost the required visual skills before reaching the normal retirement age. Also, the special glasses would be of no personal use to the employees except during working hours and would remain the property of the government. However, the purchase of eyeglasses for employees who work at video display terminals is not authorized. There is no applicable safety standard in the Occupational Safety and Health Act, 29 U.S.C. §§ 651-678, the work is not (or at least has not yet been found to be) hazardous to the eyes if proper care is used, and not all employees who work at terminals need eyeglasses. 63 Comp. Gen. 278 (1984). See also B-286137, Feb. 21, 2001 (U.S. Geological Survey may use appropriated funds to provide eye examinations for certain employees for the benefit of the government, but it may not provide these employees with prescription eyeglasses that would not be for exclusive use at work).

The 1980s saw a veritable flood of cases involving the purchase of air purifiers ("smokeeaters") as the campaign against smoking became a cause celebre. The rules, distilled from several decisions, are as follows:

- Appropriated funds are not available to purchase air purifiers for the private office of an employee who objects to tobacco smoke unless the employee's hypersensitivity to smoke qualifies him or her as handicapped under the Rehabilitation Act of 1973.

- Air purifiers may be purchased for "common areas" such as reading rooms.

- Air purifiers may be placed on the desks of employees who smoke if they will provide a general benefit to all employees working in the area.

In 2002, consistent with Executive Order No. 13058, Protecting Federal Employees and the Public From Exposure to Tobacco Smoke in the Federal Workplace, 62 Fed. Reg. 43,451 (Aug.

9, 1997), the General Services Administration prohibited the smoking of tobacco products in all interior space owned, rented, or leased by the executive branch, and in any outdoor areas under executive branch control in front of air intake ducts. 41 C.F.R. § 102-74.315.Another related line of decisions addresses the purchase of bottled drinking water for use in federal work facilities where the safety of municipal or locally provided water is at issue. Generally, appropriated funds are not available to pay for bottled water for the personal use of employees. GAO has made an exception where a building's water supply is unhealthy or unpotable. See, for example, B-247871, Apr. 10, 1992, where a problem with the water supply system in a building caused lead content to exceed the maximum contaminant level and justified the purchase of bottled water for employees until the problems with the system could be resolved.

(3) The Rehabilitation Act

The Rehabilitation Act of 1973, as amended, 29 U.S.C. §§ 701-797, establishes a federal policy in support of nondiscriminatory employment of individuals with a disability. Consistent with that policy, the federal government, its contractors, and federally funded entities are prohibited from discriminating against employees who have physical or mental impairments that substantially limit one or more major life activities but who can perform the essential functions of the position they hold (or apply for), with or without reasonable accommodation. 29 U.S.C. § 791; 29 C.F.R. §§ 1614.203, 1630(2).

The Rehabilitation Act requires federal agencies to assume an affirmative leadership role in promoting the employment of qualified handicapped individuals. 29 U.S.C. § 791(b); see also 29 U.S.C. § 701(b)(2).The Rehabilitation Act is related to the probably better known Americans With Disabilities Act (ADA) of 1990, Pub. L. No. 101-336, title I, § 101, 104 Stat. 330 (July 26, 1990), codified at 42 U.S.C. §§ 12101 et seq. Although the ADA does not apply to federal employers [42 U.S.C. § 12111(5)(B)(i); 29 C.F.R. § 1630.2(e)(2)(i)], the ADA's standards are used to determine whether agencies are in compliance with the Rehabilitation Act's requirements for employment of qualified individuals with disabilities. 29 U.S.C. § 791(g). Under Equal Employment Opportunity regulations, federal agencies are required to make "reasonable accommodations" for the known physical or mental limitations of qualified employees with disabilities, unless the accommodation(s) would impose an undue hardship on the agency's program. 29 C.F.R. §§ 1630.9(a), 1614.203(b). See B-291208, Apr. 9, 2003; B-243300, Sept. 17, 1991.

While GAO has no jurisdiction over substantive claims brought against federal agencies under the Rehabilitation Act, we have responded to agency inquiries concerning the propriety of using appropriated funds for expenditures or informal settlement awards under the Act. See 72 Comp. Gen. 111 (1993); 69 Comp. Gen. 470 (1990). Questions occasionally arise concerning whether an agency's provision of a proposed, or requested, accommodation complies with federal appropriations principles (see, e.g., B-240271, Oct. 15, 1990); whether an expense claimed by an employee is reimbursable or must be borne by the employee (see, e.g., 68 Comp. Gen. 242

(1989)); or whether an item or service may appropriately be provided under the Rehabilitation Act as a reasonable accommodation, even though not initially viewed as such (see, e.g., B-291208, Apr. 9, 2003). We discuss these three decisions, and others, below.

In addressing these questions, we recognize that agencies may expend appropriated funds to accomplish the purposes of the Rehabilitation Act when acting under the Act's authority and the regulatory standards that govern its application. B-240271, Oct. 15, 1990. An expenditure that might be viewed as personal in nature but for the Rehabilitation Act is a proper use of an agency's appropriation when incurred in satisfaction of the Act's requirements.

Thus, in B-240271, supra, GAO advised that the purchase of a motorized wheelchair for a quadriplegic employee who spent half of his time on official travel could be regarded as a "reasonable accommodation" under 29 C.F.R. § 1630.9, on condition that the wheelchair remain the property of the government. Similarly, in B-243300, Sept. 17, 1991, GAO determined that an agency could pay for wheelchair van transportation as a reasonable accommodation under the Rehabilitation Act for an employee severely handicapped by cerebral palsy. The employee needed the service for assistance in returning home when her disability affected her at work in a manner that temporarily rendered her unable to walk. Since this condition occurred only about three times a year, the cost to the agency for the service would be minimal.

The employment of reading assistants for blind employees and interpreting assistants for deaf employees is covered. Cf. 72 Comp. Gen. 305 (1993) (the Department of Education may pay for personal assistants for handicapped grant and compliance reviewers who are not federal employees as a cost of acquiring the personal services of these reviewers).

The Rehabilitation Act has also been held applicable to parking expenses. As a general matter, parking incident to an employee's commute between his residence and permanent duty station is a personal expense (see section C.13.k). However, if severely disabled employees must pay parking costs higher than those paid by nondisabled employees working at the same facility, the agency can subsidize the difference. 63 Comp. Gen. 270 (1984); (see also B-291208, Apr. 9, 2003).

Other types of personal expenses that have been recognized as reasonable accommodations under the Rehabilitation Act for employees with disabilities include—

- Baggage handling fees, to the extent they were incurred as the result of the employee's disability and exceeded similar expenses a non-disabled person would incur in a similar situation (68 Comp. Gen. 242 (1989));

- Additional subsistence expenses incurred by an employee who, with supervisory approval, began a required temporary duty assignment 3 days early, driving from Denver through mountainous terrain to San Francisco, and delayed the return trip by 2 days because of a severe snowstorm. Under the circumstances the employee exercised good judgment and prudence by extending his travel time in view of his disability (64 Comp. Gen. 310 (1985));

- Shipment of an employee's specially equipped vehicle in connection with a permanent change of duty station from California to Washington, D.C., which the agency clearly justified as a cost beneficial, reasonable accommodation under the circumstances (64 Comp. Gen. 30 (1984)); and:

- Travel expenses and per diem for an attendant accompanying an employee who was required to travel to an unfamiliar area in connection with a permanent change of duty station. The attendant's travel expense and per diem constituted a necessary expense under the circumstances. 59 Comp. Gen. 461 (1980).

The costs of structural changes to an employee's home were not considered a reasonable accommodation under the Rehabilitation Act. The employee had argued that the changes were required as a result of his assignment to a new permanent duty station. Even though the modifications were necessary to facilitate his mobility, they were made to his privately owned property, and therefore, did not constitute a "reasonable accommodation" under the statute or regulations. B-266286, Oct. 11, 1996.

d. Office Furnishings (Decorative Items)

An agency's appropriations are available without question to furnish the space it occupies with such necessary items as desks, filing cabinets, and other ordinary office equipment. Questions occasionally arise when the item to be procured is decorative rather than utilitarian.

The availability of appropriations for certain decorative items has long been recognized. In 7 Comp. Dec. 1 (1900), the Comptroller of the Treasury advised the Secretary of the Treasury that "paintings suitable for the decoration of rooms" were within the meaning of the term "furniture." Therefore, an appropriation for the furnishing of public buildings was available to purchase cases and glass coverings for paintings of deceased judges. The paintings had been donated to the government for display in a courtroom.

The Comptroller followed this decision in 9 Comp. Dec. 807 (1903), holding that Treasury appropriations were available to buy portraits as furniture for the Ellis Island immigration station if administratively determined "necessary for the public service."

Citing both of these decisions, the Comptroller General held in B-178225, Apr. 11, 1973, that the appropriation for Salaries and Expenses of the Tax Court was available for portraits of the Chief Judges of the Tax Court, to be hung (the portraits, not the judges) in the main courtroom.

Similarly, the Tax Court could purchase artwork and other decorative items for judges' individual offices. 64 Comp. Gen. 796 (1985).

Other decisions approving the use of appropriated funds for decorative items are B-143886, Sept. 14, 1960 (oil painting of agency head for "historical purposes" and public display); B-121909, Dec. 9, 1954 ("solid walnut desk mount attached to a name plate"); B-114692, May 13, 1953 (framing of Presidential Certificates of Appointment for display in the appointee's office).

Purchase of decorative items for federal buildings is now covered in the Federal Property Management Regulations, 41 C.F.R. § 101.26.103-2 (2003). The regulations authorize expenditures for pictures, objects of art, plants, flowers (both artificial and real), and other similar items. However, such items may not be purchased solely for the personal convenience or to satisfy the personal desire of an official or employee.

The regulation was discussed and the rule restated in 60 Comp. Gen. 580 (1981). Decorative items may be purchased if the purchase is consistent with work-related objectives and the items to be purchased are not "personal convenience" items. The determination of "necessity" is within the agency's discretion, subject to the regulations. The regulations apply equally to space leased by an agency in a privately owned building. See also 64 Comp. Gen. 796 (1985); 63 Comp. Gen. 110, 113 (1983).

As noted, one type of permissible decorative item is plants. A restriction in a 1980 appropriation act prohibited the use of funds for plant maintenance contracts. The Comptroller General construed this provision to apply to office space to which particular federal employees were actually assigned. The provisions legislative history suggested that it was not intended to apply to outdoor plants or to plants in common areas that were not the assigned work space of any particular employee or group of employees. 59 Comp. Gen. 428 (1980).

e. Personal Qualification Expenses

Generally, expenses necessary to qualify a government employee to do his or her job are personal expenses and not chargeable to appropriated funds. As stated in an early decision:

> "That which is required of a person to become invested with an office must be done at his own expense unless specific provision is made by law for payment by the Government."

2 Comp. Dec. 262, 263 (1895). Somewhat coldly, the Comptroller added, "if he does not desire the office, he need not accept it." Id. See also United States v. Van Duzee, 140 U.S. 169, 171 (1891) ("it is the duty of persons receiving appointments from the government ...to qualify themselves for the office").

In a 1994 decision, GAO recognized that federal law has subjected the federal government to state regulation in some areas, particularly in the area of environmental regulation, and concluded that where federal employees are required by federal law to comply with state and local licensing regulations, the employee's agency can use appropriations to cover the cost of obtaining the license necessary to perform the regulated activity. 73 Comp. Gen. 171 (1994) (asbestos abatement license required by South Carolina; water treatment foreman's license required by Texas; pesticide and herbicide application license required by North Carolina). In that decision, GAO noted that federal law required that Air Force activities in these areas conform to the regulatory requirements of the states.

> "While the license or permit is often obtained in the name of the [Air Force] member, the primary interest in obtaining the license lies with the Air Force ...Any personal benefit that Air Force members receive from the acquisition of the licenses is nominal and incidental to the performance of their official duties."

Id. at 173. GAO distinguished such licenses from the licensing requirements of professional personnel such as teachers, accountants, engineers, lawyers, doctors, and nurses.

> "These individuals are fully aware of the licensing requirements of their professions from the time they begin their professional education, and of the fact that society expects them to fully qualify themselves for the performance of their chosen professions. In that sense, the licensing requirements are considered to be more for the personal benefit of the individuals than for their employers."

Id. GAO noted, also, that driver's licenses are considered for the personal benefit of the employee. Id.

In 2001, Congress enacted legislation permitting agencies to use appropriations for "expenses for employees to obtain professional credentials, including expenses for professional accreditation, State-imposed and professional licenses, and professional certification; and examinations to obtain such credentials." Pub. L. No. 107-107, § 1112(a), 115 Stat. 1238 (Apr. 12, 2001), codified at 5 U.S.C. § 5757. The statutory language does not create an entitlement; instead, it authorizes agencies to consider such expenses as payable from agency appropriations if the agency chooses to cover them.

Neither the statute nor its legislative history defines the terms "professional credentials," "professional accreditation," and "professional certification." GAO has not had occasion to interpret and apply the statute. Nevertheless, the statute and the 1994 decision together appear to cover many, if not most, qualification expenses that GAO previously found to be personal to the employee, including actuarial accreditation (B-286026, June 12, 2001), licenses to practice medicine (B-277033, June 27, 1997), a Certified Government Financial Manager designation (B-260771, Oct. 11, 1995), and professional engineering certificates (B-248955, July 24, 1992).

It is not clear whether the statute covers driver's licenses. Historically, with a few exceptions, a driver's license was considered a personal expense. 21 Comp. Gen. 769, 772 (1942); 6 Comp.

Gen. 432 (1926); 23 Comp. Dec. 386 (1917). An exception was recognized in B-115463, Sept. 18, 1953, for Army civilian employees on temporary duty (TDY) of at least 6 months' duration in foreign countries, where the employees did not already possess drivers licenses, operating a motor vehicle was not part of the job for which the employees were hired, but the Army wanted to include driving as part of their TDY duties as a less expensive alternative to hiring additional personnel, and the license was required by the host country. See also B-257895, Oct. 28, 1994 (National Security Agency may pay for commercial licenses where the license benefited the Agency and was not a personal qualification for the employee's position); B-87138-O.M., July 19, 1949 (Virgin Islands). As noted above, in 73 Comp. Gen. 171, which concluded that agencies may pay for licenses required by certain state and local regulations, GAO expressly excluded driver's licenses. 73 Comp. Gen. at 173 ("the cost of driver's licenses are considered for the personal benefit of federal employees"). To the extent that an agency refers to the 2001 statute as authority to pay the cost of an employee's driver's license, the agency will have to find that the license is a professional credential, professional accreditation, State-imposed and professional license, or professional certification.

Another statute, 5 U.S.C. § 5945, specifically covers notary publics. It permits agencies to reimburse an employee whose job includes serving as a notary public the expense required to obtain the commission. 5 U.S.C. § 5945. The expense is reimbursable even though the employee uses the notarial power for private as well as government business. 36 Comp. Gen. 465 (1956).

This page intentionally left blank

Chapter 5: Availability of Appropriations: Time

A. General Principles--Duration of Appropriations

1. Introduction

As we have emphasized in several places in this publication, the concept of the "legal availability" of appropriations is defined in terms of three elements--purpose, time, and amount. This chapter addresses the second element, time.

The two basic authorities conferred by an appropriation law are the authority to incur obligations and the authority to make expenditures. An obligation results from some action that creates a liability or definite commitment on the part of the government to make an expenditure. The expenditure is the disbursement of funds to pay the obligation. While an obligation and expenditure may occur simultaneously, ordinarily the obligation precedes the expenditure in time. This chapter discusses the limitations on the use of appropriations relating to time--when they may be obligated and when they may be expended. Many of the rules are statutory and will be found in the provisions of Title 31, United States Code.

Our starting point is the firmly established proposition that—

> "Congress has the right to limit its appropriations to particular times as well as to particular objects, and when it has clearly done so, its will expressed in the law should be implicitly followed."

13 Op. Att'y Gen. 288, 292 (1870). The placing of time limits on the availability of appropriations is one of the primary means of congressional control. By imposing a time limit, Congress reserves to itself the prerogative of periodically reviewing a given program or agency's activities.

When an appropriation is by its terms made available for a fixed period of time or until a specified date, the general rule is that the availability relates to the authority to obligate the appropriation, and does not necessarily prohibit payments after the expiration date for obligations previously incurred, unless the payment is otherwise expressly prohibited by statute. 37 Comp. Gen. 861, 863 (1958); 23 Comp. Gen. 862 (1944); 18 Comp. Gen. 969 (1939); 16 Comp. Gen. 205 (1936). Thus, a time-limited appropriation is available to incur an obligation only during the period for which it is made. However, it remains available beyond that period, within limits, to make adjustments to the amount of such obligations and to make payments to liquidate such obligations. In this connection, 31 U.S.C. § 1502(a) provides:

> "The balance of an appropriation or fund limited for obligation to a definite period is available only for payment of expenses properly incurred during the period of availability or to complete contracts properly made within that period of availability and obligated

consistent with section 1501 of this title. However, the appropriation or fund is not available for expenditure for a period beyond the period otherwise authorized by law."

In addition, there are situations in which appropriations may be "held over" by statute and by judicial decree for obligation beyond their expiration date.

2. Types of Appropriations

Classified on the basis of duration, appropriations are of three types: annual, multiple year, and no-year appropriations.

a. Annual Appropriations

Annual appropriations (also called fiscal year or 1-year appropriations) are made for a specified fiscal year and are available for obligation only during the fiscal year for which made. The federal government's fiscal year begins on October 1 and ends on September 30 of the following year. 31 U.S.C. § 1102. For example, fiscal year 2005 begins on October 1, 2004, and ends on September 30, 2005.

All appropriations are presumed to be annual appropriations unless the appropriation act expressly provides otherwise. There are several reasons for this. First, as required by 1 U.S.C. § 105, the title and enacting clause of all regular and supplemental appropriation acts specify the making of appropriations "for the fiscal year ending September 30, (here insert the calendar year)." Thus, everything in an appropriation act is presumed to be applicable only to the fiscal year covered unless specified to the contrary. Second, 31 U.S.C. § 1301(c) provides that, with specified exceptions:

"An appropriation in a regular, annual appropriation law may be construed to be permanent or available continuously only if the appropriation...

"(2) expressly provides that it is available after the fiscal year covered by the law in which it appears."

Third, appropriation acts commonly include a general provision similar to the following:

"No part of any appropriation contained in this Act shall remain available for obligation beyond the current fiscal year unless expressly so provided herein."

Under the plain terms of this provision, the availability of an appropriation to incur a new obligation may not be extended beyond the fiscal year for which it is made absent express indication in the appropriation act itself. 71 Comp. Gen. 39 (1991); 58 Comp. Gen. 321 (1979); B-118638, Nov. 4, 1974.

A limitation item included in an appropriation (for example, a lump-sum appropriation with a proviso that not to exceed a specified sum shall be available for a particular object) is subject to the same fiscal year limitation attaching to the parent appropriation unless the limitation is specifically exempted from it in the appropriation act. 37 Comp. Gen. 246, 248 (1957); B-274576, Jan. 13, 1997.

Annual appropriations are available only to meet bona fide needs of the fiscal year for which they were appropriated. The so-called "bona fide needs rule" is covered in detail in section B.

If an agency fails to obligate its annual funds by the end of the fiscal year for which they were appropriated, they cease to be available for incurring and recording new obligations and are said to have "expired." This rule--that time-limited budget authority ceases to be available for incurring new obligations after the last day of the specified time period--has been termed an "elementary principle" of federal fiscal law. City of Houston, Texas v. Department of Housing & Urban Development, 24 F.3d 1421, 1426 (D.C. Cir. 1994); West Virginia Ass'n of Community Health Centers, Inc. v. Heckler, 734 F.2d 1570, 1576 (D.C. Cir. 1984). See also 18 Comp. Gen. 969, 971 (1939). Annual appropriations remain available for an additional five fiscal years beyond expiration, however, to adjust and make payments to liquidate liabilities arising from obligations made within the fiscal year for which the funds were appropriated. 31 U.S.C. § 1553(a), as amended by Pub. L. No. 101-510, § 1405(a), 104 Stat. 1676 (Nov. 5, 1990). The principles summarized in this paragraph are discussed in section D.

The above principles are illustrated in 56 Comp. Gen. 351 (1977). In that case, the Interior Department proposed to obtain and exercise options on certain land, obligate the full purchase price, and take immediate title to and possession of the property. Payment of the purchase price, however, would be disbursed over a period of up to 4 years. The reason being that, in view of the capital gains tax, the seller would have insisted on a higher purchase price if payment was to be made in a lump sum. The Comptroller General concluded that the proposal was not legally objectionable, provided that (a) a bona fide need for the property existed in the fiscal year in which the option was to be exercised and (b) the full purchase price was obligated against appropriations for the fiscal year in which the option was exercised. As long as these conditions were met--obligation within the period of availability for a legitimate need existing within that period--the timing of actual disbursements over a 4-year period was irrelevant.

Just as Congress can by statute expand the obligational availability of an appropriation beyond a fiscal year, it can also reduce the availability to a fixed period less than a full fiscal year. To illustrate, a fiscal year 1980 appropriation for the now defunct Community Services Administration included funds for emergency energy assistance grants. Since the program was intended to provide assistance for increased heating fuel costs, and Congress did not want the funds to be used to buy air conditioners, the appropriation specified that awards could not be made after June 30, 1980. Appropriations available for obligation for less than a full fiscal year are, however, uncommon.

Finally, Congress may pass a law to rescind the unobligated balance of a fixed (annual or multiple year) appropriation at any time prior to the accounts closing. The law may be passed at the initiation of the President pursuant to the impoundment procedures or by Congress as part of its regular legislative process.

b. Multiple Year Appropriations

Multiple year appropriations are available for obligation for a definite period in excess of one fiscal year. 37 Comp. Gen. 861, 863 (1958). For example, if a fiscal year 2005 appropriation act includes an appropriation account that specifies that it shall remain available until September 30, 2006, it is a 2-year appropriation. As a more specific illustration, the appropriation accounts for military construction are typically 5-year appropriations.

Apart from the extended period of availability, multiple year appropriations are subject to the same principles applicable to annual appropriations and do not present any special problems.

c. No-Year Appropriations

A no-year appropriation is available for obligation without fiscal year limitation. For an appropriation to be considered a no-year appropriation, the appropriating language must expressly so provide. 31 U.S.C. § 1301(c). The standard language used to make a no-year appropriation is "to remain available until expended." 40 Comp. Gen. 694, 696 (1961); 3 Comp. Dec. 623, 628 (1897); B-279886, Apr. 28, 1998; B-271607, June 3, 1996. However, other language will suffice as long as its meaning is unmistakable, such as "without fiscal year limitation." 57 Comp. Gen. 865, 869 (1978).

Unless canceled in accordance with 31 U.S.C. § 1555 or rescinded by another law, there are no time limits as to when no-year funds may be obligated and expended and the funds remain available for their original purposes until expended. 43 Comp. Gen. 657 (1964); 40 Comp. Gen. 694 (1961). This includes earmarks applicable to the use of no-year funds since they are coextensive with, and inseparable from, the period of availability of the no-year appropriation to which they relate. B-274576, Jan. 13, 1997.

A small group of decisions involves the effect of subsequent congressional action on the availability of a prior years no-year appropriation. In one case, Congress had made a no-year appropriation to the Federal Aviation Administration for the purchase of aircraft. A question arose as to the continued availability of the appropriation because, in the following year, Congress explicitly denied a budget request for the same purpose. The Comptroller General held that the subsequent denial did not restrict the use of the unexpended balance of the prior no-year appropriation. The availability of the prior appropriation could not be changed by a later act "except in such respects and to such extent as is expressly stated or clearly implied by such act." 40 Comp. Gen. 694, 696 (1961). See also Atlantic Fish Spotters Ass'n v. Evans, 321 F.3d 220 (1st Cir. 2003); B-200519, Nov. 28, 1980.

In another case, a no-year appropriation for the National Capital Park and Planning Commission included a monetary ceiling on noncontract services during the fiscal year. Based on the apparent intent of the ceiling, GAO concluded that the specific restriction had the effect of suspending the "available until expended" provision of prior unrestricted no-year appropriations as far as personal services were concerned, for any fiscal year in which the restriction was included. Thus, unobligated balances of prior unrestricted no-year appropriations could not be used to augment the ceiling. 30 Comp. Gen. 500 (1951). A similar issue was considered in 62 Comp. Gen. 692 (1983). The Nuclear Regulatory Commission received a no-year appropriation that included a prohibition on compensating intervenors. The decision held that the unobligated balance of a prior unrestricted no-year appropriation could be used to pay an Equal Access to Justice Act award to an intervenor made in a restricted year, where part of the proceeding giving rise to the award was funded by an unrestricted appropriation. Unlike the situation in 30 Comp. Gen. 500, the restriction in the 1983 case was expressly limited to "proceedings funded in this Act," and thus could have no effect on the availability of prior appropriations.

Similar issues were considered in the context of multiple year appropriations in 31 Comp. Gen. 368 (1952) and 31 Comp. Gen. 543 (1952), overruling 31 Comp. Gen. 275 (1952). In both of these cases, based on a determination of congressional intent, it was held that the current restriction had no effect on the availability of unobligated balances of prior unrestricted appropriations.

No-year appropriations have advantages and disadvantages. The advantages to the spending agency are obvious. From the legislative perspective, a key disadvantage is a loss of congressional control over actual program levels from year to year. GAO has expressed the position that no-year appropriations should not be made in the absence of compelling programmatic or budgetary reasons. See U.S. General Accounting Office, No-Year Appropriations in the Department of Agriculture, PAD-78-74 (Washington, D.C.: Sept. 19, 1978).

3. Obligation or Expenditure Prior to Start of Fiscal Year

In considering what may and may not be done before the start of a fiscal year, it is necessary to keep in mind the Antideficiency Act, which prohibits obligations or expenditures in advance of appropriations, 31 U.S.C. § 1341(a), and apportionments, 31 U.S.C. § 1517(a). By virtue of this law, certainly no obligations may be incurred before the appropriation act is enacted and amounts apportioned to the agency, unless specifically authorized by law.

There are some decisions that stand for the proposition that if the appropriation act is passed by both houses of Congress and signed by the President prior to the start of the fiscal year for which the appropriation is being made, contracts may be entered into upon enactment and before the start of the fiscal year, provided that no payments or expenditures may be made under them until the start of the fiscal year. Any such contract should make this limitation clear. 20 Comp. Gen.

868 (1941); 16 Comp. Gen. 1007 (1937); 4 Comp. Gen. 887 (1925); 2 Comp. Gen. 739 (1923); 11 Comp. Dec. 186 (1904); 4 Lawrence, First Comp. Dec. 132 (1883); B-20670, Oct. 18, 1941; A-19524, Aug. 26, 1927. GAO did not view the contract as an obligation in violation of the Antideficiency Act since, even though the time period covered by the appropriation to be charged had not yet started, the appropriation had already been enacted into law. These decisions addressed these contracts from an Antideficiency Act perspective, and did not address the bona fide needs rule.

In other decisions, the Comptroller General has expressed the opinion that, in the absence of any other statutory authority, the awarding of a "conditional contract" prior to the enactment of the appropriation act to be charged with the obligation does not raise Antideficiency Act or bona fide needs issues when the government's liability is contingent upon the future availability of appropriations. The contract must expressly provide:

1. that no legal liability on the part of the government arises until the appropriation is made available within the agency to fund the obligation and:

2. that notice is to be given by the agency to the contractor before the contractor may proceed.

See B-171798(1), Aug. 18, 1971, at 11-12. Such express provisions are necessary to make explicit what is meant by the term "contingent upon the future availability of appropriations" in order to avoid Antideficiency Act problems, and to permit the agency to maintain effective internal controls over the obligating of appropriations.

Of course, Congress may by statute authorize the actual expenditure of appropriations prior to the beginning of the fiscal year, in which event the above rule does not apply. 4 Comp. Gen. 918 (1925). This result may also follow if an appropriation is made to carry out the provisions of another law that clearly by its terms requires immediate action. E.g., 1 Comp. Dec. 329 (1895).

B. The Bona Fide Needs Rule

1. Background:

a. Introduction

Over a century ago, the Comptroller of the Treasury stated, "An appropriation should not be used for the purchase of an article not necessary for the use of a fiscal year in which ordered merely in order to use up such an appropriation." 8 Comp. Dec. 346, 348 (1901). The bona fide needs rule is one of the fundamental principles of appropriations law: A fiscal year appropriation may be obligated only to meet a legitimate, or bona fide, need arising in, or in some cases arising prior to but continuing to exist in, the fiscal year for which the appropriation was made. Citations to this principle are numerous. See, e.g., 33 Comp. Gen. 57, 61 (1953); 16 Comp. Gen. 37 (1936); B-289801, Dec. 30, 2002; B-282601, Sept. 27, 1999; B-235678, July 30, 1990.

Does the quotation above, from the Comptroller of the Treasury, mean that an agency's obligation of an annual appropriation on the last day of the fiscal year can never constitute a bona fide need of that fiscal year? While it certainly should raise a question, the answer is, "it depends." An agency may have perfectly valid reasons for year-end spending. For example, some programs have predictable 4th quarter surges due to cyclical or seasonal requirements. When using time-limited funding, an agency must dissect its ongoing business into discrete units of time in order to determine whether a particular transaction may be obligated against, or charged to, a specific appropriation. The bona fide needs rule provides an analytical framework for analyzing an agency's financial transactions to determine the period of time to which a transaction relates.

Bona fide needs questions arise in many forms. Historically, as the discussion that follows will show, bona fide needs issues have arisen most frequently in the context of the acquisition of goods or services. An agency may enter into a contract in one fiscal year, but the contractor does not complete performance until the next fiscal year. Which fiscal year should be charged? Or, an agency may modify a contract in the year following the fiscal year in which it originally entered into the contract. Sometimes, as a result of an audit, the question may be whether an obligation already recorded was a proper charge against that fiscal year's appropriation. Or, an agency may have taken certain actions that it should have recorded as an obligation but did not; when the time for payment arrives, the question again is which fiscal year to charge. These are all facets of the same basic question--whether an obligation bears a sufficient relationship to the legitimate needs of the time period of availability of the appropriation charged or sought to be charged.

Although the bona fide needs rule remains one of the bedrock principles of appropriations law, its application has changed over the years as Congress enacted statutes redefining in some instances what constitutes a bona fide need of a fiscal year appropriation. During a period of ever increasing budget constraints in the 1990s, Congress enacted laws providing civilian agencies more flexibility in their use of fiscal year appropriations, and expanded already existing authorities of defense agencies. Today, there is general authority permitting agencies to use fiscal year funds to acquire goods and services via multiyear acquisitions, and to enter into 1-year contracts for severable services that cross fiscal years. These laws have provided agencies with substantial flexibility to allocate the cost of goods and services across fiscal years, or to allocate the costs to the first fiscal year of the contract even though the goods or services may be delivered in future fiscal years.

Notwithstanding the increased flexibilities agencies now have, the bona fide needs rule remains an important and often complex consideration for an agency as it executes its budget. In this section, we discuss the basic concept underlying the rule. We then discuss the traditional application of the rule in sections B.2 through B.7, followed by a discussion of the recent statutory developments in the acquisition of goods and services area in sections B.8 and B.9. It is important to know both the traditional application as well as recently enacted flexibilities in order to understand the contracting options now available to agencies as they decide how to use their appropriations. We discuss the application of the rule in the grants and cooperative agreements context in section B.10.

b. The Concept

The bona fide needs rule has a statutory basis. The first general appropriation act in 1789 made appropriations "for the service of the present year," and this concept continues to this time. This "one-year" concept is also reflected in 31 U.S.C. § 1502(a), sometimes called the "bona fide needs statute." Originally enacted in 1870 (16 Stat. 251 (July12, 1870)), section 1502(a) provides that the balance of a fixed-term appropriation "is available only for payment of expenses properly incurred during the period of availability or to complete contracts properly made within that period...." The key word here is "properly"--expenses "properly incurred" or contracts "properly made" within the period of availability. See, e.g., 37 Comp. Gen. 155, 158 (1957). Additional statutory support for the rule is found in the Antideficiency Act, 31 U.S.C. § 1341(a), and the so-called Adequacy of Appropriations Act, 41 U.S.C. § 11. (Bona fide needs questions may involve other statutory restrictions as well.) For an early but still relevant and useful discussion, see 6 Comp. Dec. 815 (1900).

While the rule itself is universally applicable, determination of what constitutes a bona fide need of a particular fiscal year depends largely on the facts and circumstances of the particular case. B-308010, Apr. 20, 2007; 70 Comp. Gen. 469, 470 (1991); 44 Comp. Gen. 399, 401 (1965); 37 Comp. Gen. at 159.

In its most elementary form--where the entire transaction (contract or purchase, delivery or other performance, and payment) takes place during the same fiscal year--the rule means simply that the appropriation is available only for the needs of the current year. A common application of the rule in this context is that an appropriation is not available for the needs of a future year. For example, suppose that, as the end of a fiscal year approaches, an agency purchases a truckload of pencils when it is clear that, based on current usage, it already has in stock enough pencils to last several years into the future. It would seem apparent that the agency was merely trying to use up its appropriation before it expired, and the purchase would violate the bona fide needs rule.

We do not mean to suggest that an agency may purchase only those supplies that it will actually use during the fiscal year. Agencies normally maintain inventories of common use items. The bona fide needs rule does not prevent maintaining a legitimate inventory at reasonable and historical levels, the "need" being to maintain the inventory level so as to avoid disruption of operations. The problem arises when the inventory crosses the line from reasonable to excessive.

Bona fide needs questions also frequently involve transactions that cover more than one fiscal year. In the typical situation, a contract is made (or attempted to be made) in one fiscal year, with performance and payment to extend at least in part into the following fiscal year. The question is which fiscal year should be charged with the obligation. In this context, the rule is that, in order to obligate a fiscal year appropriation for payments to be made in a succeeding fiscal year, the contract imposing the obligation must have been made within the fiscal year sought to be charged, and the contract must have been made to meet a bona fide need of the fiscal year to be charged. E.g., 70 Comp. Gen. 664, 667 (1991); 64 Comp. Gen. 359, 362 (1985); 35 Comp. Gen. 692 (1956); 20 Comp. Gen. 436 (1941); 16 Comp. Gen. 37 (1936); 21 Comp. Dec. 822 (1915); 4 Comp. Dec. 553 (1898); B-289801, Dec. 30, 2002; B-257977, Nov. 15, 1995.

The principle that payment is chargeable to the fiscal year in which the obligation is incurred as long as the need arose, or continued to exist in, that year applies even though the funds are not to be disbursed and the exact amount owed by the government cannot be determined until the subsequent fiscal year. E.g., 71 Comp. Gen. 502 (1992); 21 Comp. Gen. 574 (1941). Thus, in a case where the United States entered into an agreement with a state to provide assistance for the procurement of civil defense items for the state and to pay a specified percentage of the cost, the Comptroller General found that the need arose in the year the agreement with the state was made. Therefore, appropriations current at that time were to be charged with the cost, notwithstanding the fact that the states or the United States may not have negotiated and executed the actual procurement contracts with suppliers, including the exact price, until a subsequent fiscal year. 31 Comp. Gen. 608 (1952).

The bona fide needs rule applies to multiple year as well as fiscal year appropriations. 55 Comp. Gen. 768, 773-74 (1976); B-235678, July 30, 1990. See also 64 Comp. Gen. 163, 166 (1984). In other words, an agency may use a multiple year appropriation for needs arising at any time during the period of availability.

An argument can be made, not wholly without logic, that a multiple year appropriation can be obligated at any time during its availability, but only to meet a bona fide need of the year in which the funds were appropriated. Suppose, for example, that an agency receives a 2-year appropriation every year. For fiscal year 1989, it receives an appropriation available through fiscal year 1990; for fiscal year 1990, it receives an appropriation available through fiscal year 1991, and so on. It is possible to apply the bona fide needs rule to require that the fiscal year 1990 appropriation be used only for needs arising in fiscal year 1990, although obligation may occur any time prior to the end of fiscal year 1991. The Comptroller General specifically rejected this approach in 68 Comp. Gen. 170 (1989), holding that the Defense Logistics Agency could use its fiscal year 1987 2-year Research and Development appropriation for a need arising in fiscal year 1988. "There is no requirement that 2-year funds be used only for the needs of the first year of their availability." Id. at 172.

It follows that the bona fide needs rule does not apply to no-year funds. 43 Comp. Gen. 657, 661 (1964). See also B-279886, Apr. 28, 1998. Without a prescribed period of availability, there is no fixed period during which the bona fide need must arise, and thus no fixed period in which the funds must be obligated and expended.

2. Future Years' Needs

An appropriation may not be used for the needs of some time period subsequent to the expiration of its period of availability. With respect to annual appropriations, a more common statement of the rule is that an appropriation for a given fiscal year is not available for the needs of a future fiscal year. Determining the year to which a need relates is not always easy. Some illustrative cases are listed below:

- The balance of an appropriation for salaries remaining unexpended at the end of one fiscal year could not be used to pay salaries for services rendered in the following fiscal year. 18 Op. Att'y Gen. 412 (1886).

- The Department of Housing and Urban Development recorded certain obligations for public housing subsidies on an estimated basis. At the end of the fiscal year, obligations were found to be in excess of actual needs. It was held improper to send excess funds to the state agency's operating reserve to offset the subsidy for the following year, since this amounted to using the funds for the needs of a subsequent year. The proper course of action was to deobligate the excess. 64 Comp. Gen. 410 (1985).

- Rent on property leased by the National Park Service from the National Park Foundation could be paid in advance, but the lease could not cross fiscal year lines. The proposal was for the lease to run from May 1 through April 30 and for the full annual rent to be paid in advance on May 1. However, appropriations available as of May 1 could not be used for the period from October 1 through April 30 since rent for these months constituted a need of the following fiscal year. B-207215, Mar. 1, 1983.

Any discussion of obligating for future years' needs inevitably leads to the question of year-end spending. Federal agencies as a fiscal year draws to a close are often likened to sharks on a feeding frenzy, furiously thrashing about to gobble up every appropriated dollar in sight before the ability to obligate those dollars is lost. The Comptroller of the Treasury stated the legal principle very simply in an early decision:

"An appropriation should not be used for the purchase of an article not necessary for the use of a fiscal year in which ordered merely in order to use up such appropriation. This would be a plain violation of the law."

8 Comp. Dec. 346, 348 (1901).

Thus, where an obligation is made toward the end of a fiscal year and it is clear from the facts and circumstances that the need relates to the following fiscal year, the bona fide needs rule has been violated. The obligation is not a proper charge against the earlier appropriation, but must be charged against the following year's funds. This was the result, for example, in 1 Comp. Gen. 115 (1921), in which an order for gasoline had been placed 3 days before the end of fiscal year 1921, with the gasoline to be delivered in monthly installments in fiscal year 1922. The Comptroller General stated:

> "It is not difficult to understand how the need for an article of equipment, such as a typewriter, might arise during the fiscal year 1921 and its purchase be delayed until the latter part of June [the end of the fiscal year in 1921], but as to supplies that are consumed as used, such as gasoline, it can not be held that they were purchased to supply a need of the fiscal year 1921 when the contract is made late in the month of June and expressly precludes the possibility of delivery before July 1, 1921."

Id. at 118 (explanatory information provided). See also 4 Comp. Dec. 553 (1898) (cement ordered late in one fiscal year to be delivered several months into the following fiscal year).

Yet, this is only one side of the coin. The other side is illustrated in another passage from 8 Comp. Dec. at 348:

> "An appropriation is just as much available to supply the needs of the [last day] of a particular year as any other day or time in the year."

Thus, a year-end obligation perhaps raises the possibility that the agency is trying to "dump" its remaining funds and warrants a further look, but the timing of the obligation does not, in and of itself, establish anything improper. 38 Comp. Gen. 628, 630 (1959); 6 Comp. Dec. 815, 818 (1900).

GAO has conducted several studies of year-end spending and has consistently reported that year-end spending is not inherently more or less wasteful than spending at any other time of the year. In one report, GAO suggested that year-end spending surges are really symptomatic of a larger problem--inadequate management of budget execution--and that the apportionment process could be more effectively used to provide the desired management. U.S. General Accounting Office, Federal Year-End Spending: Symptom of a Larger Problem, GAO/PAD-81-18 (Oct. 23, 1980), pp. 7-9.

GAO also noted in its October 1980 report that there are several reasons for year-end spending, some of which are perfectly valid. For example, some programs have predictable 4thquarter surges due to cyclical or seasonal fund requirements. If, for example, you are administering a fire suppression program, you should expect a 4tthuarter surge because the 4ththarter of the federal fiscal year is the major fire season in many states. GAO/PAD-81-18 at 3. In other situations, it may be desirable to delay obligations to have funds available for emergencies that may arise during the year. Id. at 4.

In evaluating a year-end obligation, it is important to determine exactly what the need is from the agency's perspective. In one case, for example, the Small Business Administration (SBA) awarded cooperative agreements to certain Small Business Development Centers on the last day of a fiscal year. The Centers then provided management and technical assistance to small businesses, all of which would obviously be done in the following year. GAO found no bona fide needs violation because the need, from the perspective of implementing SBA's appropriation, was merely to provide assistance to the Centers, and there was no reason this could not be done on the last day of the year. B-229873, Nov. 29, 1988. See also B-289801, Dec. 30, 2002.

One device Congress has employed to control year-end spending surges is legislation limiting the amount of obligations that may be incurred in the last month or 2-month period or quarter of the fiscal year. For example, the Defense Department's 1990 appropriation contained a provision limiting obligations during the last 2 months of the fiscal year to not more than 20 percent of the total fiscal year appropriations. In comments on legislative proposals of this type, GAO has pointed out that they are difficult to administer, but has supported them as temporary measures pending more fundamental improvements in budget execution management and procurement planning. In addition, there is the risk that limitations of this type may have the effect of simply moving the spending surges back a few months, accomplishing nothing.

3. Prior Years' Needs

There are situations in which it is not only proper but mandatory to use currently available appropriations to satisfy a need that arose in a prior year. We refer to this as the "continuing need." If a need arises during a particular fiscal year and the agency chooses not to satisfy it during that year, perhaps because of insufficient funds or higher priority needs, and the need continues to exist in the following year, the obligation to satisfy that need is properly chargeable to the later years funds. "An unfulfilled need of one period may well be carried forward to the next as a continuing need with the next periods appropriation being available for funding." B-197274, Sept. 23, 1983. Thus, an important corollary to the bona fide needs rule is that a continuing need is chargeable to funds current for the year in which the obligation is made, regardless of the fact that the need may have originated in a prior year.

An illustration is B-207433, Sept. 16, 1983. The Army contracted for a specific quantity of thermal viewers. The contract provided for a downward adjustment in the contract price in the case of an "underrun," that is, if the contractor was able to perform at less than the contract price. After the appropriation charged with the contract had expired, the contractor incurred an underrun and proposed to use the excess funds to supply an additional quantity of viewers. It was undisputed that the need for additional viewers could be attributed to the year in which the contract was entered into, and that the need continued to exist. GAO agreed with the Army that the proper course of action was to deobligate the excess funds and, if the Army still wished to procure them, to charge the obligation for the additional quantity to current years appropriations. The fact that the need arose in a prior year was immaterial. The decision, at pages 4-5, offered the following explanation:

"Certainly the Army could have used underrun funds to procure additional viewers at any time during the period those funds remained available for obligation. Also, we are of course aware that an unmet need does not somehow evaporate merely because the period of availability has expired. However, nothing in the bona fide needs rule suggests that expired appropriations may be used for an item for which a valid obligation was not incurred prior to expiration merely because there was a need for that item during that period ...Once the obligational period has expired, the procurement of an increased quantity must be charged to new money, and this is not affected by the fact that the need for that increased quantity may in effect be a 'continuing need' that arose during the prior period."

Another illustration is B-226198, July 21, 1987. In late fiscal year 1986, the U.S. Geological Survey ordered certain microcomputer equipment, to be delivered in early fiscal year 1987, charging the purchase to fiscal year 1986 funds. The equipment was delivered and accepted, but was stolen before reaching the ordering office. The decision held that a reorder, placed in fiscal year 1987, had to be charged to fiscal year 1987 funds. As with the thermal viewers in B-207433, the fact that the need for the equipment arose in 1986 was immaterial. See also B-286929, Apr. 25, 2001; B-257617, Apr. 18, 1995.

In another case, cost overruns caused the Army to delete certain items from a fiscal year 1979 procurement. The Army repurchased the canceled items in 1981, charging 1981 appropriations. GAO agreed that the repurchase was properly chargeable to 1981, rather than 1979 funds. B-206283-O.M., Feb. 17, 1983.

The essential requirements of the "continuing need" corollary are that (1) the need, unmet in the year in which it arose, must continue to exist in the subsequent obligational period; (2) the incurring of an obligation must have been discretionary with the agency to begin with; and (3) no obligation was in fact incurred during the prior year.

If the agency has no discretion as to the timing of an obligation (for example, in situations where the obligation arises by operation of law), or, even in discretionary situations, if the agency has actually incurred a valid obligation in the prior year (whether recorded or unrecorded), then the "continuing need" concept has no application and the obligation must be charged to the prior year. Absent statutory authority, current appropriations are not available to fund an obligation or liability (as opposed to an unmet and unobligated-for need) of a prior obligational period. If insufficient funds remain in the prior years' appropriation, the agency must seek a supplemental or deficiency appropriation and must further consider the possibility that the Antideficiency Act, 31 U.S.C. § 1341(a), has been violated.

In an early case, for example, an agency had contracted for repairs to a building toward the end of fiscal year 1904. Since it was clear that the repairs were needed at the time they were ordered, they were chargeable to fiscal year 1904 appropriations, and the exhaustion of the 1904 appropriation did not permit use of 1905 funds. 11 Comp. Dec. 454 (1905). See also 21 Comp. Dec. 822 (1915).

In B-226801, Mar. 2, 1988, GAO considered various entitlement programs administered by the Department of Veterans Affairs (VA). Under these programs, the obligation arises when VA determines eligibility through its adjudication process and must be recorded at that time. If the obligations would exceed available funds, it is not proper to defer the recording and charge the following year's appropriation. Since the obligations are required by law, overobligation would not violate the Antideficiency Act, but they must still be recognized and recorded when they arise. Congress subsequently began including an administrative provision in VA's appropriation act permitting the use of appropriations for these programs to pay obligations required to be recorded in the last quarter of the preceding fiscal year. See also B-287619, July 5, 2001.

For additional cases, see 55 Comp. Gen. 768, 773-74 (1976) (current year's appropriations not available to fund prior year's Antideficiency Act violation); 54 Comp. Gen. 393, 395 (1974) (deficiency appropriation necessary to pay claims against exhausted appropriation); B-133001, Mar. 9, 1979 (fiscal year refugee assistance appropriation not available to pay for services performed in prior year); B-14331, Jan. 24, 1941; A-76081, June 8, 1936 (appropriations not available for past obligations unless clearly indicated by language and intent of appropriation act); B-221204-O.M., Jan. 31, 1986 (meals under child nutrition program served in September of one fiscal year may not be charged to subsequent year's appropriation). Congressional denial of a request for a deficiency appropriation does not make current appropriations available to satisfy the prior year's obligation. B-114874, Sept. 16, 1975 (postage charges under 39 U.S.C. § 3206).

4. Delivery of Materials beyond the Fiscal Year

When the government purchases goods or materials in one fiscal year and delivery occurs in whole or in part in a subsequent fiscal year, the question is whether the contract meets a bona fide need of the fiscal year in which it was made. This was the central legal issue in our discussion of year-end spending in section B.2, but the issue exists regardless of when in the fiscal year the contract is made. In this section we will explore those contracts where the agency intends to meet the needs of the fiscal year in which it entered into the contract. We will discuss multiyear contracts, where an agency intends to meet its needs for more than one fiscal year, in sections B.8 and B.9.

An agency may not obligate funds when it is apparent from the outset that there will be no requirement until the following fiscal year. For example, it was found that annual appropriations obligated to fund an agreement between the General Services Administration (GSA) and the Federal Power Commission (FPC), whereby GSA agreed to renovate space in a federal building incident to relocation of FPC personnel, were not available since the relocation was not required to, and would not, take place by the end of the fiscal year, and because the space in question would not be made "tenantable" until the following fiscal year. B-95136-O.M., Aug. 11, 1972.

If deliveries are scheduled only for a subsequent fiscal year, or if contract timing effectively precludes delivery until the following fiscal year, one could question whether the contract was made in the earlier fiscal year only to obligate funds from an expiring appropriation and that the goods or materials were not intended to meet a bona fide need of that year. See 38 Comp. Gen. 628, 630 (1959); 35 Comp. Gen. 692 (1956); 33 Comp. Gen. 57, 60-61 (1953); 21 Comp. Gen. 1159 (1941); 1 Comp. Gen. 115 (1921); 27 Comp. Dec. 640 (1921).

However, the timing of delivery, while obviously a relevant factor, is not conclusive. There are perfectly legitimate situations in which an obligation may be incurred in one fiscal year with delivery to occur in a subsequent year. Thus, where materials cannot be obtained in the same fiscal year in which they are needed and contracted for, provisions for delivery in the subsequent fiscal year do not violate the bona fide needs rule as long as the time intervening between contracting and delivery is not excessive and the procurement is not for standard commercial items readily available from other sources. 38 Comp. Gen. at 630.

Similarly, an agency may contract in one fiscal year for delivery in a subsequent year if the material contracted for will not be obtainable on the open market at the time needed for use, provided the intervening period is necessary for production or fabrication of the material. 37 Comp. Gen. 155, 159 (1957).

If an obligation is proper when made, unforeseen delays that cause delivery or performance to extend into the following fiscal year will not invalidate the obligation. In one case, for example, although work under a construction contract was performed during the fiscal year following its execution, the Comptroller General approved payment to the contractor under the original obligation since the agency had awarded the contract as expeditiously as possible and had made provision for the work to begin within the current fiscal year, but experienced a delay in obtaining certain materials the government had agreed to provide. 1 Comp. Gen. 708 (1922). See also 23 Comp. Gen. 82 (1943); 20 Comp. Gen. 436 (1941).

An order or contract for the replacement of stock is viewed as meeting a bona fide need of the year in which the contract is made as long as it is intended to replace stock used in that year, even though the replacement items will not be used until the following year. See 44 Comp. Gen. 695 (1965). "Stock" in this context refers to "readily available common-use standard items." Id. at 697. See also 73 Comp. Gen. 259 (1994); 32 Comp. Gen. 436 (1953). Generally, scheduling delivery for the following year would seem irrelevant. There are limits, however. GAO has questioned the propriety, from the bona fide needs perspective, of purchases of materials carried in stock for more than a year prior to issuance for use. B-134277, Dec. 18, 1957.

5. Services Rendered beyond the Fiscal Year

Services procured by contract are generally viewed as chargeable to the appropriation current at the time the services are rendered. 38 Comp. Gen. 316 (1958). However, a need may arise in one fiscal year for services that, by their nature, cannot be separated for performance in separate fiscal years. The Comptroller General has held that the question of whether to charge the appropriation current on the date the contract is made, or to charge funds current at the time the services are rendered, depends upon whether the services are "severable" or "entire":

> "The fact that the contract covers a part of two fiscal years does not necessarily mean that payments thereunder are for splitting between the two fiscal years involved upon the basis of services actually performed during each fiscal year. In fact, the general rule is that the fiscal year appropriation current at the time the contract is made is chargeable with payments under the contract, although performance thereunder may extend into the ensuing fiscal year."

23 Comp. Gen. 370, 371 (1943). A contract that is viewed as "entire" is chargeable to the fiscal year in which it was made, notwithstanding that performance may have extended into the following fiscal year. The determining factor for whether services are severable or entire is whether they represent a single undertaking. Thus, in 23 Comp. Gen. 370, a contract for the cultivation and protection of a tract of rubber-bearing plants, payable on completion of the services, was chargeable against fiscal year funds for the year in which the contract was made. Because the services necessarily covered the entire growing period, which extended into the following fiscal year, the Comptroller General characterized them as a single undertaking, which "although extending over a part of two fiscal years, nevertheless was determinable both as to the services needed and the price to be paid therefor at the time the contract was entered into." Id. at 371.

The rationale of 23 Comp. Gen. 370 was applied in 59 Comp. Gen. 386 (1980) (requisition for printing accompanied by manuscript sufficient for Government Printing Office to proceed with job). See, e.g., 65 Comp. Gen. 741 (1986) (contract for study and final report on psychological problems among Vietnam veterans); B-257977, Nov. 15, 1995 (contract for 2-year intern training program since interns are required to complete entire training program to be eligible for noncompetitive Presidential Management Intern appointment). See also 73 Comp. Gen. 77 (1994) (subsequent modifications to Fish and Wildlife Service research work orders should be charged to the fiscal year current when the work orders were issued since the purpose of the research is to provide a final research report and the services under the contract are nonseverable). The last opinion is noteworthy because it pointed out that a limitation of funds clause does not affect the application of the bona fide needs rule and the severable test. 73 Comp. Gen. at 80.

However, where the services are continuing and recurring in nature, the contract is severable. Service contracts that are "severable" may not cross fiscal year lines unless authorized by statute. 71 Comp. Gen. 428 (1992); 58 Comp. Gen. 321, 324 (1979); B-192518, Aug. 9, 1979; B-133001, Mar. 9, 1979; B-187881, Oct. 3, 1977. See also B-287619, July 5, 2001 (TRICARE contractors provide on-going services such as enrolling beneficiaries, adjudicating claims, etc., that are severable into components that independently provide value). Most federal agencies have authority to enter into a 1-year severable service contract, beginning at any time during the fiscal year and extending into the next fiscal year, and to obligate the total amount of the contract to the appropriation current at the time the agency entered into the contract. 10 U.S.C. § 2410a (defense agencies); 41 U.S.C. § 2531 (civilian agencies); 41 U.S.C. § 2531-1 (Comptroller General); 41 U.S.C. § 2531-2 (Library of Congress); 41 U.S.C. § 2531-3 (Chief Administrative Officer of the House of Representatives); 41 U.S.C. § 2531-4 (Congressional Budget Office). See also B-259274, May 22, 1996. Otherwise, the services must be charged to the fiscal year(s) in which they are rendered. 65 Comp. Gen. at 743; 33 Comp. Gen. 90 (1953) (trucking services); 10 Comp. Dec. 284 (1903) (contract for services of various categories of skilled laborers in such quantities and at such times as may be deemed necessary is severable). As stated in 33 Comp. Gen. at 92:

> "The need for current services, such as those covered by the contract here under consideration, arises only from day to day, or month to month, and the Government cannot, in the absence of specific legislative authorization, be obligated for such services by any contract running beyond the fiscal year."

See also 35 Comp. Gen. 319 (1955), amplified by B-125444, Feb. 16, 1956 (gardening and window cleaning services).

In addition to the recurring nature of the services, another factor identified in some of the decisions is whether the contracted-for services are viewed as personal or nonpersonal. Personal services are presumptively severable by their nature and are properly chargeable to the fiscal year in which the services are rendered. B-174226, Mar. 13, 1972 (performance on an evaluation team). Legal services have been viewed as either personal or nonpersonal, depending on the nature of the work to be done. B-122596, Feb. 18, 1955; B-122228, Dec. 23, 1954.

The distinction appears to have derived from the distinction inherent in 5 U.S.C. § 3109, which authorizes agencies to procure services of experts or consultants by employment (personal) or contract (nonpersonal). B-174226, supra. In the context of applying the bona fide needs rule, however, the distinction is not particularly useful since it is still necessary to look at the nature of the services involved in the particular case. In other words, characterizing services as personal or nonpersonal does not provide you with an automatic answer. In fact, some of the more recent cases have merely considered the nature of the work without characterizing it as personal or nonpersonal, which would have added nothing to the analysis. E.g., 50 Comp. Gen. 589 (1971) (fees of attorneys contracted for under Criminal Justice Act chargeable to appropriations current at time of appointment); B-224702, Aug. 5, 1987 (contract for legal support services held severable since it consisted primarily of clerical tasks and required no final report or end product).

A 1981 decision applied the above principles to agreements made by the Small Business Administration (SBA) with private organizations to provide technical and management assistance to businesses eligible for assistance under the Small Business Act. The typical agreement covered one calendar year and crossed fiscal year lines. Under the agreement, payment was to be made only for completed tasks and SBA was under no obligation to place any orders, or to place all orders with any given contractor. The question was whether the "contract" was chargeable to the fiscal year in which it was executed. The Comptroller General found that the services involved were clearly severable and that the agreement was not really a contract since it lacked mutuality of obligation. Accordingly, SBA created a contract obligation only when it placed a definite order, and could charge each fiscal year only with obligations incurred during that fiscal year. 60 Comp. Gen. 219 (1981). The principles were reiterated in 61 Comp. Gen. 184 (1981).

In another 1981 case, GAO considered the District of Columbia's recording of obligations for social security disability medical examinations. A person seeking to establish eligibility for disability benefits is given an appointment for a medical examination and a purchase order is issued at that time. However, for a number of reasons beyond the District's control, the examination may not take place until the following fiscal year (for example, a person makes an application at end of fiscal year or does not show up for initial appointment). Nevertheless, the need for the examination arises when the applicant presents his or her claim for disability benefits. The decision concluded that the obligation occurs when the purchase order is issued and is chargeable to that fiscal year. 60 Comp. Gen. 452 (1981).

Training tends to be nonseverable. Thus, where a training obligation is incurred in one fiscal year, the entire cost is chargeable to that year, regardless of the fact that performance may extend into the following year. B-233243, Aug. 3, 1989; B-213141-O.M., Mar. 29, 1984. In 70 Comp. Gen. 296 (1991), training that began on the first day of fiscal year 1990 was held chargeable to 1989 appropriations where the training had been identified as a need for 1989, scheduling was beyond the agency's control, and the time between procurement and performance was not excessive. If some particular training were severable (it is not entirely clear when this might be the case), the contract could not cross fiscal year lines and payment would have to be apportioned between the fiscal years in which the training is actually conducted. See 34 Comp. Gen. 432 (1955).

After a confusing start, we have determined that the type of contract does not affect the severable versus nonseverable distinction. For example, "level-of-effort" contracts may be severable or nonseverable. A level-of-effort contract is a type of cost-reimbursement contract in which the scope of work is defined in general terms, with the contractor being obligated to provide a specified level of effort (e.g., a specified number of person-hours) for a stated time period. Federal Acquisition Regulation, 48 C.F.R. § 16.306(d)(2). The bona fide needs determination is based not on the contract type but on the nature of the work being performed and is, in the first instance, the responsibility of the contracting agency. B-235678, July 30, 1990. A 1985 case, 65 Comp. Gen. 154, had implied that all level-of-effort contracts were severable by definition (id. at 156), and to that extent was modified by B-235678. See also B-277165, Jan. 10, 2000 (cost-plus-fixed-fee contracts are presumptively severable unless the actual nature of the work warrants a different conclusion).

The Comptroller General has noted that to some degree an agency can control whether services are severable or nonseverable by selecting the type of contract and crafting the statement of work. B-277165, supra ("one might reasonably conclude that the initial agency determination whether the contract is for funding purposes severable or nonseverable takes place roughly contemporaneously with agency selection of contract type").

As a final thought, there is a fairly simple test that is often helpful in determining whether a given service is severable or nonseverable. Suppose that a service contract is to be performed half in one fiscal year and half in the next. Suppose further that the contract is terminated at the end of the first fiscal year and is not renewed. What do you have? In the case of a window-cleaning contract, you have half of your windows clean, a benefit that is not diminished by the fact that the other half is still dirty. What you paid for the first half has not been wasted. These services are clearly severable. Now consider a contract to conduct a study and prepare a final report, as in 65 Comp. Gen. 741 (1986). If this contract is terminated halfway through, you essentially have nothing. The partial results of an incomplete study, while perhaps beneficial in some ethereal sense, do not do you very much good when what you needed was the complete study and report. Or suppose the contract is to repair a broken frammis. If the repairs are not completed, certainly some work has been done but you still don't have an operational frammis. The latter two examples are nonseverable.

6. Replacement Contracts

In an early decision, the Comptroller of the Treasury was asked whether fiscal year 1902 funds, originally obligated under a contract but unexpended because of contractor default, could be used in the following year to continue the original object of the contract. The Comptroller stated:

"A contract was properly made within the fiscal year 1902, and it would seem that any part of the consideration of that contract which failed of use owing to the default of the contractor could still be used in carrying out the object of the original contract within the meaning of

[31 U.S.C. § 1502(a)]. Appropriations are made to be used and not to be defeated in their use, and it would be a narrow construction to hold that a default on a properly made contract would prevent the use of the appropriation for the object for which it was made and for carrying out which the contract was executed."

9 Comp. Dec. 10, 11 (1902). This marked the beginning of the replacement contract theory.

In its traditional form, the rule is well settled that, where it becomes necessary to terminate a contract because of the contractor's default, the funds obligated under the original contract are available, beyond their original period of obligational availability, for the purpose of engaging another contractor to complete the unfinished work. 60 Comp. Gen. 591 (1981); 55 Comp. Gen. 1351 (1976); 44 Comp. Gen. 623 (1965); 40 Comp. Gen. 590 (1961); 32 Comp. Gen. 565 (1953); 2 Comp. Gen. 130 (1922); 21 Comp. Dec. 107 (1914); B-160834, Apr. 7, 1967; B-105555, Sept. 26, 1951; A-22134, Apr. 12, 1928.

Implicit in the rule is the premise that the original contract validly obligated then current funds. See 34 Comp. Gen. 239 (1954). In addition, the rule is based on the notion that the default termination does not eliminate the bona fide need of the fiscal year in which the original contract was executed. 44 Comp. Gen. 399, 401 (1965). In accordance with 31 U.S.C. § 1502, amounts from the appropriation available at the time the original contract was entered would remain available to fund costs properly chargeable to that appropriation. See B-242274, Aug. 27, 1991. Accordingly, the replacement contract seeks only to meet the agency's preexisting and continuing need relying on the budget authority obligated by the original contract.

In order for funds to remain available beyond expiration for a replacement contract, three conditions must be met:

- A bona fide need for the work, supplies, or services must have existed when the original contract was executed, and it must continue to exist up to the award of the replacement contract. E.g., 55 Comp. Gen. 1351, 1353 (1976); 34 Comp. Gen. 239, 240 (1954). If a terminated contract is found to have been improperly made to fulfill a need of a fiscal year other than the year against which the obligation was recorded, it would also be improper to charge that same appropriation for obligations incident to a replacement contract. 35 Comp. Gen. 692 (1956). In addition, if contracts made in a subsequent fiscal year do not satisfy a continuing need for the goods and/or services provided under the original contract from a prior fiscal year, then the subsequent fiscal year contracts are not replacements and those contracts are not chargeable to the prior fiscal year appropriation. See B-242274, Aug. 27, 1991.

- The replacement contract must not exceed the scope of the original contract. If it does, it is a new obligation and must be charged to funds currently available for obligation at the time the replacement contract is entered into. E.g., 44 Comp. Gen. 399 (1965); B-181176-O.M., June 26, 1974.

- The replacement contract must be awarded within a reasonable time after termination of the original contract. E.g., 60 Comp. Gen. at 593. Excessive delay raises the presumption that the original contract was not intended to meet a then existing bona fide need. The same result may follow if there is unwarranted delay in terminating the original contract. 32 Comp. Gen. 565 (1953).

At one time, the replacement contract rule was mostly (but not exclusively) limited to the default situation. E.g., 24 Comp. Gen. 555 (1945), overruled by 55 Comp. Gen. 1351. It has, however, been expanded. In 34 Comp. Gen. 239 (1954), a default termination was found to be erroneous and was converted to a termination for convenience by agreement of the parties to permit settlement of the contractor's claim for damages. The decision held that, in view of the original termination, the funds originally obligated were available for the timely execution of a new contract for the performance of the unfinished work. A further question in that case was whether the replacement contract rule was affected by the newly enacted 31 U.S.C. § 1501(a), which requires that contractual obligations be supported by a binding agreement in writing executed prior to expiration of the appropriations availability. The decision held that the original contract met these requirements. 34 Comp. Gen. at 241.

In a later case, a contract for flooring repairs was awarded in fiscal year 1975, obligating fiscal year 1975 funds, conditioned upon a determination from the Small Business Administration (SBA) that the contractor qualified as a small business. SBA found the contractor not to be a small business. Concluding that the original award was sufficient to support an obligation under 31 U.S.C. § 1501(a), the Comptroller General applied the replacement contract rule and held that the funds obligated for the contract in fiscal year 1975 could be used to resolicit in fiscal year 1976. 55 Comp. Gen. 1351 (1976).

In 66 Comp. Gen. 625 (1987), however, the Comptroller General declined to extend the rule in a situation involving a voluntary modification that reduced the scope of a contract. The Navy had contracted for the construction of 12 ships. The contractor encountered financial difficulties and filed for reorganization under Chapter 11 of the Bankruptcy Act under which the contractor could, with court approval, reject the contract. See 11 U.S.C. §§ 365(a) and (d)(2). To avert this possibility, the Navy agreed to a contract modification that, among other things, reduced the number of ships to be provided from 12 to 10. The question was whether the funds originally obligated for the 2 ships deleted by the modification were available after expiration to fund a reprocurement. GAO concluded that they were not because there had been no default, nor was there an actual rejection under the Bankruptcy Code. "[T]he modification was an essentially voluntary act on the part of the Navy, and as such is beyond the scope of the replacement contract rule." Id. at 627. Therefore, any replacement contract for the 2 deleted ships would have to be charged to appropriations current at the time it was made.

Cases involving the termination of erroneously or improperly awarded contracts have been less than consistent, although a clear direction now appears evident. The earliest decisions applied the replacement contract rule. Thus, 17 Comp. Gen. 1098 (1938) held, without much discussion, that funds obligated by an award to a bidder subsequently determined not to have been the low bidder could be used for an award to the otherwise low bidder in the following fiscal year. In a 1953 case, a contract had to be partially canceled because the contractor's bid had not conformed to the advertised specifications. GAO noted that "the obligating instrument was legally defective in such a way as to render the contract voidable at the election of the Government," but nevertheless applied the replacement contract rule. B-116131, Oct. 19, 1953. See also B-89019, May 31, 1950.

GAO's position seemed to change with the enactment of 31 U.S.C. § 1501(a) in 1954, on the theory that a contract award found to be invalid did not constitute a binding agreement so as to support a recordable obligation. 38 Comp. Gen. 190 (1958); B-118428, Sept. 21, 1954, overruling B-116131 and B-89019. However, B-116131 was at least arguably "reinstated" by B-152033, May 27, 1964, which followed both the "voidable at the election of the government" rationale and the result of B-116131, without citing either it or the case that presumably overruled it. See also B-173244(2), Aug. 10, 1972; B-158261, Mar. 9, 1966. This latter group of cases was in turn cited with approval in 55 Comp. Gen. 1351, 1353 (1976).

The apparent direction indicated by 55 Comp. Gen. 1351 (1976) and the cases it cited was called into question by statements in 60 Comp. Gen. 591 (1981) to the effect that the replacement contract rule does not apply to terminations for the convenience of the government, whether initiated by the contracting agency or on recommendation of some other body such as GAO. Of course, the typical situation in which a replacement contract is needed following a termination for convenience is where the original contract is found to have been improperly awarded. An important clarification occurred in 68 Comp. Gen. 158 (1988), which modified 60 Comp. Gen. 591 and held the replacement contract rule applicable where a contract must be terminated for convenience, without a prior default termination, pursuant to a determination by competent administrative or judicial authority (court, board of contract appeals, GAO) that the contract award was improper. As noted previously, the bona fide need of the original contract must continue, and the replacement contract must be made without undue delay after the original contract is terminated and must be awarded on the same basis as, and be substantially similar in scope and size to, the original contract.

Logically and inevitably, the next question would be why the rule should not be the same regardless of whether the defect leading to termination is determined by an external reviewing body or by the contracting agency itself. It should make no difference, GAO concluded in 70 Comp. Gen. 230 (1991). The essence of the problem--a legal impropriety in the procurement process requiring corrective action--is no different. Thus, the replacement contract rule, with its attendant conditions, applies where the contracting agency determines that a contract award was improper and terminates the contract for the convenience of the government, provided there is clear evidence that the award was erroneous and the agency documents its determination with appropriate findings of fact and law. Id.

It is worth noting that with regard to agencies that terminate their contracts based on improper awards, the 1991 GAO decision added a fourth condition to the three articulated earlier in this section that determine whether funds remain available in a subsequent fiscal year for replacement contracts. In addition to the existence of a continuing bona fide need, a replacement contract of the same size and scope as the original, and the execution of the replacement without undue delay, the decision added that the original contract had to be made in "good faith" before an agency could use prior year appropriations to fund a replacement contract after terminating the original for convenience due to an improper award. 70 Comp. Gen. at 232; 70 Comp. Gen. 287, 289 (1991).

The issue of whether an agency is required to avail itself of the replacement contract rule arose in a protest submitted to GAO alleging the improper award of a contract. GAO found that the agency properly awarded the contract and that, even when available, the replacement contract rule is not mandatory on an agency. B-270723, Apr. 15, 1996. The 1996 decision stated that since the replacement contract rule "provides a mechanism to allow agencies to administer their contract effectively when there is a reason to terminate a contract, its use is solely at the government's discretion." Id. At least one federal district court has adopted the position that the availability of funds for a replacement contract does not require the agency to procure a replacement contract. LeBoeuf, Lamb, Greene & MacRae, L.L.P. v. Abraham, 215 F. Supp. 2d 73, 81 (D.D.C. 2002). See, e.g., B-276334.2, Oct. 27, 1997.

7. Contract Modifications and Amendments Affecting Price

Contract performance may extend over several years. During this time, the contract may be modified or amended for a variety of reasons at the instigation of either party. An amendment within the general scope of the contract that does not increase the contract price remains an obligation of the year in which the contract was executed. B-68707, Aug. 19, 1947. If the modification results in an increase in contract price, the question from the bona fide needs perspective is which fiscal year to charge with the modification.

If the modification exceeds the general scope of the original contract, for example, by increasing the quantity of items to be delivered, the modification amounts to a new obligation and is chargeable to funds current at the time the modification is made. 37 Comp. Gen. 861 (1958); B-207433, Sept. 16, 1983. When the Internal Revenue Service (IRS) benefited from a contractual provision that allowed its contractor to pass along cost savings to the agency in a fiscal year subsequent to when it entered the contract, IRS could not use those cost savings to increase the quantity of items that the contract required the contractor to deliver. B-257617, Apr. 18, 1995. Although there was a bona fide need for an increased quantity of items that had continued from the fiscal year that IRS entered the contract, it was not within the scope of the contract to increase the quantity of items delivered. If the contractual provision had stated that a cost savings would be passed on to IRS in the form of an increased quantity of items delivered, then increasing the quantity would not have constituted a contract modification creating a new obligation. Id.

In the case of a contract for severable services, a modification providing for increased services must be charged to the fiscal year or years in which the services are rendered, applying the principles discussed in section B.5. 61 Comp. Gen. 184 (1981), aff'd upon reconsideration, B-202222, Aug. 2, 1983; B-224702, Aug. 5, 1987. See also B-235086, Apr. 24, 1991. In 61 Comp. Gen. 184, for example, a contract to provide facilities and staff to operate a project camp was modified in the last month of fiscal year 1980. The modification called for work to be performed in fiscal year 1981. Regardless of whether the contract was viewed as a service contract or a contract to provide facilities, the modification did not meet a bona fide need of fiscal year 1980. The modification amounted to a separate contract and could be charged only to fiscal year 1981 funds, notwithstanding that it purported to modify a contract properly chargeable to fiscal year 1980 funds.

For modifications within the general scope of the original contract, the situation is a bit more complicated. Most government contracts contain provisions which, under certain conditions, render the government liable to make equitable adjustments in the contract price. Such liability may arise due to changes in specifications, government-caused delay, changed conditions, increased overhead rates, etc. These conditions are set out in standard contract clauses such as the "Changes" clause, "Government Property" clause, or "Negotiated Overhead Rates" clause.

Because there is no way to know whether the government will actually incur liability under these provisions, and if so, the amount of such liability, until the occurrence of the specified conditions (cf. 50 Comp. Gen. 589, 591 (1971)), the appropriations charged with the cost of the contract are not firmly obligated to cover future price increases, which arise due to the operation of these clauses. Nevertheless, as noted, government contracts frequently contemplate that performance will extend into subsequent fiscal years. When an upward price adjustment is necessitated in a subsequent year, the general approach is to ask whether the adjustment is attributable to an "antecedent liability"--that is, whether the government's liability arises and is enforceable under a provision in the original contract. If the answer to this question is yes, then a within-scope price adjustment, which is requested and approved in a subsequent fiscal year, for example, under the "Changes" clause, will--with one important qualification to be noted later--be charged against the appropriation current at the time the contract was originally executed. Cases supporting this proposition in various contexts are 59 Comp. Gen. 518 (1980); 23 Comp. Gen. 943 (1944); 21 Comp. Gen. 574 (1941); 18 Comp. Gen. 363 (1938); A-15225, Sept. 24, 1926; B-146285-O.M.,

Sept. 28, 1976. See also B-197344, Aug. 21, 1980, where supplemental work was done without issuance of a formal contract modification. This principle is occasionally referred to as the doctrine of "relation back." E.g., 37 Comp. Gen. 861, 863 (1958).

The reasoning is that a change order does not give rise to a new liability, but instead only renders fixed and certain the amount of the government's preexisting liability to adjust the contract price. Since that liability arises at the time the original contract is executed, the subsequent price adjustment is viewed as reflecting a bona fide need of the same year in which funds were obligated for payment of the original contract price. The concept was stated as follows in 23 Comp. Gen. 943, 945 (1944) (explanatory information provided):

> "It is true that at the time the contract was executed it was not known that there would, in fact, be any changes ordered ...for which the contractor would be entitled to be paid an amount in addition to amounts otherwise payable under the contract. Also, it is true that [the Changes clause] contemplates the execution of amendments to the contract from time to time covering such changes. However, the fact remains that the obligations and liabilities of the parties respecting such changes are fixed by the terms of the original contract, and the various amendments merely render definite and liquidated the extent of the Government's liability in connection with such changes."

In order to avoid overobligating the original appropriation, the contracting officer must estimate the expected net additional obligations to insure that available appropriations are not committed to other purposes. E.g., 61 Comp. Gen. 609, 612 (1982); B-192036, Sept. 11, 1978. It is also true, however, that estimated liabilities of this type require constant review to ensure that appropriations do not remain encumbered in excess of the amounts that will actually be needed to meet the total liability under the contract.

For contracts spanning lengthy periods of time, funding of within scope modifications involves the use of expired appropriations. The balances in expired accounts prior to closing are available without further congressional action.

Not all price adjustments arising from contract modifications or amendments represent a bona fide need of the year in which the agreement was made. If, as noted above, the change or amendment exceeds the general scope of the contract, or is not made pursuant to a provision in the original contract, then it is not based on any antecedent liability, in which event it may obligate only appropriations current at the time it is issued. 56 Comp. Gen. 414 (1977). See also 25 Comp. Gen. 332 (1945) (purported change order issued after completion of contract, covering work the contractor was not legally bound to do under the original contract, amounted to a new contract).

As noted above, there is an important exception or qualification to the antecedent liability rule. In cost reimbursement contracts, discretionary cost increases (i.e., increases that are not enforceable by the contractor), which exceed funding ceilings established by the contract, may be charged to funds currently available when the discretionary increase is granted by the contracting officer. 61 Comp. Gen. 609 (1982). It would be unreasonable, the decision pointed out, to require the contracting officer to reserve funds in anticipation of increases beyond the contract's ceiling. Id. at 612. Changes that do not exceed the stipulated ceiling continue to be chargeable to funds available when the contract was originally made (id. at 611), as do amounts for final overhead in excess of the ceiling where the contractor has an enforceable right to those amounts (id. at 612). Since prior decisions such as 59 Comp. Gen. 518 had not drawn the below-ceiling/above-ceiling distinction, 61 Comp. Gen. 609 modified them to that extent. A more recent case applying 61 Comp. Gen. 609 is 65 Comp. Gen. 741 (1986).

Once an appropriation account has closed (generally five fiscal years after the expiration of obligational availability), questions of antecedent liability or relation back are no longer relevant for purposes of determining the availability of amounts in the closed accounts since, at that time, appropriation balances cease to be available for expenditure. However, questions of antecedent liability or relation back are used to determine the extent to which current funds are available since, once an appropriation closes, only current funds may be used, up to specified limits, for such obligations. 31 U.S.C. §§ 1552 and 1553.

8. Multiyear Contracts

a. Introduction

(3 yr contract, 7/2 mo.) funding in the current yr

The term "multiyear contract" has been used in a variety of situations to describe a variety of contracts touching more than one fiscal year. To prevent confusion, we think it is important to start by establishing a working definition. A multiyear contract, as we use the term in this discussion, is a contract covering the requirements, or needs, of more than one fiscal year. A contract for the needs of the current year, even though performance may extend over several years, is not a multiyear contract. Thus, a contract to construct a ship that will take 3 years to complete is not a multiyear contract; a contract to construct one ship a year for the next 3 years is.

Multiyear contracting, like most things in life, has advantages and disadvantages. Some of the potential benefits are:

- Multiyear contracting can reduce costs by permitting the contractor to amortize nonrecurring "start up" costs over the life of the contract. Without multiyear authority, the contractor may insist on recovering these costs under the 1-year contract (since there is no guarantee of getting future contracts), thus resulting in increased unit prices.

- Multiyear contracting may enhance quality by reducing the uncertainty of continued government business and enabling the contractor to maintain a stable workforce.

- Multiyear contracting may increase competition by enabling small businesses to compete in situations where nonrecurring start-up costs would otherwise limit competition to larger concerns.

However, the situation is not one-sided. Multiyear contracting authority also has potential disadvantages:

- Competition may decrease because there will be fewer opportunities to bid.

- A contractor who is able to amortize start-up costs in a multiyear contract has, in effect, a government-funded competitive price advantage over new contractors in subsequent solicitations. This could evolve into a sole-source posture.

- Being locked into a contract for several years is not always desirable, particularly where the alternative is to incur cancellation charges that could offset initial savings.

An agency may engage in multiyear contracting only if it has (1) no-year funds or multiple year funds covering the entire term of the contract or (2) specific statutory authority. Cray Research, Inc. v. United States, 44 Fed. Cl. 327, 332 (1999); 67 Comp. Gen. 190, 192 (1988); B-171277, Apr. 2, 1971 (multiyear contract permissible under no-year trust fund). An agency may enter into a multiyear contract with fiscal year appropriations (or for a term exceeding the period of availability of a multiple year appropriation) only if it has specific statutory authority to do so. See 71 Comp. Gen. 428, 430 (1992); B-259274, May 22, 1996. Most agencies now have some form of multiyear contracting authority, as we will describe in the next section.

b. Multiple Year and No-Year Appropriations

If an agency does not have specific multiyear contracting authority but enters into a multiyear contract solely under authority of a multiple year or no-year appropriation, the full contract amount must be obligated at the time of contract award. B-195260, July 11, 1979. This is also true for revolving funds, which authorize expenditures without fiscal year limitation. Revolving funds must have sufficient budget authority against which to record the entire amount of long-term contracts at the time of the obligation. 72 Comp. Gen. 59, 61 (1992). A revolving fund may not count anticipated receipts from future customer orders as budget authority. B-288142, Sept. 6, 2001. See also U.S. General Accounting Office, The Air Force Has Incurred Numerous Overobligations In Its Industrial Fund, AFMD-81-53 (Washington, D.C.: Aug. 14, 1981).

However, there have been some circumstances under which GAO approved the incremental funding of a multiyear contract using no-year funds. For example, 43 Comp. Gen. 657 (1964) involved a scheme in which funds would be made available, and obligated, on a year-by-year basis, together with a "commitment" to cover maximum cancellation costs. The cancellation costs represented amortized start-up costs, which would be adjusted downward each year. Thus, funds would be available to cover the government's maximum potential liability in each year. See also 62 Comp. Gen. 143 (1983) (similar approach for long-term vessel charters under the Navy Industrial Fund); 51 Comp. Gen. 598, 604 (1972) (same); 48 Comp. Gen. 497, 502 (1969) (either obligational approach acceptable under revolving fund). (As we will see later, this type of arrangement under a fiscal year appropriation presents problems.)

If an agency has neither multiple year or no-year funds, nor uses multiyear contracting authority, a multiyear contract violates statutory funding restrictions, including the Antideficiency Act (prohibiting obligations in advance of an appropriation for that fiscal year, 31 U.S.C. § 1341(a)) and the bona fide needs statute (prohibiting the obligation of an appropriation in advance of need, 31 U.S.C. § 1502(a)). See Cray Research, Inc. v. United States, 44 Fed. Cl. 327,332 (1999). E.g., 67 Comp. Gen. 190 (1988); 66 Comp. Gen. 556 (1987); 64 Comp. Gen. 359 (1985); 48 Comp. Gen. 497 (1969); 42 Comp. Gen. 272 (1962); 27 Op. Att'y Gen. 584 (1909). Multiyear commitments were found illegal in various contexts in each of these cases, although each case does not necessarily discuss each funding statute.

In 42 Comp. Gen. 272, for example, the Air Force, using fiscal year appropriations, awarded a 3-year contract for aircraft maintenance, troop billeting, and base management services on Wake Island. Because an agency typically incurs an obligation at the time it enters into a contract, and must charge that obligation to an appropriation current at that time, the Air Force contract raised two issues: (1) whether the services to be provided in the second and third years of the contract constituted a bona fide need of the Air Force's fiscal year appropriation, and (2) if not, whether the Air Force had incurred an obligation in the first fiscal year for the needs of the second and third years in advance of appropriations for those 2 years. The Air Force contended that no funds were obligated at time of contract award; instead, the Air Force argued that it had a "requirements" contract, and that it incurred no obligation unless and until it issued requisitions, thereby exempting the contract from the statutory funding restrictions. However, the Comptroller General refused to adopt this characterization of the contract. Although the contractor had expressly agreed to perform only services for which he had received the contracting officer's order, GAO found that there was no need for an administrative determination that requirements existed since the contract services were "automatic incidents of the use of the air field." Id. at 277. Only a decision to close the base would eliminate the requirements. Consequently, the contract was found to be an unauthorized multiyear contract--the Air Force, using fiscal year appropriations, had entered into a contract for its needs of subsequent fiscal years in advance of appropriations for those years.

c. Fiscal Year Appropriations

If an agency is contracting with fiscal year appropriations and does not have multiyear contracting authority, the only authorized course of action, apart from a series of separate fiscal year contracts, is a fiscal year contract with renewal options, with each renewal option (1) contingent on the availability of future appropriations and (2) to be exercised only by affirmative action on the part of the government (as opposed to automatic renewal unless the government refuses). Leiter v. United States, 271 U.S. 204 (1926); 66 Comp. Gen. 556 (1987); 36 Comp. Gen. 683 (1957); 33 Comp. Gen. 90 (1953); 29 Comp. Gen. 91 (1949); 28 Comp. Gen. 553 (1949); B-88974, Nov. 10, 1949. The inclusion of a renewal option is key; with a renewal option, the government incurs a financial obligation only for the fiscal year, and incurs no financial obligation for subsequent years unless and until it exercises its right to renew. The government records the amount of its obligation for the first fiscal year against the appropriation current at the time it awards the contract. The government also records amounts of obligations for future fiscal years against appropriations current at the time it exercises its renewal options. The mere inclusion of a contract provision conditioning the government's obligation on future appropriations without also subjecting the multiyear contract to the government's renewal option each year would be insufficient. Cray Research, Inc. v. United States, 44 Fed. Cl. 327, 332 (1999). Thus, in 42 Comp. Gen. 272 (1962), the Comptroller General, while advising the Air Force that under the circumstances it could complete that particular contract, also advised that the proper course of action would be either to use an annual contract with renewal options or to obtain specific multiyear authority from Congress. Id. at 278.

In a 1-year contract with renewal options, the contractor can never be sure whether the renewal options will be exercised, thereby preventing the contractor from amortizing initial investment costs. To protect against this possibility, contractors occasionally seek a contract termination penalty equal to the unamortized balance of initial investment costs if the government fails to renew the contract for any fiscal year. However, the Comptroller General has held that these provisions contravene the bona fide needs rule:

"The theory behind such obligations (covering amortized facility costs unrecovered at time of termination) has been that a need existed during the fiscal year the contracts were made for the productive plant capacity represented by the new facilities which were to be built by the contractor to enable him to furnish the supplies called for by the contracts. After thorough consideration of the matter, we believe that such obligations cannot be justified on the theory of a present need for productive capacity".

" …The real effect of the termination liability is to obligate the Commission to purchase a certain quantity of magnesium during each of five successive years or to pay damages for its failure to do so. In other words, the termination charges represent a part of the price of future, as distinguished from current, deliveries and needs under the contract, and for that reason such charges are not based on a current fiscal year need."

36 Comp. Gen. 683, 685 (1957). See also 37 Comp. Gen. 155 (1957).

Attempts to impose penalty charges for early termination (sometimes called "separate charges") have occurred in a number of cases involving automated data processing (ADP) procurements. In one case, a competitor for a contract to acquire use of an ADP system for a 65-month period proposed to include a provision under which the government would be assessed a penalty if it failed to exercise its annual renewal options. The Comptroller General noted that the penalty was clearly intended to recapitalize the contractor for its investment based on the full life of the system in the event the government did not continue using the equipment. Accordingly, the Comptroller General concluded that the penalty did not reasonably relate to the value of the equipment's use during the fiscal year in which it would be levied. The penalty charges would, therefore, not be based on a bona fide need of the current fiscal year and their payment would violate statutory funding restrictions. 56 Comp. Gen. 142 (1976), aff'd in part, 56 Comp. Gen. 505 (1977). See also 56 Comp. Gen. 167 (1976); B-190659, Oct. 23, 1978.

One scheme, however, has been found to be legally sufficient to permit the government to realize the cost savings that may accrue through multiyear contracting. The plan approved by the Comptroller General in 48 Comp. Gen. 497, 501-02 (1969) provided for a 1-year rental contract with an option to renew each subsequent year. If the government completed the full rental period by continuing the contract on a year-by-year basis, it would be entitled to have monthly rental credits applied during the final months of the rental period. The Comptroller General noted that:

> "Under this arrangement the Government would not be obligated to continue the rental beyond the fiscal year in which made, or beyond any succeeding fiscal year, unless or until a purchase order is issued expressly continuing such rental during the following fiscal year. In effect, the company is proposing a 1 year rental contract with option to renew. Also, under this proposal rental for any contract year would not exceed the lowest rental otherwise obtainable from [the contractor] for one fiscal year. We have no legal objection to this type of rental plan for ADP equipment."

d. Contracts with No Financial Obligation

Multiyear arrangements may be permissible, even without specific statutory authority, if they are structured in such a way that the agency, at time of contract award, incurs no financial obligation. Without a financial obligation, the agency does not violate the Antideficiency Act or the bona fide needs rule. In 63 Comp. Gen. 129 (1983), the Comptroller General considered the General Services Administration proposal to use 3-year "Multiple Award Schedule" (MAS) contracts for Federal Supply Schedule items. There was no commitment to order any specific quantity of items. Rather, the commitment was for an agency with a requirement for a scheduled item to order it from the contractor if the contractor has offered the lowest price. If an agency found the item elsewhere for less than the contract price, it was free to procure the item from that other source without violating the contract. Since entering into the MAS contracts did not require the obligation of funds, there was no violation of statutory funding restrictions. Obligations would occur only when agencies placed specific orders, presumably using funds currently available to them at the time. Another example is a 1935 decision, A-60589, July 12, 1935, which concerned a requirements contract for supplies in which no definite quantity was required to be purchased and under which no financial obligation would be imposed on the government until an order was placed. In order to retain the availability of the vendor and a fixed price, the government agreed not to purchase the items elsewhere. See also B-259274, May 22, 1996.

Also, contracts that do not require the expenditure of appropriated funds are not subject to the same fiscal year strictures. E.g., 10 Comp. Gen. 407 (1931) (no legal objection to multiyear leases or contracts for the operation of concessions on federal property).

9. Specific Statutes Providing for Multiyear and Other Contracting Authorities

As we noted at the beginning of our discussion of the bona fide needs rule, a fixed-term appropriation is available only "to complete contracts properly made within that period of availability." See 31 U.S.C. § 1502 (a). For multiyear contracts, "properly made" means that the bona fide needs rule is satisfied if an agency has statutory authority to obligate its fiscal year funds for a contract that crosses fiscal years or is for multiple years. While these statutes are sometimes referred to as exceptions to the bona fide needs statute, it is clear that by using the phrase "contracts properly made," the bona fide needs statute anticipates that Congress may authorize agencies to obligate funds across fiscal years, either generally or for a particular agency or program. In so doing, Congress defines the bona fide need in the particular statute.

a. Severable Services Contracts *(can cross between physical yrs now) new charge by Congress.*

There are several general authorities to contract across a fiscal year or to enter into multiyear contracts. For example, 41 U.S.C. § 2531 authorizes the heads of executive agencies to enter into procurement contracts for severable services for periods beginning in one fiscal year and ending in the next fiscal year as long as the contracts do not exceed 1 year. It permits agencies to obligate the total amount of the contract to appropriations of the first fiscal year. Without specific statutory authority such as this, such action would violate the bona fide needs rule. Section 2531, in effect, redefines for an agency that elects to contract under authority of section 2531 its bona fide need for the severable services for which it is contracting. Related statutes extend this authority to various legislative branch entities. Similarly, 10 U.S.C. § 2410a authorizes the military departments to use current fiscal year appropriations to finance severable service contracts into the next fiscal year for a total period not to exceed 1 year. GAO states in B-259274, May 22, 1996, that "[t]he purpose of 10 U.S.C. § 2410a is to overcome the bona fide needs rule," which is another way of saying that Congress has provided the military departments with authority to properly enter into a contract not to exceed 1 year that crosses fiscal years. The statute specifically authorizes the departments to obligate "[f]unds made available for a fiscal year … for the total amount of a contract entered into" under section 2410a(a).

In B-259274, May 22, 1996, the Air Force took full advantage of this authority to maximize efficient use of fiscal year appropriations. The Air Force had intended to award a 12-month severable services contract for vehicle maintenance beginning on September 1, 1994 (fiscal year 1994), and running until August 31, 1995 (fiscal year 1995). Using 10 U.S.C. § 2410a, the Air Force had planned to obligate the contract against its fiscal year 1994 appropriation, until it learned that it did not have sufficient unobligated amounts to cover the contract. To avoid Antideficiency Act problems, but taking advantage of section 2410a, the Air Force entered into a 4-month contract, beginning September 1, 1994, and running until December 31, 1994, and included an option to renew the contract at that time. The option, as in the Leiter decision we discussed in section B.8, could be exercised only by the Air Force, not the contractor, by affirmative written notification to the contractor. GAO concluded that the Air Force's obligation was only for 4 months, and under authority of section 2410a, it constituted a bona fide need of fiscal year 1994 and was properly chargeable to fiscal year 1994. Also, GAO found no Antideficiency Act violation. GAO said that with the option to renew for 8 months, the Air Force had incurred "a naked contractual obligation that carries with it no financial exposure to the government."

b. 5-year Contract Authority

(1) 10 U.S.C. §§ 2306b, 2306c:

In addition to the severable services contracting authority, Congress has provided executive, legislative, and judicial entities substantial authority for multiyear contracting for goods and services using annual funds. The military departments are authorized by 10 U.S.C. §§ 2306b and 2306c to enter into multiyear contracts for goods and services, respectively, for periods of not more than 5 years if certain administrative determinations are made. Section 2306b applies not only to routine supplies, but also to the military departments acquisition of weapon systems and items and services associated with such systems. Section 2306c, enacted in response to the Wake Island decision (see 67 Comp. Gen. 190, 193 (1988)), applies to such services as installation maintenance and support, maintenance or modification of aircraft and other complex military equipment, specialized training, and base services. Sections 2306b and 2306c permit the military departments to obligate the entire amount of the 5-year contract to the fiscal year appropriation current at the time of contract award, even though the goods or services procured for the final 4 years of the contract do not constitute needs of that fiscal year. Alternatively, sections 2306b and 2306c permit the military departments to obligate the amount for each of the 5 years against appropriations enacted for each of those years. If funds are not made available for continuation in a subsequent fiscal year, cancellation or termination costs may be paid from appropriations originally available for the contract, appropriations currently available for the same general purpose, or appropriations made specifically for those payments. 10 U.S.C. §§ 2306b(f) and 2306c(e). The authority contained in sections 2306b and 2306c is also available to the Coast Guard and the National Aeronautics and Space Administration. 10 U.S.C. § 2303.

A multiyear contract entered into under authority of 10 U.S.C. §§ 2306b or 2306c is binding on both parties for the full term of the contract unless terminated as provided in the statute. See Beta Systems, Inc. v. United States, 838 F.2d 1179, 1183 n.2 (Fed. Cir. 1988); Beta Systems, Division of Velcon Filters, Inc.v. United States, 16 Cl. Ct. 219, 228 (1989).

A contract under sections 2306b or 2306c must relate to the bona fide needs of the contract period as opposed to the need only of the first fiscal year of the contract period. The statute does not authorize the advance procurement of materials not needed during the 5-year term of the contract. See 64 Comp. Gen. 163 (1984); B-215825-O.M., Nov. 7, 1984. See also 35 Comp. Gen. 220 (1955).

(2) 41 U.S.C. § 254c

The Federal Acquisition Streamlining Act of 1994 (FASA) and related statutes extended multiyear contracting authority with annual funds to nonmilitary departments. FASA authorizes an executive agency to enter into a multiyear contract for the acquisition of property or services for more than 1, but not more than 5 years, if the agency makes certain administrative determinations. 41 U.S.C. § 254c. Related laws extend this authority to various legislative branch agencies. Through FASA and the related laws, Congress has relaxed the constraints of the bona fide needs rule by giving agencies the flexibility to structure contracts to fund the obligations up front, incrementally, or by using the standard bona fide needs rule approach. B-277165, Jan. 10, 2000. To the extent an agency elects to obligate a 5-year contract incrementally, it must also obligate termination costs.

The enactment of FASA satisfied the GAO recommendation for the enactment of legislation to authorize all federal agencies to engage in limited multiyear procurement. See U.S. General Accounting Office, Federal Agencies Should Be Given General Multiyear Contracting Authority For Supplies and Services, PSAD-78-54 (Washington, D.C.: Jan. 10, 1978). See also B-214545, Aug. 7, 1985 (comments on proposed legislation).

c. Examples of Agency-Specific Multiyear Contracting Authorities

An example of a specific authority is 41 U.S.C. § 11a, which authorizes the Secretary of the Army "to incur obligations for fuel in sufficient quantities to meet the requirements for one year without regard to the current fiscal year," and to pay from appropriations either for the fiscal year in which the obligation is incurred or for the ensuing fiscal year. See 28 Comp. Gen. 614 (1949) (construing the term "fuel" in that statute to include gasoline and other petroleum fuel products).

Another example is 31 U.S.C. § 1308, which permits charges for telephone and other utility services for a time period beginning in one fiscal year and ending in another to be charged against appropriations current at the end of the covered time period. In addition, 42 U.S.C. § 2459a authorizes the National Aeronautics and Space Administration to enter into contracts for certain "services provided during the fiscal year following the fiscal year in which funds are appropriated."

A further example of statutory authority for multiyear contracting is 40 U.S.C. § 481(a)(3), which authorizes contracts for public utility services for periods not exceeding 10 years. The purpose of the statute is to enable the government to take advantage of discounts offered under long-term contracts. 62 Comp. Gen. 569, 572 (1983); 35 Comp. Gen. 220, 222-3 (1955). For purposes of applying this statute, the nature of the product or service and not the nature of the provider is the governing factor. 70 Comp. Gen. 44, 49 (1990). Thus, the statute applies to obtaining utility services from other than a "traditional" form of public utility. 62 Comp. Gen. 569. When entering into a contract under 40 U.S.C. § 481(a)(3), the contracting agency needs to have sufficient budget authority only to obligate the first years costs. 62 Comp. Gen. at 572; 44 Comp. Gen. 683, 687-88 (1965).

Other examples of specific multiyear authority are 40 U.S.C. § 490(h), which authorizes the General Services Administration (GSA) to enter into leases for periods of up to 20 years; 40 U.S.C. § 757(c), which authorizes GSA to use the Information Technology Fund for contracts up to 5 years for information technology hardware, software, or services; and 10 U.S.C. § 2828(d), under which the military departments may lease family housing united in foreign countries for periods up to 10 years, to be paid from annual appropriations.

10. Grants and Cooperative Agreements

The bona fide needs rule applies to all federal government activities carried out with appropriated funds, not just contracts, including grants and cooperative agreements. B-289801, Dec. 30, 2002; 73 Comp. Gen. 77, 78-79 (1994). Because of the fundamentally different purposes of contracts and grants, a bona fide needs analysis in the context of grants and cooperative agreements is different from an analysis in a contract context. The purpose of a contract is to acquire goods or services; the purpose of a grant is to provide financial assistance. It is for that reason that we do not import into a grant analysis the contract concepts of supplies and services, particularly severable and nonseverable services. In the world of contracts, the analysis focuses, necessarily, on the agency's need for the goods or services for which it has contracted. In that context, these concepts have particular relevance. The agency's "need" in the grant context, however, is to make a grant in furtherance of the goals Congress hoped to achieve when it enacted the grant-making authority. In this context, the agency's "need" is to make a grant, and the grantee's use of grant funds has no relevance in the assessment of agency needs.

For that reason, a bona fide needs analysis in the grant context focuses on whether the grant was made during the period of availability of the appropriation charged and furthers the authorized purpose of program legislation. B-289801, Dec. 30, 2002. Thus, where a statute authorizes grants to be made for up to 5 years to support childhood education, an award of a 5-year grant fulfills a bona fide need in the year that the grant is awarded even though the 5-year grant is funded with a fiscal year appropriation. Id. However, where the "School Improvement Programs" appropriation for fiscal year 2002 authorizes grants only for "academic year 2002-2003," only grants providing funding for the 2002-03 academic year are a bona fide need of the fiscal year 2002 appropriation, notwithstanding that the program statute authorizes grants for up to 4 years. Id.

The application of contract concepts to grants has not been without doubt. Prior to our 2002 decision, the application of the severability concept to grants and cooperative agreements had evolved over the years. In cases where agencies did not have explicit multiyear award authority, GAO used to treat grants and cooperative agreements in much the same way that it treated service contracts with regard to severability. In 64 Comp. Gen. 359 (1985), GAO held that since the National Institutes of Health (NIH) grant program did not contemplate a required outcome or product but, instead, sought to stimulate research that would be needed year after year, NIH was required to use appropriations available in the year that services were rendered to fund the grants.

However, GAO significantly departed from that reasoning in a 1988 decision involving Small Business Administration (SBA) grants. In that decision, GAO stated that when reviewing grants or cooperative agreements in the context of the bona fide needs rule, the principle of severability is irrelevant. B-229873, Nov. 29, 1988. GAO held that SBA did not violate the bona fide needs rule when it used its current appropriation on September 30, the last day of the fiscal year, to award cooperative agreements to Small Business Development Centers that would use the money in the next fiscal year. GAO concluded that, unlike a contract, a cooperative agreement satisfies the bona fide need of the agency--to financially assist the awardee--at the time SBA makes the award to the Small Business Development Centers. Id. Thus, the dates on which the Centers actually used the financial assistance are irrelevant for purposes of assessing SBA's bona fide need. Id.

Building on the SBA decision, GAO held that the Department of Education could use 1-year appropriations to award multiyear grants where the legislation creating the grant program explicitly stated that the grants could last multiple years and even in instances where the legislation did not address the duration of the grants. B-289801, Dec. 30, 2002. The determining factor is that the grants, at the time of award, further the objective of the grant legislation. Thus, GAO held that Education could use its fiscal year appropriations to fund a 4-year grant when the statute directed the agency to award grants "for periods of not more than 4 years." See 20 U.S.C. § 6651(e)(2)(B)(i). Furthermore, GAO determined that Education could use its fiscal year appropriation to provide 5-and 2-year grants even though the statutes creating the grants were silent with regard to grant duration. See 20 U.S.C. §§ 1070a-21 et seq. and Pub. L. No. 106-554, app. A, 114 Stat. 2763A-33-34 (Dec. 21, 2000). GAO reasoned that, in addition to authorizing awards, the grant statutes conferred broad discretion on Education to help ensure the accomplishment of grant objectives; and it was within that discretion for Education to determine whether the grant objectives would best be accomplished through the use of multiyear grant awards. B-289801, Dec. 30, 2002.

C. Advance Payments

1. The Statutory Prohibition

Advance payments in general are prohibited by 31 U.S.C. § 3324, which provides in part:

> "(a) Except as provided in this section, a payment under a contract to provide a service or deliver an article for the United States Government may not be more than the value of the service already provided or the article already delivered."

> (b) An advance of public money may be made only if it is authorized by—"

> > "(1) a specific appropriation or other law ...."

The quoted portion of 31 U.S.C. § 3324 is derived from legislation originally enacted in 1823 (3 Stat. 723).

The primary purpose of 31 U.S.C. § 3324 is to protect the government against the risk of nonperformance--"to preclude the possibility of loss to the Government in the event a contractor--after receipt of payment--should fail to perform his contract or refuse or fail to refund moneys advanced." 25 Comp. Gen. 834, 835 (1946). See also 65 Comp. Gen. 806, 809 (1986); B-256692, June 22, 1995; B-249006, Apr. 6, 1993; B-180713, Apr. 10, 1974. Thus, in its simplest terms, the statute prohibits the government from paying for goods before they have been received or for services before they have been rendered. The Floyd Acceptances, 74 U.S. (7 Wall.) 666, 682 (1868); 10 Op. Att'y Gen. 288, 301 (1862). The statute has been described as "so plain that construction of it is unnecessary." 27 Comp. Dec. 885, 886 (1921). While that may be true if section 3324 is viewed in isolation, the situation today is nowhere near that simple. Advance payments are now permissible in a number of situations. What we now have is a basic statutory prohibition with a network of exceptions, both statutory and nonstatutory, some of which are of major importance.

Exceptions to the advance payment prohibition may be found in appropriation acts or in "other law." Examples of specific exceptions are: 10 U.S.C. § 2396 (for compliance with foreign laws, rent in foreign countries, tuition, pay, and supplies of armed forces of friendly countries); 31 U.S.C. §§ 3324(b)(2) and (d)(2) (pay and allowances of members of the armed forces at distant stations and publications); and 19 U.S.C. §§ 2076-2077 and 2080 (Customs Service payments). Numerous other statutory exceptions exist in various contexts. A major exception permits advance and progress payments under procurement contracts in certain situations.

Payments to or on behalf of federal civilian employees and members of the uniformed service constitute another area in which exceptions exist. Advances of travel and transportation allowances for federal civilian employees are authorized by, e.g., 5 U.S.C. §§ 5705 and 5724(f). In addition, advances of allowances for basic housing, travel, and transportation, to members of the uniformed services (for themselves and in specified situations their dependents) are authorized by several statutes, e.g., 37 U.S.C. §§ 403(a), 404(b)(1)(A), 404a(b), 405(a), 405a(a), 406(a)(3), and 409(b).

Prior to late 1990, the advance payment of salary, as opposed to the various allowances discussed in the preceding paragraph, remained prohibited, with a limited exception in 5 U.S.C. § 5522 for certain emergency or "national interest" evacuations. This situation caused occasional hardship for new employees resulting from delay in receiving their first regular paycheck. In 58 Comp. Gen. 646 (1979), GAO had concurred in a proposal to minimize this hardship by using imprest funds to make partial salary payments to new federal employees early in the week following the first week of employment, but cautioned that, in view of 31 U.S.C. § 3324, no payments could be made before the work had been performed. Section 107 of the Federal Employees Pay Comparability Act of 1990 added a new 5 U.S.C. § 5524a, authorizing agencies to make advance payments of up to two pay periods of basic pay to new employees.

Advance payment of salary remains prohibited in situations not covered by statutory exceptions. Thus, GAO has advised that partial or emergency salary payments can be made if a salary check is lost in the mail or an electronic deposit goes astray, but must be subject to "advance payment" safeguards similar to those discussed in 58 Comp. Gen. 646. B-193867.2, Jan. 12, 1990 (nondecision letter). Similarly, GAO concluded that the Nuclear Regulatory Commission could reschedule its commissioners' pay days that fall on weekends or holidays to the preceding workday, provided that payments made prior to the end of a pay period did not include salary applicable to days remaining in the pay period. B-237963, June 28, 1990.

Tuition payments may be paid in advance. The Government Employees Training Act, 5 U.S.C. § 4109, provides general authority for advance tuition payments for civilian employees. Also, 10 U.S.C. § 2396(a)(3) authorizes advance tuition payments for military personnel. Prior to the enactment of these provisions, the Comptroller General held that certain tuition payments could be made in advance. For example, legislation authorizing the Coast Guard to provide training for its personnel at private or state colleges and universities and to pay certain expenses, including tuition, was viewed as authorization by "other law" within the meaning of 31 U.S.C. § 3324. Tuition could therefore be paid at the time of enrollment if required by the educational institution. 41 Comp. Gen. 626 (1962). See also B-70395, Oct. 30, 1947 (tuition payments by Public Health Service in connection with research fellowships); B-56585, May 1, 1946 (tuition payments by the former Veterans Administration in connection with schooling of veterans).

Exceptions to the advance payment prohibition may appear in appropriation acts as well as other legislation. The extent of the authority conferred and its duration will of course be determined in accordance with rules applicable to construing appropriations language. Some may be limited by duration and some may be limited to a particular agency. Also, the bona fide needs rule applies. In one case, a fiscal year 1955 appropriation for an Indian education program included authority for the Bureau of Indian Affairs to make certain payments in advance. The Comptroller General held that the funds could be obligated only for the bona fide needs of the period for which appropriated. Therefore, the advance payment authority was limited to the portion of the program to be furnished during fiscal year 1955 and could not operate to extend the period of availability of the appropriation, that is, could not be used to pay for portions of the program extending into fiscal year 1956. 34 Comp. Gen. 432 (1955). This principle would be equally applicable to advance payment authority contained in permanent legislation.

If a given situation does not fall within any existing exception, the statutory prohibition will apply. E.g., 65 Comp. Gen. 806 (1986) (advance payment for published advertisement); 64 Comp. Gen. 710 (1985) (advance payments under contract for office equipment maintenance found to violate statute notwithstanding Federal Supply Schedule contract language to the contrary).

The statutory prohibition on the advance payment of public funds, 31 U.S.C. § 3324, does not apply to grants. Since assistance awards are made to assist authorized recipients and are not primarily for the purpose of obtaining goods or services for the government, the policy behind the advance payment prohibition has less force in the case of assistance awards than in the case of procurement contracts. Accordingly, it has been held that 31 U.S.C. § 3324 does not preclude advance funding in authorized grant relationships. Unless restricted by the program legislation of the applicable appropriation, the authority to make grants is sufficient to satisfy the requirements of 31 U.S.C. § 3324. 60 Comp. Gen. 208 (1981); 59 Comp. Gen. 424 (1980); 41 Comp. Gen. 394 (1961). As stated in 60 Comp. Gen. 209, "[t]he policy of payment upon receipt of goods or services is simply inconsistent with assistance relationships where the government does not receive anything in the usual sense."

In 70 Comp. Gen. 701 (1991), the Comptroller General held that payments by the Bureau of Indian Affairs for McDonald's gift certificates and movie tickets, which would be redeemed at a later date for their full value, would not violate 31 U.S.C. § 3324, provided that adequate administrative safeguards for the control of the certificates and tickets were maintained, the purchase of the certificates was in the government's interest, and the certificates and tickets were readily redeemable for cash.

2. Government Procurement Contracts

a. Background

First, it is important to define a few terms. We take our definitions from the Federal Acquisition Regulation (FAR), 48 C.F.R. § 32.102. In the context of government contracting, "advance payments" are payments to a prime contractor "before, in anticipation of, and for the purpose of complete performance under one or more contracts." Advance payments are not measured by performance. "Progress payments" are payments made to the contractor as work progresses on the contract. They may be based on costs incurred by the contractor or a percentage or stage of completion. "Partial payments" are payments "for accepted supplies and services that are only a part of the contract requirements." Advance payments and progress payments based on costs incurred are regarded as forms of "contract financing." Partial payments and progress payments based on a percentage or stage of completion are viewed simply as payment methods.

The extent to which various forms of contract financing are permissible under the advance payment statute was the subject of many early decisions. In one early case, the advance payment statute was applied to a question regarding the legality of government partial (progress) payments for materials that had not been delivered. The Comptroller General held that the statute does not necessarily require withholding of payment under a contract until it has been entirely completed and all deliverables have been provided to the government. The statute "was not intended to prevent a partial payment in any case in which the amount of such payment had been actually earned by the contractor and the United States had received an equivalent therefor." 1 Comp. Gen. 143, 145 (1921). The partial payments proposed in that case were not in excess of the amount actually expended by the contractor in performance of the contract, and because the contract provided that title to all property on which payment was made vested in the government, the government would receive the corresponding benefit. Partial payments in advance of complete delivery were therefore permissible.

In 20 Comp. Gen. 917 (1941), the Comptroller General approved a proposed contract amendment to provide for partial payment of the contract price prior to delivery to the government on the condition that title to the materials would pass to the government at the time of payment.

From these and similar cases, a rule evolved, applied both by the accounting officers and by the Attorney General, that partial payments for equipment or land made in advance of their delivery into the actual possession of the United States would not violate the advance payment statute if title therein had vested in the government at the time of payment, or if the equipment or land was impressed with a valid lien in favor of the United States in an amount at least equal to the payment. 28 Comp. Gen. 468 (1949); 20 Comp. Gen. 917 (1941).

Applying this rule, GAO has approved the payment of "earnest money" under a contract for the sale of real estate to the government. The arrangement was found sufficient to protect the government's interests because the contract (a) vested equitable title in the government prior to the vesting of legal title, which remained in the seller only to secure payment of the purchase price, and (b) obligated the seller to deliver title insurance commitment. 34 Comp. Gen. 659 (1955).

b. Contract Financing

"Contract financing payment" is defined by the Federal Acquisition Regulation (FAR) as an authorized government disbursement of moneys to a contractor prior to acceptance of supplies or services by the government. Such payments include: advance payments; performance-based payments; commercial advance and interim payments; certain cost-based progress payments; certain percentage-or stage-of-completion-based progress payments; and interim payments under certain cost reimbursement contracts. 48 C.F.R. § 32.001. "Advance payments" are payments made to a prime contractor before, in anticipation of, and for the purpose of complete performance under one or more contracts. Such payments are not measured by performance. 48 C.F.R. § 32.102(a). "Progress payments based on costs" are made on the basis of costs incurred by the contractor as work progresses under the contract. 48 C.F.R. § 32.102(b). Progress payments based on percentage or stage of completion are to be made under agency procedures that ensure that payments are commensurate with the work accomplished that meets the quality standards established under the contract. 48 C.F.R. § 32.102(e).

The major laws governing acquisition by most agencies of the executive branch of government have for over a half century included provisions relating to agencies making advance and progress payments under contracts for supplies or services. See 10 U.S.C. § 2307 (Department of Defense) and 41 U.S.C. § 255 (most civilian agencies). Both provisions permit agencies to make advance, partial, progress, or other payments under contracts for property or services that do not exceed the unpaid contract price. Within their discretion, the agencies may include in bid solicitations a provision limiting advance or progress payments to small business concerns. 10 U.S.C. § 2307(a)(c); 41 U.S.C. § 255(a)(c). The Comptroller General views the authority conferred by both these provisions to apply to both advertised and negotiated procurements. B-158487, Apr. 4, 1966.

Both provisions provide that whenever practicable, payments are to be made based on (1) performance, using quantifiable methods such as delivery of acceptable items, work measurement, or statistical process controls; (2) accomplishment of events defined in a program management plan; or (3) other quantifiable measures of results. 10 U.S.C. § 2307(b); 41 U.S.C. § 255(b). Both provisions establish conditions for progress payments for work in process and limit such payments to 80 percent of the contract price for contracts over $25,000. 10 U.S.C. § 2307(e); 41 U.S.C. § 255(e).

Both provisions provide that advance payments may be made only upon adequate security and a determination by the agency head that such would be in the public interest. Such security interest may be in the form of a lien in favor of the government on the property contracted for, on the balance in an account in which such payments are deposited, and such of the property acquired for performance of the contract as agreed to by the parties. The lien is to be paramount to all other liens and effective immediately upon the first advance of funds without filing, notice, or any other action by the government. 10 U.S.C. § 2307(d); 41 U.S.C. § 255(d). Advance payments for commercial items may not exceed 15 percent of the contract price in advance of any performance of work under the contract. 10 U.S.C. § 2307(f)(2); 41 U.S.C. § 255(f)(2). Section 2307(h) provides that if a contract calls for advance, partial, progress, or other payments and provides for title to property to vest in the United States, the title vests in accordance with the terms of the contract, regardless of any security interest in the property that is asserted before or after entering into the contract.

Section 2307(g) of title 10 of the United States Code contains special provisions relating to Navy contracts, for example, that progress payments under contracts for repair, maintenance, or overhaul of a naval vessel may not be less than 95 percent for small businesses and 90 percent for any other business.

Generally speaking, the government's preference is that the contractor be able to perform using private financing, that is, the contractor's own resources or financing obtained in the private market. 48 C.F.R. § 32.106. The advance payment authority of 10 U.S.C. § 2307 and 41 U.S.C. § 255 is a financing tool to be used sparingly. It is considered the least preferred method of contract financing. 48 C.F.R. §§ 32.106 and 32.402(b); 57 Comp. Gen. 89, 94 (1977). However, the need for government assistance in various situations has long been recognized. In this context, government contracting, while primarily intended to serve the government's needs, is also designed to foster a variety of social and economic objectives.

The FAR prescribes policies and procedures for agencies to apply in using contract financing. 48 C.F.R. pt. 32. For example, subparts 32.1 and 32.2 provide guidance on the use of such authority when purchasing noncommercial and commercial items, respectively. Subpart 32.4 provides guidance on the use of advance payment authority when contracting for noncommercial items. Subpart 32.5 provides guidance on the use of progress payments based on cost, and subpart 32.10 provides guidance on the use of performance-based payments for noncommercial items. Various provisions of the FAR elaborate further on the statutory requirements with respect to adequate security for advance payments. See, e.g., 48 C.F.R. §§ 32.202-4, 32.409-3. Application for advance payments under contracts to acquire noncommercial items may be made before or after the award of the contract under 48 C.F.R. § 32.408.

Security requirements may vary to fit the circumstances of the particular case. 48 C.F.R. § 32.409-3(d). In B-214446, Oct. 29, 1984, GAO considered a proposal to certify payment before the services were rendered. The check would be held in escrow under the government's control until contract obligations were met, at which time it would be released to the contractor. This arrangement was deemed adequate for purposes of 41 U.S.C. § 255. In an earlier case, GAO declined approval of a "purchase order draft" procedure, which called for the government to send a blank check to the supplier upon placing an order. The supplier was to fill in the check for the actual amount due, not to exceed a sum specified on the check, thereby effecting immediate payment and eliminating the need for the supplier to bill the government. GAO concluded that an agency head could not reasonably find that this plan would provide adequate security for the government. B-158873, Apr. 27, 1966. In B-288013, Dec. 11, 2001, a case involving whether the Department of Defense could make payment of membership fees to a private fitness center at the beginning of each option year, GAO found that permitting membership transfers did not provide adequate security to the government to justify an advance payment.

Advance payments are also authorized under Public Law 85-804, 50 U.S.C. §§ 1431-1435. This law permits agencies designated by the President to enter into contracts, or to modify or amend existing contracts, and to make advance payments on those contracts, "without regard to other provisions of law relating to the making, performance, amendment, or modification of contracts, whenever [the President] deems that such action would facilitate the national defense." 50 U.S.C. § 1431. Agencies authorized to utilize Public Law 85-804 are listed in Executive Order No. 10789, Nov. 14, 1958, as amended (reprinted as note following 50 U.S.C. § 1431). The FAR subpart on advance payments includes provisions addressing Public Law 85-804, which applies only during a declared national emergency. 50 U.S.C. § 1435.

Progress payments, where authorized, are made periodically based on costs incurred, with the total not to exceed 80 percent of the total contract price. 48 C.F.R. §§ 32.5011 and 52.232-16 (required contract clause for fixed-price contracts). In an incrementally funded fixed-price contract, GAO has construed "total contract price" as the price for complete performance rather than the amount already allotted to the contract, provided that payment may not exceed the total amount allotted. 59 Comp. Gen. 526 (1980). See also 48 C.F.R. § 32.5013.

A key condition where cost-based progress payments are authorized is the vesting in the government of title to work in process and certain other property allocable to the contract. 48 C.F.R. §§ 32.503-14 and 52.232-16. These title provisions are an outgrowth of the case law noted earlier in this section.

The nature of the government's interest under this title-vesting provision has produced disagreement among the courts. One view is that title means full, absolute title, which cannot be defeated by subsequent liens. In re Reynolds Manufacturing Co., 68 B.R. 219 (Bankr. W.D. Penn. 1986); In re Denalco Corp., 51 B.R. 77 (Bankr. N.D. Ill. 1985); In re Economy Cab and Tool Co., 47 B.R. 708 (Bankr. D. Minn. 1985); In re American Pouch Foods, Inc., 30 B.R. 1015 (Bankr. N.D. Ill. 1983), aff'd, 769 F.2d 1190 (7th Cir.), cert. denied, 475 U.S. 1082 (1985); McDonnell Douglas Corp. v. Director of Revenue, 945 S.W.2d 437 (Mo. 1997). See also In re Wincom Corp., 76 B.R. 1 (Bankr. D. Mass. 1987), reaching the same result. Another view is that the title-vesting provision gives the government a security interest in the form of a lien relative to progress payments identified with specific property, paramount to the liens of general creditors. United States v. Dominicci, 899 F. Supp. 42 (D.P.R. 1995); United States v. Hartec Enterprises, Inc., 967 F.2d 130 (5th Cir. 1992); Fairchild Industries, Inc. v. United States, 71 F.3d 868 (Fed. Cir. 1995); Marine Midland Bank v. United States, 687 F.2d 395 (Ct. Cl. 1982), cert. denied, 460 U.S. 1037 (1983); Welco Industries, Inc. v. United States, 8 Cl. Ct. 303 (1985), aff'd mem., 790 F.2d 90 (Fed. Cir. 1986). The American Pouch and Marine Midland decisions, while reaching different conclusions, contain detailed discussions of the evolution of contract financing in relation to the advance payment statute.

c. Payment

Under a strict interpretation of 31 U.S.C. § 3324 standing alone, payment could not be made until property being acquired was actually received and accepted by the government. Thus, in one early case, a supply contract provided for payment "for articles delivered and accepted" and for the contractor to retain responsibility for the supplies or materials until they were actually in the possession of a government representative at their destination. The Comptroller General held that payments on the basis of vouchers or invoices supported by evidence of shipment only, without evidence of arrival of the supplies at the destination and without assurance of receipt or acceptance by the government, would be unauthorized. 20 Comp. Gen. 230 (1940).

As with the forms of contract financing discussed above, the enactment of 10 U.S.C. § 2307 and 41 U.S.C. § 255 permitted more latitude in payment procedures. In view of this statutory authority, the Comptroller General, in B-158487, Apr. 4, 1966, approved an advance payment procedure under which the General Services Administration (GSA) would make payments on direct delivery vouchers prior to the receipt of "receiving reports" from the consignees. The proposal was designed to effect savings to the government by enabling GSA to take advantage of prompt payment discounts. GAO's approval was conditioned on compliance with the conditions specified in 41 U.S.C. § 255 that advance payment be in the public interest and that adequate security be provided.

GAO has since approved similar accelerated payment or "fast pay" procedures for other agencies in B-155253, Mar. 20, 1968 (Defense Department) and B-155253, Aug. 20, 1969 (Federal Aviation Administration), and reaffirmed them for GSA in 60 Comp. Gen. 602 (1981). See also B-279620, Mar. 31, 1998, for an extensive discussion of the background of, and adequate controls required for, fast pay.

The Federal Acquisition Regulation provides guidance in using fast payment procedures in 48 C.F.R. subpt. 13.4. An agency may pay for supplies based on the contractor's submission of an invoice under, among others, the following conditions:

- The individual order does not exceed $25,000. Agencies have discretionary authority to set higher limits for specified items or activities.

- Geographical separation and lack of adequate communications facilities between receiving and disbursing activities make it impractical to make timely payment based on evidence of acceptance.

- Title vests in the government upon delivery to a post office or common carrier or, if shipment is by means other than Postal Service or common carrier, upon receipt by the government.

- The contractor agrees to repair, replace, or otherwise correct any items not received at destination, damaged in transit, or not conforming to purchase requirements.

The invoice is the contractor's representation that the goods have been delivered to a post office, common carrier, or point of first receipt by the government.

Accelerated payment procedures should have adequate internal controls. GAO's recommended controls are outlined in 60 Comp. Gen. 602 (1981) and B-205868, June 14, 1982. Fast pay procedures should be subject to monetary ceilings (now required by the FAR), limited to contractors which have an ongoing relationship with the agency, and reviewed periodically to ensure that benefits outweigh costs. The agency must keep records adequate to determine that the agency is getting what it pays for. The system should permit the timely discovery of discrepancies and require prompt follow-up action. GAO has also recommended that an agency test the procedure before agencywide implementation. B-205868, supra at 3.

It has also been held that the use of imprest or petty cash funds to purchase supplies under C.O.D. [cash on delivery] procedures does not violate 31 U.S.C. § 3324, even where payment is made prior to examination of the shipment. 32 Comp. Gen. 563 (1953).

Another fast pay issue was discussed in B-203993-O.M., July 12, 1982, in which GAO's General Counsel advised the GAO finance office that it could pay the invoice amount, without the need for further verification, if goods are shipped "f.o.b. [freight on board] origin" and the difference between the estimated price in the purchase order and the amount shown on the invoice is based solely on transportation costs. Any discrepancy regarding the transportation costs could be determined and adjusted through post-audit procedures under 31 U.S.C. § 3726. This would not apply to goods shipped "f.o.b. destination" because transportation charges are included as part of the purchase price.

As a general proposition, since fast pay procedures permit the agency to dispense with prepayment voucher audits, GAO's approval of fast pay procedures has been based on the assumption that the agency would conduct 100 percent post-payment audits. In 67 Comp. Gen. 194 (1988), GAO approved in concept a GSA proposal to combine fast pay procedures with the use of statistical sampling in post-audit for utility invoices. "We see no reason why these two techniques cannot be combined in appropriate circumstances if they result in economies and adequately protect the interests of the government." Id. at 199. However, GAO found that the specific proposal did not provide adequate controls. GSA modified its proposal, and the Comptroller General approved it in 68 Comp. Gen. 618 (1989).

3. Lease and Rental Agreements

The advance payment statute has been consistently construed as applicable to lease or rental agreements as well as purchases, and applies with respect to both real and personal property. 18

Comp. Gen. 839 (1939); 3 Comp. Gen. 542 (1924); B-188166, June 3, 1977. Thus, when the government acquires land by leasing, payments must be made "in arrears" unless the applicable appropriation act or other law provides an exemption from 31 U.S.C. § 3324. 19 Comp. Gen. 758, 760 (1940). The Federal Acquisition Regulation advance payment provisions do not apply to rent. 48 C.F.R. § 32.404(a)(1).

In 57 Comp. Gen. 89 (1977), the Comptroller General held that a leasing arrangement of telephone equipment called "tier pricing," under which the government would be obligated to pay the contractor's entire capital cost at the outset of the lease, would violate 31 U.S.C. § 3324. See also 58 Comp. Gen. 29 (1978).

The advance payment of annual rent on property leased from the National Park Foundation, a statutorily created charitable nonprofit organization, was found permissible in B-207215, Mar. 1, 1983, based on the "unique status" of the lessor.

Certain long-term lease/rental agreements may present more complicated problems in that they may involve not only 31 U.S.C. § 3324 but also the Antideficiency Act, 31 U.S.C. § 1341. Since appropriations are made only for the bona fide needs of a particular fiscal year, and since a lease purporting to bind the government for more than one fiscal year would necessarily include the needs of future years, such a lease would be contrary to the Antideficiency Act prohibition against contracting for any purpose in advance of appropriations made for such purpose. Thus, a lease agreement for the rental of nitrogen gas cylinders for a 25-year period, the full rental price to be paid in the first year, would violate both statutes. 37 Comp. Gen. 60 (1957). A contractual arrangement on an annual basis with an option in the government to renew from year to year was seen as the only way to accomplish the desired objective. Id. at 62. See also 19 Comp. Gen. 758 (1940).

4. Publications

Advance payment is authorized for "charges for a publication printed or recorded in any way for the auditory or visual use of the agency." 31 U.S.C. § 3324(d)(2).

The original exemption for publications was enacted in 1930 (46 Stat. 580 (June 12, 1930)) and amended in 1961 (Pub. L. No. 87-91, 75 Stat. 211 (July 20, 1961)). It authorized advance payments for "subscriptions or other charges for newspapers, magazines, periodicals, and other publications for official use." Prior to 1974, a seemingly endless stream of cases arose over the meaning of the terms "publications" or "other publications" as used either in the general exemption or in specific appropriation acts. Based on judicial precedent, GAO construed the terms to mean publications in the customary and commonly understood sense of the word, that is, books, pamphlets, newspapers, periodicals, or prints. B-125979, June 14, 1957. The exemption was also held to include other types of "visual" material such as microfilm products, (41 Comp. Gen. 211 (1961)); 35-millimeter slides (48 Comp. Gen. 784 (1969)); CD-Rom technical databases, online databases that include technical articles updated daily, and a newsletter (B-256692, June 22, 1995). However, the term "publications" was held not to include items made to be heard rather than read, such as phonograph records (21 Comp. Gen. 524 (1941); B-125979, June 14, 1957) or tape-recorded material (46 Comp. Gen. 394 (1966); B-137516, Oct. 28, 1958). In 35 Comp. Gen. 404 (1956), the use of advance payments for the procurement of books through "book club" facilities was held permissible.

In 1974, Congress resolved the problems over the interpretation of "other publications" by enacting legislation to codify some of the GAO decisions and modify others, by defining "other publications" as including "any publication printed, microfilmed, photocopied, or magnetically or otherwise recorded for auditory or visual usage" (Pub. L. No. 93-534, 88 Stat. 1731 (Dec. 22, 1974)). This was condensed into the present version of 31 U.S.C. § 3324(d)(2) when Title 31 was recodified in 1982.

A 1978 decision considered the question of whether a microfilm library could be acquired under a lease/rental arrangement or whether the advance payments were authorized only where the government actually purchased the library. The Comptroller General concluded that in the absence of statutory language or evidence of legislative intent to the contrary, there is no meaningful difference between the purchase and rental of publications needed by the government, and that the rental or leasing of a microfilm library for official government use fell within the purview of the publications exemption. 57 Comp. Gen. 583 (1978). However, advance payments for items of equipment necessary for use in conjunction with a microfilm library are still prohibited. B-188166, June 3, 1977. (The cited decision, although not clear from the text itself, dealt with reader/printers.)

More recent decisions have construed the publications exemption found in 31 U.S.C. § 3324(d)(2) as permitting advance payment for coupons to be used for the purchase of articles from medical journals and redeemable for cash if unused (67 Comp. Gen. 491 (1988)); verification reports of physicians' board certifications (B-231673, Aug. 8, 1988); and hospital evaluation reports based on data submitted by participating government hospitals and including, as part of the subscription price, a laboratory kit for use in obtaining the data required for the reports, the kit being regarded as "a part of the publication process" (B-210719, Dec. 23, 1983).

In B-256692, June 22, 1995, the Comptroller General held that the Centers for Disease Control and Prevention (CDC) could not, under 31 U.S.C. § 3324(d)(2), make an advance payment for telephonic support services offered as part of a technical support package for computer software products. The telephonic support did not constitute a publication under section 3324(d)(2), and because it had significant value to the CDC independent of the package, it could not be classified as so necessary to the other publications in the package that advance payment authority would be available.

The Federal Acquisition Regulation advance payment provisions do not apply to subscriptions to publications. 48 C.F.R. § 32.404(a)(6).

5. Other Governmental Entities

The Comptroller General has not applied the advance payment prohibition to payments to other federal agencies. As noted previously, the primary purpose of the prohibition is to preclude the possibility of loss in the event a contractor, after receipt of payment, should fail to perform and fail or refuse to refund the money to the United States. The danger of such a loss is minimized when the contractor is another government agency. Thus, 31 U.S.C. § 3324 does not prohibit advance payment of post office box rentals. 25 Comp. Gen. 834 (1946). Also, the Economy Act, 31 U.S.C. § 1535, expressly authorizes advance payments for transactions within its scope.

GAO has applied the same rationale to exempt state and local governments from the advance payment prohibition. E.g., 57 Comp. Gen. 399 (1978) (no objection to advance payment of rent under lease of land from state of Idaho). This exception, however, applies only where the state is furnishing noncommercial services reasonably available only from the state. 39 Comp. Gen. 285 (1959); B-250935, Oct. 12, 1993 (sewer service charge); B-118846, Mar. 29, 1954 (expenses of state water commissioner administering Indian irrigation project pursuant to court order); B-109485, July 22, 1952 (repair, operation, and maintenance of roads in conjunction with permanent transfer of federal roads to county); B-65821, May 29, 1947, and B-34946, June 9, 1943 (state court fees and other items of expense required to litigate in state courts in compliance with the requirements of state law); B-36099, Aug. 14, 1943 (lease of state lands); B-35670, July 19, 1943 (state forest fire prevention and suppression services).

Conversely, where a state provides the federal government with services that are freely and readily available in the commercial market, the statutory advance payment restrictions applicable to private contractors govern. 58 Comp. Gen. 29 (1978) (telephone services).

In B-207215, Mar. 1, 1983, GAO advised the National Park Service that it could make advance payments of annual rent on property leased from the National Park Foundation. The National Park Foundation is a charitable nonprofit organization created by statute to accept and administer gifts to the National Park Service, and its board of directors includes the Secretary of the Interior and the Director of the Park Service. GAO concluded that the Foundation's "unique status virtually assures that there is no threat of loss to the Government." Even though technically the Foundation is neither a state nor a federal agency, it is, in effect, tantamount to one for advance payment purposes.

The exception recognized in the case of state and local governments has not been extended to public utilities. 42 Comp. Gen. 659 (1963) (telephone services). See also 27 Comp. Dec. 885 (1921). Thus, a government agency cannot use a utility "budget plan" which would provide for level monthly payments in a predetermined amount throughout the year. B-237127, Dec. 12,

1989 (nondecision letter). In subscribing to a cable service, the National Park Service could only make payment after the service has been rendered. B-254295, Nov. 24, 1993. Similarly, monthly charges under a utility service contract for cable television service to a Naval hospital may not be paid in advance. B-237789, Dec. 10, 1990. The Federal Aviation Administration (FAA) violated 31 U.S.C. § 3324 by making an advance payment to Pacific Gas and Electric Company for connecting electrical utility service to a remote FAA facility because it failed to obtain "adequate security" as required by 41 U.S.C. § 255 or to follow Federal Acquisition Regulation advance payment requirements. B-260063, June 30, 1995.

D. Disposition of Appropriation Balances

1. Terminology

Annual appropriations that are unobligated at the end of the fiscal year for which they were appropriated are said to "expire" for obligational purposes. In other words, they cease to be available for the purposes of incurring and recording new obligations. The same principle applies to multiple year appropriations as of the end of the last fiscal year for which they were provided. For purposes of this discussion, annual and multiple year appropriations are referred to cumulatively as "fixed appropriations." 31 U.S.C. § 1551(a)(3).

The portion of an appropriation that has not actually been spent at the end of the fiscal year (or other definite period of availability) is called the "unexpended balance."

It consists of two components--the obligated balance and the unobligated balance. The obligated balance is defined as "the amount of unliquidated obligations applicable to the appropriation less amounts collectible as repayments to the appropriation." 31 U.S.C. § 551(a)(1). Restated, obligated balance means the amount of undisbursed funds remaining in an appropriation against which definite obligations have been recorded.

The unobligated balance is "the difference between the obligated balance and the total unexpended balance." Id. at § 1551(a)(2). It represents that portion of the unexpended balance unencumbered by obligations recorded under 31 U.S.C. § 1501.

2. Evolution of the Law

Congressional treatment of unexpended balances has changed a number of times over the years, most recently in November 1990. Some knowledge of the past is useful in understanding the pre-1991 decisions and in determining which portions of them remain applicable.

Prior to 1949, unexpended balances of annual appropriations retained their fiscal year identity for two full fiscal years following expiration, after which time the remaining undisbursed balance had to be covered into the surplus fund of the Treasury. The agency involved no longer had access to the balance for any purpose, and subsequent claims against the appropriation had to be settled by GAO. E.g., B-24565, Apr. 2, 1942; B-18740, July 23, 1941. The appropriation was said to "lapse" when it was covered into the surplus fund of the Treasury. See 24 Comp. Gen. 942, 945 (1945); 21 Comp. Gen. 46 (1941).

The problem with this arrangement was that, in view of article I, section 9 of the United States Constitution, once the money was covered into the Treasury, another appropriation was needed to get it back out. E.g., 23 Comp. Gen. 689, 694 (1944). This was true even for simple, undisputed claims. Congress tried various devices to pay claims against lapsed appropriations-- reappropriation of lapsed funds, definite and indefinite appropriations for the payment of claims under $500, and appropriations for specific claims--but none proved entirely satisfactory.

In 1949, Congress enacted the Surplus Fund-Certified Claims Act (ch. 299, 63 Stat. 407 (July 6, 1949)), intended to permit payment of claims against lapsed appropriations without the need for specific appropriations or reappropriations. The statute provided for the transfer of unexpended balances remaining after 2 years to a Treasury account designated "Payment of Certified Claims." Funds in this account remained available until expended for the payment of claims certified by the Comptroller General to be lawfully due and chargeable to the respective balances in the account. See B-61937, Sept. 17, 1952. Like the pre-1949 system, this arrangement too proved unsatisfactory in that all claims payable from the certified claims account, undisputed invoices included, still had to come through GAO.

The system changed again in 1956 (Pub. L. No. 84-798, 70 Stat. 647 (July 25, 1956)), on the recommendation of the second Hoover Commission. One of the significant changes made by the 1956 law was to pass the direct responsibility for making payments from lapsed appropriations from GAO to the cognizant agencies. For the first time, agencies could dispose of clearly valid claims against prior year appropriations without the need for any action by either Congress or GAO. The statutory evolution is discussed in more detail in B-179708, Nov. 20, 1973.

The 1956 law, which was to remain in effect until late 1990, prescribed different procedures for obligated and unobligated balances. The obligated balance retained its fiscal year identity for two full fiscal years following the expiration date, at which time any remaining obligated but unexpended balance was transferred to a consolidated successor account, where it was merged with the obligated balances of all other appropriation accounts of that department or agency for the same general purpose. These successor accounts were known as "M" accounts. Funds in an "M" account were available indefinitely to liquidate obligations properly incurred against any of the appropriations from which the account was derived. Upon merger in the "M" account, the obligated but unexpended balances of all annual and multiple year appropriations of the agency lost their fiscal year identity for expenditure purposes.

With fiscal year identity no longer a concern, there was no need to relate a payment from the "M" account to the specific balance that had been transferred from the particular year in which the obligation had occurred. Thus, as a practical matter, once an appropriation balance reached the "M" account, the potential for violations of the Antideficiency Act became highly remote. B-179708, June 24, 1975. An Antideficiency Act violation could occur only if identifiable obligations exceeded the entire "M" account balance plus the aggregate of all funds potentially restorable from withdrawn unobligated balances.

The unobligated balances of fixed-year appropriations were "withdrawn" upon expiration of the period of obligational availability and were returned to the general fund of the Treasury. A withdrawn unobligated balance retained its fiscal year identity on the books of the Treasury for two fiscal years, during which time it was called "surplus authority." At the end of the 2-year period, the balances were transferred to "merged surplus" accounts, at which point they lost their fiscal year identity.

Withdrawn unobligated balances could be restored to adjust previously recorded obligations where the amount originally recorded proved to be less than the actual obligation, or to liquidate obligations that arose but were not formally recorded prior to the appropriations expiration, provided that the obligations met one of the criteria specified in 31 U.S.C. § 1501(a) and were otherwise valid. Some cases discussing this restoration authority are 68 Comp. Gen. 600 (1989); 63 Comp. Gen. 525 (1984); B-236940, Oct. 17, 1989; B-232010, Mar. 23, 1989; B-164031(3).150, Sept. 5, 1979.

From the perspective of congressional control, one weakness of the system described above was that it permitted the accumulation of large amounts in "M" accounts. While agencies were supposed to review their "M" accounts annually and return any excess to the Treasury, this was not always done. This situation, in conjunction with the previously discussed rules on the funding of contract modifications, created the potential for large transactions with minimal congressional oversight. For example, a 1989 GAO report discussed an Air Force proposal, completely legal under existing legislation, to use over $1 billion from expired accounts to fund B-1B contract modifications. U.S. General Accounting Office, Strategic Bombers: B-1B Programs Use of Expired Appropriations, GAO/NSIAD-89-209 (Washington, D.C.: Oct. 5, 1989).

Congressional concern mounted during 1990, and the treatment of expired appropriations was changed once again by section 1405 of the National Defense Authorization Act for Fiscal Year 1991, Pub. L. No. 101-510, 104 Stat. 1485, 1675 (Nov. 5, 1990). Section 1405 applies to both military and civilian agencies, and includes transition provisions that dealt with the then-existing merged surplus and "M" accounts. Unrestored merged surplus authority was canceled as of December 5, 1990, with no further restorations authorized after that date. The "M" accounts were phased out over a 3-year period, with any remaining "M" account balances canceled on September 30, 1993.

3. Expired Appropriation Accounts

The current account closing procedures are set forth in 31 U.S.C. §§ 1551-1558. Two of the key provisions provide:

> "On September 30th of the 5th fiscal year after the period of availability for obligation of a fixed appropriation account ends, the account shall be closed and any remaining balance (whether obligated or unobligated) in the account shall be canceled and thereafter shall not be available for obligation or expenditure for any purpose."

31 U.S.C. § 1552(a).

> "After the end of the period of availability for obligation of a fixed appropriation account and before the closing of that account under section 1552(a) of this title, the account shall retain its fiscal-year identity and remain available for recording, adjusting, and liquidating obligations properly chargeable to that account."

31 U.S.C. § 1553(a).

Just as under the prior system, a 1-year or multiple year appropriation expires on the last day of its period of availability and is no longer available to incur and record new obligations. However, the unobligated balance no longer reverts immediately to the general fund of the Treasury.

Upon expiration of a fixed appropriation, the obligated and unobligated balances retain their fiscal year identity in an "expired account" for that appropriation for an additional five fiscal years. As a practical matter, agencies must maintain separate obligated and unobligated balances within the expired account as part of their internal financial management systems in order to insure compliance with the Antideficiency Act. Also relevant in this connection is 31 U.S.C. §1554(a), under which applicable audit requirements, limitations on obligations, and reporting requirements remain applicable to the expired account.

During the 5-year period, the expired account balance may be used to liquidate obligations properly chargeable to the account prior to its expiration. The expired account balance also remains available to make legitimate obligation adjustments, that is, to record previously unrecorded obligations and to make upward adjustments in previously under recorded obligations. For example, Congress appropriated funds to provide education benefits to veterans under the so-called "GI bill," codified at 38 U.S.C. § 1662. Prior to the expiration of the appropriation, the Veterans Administration (VA) denied the benefits to certain Vietnam era veterans. The denial was appealed to the courts. The court determined that certain veterans may have been improperly denied benefits and ordered VA to entertain new applications and reconsider the eligibility of veterans to benefits. VA appealed the court order. Prior to a final resolution of the issue, the appropriation expired. GAO determined that, consistent with 31 U.S.C. § 1502(b), the unobligated balance of VA's expired appropriation was available to pay benefits to veterans who filed applications prior to the expiration of the appropriation or who VA determined were improperly denied education benefits. 70 Comp. Gen. 225 (1991). See also B-265901, Oct. 14, 1997.

Unobligated balances in the expired account cannot be used to satisfy an obligation properly chargeable to current appropriations (50 Comp. Gen. 863 (1971)), or to any other expired account. The authority of 31 U.S.C. § 1553(a) is intended to permit agencies to adjust their accounts to more accurately reflect obligations and liabilities actually incurred during the period of availability. 63 Comp. Gen. 525, 528 (1984). However, arbitrary deobligation in reliance upon the authority to make subsequent adjustments is not consistent with the statutory purpose. B-179708, July 10, 1975.

During the 5-year period, the potential for an Antideficiency Act violation exists if the amount of adjustments to obligations chargeable to the expired account during a year exceeds the adjusted balance available in the expired account against which to charge such adjustments. Should this happen, the excess can be liquidated only pursuant to a supplemental or deficiency appropriation or other congressional action. 73 Comp. Gen. 338, 342 (1994); 71 Comp. Gen. 502 (1992).

4. Closed Appropriation Accounts

At the end of the 5-year period, the account is closed. Any remaining unexpended balances, both obligated and unobligated, are canceled, returned to the general fund of the Treasury, and are thereafter no longer available for any purpose.

Once an account has been closed:

> "[O]bligations and adjustments to obligations that would have been properly chargeable to that account, both as to purpose and in amount, before closing and that are not otherwise chargeable to any current appropriation account of the agency may be charged to any current appropriation account of the agency available for the same purpose."

31 U.S.C. § 1553(b)(1).

This is a major exception to the rule previously discussed that current appropriations are not available to satisfy obligations properly chargeable to a prior year. For example, the Office of Surface Mining (OSM) entered into an Economy Act agreement with the Department of Energy (DOE) for services that DOE provided through a contractor. DOE funded the service from no-year accounts. The final audit of the contractor that was performed after the OSM account obligated by the Economy Act agreement closed revealed that DOE owed the contractor an additional amount for performing services for OSM. DOE asked whether OSM was liable to reimburse it for the additional amount under the Economy Act. GAO replied that the account closing law required OSM to reimburse DOE the additional amounts using current appropriations available for the same general purpose as the closed account. B-260993, June 26,

1996. Compare B-257825, Mar. 15, 1995 (Treasury properly refused to restore amount of canceled "M" account to Federal Aviation Administration (FAA) appropriation in order for FAA to reimburse the Federal Highway Administration (FHWA) for services provided that were properly chargeable to the canceled account. This was true notwithstanding the fact that FHWA inadvertently neglected to bill for the services at the time they were rendered. GAO pointed out that the law provided that FAA reimbursement to FHWA was chargeable to current appropriations).

The authority to use current year appropriations to pay obligations chargeable to closed accounts is not unlimited, however. The cumulative total of old obligations payable from current appropriations may not exceed the lesser of 1 percent of the current appropriation or the remaining balance (whether obligated or unobligated) canceled when the appropriation account is closed. 31 U.S.C. § 1553(b). In view of the limitations on the amount of current appropriations that may be used to pay obligations properly charged to closed accounts, agencies must maintain records of the appropriation balances canceled beyond the end of the 5-year period and adjust these balances as subsequently presented obligations are liquidated. 73 Comp. Gen. 338, 341-342 (1994). Otherwise, there is no way for agencies to ensure that payments do not exceed the original appropriation.

Because of the need to keep accurate records, agencies may, in limited circumstances, adjust their records pertaining to closed appropriation accounts. For example, if an agency determines that the balances reflected in the records of a closed account are erroneous because of reporting and clerical errors, it may adjust its records if it discovers that a disbursement actually made before the appropriation account closed and properly chargeable to an obligation incurred during the appropriations period of availability was either not recorded at all or was charged to the wrong appropriation.

Neither of these types of adjustments constitutes charging obligations against or disbursing funds from closed appropriation accounts. They represent corrections of the accounting records. Since the appropriations, in effect, no longer exist, these adjustments affect only the agency's records. They have no effect on the availability or use of obligated or unobligated balances formerly contained in those appropriation accounts. U.S. General Accounting Office, Canceled DOD Appropriations: $615 Million of Illegal or Otherwise Improper Adjustments, GAO-01-697 (Washington, D.C.: July 26, 2001) at 7. However, adjustments may not be made to the records of the balances of closed accounts when the initial disbursements:

1. occurred after the appropriation being charged has already been closed,

2. occurred before the appropriation being charged was enacted, or:

3. were charged to the correct appropriation in the first place and no adjustment is necessary.

5. Exemptions from the Account Closing Procedures

Congress may, by specific legislation, exempt an appropriation from the above rules and may otherwise fix the period of its availability for expenditure. 31 U.S.C. §§ 1551(b), 1557. An agency should consider seeking an exemption if it administers a program that by its nature requires disbursements beyond the 5-year period. One form of exemption simply preserves the availability for disbursement of obligated funds. For example, section 511 of the Foreign Operations Appropriation Act, 2001, authorized that the 2-year appropriation made for "Assistance for Eastern Europe and the Baltic States" would remain available until expended if properly obligated before the appropriation would otherwise have expired on September 30, 2002.

Section 1558(a) of Title 31 of the United States Code provides an automatic stay to the closing of an appropriation account under section 1552 when a protest is filed against the solicitation for, proposed award of, or award of a contract. The appropriation that would have funded the contract remains available for obligation for 100 days after a final ruling on the protest.

To the extent of its applicability, the statutory scheme found at 31 U.S.C. §§ 1551-1558 provides the exclusive method for the payment of obligations chargeable to expired appropriations. B-101860, Dec. 5, 1963. Thus, there is generally no authority to transfer appropriations to some form of trust fund or working fund for the purpose of preserving their availability. Id. See also 31 U.S.C. §1532, which prohibits the transfer of appropriations to a working fund without statutory authority. In B-288142, Sept. 6, 2001, customer agencies made advances from their fixed period appropriations to the Library of Congress for deposit to the credit of the no-year FEDLINK revolving fund. The advances were used by the Library of Congress to pay the cost of service provided to the agencies by Library of Congress contractors. Once the service was provided and the cost determined, the Library discovered that some agencies had advanced amounts in excess of the cost of the service ordered. We determined that the Library of Congress lacked authority to apply the excess amount to pay for orders for service placed after the expiration of the fixed period appropriation charged with the advance.

The rules for certain legislative branch appropriations are a bit different. The provisions of 31 U.S.C. §§ 1551-1558 do not apply to appropriations to be disbursed by the Secretary of the Senate, the Clerk of the House of Representatives, and the District of Columbia. 31 U.S.C. § 1551(c). For appropriations of the House and Senate, unobligated balances more than 2 years old cannot be used short of an act of Congress. Instead, obligations chargeable to appropriations that have been expired for more than 2 years "shall be liquidated from any appropriations for the same general purpose, which, at the time of payment, are available for disbursement." 2 U.S.C. § 102a. See B-213771.3, Sept. 17, 1986. There is no comparable account closing procedure currently in effect for the appropriations made to the District of Columbia from its local revenues.

6. No-Year Appropriations

There is one important statutory restriction on the availability of no-year funds. Under 31 U.S.C. § 1555, a no-year account is to be closed if (a) the agency head or the President determines that the purposes for which the appropriation was made have been fulfilled and (b) no disbursement has been made against the appropriation for two consecutive fiscal years. The purpose of section 1555 is to permit the closing of inactive appropriations. 39 Comp. Gen. 244 (1959); B-271607, June 3, 1996; B-182101, Oct. 16, 1974.

Any attempt by an agency to close a no-year account that does not satisfy the requirements of section 1555 is without legal effect and the funds remain available for obligation. B-256765, Jan. 19, 1995. An interesting example of a misplaced attempt to close a permanent appropriation involved the check forgery insurance fund. The check forgery insurance fund was established in 1941 to authorize the Treasury to issue and pay a replacement check to payees whose original check was lost or stolen through no fault of their own and paid on a forged endorsement. 31 U.S.C. § 3343 (1994). In the absence of the fund, the payee would have had to wait for the government to recover the amount paid on the forged endorsement in order to issue a replacement check to the payee. The fund was financed by appropriations made to the fund and recoveries of amounts paid on forged endorsements (reclamations). 31 U.S.C. §§ 3343(a) and (d) (1994). In 1992, the Treasury's Financial Management Service (FMS) closed the fund asserting that it was authorized to do so by 31 U.S.C. § 1555. FMS claimed that the fund was inadequate and obsolete and had been impliedly repealed by the Competitive Equality Banking Act.

In response to a request for an advance decision from the Department of the Navy, GAO determined that Treasury lacked the authority to close the fund. 72 Comp. Gen. 295 (1993). First, GAO determined that nothing in the language of the Competitive Equality Banking Act or its legislative history reflected the intent by Congress to eliminate the fund. Next, GAO determined that the fund was the only appropriation available to pay forged check claims. While the volume of forged check claims may have become large and exceeded the amount recovered by reclamation that was available to cover issuance of the replacement check, the remedy was for Treasury to request increased funding, not to cancel the only appropriation that was available to make such payments. Finally, GAO determined that the purpose for which the fund was established continued to exist and that Treasury lacked sufficient justification to close the fund under 31 U.S.C. § 1555. Thus, GAO determined that Treasury should restore the balance to the fund and charge all check forgery claims to the fund. Once the fund balance was restored GAO recommended that Treasury request sufficient appropriations or a permanent indefinite appropriation to pay claims. The law was amended in 1995 to make a permanent indefinite appropriation to the fund of amounts necessary to issue and pay replacement checks to payees whose original check was paid on a forged endorsement. 31 U.S.C. § 3343(a).

As with fixed appropriations, obligations attributable to the canceled balance of a no-year account may be paid from current appropriations for the same purpose, and subject to the same 1 percent limitation. 31 U.S.C. § 1553(b).

Like a no-year appropriation, a permanent indefinite appropriation (e.g., 31 U.S.C. §1304) is not subject to fiscal year limitations. However, 31 U.S.C. § 1555 does not apply to permanent indefinite appropriations since the "remaining balance" by definition is the general fund of the Treasury. Cf. 11 Comp. Dec. 400 (1905) (applying a prior version of the account closing law to a permanent indefinite appropriation).

7. Repayments and Deobligations

a. Repayments

To prevent the overstatement of obligated balances, the term "obligated balance" is defined in 31 U.S.C. § 1551(a)(1), for purposes of 31 U.S.C. §§ 1551-1557, as the amount of unliquidated obligations applicable to the appropriation, "less amounts collectible as repayments to the appropriation." Once an account has been closed pursuant to either 31 U.S.C. § 1552(a) or 31 U.S.C. § 1555, collections received after closing, which could have been credited to the appropriation account if received prior to closing, must be deposited in the Treasury as miscellaneous receipts. 31 U.S.C. § 1552(b).

The term "repayment" is a general term referring to moneys received by a federal agency that are authorized to be credited to the receiving agency's appropriation and are not required to be deposited in the Treasury as miscellaneous receipts. Treasury Department-General Accounting Office Joint Regulation No. 1, Sept. 22, 1950, reprinted at 30 Comp. Gen. 595 (1950). Section 2 of Joint Regulation No. 1 divides repayments into two subcategories: (1) reimbursements for services or items provided outside parties that the agency is authorized by independent statutory authority to retain and disburse for an authorized purpose and (2) refunds of overpayments and erroneous payments that the agency is authorized to retain and use even in the absence of independent statutory authority.

Generally, in the absence of some other authority, when the appropriation to be credited has expired, reimbursements must be credited to the expired account and not to the current account. For example, reimbursements for items or services provided another agency under the Economy Act are credited to the fiscal year appropriation that earned them regardless of when the reimbursements are collected. If the appropriation that earned the reimbursement remains available for obligation at the time of collection, there is no distinction between a credit to the year earned or to the year collected. If, however, the appropriation that earned the reimbursement has expired for obligation purposes at the time of collection, then reimbursement can be credited only to the expired account. B-194711, June 23, 1980; B-179708, Dec. 1, 1975. After closing, the reimbursement would have to go to miscellaneous receipts.

The same treatment is accorded to refunds. For example, recoveries of amounts paid under a fraudulent contract constitute refunds that may be deposited to the credit of the appropriations charged with the payments until the appropriation account is closed. Once the account is closed, recoveries should be deposited to the general fund of the Treasury to the credit of the appropriate receipt account. B-257905, Dec. 26, 1995; B-217913.2, Feb. 19, 1993. Certain exceptions to these rules have been recognized in the treatment of de minimis amounts. For example, we did not object to an agency accepting a credit of less than $100 from a vendor against the amount owed on a current year obligation to offset an overpayment made to the vendor on a prior year obligation without adjusting the accounts. 72 Comp. Gen. 63 (1992). See also B-217913.3, June 24, 1994.

b. Deobligations

The amount of an obligation that is recorded against appropriations in excess of the amount necessary to pay the obligation is accounted for as follows: If the agency deobligated the appropriation before the expiration of the period of availability, the deobligated amount is available to incur new obligations. If an agency deobligates the appropriation after the expiration of the period of availability, the deobligated amount is not available to incur a new obligation, but is available to cover appropriate adjustments to obligations in the expired account. B-286929, Apr. 25, 2001. See also 52 Comp. Gen. 179 (1972).

Deobligated no-year funds, as well as no-year funds recovered as a result of cost reductions, are available for obligation on the same basis as if they had never been obligated, subject to the restrictions of 31 U.S.C. § 1555. 40 Comp. Gen. 694, 697 (1961); B-211323, Jan. 3, 1984; B-200519, Nov. 28, 1980. One early decision concerned the disposition of liquidated damage penalties deducted from payments made to a contractor. The Comptroller General concluded that, if the contractor had not objected to the deduction within 2 years, the funds could be treated as unobligated balances available for expenditure in the same manner as other funds in the account, assuming the no-year account contained a sufficient balance for the discharge of unanticipated claims. 23 Comp. Gen. 365 (1943). There was nothing magic about the suggested 2-year period. It was simply GAO's estimate of a point beyond which the likelihood of a claim by the contractor would be sufficiently remote. Id. at 367.

Legislation on rare occasion has authorized an agency to reobligate amounts that are deobligated after the appropriation has expired. This has been referred to as deobligation-reobligation ("deob-reob") authority. We mention this only to emphasize that deob-reob authority should not be confused with the general authority conferred on agencies by the account closing law to use amounts freed up as a result of the downward adjustment of obligations occurring prior to closing that are now generally referred to as deobligated amounts.

E. Effect of Litigation on Period of Availability

If the entitlement to unobligated funds is tied up in litigation, the statutory expiration and closing procedures could come into conflict with a claimants right to pursue a claim with the courts.

Suppose, for example, Congress made an appropriation directing the Comptroller General to pay a huge bonus to the editors of this manual. Suppose further that the agency refused to make payment because it thought the idea economically unsound or just plain ridiculous. Maybe the agency would rather use the money for other purposes or simply let it revert to the Treasury. The editors of course could sue and would presumably be entitled to pursue the suit through the appellate process if necessary. But this could take years. If the obligational availability of the appropriation were to expire at the end of the fiscal year, the suit might very well have to be dismissed as moot. See, e.g., Township of River Vale v. Harris, 444 F. Supp. 90, 93 (D.D.C. 1978). What, then, can be done to prevent what one court has termed (presumably with tongue in judicial cheek) "the nightmare of reversion to the federal treasury"?

The answer is two-fold: the equitable power of the federal judiciary and a statute, 31 U.S.C. § 1502(b). While the cases discussed in this section predate the 1990 revision of 31 U.S.C. §§ 1551-1557 and thus use language that is in some respects obsolete, the concepts would appear applicable either directly or by analogy to the new procedures. For example, if a court could enjoin reversion to the Treasury under the old law, it can presumably equally enjoin expiration under the new law.

The cases establishing the equitable power of the courts involve two distinct situations--the normal expiration of annual appropriations at the end of the fiscal year and the expiration of budget authority in accordance with the terms of the applicable authorizing legislation. For purposes of the principles to be discussed, the distinction is not material. See B-115398.48, Dec. 29, 1975 (nondecision letter). Thus, we have generally not specified which of the two each case involves.

The concept of applying the courts' equity powers to stave off the expiration of budget authority seems to have first arisen, at least to any significant extent, in a group of impoundment cases in the early 1970s. A number of potential recipients under various grant and entitlement programs filed suits to challenge the legality of executive branch impoundments. The device the courts commonly used was a preliminary injunction for the express purpose of preventing expiration of the funds. For example, in National Council of Community Mental Health Centers, Inc.v. Weinberger, 361 F. Supp. 897 (D.D.C. 1973), plaintiffs challenged the impoundment of grant funds under the Community Mental Health Centers Act. Pending the ultimate resolution on the merits, the court issued a preliminary injunction to prevent expiration of unobligated funds for the grant programs in question. Id. at 900.

Other cases employing similar devices to preserve the availability of funds are: Maine v. Fri, 486 F.2d 713 (1st Cir. 1973); Bennett v. Butz, 386 F. Supp. 1059 (D. Minn. 1974); Guadamuz v. Ash, 368 F. Supp. 1233 (D.D.C. 1973); Community Action Programs Executive Directors Ass'n of New Jersey, Inc. v. Ash, 365 F. Supp. 1355 (D.N.J. 1973); Oklahoma v. Weinberger, 360 F. Supp. 724 (W.D. Okla. 1973).

In several of the cases (e.g., National Council of Community Mental Health Centers v. Weinberger, Community Action Programs Executive Directors Ass'n v. Ash, Bennett v. Butz), the court not only enjoined expiration of the funds but directed the agency to record an obligation under 31 U.S.C. § 1501(a). One of these cases, Bennett v. Butz, spawned a decision of the Comptroller General, 54 Comp. Gen. 962 (1975), in which GAO confirmed that such an order would constitute a valid obligation under 31 U.S.C. § 1501(a)(6), which says that no amount shall be recorded as an obligation unless it is supported by documentary evidence of a liability that may result from pending litigation.

The concept has also been applied in nonimpoundment cases. An example is City of Los Angeles v. Adams, 556 F.2d 40 (D.C. Cir. 1977). The Airport and Airway Development Act of 1970 established a formula for the apportionment of airport development grant funds. The statute also established minimum aggregate amounts for the grants, but subsequent appropriation acts imposed monetary ceilings lower than the authorized amounts. The court held that the appropriation ceilings controlled, but that the money still had to be apportioned in accordance with the formula in the enabling legislation. To preserve the availability of the additional grant funds the plaintiff was seeking, the district court had ordered the Federal Aviation Administration to obligate the amount in question prior to the statutory deadline, and the court of appeals confirmed this as proper. Id. at 51.

Thus, what we may view as the "first wave" of cases firmly established the proposition that a federal court can enjoin the statutory expiration of budget authority. Inevitably, the next group of cases to arise would involve the power of the courts to act after the funds have expired for obligational purposes--in other words, the power of the courts to "revive" expired budget authority.

The "leading case" in this area appears to be National Ass'n of Regional Councils v. Costle, 564 F.2d 583 (D.C. Cir. 1977). The plaintiff sued to force the Environmental Protection Agency to make available unobligated contract authority under the Federal Water Pollution Control Act Amendments of 1972. The court first noted that contract authority is a form of budget authority, and when made available for a definite period, terminates at the end of that period the same as direct appropriations. The court then reaffirmed the proposition that courts may "order that funds be held available beyond their statutory lapse date if equity so requires." Id. at 588. However, the court found the rule inapplicable because the suit had not been filed prior to the relevant expiration date, and the court therefore did not acquire jurisdiction of the case prior to expiration. The essence of the Costle decision is the following excerpt:

"Decisions that a court may act to prevent the expiration of budget authority which has not terminated at the time suit is filed are completely consistent with the accepted principle that the equity powers of the courts allow them to take action to preserve the status quo of a dispute and to protect their ability to decide a case properly before them. In such situations, the courts simply suspend the operation of a lapse provision and extend the term of already existing budget authority. If, however, budget authority has lapsed before suit is brought, there is no underlying congressional authorization for the court to preserve. It has vanished, and any order of the court to obligate public money conflicts with the constitutional provision vesting sole power to make such authorizations in the Congress. Equity empowers the courts to prevent the termination of budget authority which exists, but if it does not exist, either because it was never provided or because it has terminated, the Constitution prohibits the courts from creating it no matter how compelling the equities."

Id. at 588-89.

Costle is also significant in that it explained and clarified several prior cases that had purported to establish a similar, and in one instance even broader, principle. Specifically:

- National Ass'n of Neighborhood Health Centers, Inc. v. Mathews, 551 F.2d 321 (D.C. Cir. 1976). This was a suit challenging the administration of the Hill-Burton Act. The court found that certain funds had been improperly used, and directed their recovery and reallocation. The court further noted that the district court could order that the funds be held available if necessary to prevent their expiration upon recovery. However, the Costle court pointed out that the funds in Mathews had already been obligated and thus had not expired before suit was filed. Costle, 564 F.2d at 588.

- Jacksonville Port Authority v. Adams, 556 F.2d 52 (D.C. Cir. 1977). The plaintiff, in a suit to obtain additional funds under the Airport and Airway Development Program, had sought a temporary restraining order (TRO) to prevent expiration of the funds, which the district court denied. The court of appeals found denial of the TRO to be an abuse of discretion and held that, in the words of the Costle court, "relief was still available because it would have been available if the district court had initially done what should have been done," that is, grant the preservation remedy. Costle, 564 F.2d at 588. A similar case is Wilson v. Watt, 703 F.2d 395 (9thCir. 1983) (reversing the district court's denial of preliminary injunction and directing preservation of funds as necessary).

- Pennsylvania v. Weinberger, 367 F. Supp. 1378 (D.D.C. 1973). This was an impoundment suit involving the Elementary and Secondary Education Act of 1965, Pub. L. No. 89-10, 79 Stat. 27 (Apr. 11, 1965). Noting the then-existing authority of agencies to restore expired unobligated balances, the court concluded that it had even broader equitable power to order the restoration of expired appropriations. The Costle court expressly rejected the broad view that "once it is shown that Congress has authorized the restoration of lapsed authority under some circumstances then the courts may order the restoration and obligation of lapsed authority whenever they deem it appropriate." Costle, 564 F.2d at 589. The Pennsylvania decision was nevertheless correct, however, in that a separate statutory provision had extended the availability of the funds in question. Costle, 564 F.2d at 589 n.12. A case similar to Pennsylvania is Louisiana v. Weinberger, 369 F. Supp. 856 (E.D. La. 1973). The analog under current legislation would be obligation adjustments under 31 U.S.C. § 1553(a).

Thus, under Costle, the crucial test is not whether the court actually acted before the budget authority expired, but whether it had jurisdiction to act. As long as the suit is filed prior to the expiration date, the court acquires the necessary jurisdiction and has the equitable power to "revive" expired budget authority, even where preservation is first directed at the appellate level.

The principles set forth in Costle have been followed and applied in several later cases. Connecticut v. Schweiker, 684 F.2d 979 (D.C. Cir. 1982), cert. denied, 459 U.S. 1207 (1983); United States v. Michigan, 781 F. Supp. 492 (E.D. Mich. 1991); Burton v. Thornburgh, 541 F. Supp. 168 (E.D. Pa. 1982); Grueschow v. Harris, 492 F. Supp. 419 (D.S.D.), aff'd, 633 F.2d 1264 (8thCir. 1980); Sodus Central School District v. Kreps, 468 F. Supp. 884 (W.D. N.Y. 1978); Township of River Vale v. Harris, 444 F. Supp. 90 (D.D.C. 1978). See also Dotson v. Department of Housing& Urban Development, 731 F.2d 313, 317 n.2 (6tthir. 1984).

The application of the Costle doctrine "assumes that funds remain after the statutory lapse date." West Virginia Ass'n of Community Health Centers, Inc. v. Heckler, 734 F.2d 1570, 1577 (D.C. Cir. 1984). See Heleba v. Allbee, 628 A.2d 1237, 1240 (Vt. 1992). Consequently, where all funds have properly been disbursed (the key word here is "properly"), the Costle doctrine no longer applies. Id. To an extent, this gives agencies the potential to circumvent the Costle doctrine simply by spending the money, as long as the obligations and disbursements are "proper." Recognizing this, the West Virginia Association court cautioned that "we do not mean to suggest our approval, in every case, of government decisions to expend funds over which a legal controversy exists." 734 F.2d at 1577 n.8. In addition, to prevent this potential loophole from swallowing up the rule, there is a logical corollary to the Costle doctrine to the effect that courts may enjoin the obligation of funds or even the disbursement of funds already obligated where disbursement would have the effect of precluding effective relief and thereby rendering the case moot. See City of Houston v. Department of Housing & Urban Development, 24 F.3d 1421, 1426-27 (D.C. Cir. 1994); Population Institute v. McPherson, 797 F.2d 1062 (D.C. Cir. 1986). Similarly, the district court's injunction in Bennett v. Butz, quoted in 54 Comp. Gen. 962, supra, included a provision mandating retention of the obligated balances until further order of the court.

When Congress acts to rescind an appropriation, those amounts are no longer available to the court for award. City of Houston, 24 F.3d at 1426. It does not matter that the court has issued a temporary restraining order requiring the agency to set aside funds pending the resolution of the plaintiff's timely filed claim. Rochester Pure Waters District v. EPA, 960 F.2d 180, 183-84 (D.C. Cir. 1992). A temporary restraining order is not binding on Congress, which has "absolute control of the moneys of the United States." Id. at 185. See Harrington v. Bush, 553 F.2d 190, 194 n.7 (D.C. Cir. 1977). Thus, after Congress has rescinded an appropriation, a court may not order a permanent injunction awarding the rescinded funds to the plaintiff, as the court cannot order the obligation of funds for which there is no appropriation. Rochester, 960 F.2d at 184.

In addition to the judicial authority in Costle and the cases that follow, there is a statute that seems to point in the same direction, 31 U.S.C. § 1502(b), which provides:

"A provision of law requiring that the balance of an appropriation or fund be returned to the general fund of the Treasury at the end of a definite period does not affect the status of lawsuits or rights of action involving the right to an amount payable from the balance."

The statute was enacted as part of a continuing resolution in 1973. Pub. L. No. 93-52, § 111, 87 Stat. 134 (July 1, 1973). Its legislative history, which is extremely scant, is found at 119 Cong. Rec. 22326 (June 29, 1973), and indicates that it was generated by certain impoundment litigation then in process.

For the most part, the courts have relied on their equitable powers and have made little use of 31 U.S.C. § 1502(b). Connecticut v. Schweiker cited the statute in passing in a footnote. 684 F.2d 979, at 996 n.29. The court in Township of River Vale v. Harris, 444 F. Supp. at 94, noted the statute but found it inapplicable because the funds in that case would have reverted to a revolving fund rather than to the general fund of the Treasury. In Population Institute v. McPherson, 797 F.2d at 1081, and International Union, United Automobile, Aerospace & Agricultural Implement Workers of America v. Donovan, 570 F. Supp. 210,220 (D.D.C. 1983), the court cited section 1502(b) essentially as additional support for the rule that courts have the equitable power to prevent the expiration of budget authority in appropriate cases.

Note that the statute uses the words "lawsuits or rights of action." One court has relied on this language to reach a result perhaps one step beyond Costle. In Missouri v. Heckler, 579 F. Supp. 1452 (W.D. Mo. 1984), the plaintiff state sued the Department of Health and Human Services (HHS) for reimbursement of expenditures under the Medicaid program. Based on Connecticut v. Schweiker, supra, the court concluded that the plaintiff was clearly entitled to be paid. The court then reviewed a provision of the Department's fiscal year 1983 continuing resolution and directed that the claims be paid in fiscal years 1984 through 1986. Alternatively, the court applied 31 U.S.C. § 1502(b) and held that the claims were payable from and to the extent of the unobligated balance of fiscal year 1981 funds. Although Missouri had not filed its lawsuit prior to the end of fiscal year 1981, it had filed its claims for reimbursement with HHS before then.

The court found that "Missouri's right to reimbursement arose when it filed its claims in a timely fashion ...and otherwise complied with the law and regulations then in effect. With this right to reimbursement came the concomitant right of action to enforce the claim for reimbursement." Missouri, 579 F. Supp. at 1456.

The Missouri court further noted that if section 1502(b) is to meaningfully preserve the "status" of rights of action, it should also be construed as preserving the availability of funds. Id. at 1456 n.4.

The Comptroller General followed a similar approach in 62 Comp. Gen. 527 (1983). A labor union had filed an unfair labor practice charge with the statutorily created Foreign Service Labor Relations Board, based on a refusal by the United States Information Agency to implement a decision of the Foreign Service Impasse Disputes Panel. The dispute concerned fiscal year 1982 performance pay awards for members of the Senior Foreign Service. The question presented to GAO was the availability of fiscal year 1982 funds to pay the awards after the end of the fiscal year. GAO first found 31 U.S.C. § 1501(a)(6) (which provides that an obligation may be recorded when supported by documentary evidence of a liability that may result from pending litigation) inapplicable, then concluded that, by virtue of 31 U.S.C. § 1502(b), the unobligated balance of fiscal year 1982 funds remained available for the awards. The unfair labor practice proceeding was a "right of action," and the statute therefore operated to preserve the availability of the funds.

Under 31 U.S.C. §§ 1551-1557, funds are "returned to the general fund of the Treasury" only when the account is closed, raising the question whether section 1502(b) continues to apply to expiration in addition to closing. If section 1502(b) is to be construed in light of its purpose, then the answer is that expired appropriations will continue to be available to liquidate obligations that arise from injunctive relief ordered by a court or agreed to by an agency in settlement of a legal dispute. See 70 Comp. Gen. 225, 229-30 (1991). In general, section 1553(a) "provides that an expired account retains its fiscal year identity and remains available for recording, adjusting, and liquidating obligations properly chargeable to that account." 71 Comp. Gen. 502, 505 (1992).

However, pursuant to section 1552(a), an appropriation may only be used to pay properly chargeable obligations during the period of the appropriation's availability and during the five fiscal years immediately following the period of availability. After that, the appropriation account is closed and the remaining balance is canceled. 73 Comp. Gen. 338, 342 (1994). If a valid obligation arises after the appropriation account is closed, section 1553(b) authorizes payment of the obligation from current appropriations if account records show that sufficient funds remained available to cover the obligation when the account was closed by operation of law. Id.; 71 Comp. Gen. at 505-506.

Similar problems exist in the case of bid protests. If a protest is filed near the end of a fiscal year and the contract cannot be awarded until the protest is resolved, the contracting agency risks expiration of the funds.Congress addressed this situation in late 1989 by enacting a new 31 U.S.C. § 1558(a), which currently reads as follows:

> "(a) ...[F]unds available to an agency for obligation for a contract at the time a protest ...is filed in connection with a solicitation for, proposed award of, or award of such contract shall remain available for obligation for 100 days after the date on which the final ruling is made on the protest.... A ruling is considered final on the date on which the time allowed for filing an appeal or request for reconsideration has expired, or the date on which a decision is rendered on such an appeal or request, whichever is later."

This provision applies to protests filed with GAO, the contracting agency, or a court under 31 U.S.C. §§ 3552 and 3556, and to protests filed with the General Services Board of Contract Appeals, the contracting agency, or a court under 40 U.S.C. § 759(f). 31 U.S.C. § 1558(b).

However, the fiscal principles inherent in the Antideficiency Act are really quite simple. Government officials may not make payments or commit the United States to make payments at some future time for goods or services unless there is enough money in the "bank" to cover the cost in full. The "bank," of course, is the available appropriation.

The combined effect of the Antideficiency Act, in conjunction with the other funding statutes discussed throughout this publication, was summarized in a 1962 decision. The summary has been quoted in numerous later Antideficiency Act cases and bears repeating here:

> "These statutes evidence a plain intent on the part of the Congress to prohibit executive officers, unless otherwise authorized by law, from making contracts involving the Government in obligations for expenditures or liabilities beyond those contemplated and authorized for the period of availability of and within the amount of the appropriation under which they are made; to keep all the departments of the Government, in the matter of incurring obligations for expenditures, within the limits and purposes of appropriations annually provided for conducting their lawful functions, and to prohibit any officer or employee of the Government from involving the Government in any contract or other obligation for the payment of money for any purpose, in advance of appropriations made for such purpose; and to restrict the use of annual appropriations to expenditures required for the service of the particular fiscal year for which they are made."

42 Comp. Gen. 272, 275 (1962).

To the extent it is possible to summarize appropriations law in a single paragraph, this is it. Viewed in the aggregate, the Antideficiency Act and related funding statutes "[restrict] in every possible way the expenditures and expenses and liabilities of the government, so far as executive offices are concerned, to the specific appropriations for each fiscal year." Wilder's Case, 16 Ct. CL 528, 543 (1880).

2. Obligation/Expenditure in Excess or Advance of Appropriations

The key provision of the Antideficiency Act is 31 U.S.C. § 1341(a)(1):

> "(a)(1) An officer or employee of the United States Government or of the District of Columbia government may not:

>> "(A) make or authorize an expenditure or obligation exceeding an amount available in an appropriation or fund for the expenditure or obligation; or;

>> "(B) involve either government in a contract or obligation for the payment of money before an appropriation is made unless authorized by law."

Not only is section 1341(a)(1) the key provision of the Act, it was originally the only provision, the others being added to ensure enforcement of the basic prohibitions of section 1341.

The law is not limited to the executive branch, but applies to any "officer or employee of the United States Government" and thus extends to all branches. Examples of legislative branch applications are B-303964, Feb. 3, 2005 (Capitol Police use of the Legislative Branch Emergency Response Fund); B-303961, Dec. 6, 2004 (Architect of the Capitol); B-107279, Jan. 9, 1952 (Office of Legislative Counsel, House of Representatives); B-78217, July 21, 1948 (appropriations to Senate for expenses of Office of Vice President); 27 Op. Att'y Gen. 584 (1909) (Government Printing Office). Within the judicial branch, it applies to the Administrative Office of the United States Courts. E.g., 50 Comp. Gen. 589 (1971). However, whether a federal judge is an officer or employee for purposes of 31 U.S.C. § 1341(a)(1) appears to remain an open question, at least in some contexts. See Armster v. United States District Court, 792 F.2d 1423, 1427 n.7 (9th Cir. 1986) (the Seventh Amendment of the Constitution prohibits suspension of civil jury trials for lack of funds, whether or not a judge is considered an employee or officer under the Antideficiency Act). The Antideficiency Act also applies to officers of the District of Columbia Courts. B-284566, Apr. 3, 2000.

Some government corporations are also classified as agencies of the United States Government, and to the extent they operate with funds which are regarded as appropriated funds, they too are subject to 31 U.S.C. § 1341(a)(1). E.g., B-223857, Feb. 27, 1987 (Commodity Credit Corporation); B-135075-0.M., Feb. 14, 1975 (Inter-American Foundation). It follows that section 1341(a)(1) does not apply to a government corporation that is not an agency of the United States Government. E.g., B-175155-0.M., July 26, 1976 (Amtrak). These principles are, of course, subject to variation if and to the extent provided in the relevant organic legislation.

There are two distinct prohibitions in section 1341(a)(1). Unless otherwise authorized by law, no officer or employee of the United States may (1) make any expenditure or incur an obligation in excess of available appropriations, or (2) make an expenditure or incur an obligation in advance of appropriations.

The distinction between obligating in excess of an appropriation and obligating in advance of an appropriation is clear in the majority of cases, but can occasionally become blurred. For example, an agency which tries to meet a current shortfall by "borrowing" from (i.e., obligating against) the unenacted appropriation for the next fiscal year is clearly obligating in advance of an appropriation. E.g., B-236667, Jan. 26, 1990. However, it is also obligating in excess of the currently available appropriation. Since both are equally illegal, determining precisely which subsection of event, the point to be stressed here is that the law is violated not just when there are insufficient funds in an account when a payment becomes due. The very act of obligating the United States to make a payment when the necessary funds are not already in the account is also a violation of 31 U.S.C. § 1341(a). E.g., B-300480, Apr. 9, 2003.

In B-290600, July 10, 2002, both the Office of Management and Budget (OMB) and the Airline Transportation Stabilization Board (ATSB) violated the Antideficiency Act when OMB apportioned, and ATSB obligated an appropriation, in advance of, and thus in excess of, its availability. The Air Transportation Safety and System Stabilization Act authorized the President to issue up to $10 billion in loan guarantees, and to provide the subsidy amounts necessary for such guarantees, to assist air carriers who incurred losses resulting from the September 11, 2001, terrorist attacks on the United States. Pub. L. No. 107-42, title I, § 101(a)(1), 115 Stat. 230 (Sept. 22, 2001). Congress established the ATSB to review and decide on applications for these loan guarantees. The budget authority for the guarantees was available only "to the extent that a request, that includes designation of such amount as an emergency requirement ... is transmitted by the President to Congress." Id. at § 101(b). The President had not submitted such a request at the time OMB apportioned the funds to ATSB and the ATSB obligated the funds; therefore, both OMB and ATSB made funds available in advance of their availability, violating the Antideficiency Act.

Note that 31 U.S.C. § 1341(a) refers to overobligating and overspending the amount available in an "appropriation or fund." The phrase "appropriation or fund" refers to appropriation and fund accounts. An appropriation account is the basic unit of an appropriation generally reflecting each unnumbered paragraph in an appropriation act. Fund accounts include general fund accounts, intragovernmental fund accounts, special fund accounts, and trust fund accounts. See, e.g., 72 Comp. Gen. 59 (1992) (Corps of Engineers was prohibited by the Antideficiency Act from overobligating its Civil Works Revolving Fund's available budget authority).

Thus, for example, the Antideficiency Act applies to Indian trust funds managed by the Bureau of Indian Affairs However, the investment of these funds in certificates of deposit with federally insured banks under authority of 25 U.S.C. § 162a does not, in GAO's opinion, constitute an obligation or expenditure for purposes of 31 U.S.C. § 1341. Accordingly, overinvested trust funds do not violate the Antideficiency Act unless the overinvested funds, or any attributable interest income, are obligated or expended by the Bureau. B-207047-O.M., June 17, 1983. Cf. B-303413, Nov. 8, 2004 (the Federal Communications Commission's (FCC) regulatory action to provide spectrum rights through a license modification instead of an auction did not violate section 1341; spectrum licenses that impose costs and expenses on the licensee do not constitute an obligation and expenditure of the FCC). GAO also views the Antideficiency Act as applicable to presidential and vice-presidential "unvouchered expenditure" accounts. B-239854, June 21, 1990 (internal memorandum).

a. Exhaustion of an Appropriation

When we talk about an appropriation being "exhausted," we are really alluding to any of several different but related situations:

- Depletion of appropriation account (i.e., fully obligated and/or expended).

- Similar depletion of a maximum amount specifically earmarked in a lump-sum appropriation.

- Depletion of an amount subject to a monetary ceiling imposed by some other statute (usually, but not always, the relevant program legislation).

(1) Making further payments

In simple terms, once an appropriation is exhausted, the making of any further payments, apart from using expired balances to liquidate or make adjustments to valid obligations recorded against that appropriation, violates 31 U.S.C. § 1341. When the appropriation is fully expended, no further payments may be made in any case. If an agency finds itself in this position, unless it has transfer authority or other clear statutory basis for making further payments, it has little choice but to seek a deficiency or supplemental appropriation from Congress, and to adjust or curtail operations as may be necessary. E.g., B-285725, Sept. 29, 2000; 61 Comp. Gen. 661 (1982); 38 Comp. Gen. 501 (1959). For example, when the Corporation for National and Community Service obligated funds in excess of the amount available to it in the National Service Trust, the Corporation suspended participant enrollment in the AmeriCorps program and requested a deficiency appropriation from Congress.

In many ways, the prohibitions in the Adequacy of Appropriations Act, 41 U.S.C. § 11, parallel those of 31 U.S.C. § 1341(a). The Adequacy of Appropriations Act states in part that:

"No contract or purchase on behalf of the United States shall be made, unless the same is authorized by law or is under an appropriation adequate to its fulfillment, except in the Department of Defense and in the Department of Transportation with respect to the Coast Guard when it is not operating as a service in the Navy, for clothing, subsistence, forage, fuel, quarters, transportation, or medical and hospital supplies, which, however, shall not exceed the necessities of the current year."

41 U.S.C. § 11(a).

For example, a contract in excess of the available appropriation violates both statutes. E.g., 9 Comp. Dec. 423 (1903). However, a contract in compliance with 41 U.S.C. § 11 can still result in a violation of the Antideficiency Act. Assessment of Antideficiency Act violations is not frozen at the point when the obligation is incurred. Even if the initial obligation was well within available funds, the Antideficiency Act can still be violated if upward adjustments cause the obligation to exceed available funds. E.g., 55 Comp. Gen. 812, 826 (1976).

What one authority termed the "granddaddy of all violations occurred when the Navy overobligated and overspent nearly $110 million from its "Military Personnel, Navy" appropriation during the years 1969-1972. GAO summarized the violation in a letter report, B-177631, June 7, 1973. While there may have been some concealment, GAO concluded that the violation was not the result of some evil scheme; rather, the "basic cause of the violation was the separation of the authority to create obligations from the responsibility to control them." The authority to create obligations had been decentralized while control was centralized in the Bureau of Naval Personnel.

Granddaddy was soon to lose his place of honor on the totem pole. Around November of 1975, the Department of the Army discovered that, for a variety of reasons, it had overobligated four procurement appropriations in the aggregate amount of more than $160 million and consequently had to halt payments to some 900 contractors. The Army requested the Comptroller General's advice on a number of potential courses of action it was considering. The resulting decision was 55 Comp. Gen. 768 (1976). The Army recognized its duty to mitigate the Antideficiency Act violation. It was clear that without a deficiency appropriation, all the contractors could not be paid. One option—to use current appropriations to pay the deficiencies—had to be rejected because there is no authority to apply current funds to pay off debts incurred in a previous year. Id. at 773. An option GAO endorsed was to reduce the amount of the deficiencies by terminating some of the contracts for convenience, although the termination costs would still have to come from a deficiency appropriation unless there was enough left in the appropriation accounts to cover them. Id.

(2) Limitations on contractor recovery

If the Antideficiency Act prohibits any further payments when the appropriation is exhausted, where does this leave the contractor? Is the contractor expected to know how and at what rate the agency is spending its money? There is a small body of judicial case law which discusses the effect of the exhaustion of appropriations on government obligations. The fate of the contractor seems to depend on the type of appropriation involved and the presence or absence of notice, actual or constructive, to the contractor on the limitations of the appropriation.

Where a contractor is but one party out of several to be paid from a general appropriation, the contractor is under no obligation to know the status or condition of the appropriation account on the government's books. If the appropriation becomes exhausted, the Antideficiency Act may prevent the agency from making any further payments, but valid obligations will remain enforceable in the courts. For example, in Ferris v. United States, 27 Ct. Cl. 542 (1892), the plaintiff had a contract with the government to dredge a channel in the Delaware River. The Corps of Engineers made him stop work halfway through the job because it had run out of money. In discussing the contractor's rights in a breach of contract suit, the court said:

"A contractor who is one of several persons to be paid out of an appropriation is not chargeable with knowledge of its administration, nor can his legal rights be affected or impaired by its maladministration or by its diversion, whether legal or illegal, to other objects. An appropriation per se merely imposes limitations upon the Government's own agents; it is a definite amount of money entrusted to them for distribution; but its insufficiency does not pay the Government's debts, nor cancel its obligations, nor defeat the rights of other parties."

Id. at 546.

The rationale for this rule is that "a contractor cannot justly be expected to keep track of appropriations where he is but one of several being paid from the fund." Ross Construction Corp. v. United States, 392 F.2d 984, 987 (Ct. Cl. 1968). Other illustrative cases are Dougherty ex rel. Slavens v. United States, 18 Ct. Cl. 496 (1883), and Joplin v. United States, 89 Ct. Cl. 345 (1939). The Antideficiency Act may "apply to the official, but [does] not affect the rights in this court of the citizen honestly contracting with the Government." Dougherty, 18 Ct. Cl. at 503. Thus, it is settled that contractors paid from a general appropriation are not barred from recovering for breach of contract even though the appropriation is exhausted.

However, under a specific line-item appropriation, the answer is different. The contractor in this situation is deemed to have notice of the limits on the spending power of the government official with whom he contracts. A contract under these circumstances is valid only up to the amount of the available appropriation. Exhaustion of the appropriation will generally bar any further recovery beyond that limit. E.g., Sutton v. United States, 256 U.S. 575 (1921); Hooe v. United States, 218 U.S. 322 (1910); Shipman v. United States, 18 Ct. Cl. 138 (1883); Dougherty, 18 Ct. Cl. at 503.

The distinction between the Ferris and Sutton lines of cases follows logically from the old maxim that ignorance of the law is no excuse. If Congress appropriates a specific dollar amount for a particular contract, that amount is specified in the appropriation act and the contractor is deemed to know it. It is certainly not difficult to locate. If, on the other hand, a contract is but one activity under a larger appropriation, it is not reasonable to expect the contractor to know how much of that appropriation remains available for it at any given time. A requirement to obtain this information would place an unreasonable burden on the contractor, not to mention a nuisance for the government as well.

In two cases in the 1960s, the Court of Claims permitted recovery on contractor claims in excess of a specific monetary ceiling. See Anthony P Miller, Inc. v. United States, 348 F.2d 475 (Ct. Cl. 1965) (claim by Capehart Housing Act contractor); Ross Construction Corp. v. United States, 392 F.2d 984 (Ct. Cl. 1968) (claim by contractor for "off-site" construction ancillary to Capehart Act housing). The court distinguished between matters not the fault or responsibility of the contractor (for example, defective plans or specifications or changed conditions under the "changed conditions" clause), in which case above-ceiling claims are allowable, and excess costs resulting from what it termed "simple extras," in which case they are not. Without attempting to detail the fairly complex Capehart legislation here, we note merely that Ross is more closely analogous to the Ferris situation (392 F.2d at 986), while Anthony P Miller is more closely analogous to the Sutton situation (392 F.2d at 987). The extent to which the approach reflected in these cases will be applied to the more traditional form of exhaustion of appropriations remains to be developed, although the Ross court intimated that it saw no real distinction for these purposes between a specific appropriation and a specific monetary ceiling imposed by other legislation (id.).

b. Contracts or Other Obligations in Excess or Advance of Appropriations

It is easy enough to say that the Antideficiency Act prohibits you from obligating a million dollars when you have only half a million left in the account, or that it prohibits you from entering into a contract in September purporting to obligate funds for the next fiscal year that have not yet been appropriated. Many of the situations that actually arise from day to day, however, are not quite that simple. A useful starting point is the relationship of the Antideficiency Act to the recording of obligations under 31 U.S.C. § 1501.

(1) Proper recording of obligations

Proper recording practices are essential to sound funds control. An amount of recorded obligations in excess of the available appropriation is prima facie evidence of a violation of the Antideficiency Act, but is not conclusive. B-134474-O.M., Dec. 18, 1957.

An example of this is B-300480, Apr. 9, 2003, in which the Corporation for National and Community Services failed to recognize and record obligations for national service educational benefits of AmeriCorps participants when it incurred that obligation. In that case, the Corporation made grant awards to state corporations, who, in turn, made subgrants to nonprofit entities, who enrolled participants. In its grant awards to the state corporations, the Corporation approved the enrollment of a specified number of new program participants. Because the Corporation in the grant agreement had committed to a specified number of new participants, the Corporation incurred an obligation for the participants' educational benefits at that time; without further action by the Corporation, the Corporation was legally required to pay education benefits of all participants, up to the number the Corporation had specified in the grant agreement, if the grantee and subgrantee, who needed no further approval from the Corporation, enrolled that number of new participants, and if they satisfied the criteria for benefits. The Corporation's failure to recognize and record its obligation did not ameliorate its violation of the Act. See also B-300480.2, June 6, 2003.

Also, in many situations, the amount of the government's liability is not definitely fixed at the time the obligation is incurred. An example is a contract with price escalation provisions. A violation would occur if sufficient budget authority is not available when an agency must adjust a recorded obligation. See, e.g., B-240264, Feb. 7, 1994 (an agency would incur an Antideficiency Act violation if it must adjust an obligation for an incrementally funded contract to fully reflect the extent of the bona fide need contracted for and sufficient appropriations are not available to support the adjustment).

This is illustrated in B-289209, May 31, 2002. After holding that the Coast Guard had wrongly used no-year funds from the Oil Spill Liability Trust Fund for administrative expenses, GAO concluded that the agency should adjust its accounting records by deobligating the incorrectly charged expenses and charging them instead to the proper appropriation. GAO advised the Coast Guard that these adjustments could result in a violation of the Antideficiency Act to the extent that there was insufficient budget authority, and that the agency should report any deficiency in accordance with the Antideficiency Act.

The incurring of an obligation in excess or advance of appropriations violates the Act, and this is not affected by the agency's failure to record the obligation. E.g., 71 Comp. Gen. 502, 509 (1992); 65 Comp. Gen. 4, 9 (1985); 62 Comp. Gen. 692, 700 (1983); 55 Comp. Gen. 812, 824 (1976); B-245856.7, Aug. 11, 1992.

(2) Obligation in excess of appropriations

Incurring an obligation in excess of the available appropriation violates 31 U.S.C. § 1341(a)(1). As the Comptroller of the Treasury advised an agency head many years ago, "your authority in the matter was strictly limited by the amount of the appropriation; otherwise there would be no limit to your power to incur expenses for the service of a particular fiscal year." 9 Comp. Dec. 423, 425 (1903). If you want higher authority, the Supreme Court has stated that, absent statutory authorization, "it is clear that the head of the department cannot involve the government in an obligation to pay any thing in excess of the appropriation." Bradley v. United States, 98 U.S. 104, 114 (1878).

To take a fairly simple illustration, the statute was violated by an agency's acceptance of an offer to install automatic telephone equipment for $40,000 when the unobligated balance in the relevant appropriation was only $20,000. 35 Comp. Gen. 356 (1955).

In a 1969 case, the Air Force wanted to purchase computer equipment but did not have sufficient funds available. It attempted an arrangement whereby it made an initial down payment, with the balance of the purchase price to be paid in installments over a period of years, the contract to continue unless the government took affirmative action to terminate. This was nothing more than a sale on credit, and since the contract constituted an obligation in excess of available funds, it violated the Antideficiency Act. 48 Comp. Gen. 494 (1969).

(3) Variable quantity contracts

A leading case discussing the Antideficiency Act ramifications of "variable quantity" contracts (requirements contracts, indefinite quantity contracts, and similar arrangements) is 42 Comp. Gen. 272 (1962). That decision considered a 3-year contract the Air Force had awarded to a firm to provide any service or maintenance work necessary for government aircraft landing on Wake Island. GAO questioned the legality of entering into a contract of more than 1 year since the Air Force had only a 1-year appropriation available. The Air Force argued that it was a "requirements" contract, that no obligation would arise unless or until some maintenance work was ordered, and that the only obligation was a negative one—not to buy service from anyone else but the contractor should the services be needed. GAO disagreed. The services covered were "automatic incidents of the use of the air field." There was no place for a true administrative determination that the services were or were not needed. There was no true "contingency" as the services would almost certainly be needed if the base were to remain operational. Accordingly, the contract was not a true requirements contract but amounted to a firm obligation for the needs of future years, and was therefore an unauthorized multiyear contract. As such, it violated the Antideficiency Act. The solution was to contract on an annual basis with renewal options from year to year, and, if that did not meet the Air Force's needs, then ask Congress for multiyear procurement authority.

The Wake Island decision noted that the contract contained no provision permitting the Air Force to reduce or eliminate requirements short of a termination for convenience. Id. at 277. If the contract had included such a provision—and in the unlikely event that, given the nature of the contract, such a provision could have been meaningful—a somewhat different analysis might have resulted. Compare, for example, the situation in 55 Comp. Gen. 812 (1976). The exercise of a contract option required the Navy to furnish various items of government-furnished property (GFP), but another contract clause authorized the Navy to unilaterally delete items of GFP. If the entire quantity of GFP had to be treated as a firm obligation at the time the option was exercised, the obligation would have exceeded available appropriations, resulting in an Antideficiency Act violation. However, since the Navy was not absolutely obligated to furnish all the GFP items at the time the option was exercised, the Navy could avert a violation if it were able to delete enough GFP to stay within the available appropriation; if it found that it could not do so, the violation would then exist. See also B-134474-0.M., Dec. 18, 1957.

In 47 Comp. Gen. 155 (1967), GAO considered an Air Force contract for mobile generator sets which specified minimum and maximum quantities to be purchased over a 12-month period. Since the contract committed the Air Force to purchase only the minimum quantity, it was necessary to obligate only sufficient funds to cover that minimum. See also B-287619, July 5, 2001. Subsequent orders for additional quantities up to the maximum were not legally objectionable as long as the Air Force had sufficient funds to cover the cost when it placed those orders. See also 19 Comp. Gen. 980 (1940). The fact that the Air Force, at the time it entered into the contract, did not have sufficient funds available to cover the maximum quantity was, for Antideficiency Act purposes, irrelevant. The decision distinguished the Wake Island case on the basis that nothing in the mobile generator contract purported to commit the Air Force to obtain any requirements over and above the specified minimum from the contractor.

In 63 Comp. Gen. 129 (1983), GAO found no Antideficiency Act problems with a General Services Administration "Multiple Award Schedule" contract under which no minimum purchases were guaranteed and no binding obligation would arise unless and until a using agency made an administrative determination that it had a requirement for a scheduled item.

Regardless of whether we are dealing with a requirements contract, indefinite quantity contract, or some variation, two points apply as far as the Antideficiency Act is concerned:

- Whether or not there is a violation at the time the contract is entered into depends on exactly what the government is obligated to do under the contract.

- Even if there is no violation at the time the contract is entered into, a violation may occur later if the government subsequently incurs an obligation under the contract in excess of available funds, for example, by electing to order a maximum quantity without sufficient funds to cover the quantity ordered.

A conceptually related situation is a contract that gives the government the option of two performances at different prices. The government can enter into such a contract without violating the Antideficiency Act as long as it has sufficient appropriations available at the time the contract is entered into to pay the lesser amount. For example, the Defense Production Act of 1950 authorizes the President to contract for synthetic fuels, but the contract must give the President the option to refuse delivery and instead pay the contractor the amount by which the contract price exceeds the prevalent market price at the time of the delivery. Such a contract would not violate the Antideficiency Act at the time it is entered into as long as sufficient appropriations are available to pay any anticipated difference between the contract price and the estimated market price at the time of performance. 60 Comp. Gen. 86 (1980). Of course, the government could choose not to accept delivery unless there were sufficient appropriations available at that time to cover the full cost of the fuel under the contract.

An agreement to pay "special termination" costs under an incrementally funded contract creates a firm obligation, not a contingent liability, to pay the contractor because the contracting agency remains liable for the costs even if it decides not to fund the contract further. B-238581, Oct. 31, 1990.

(4) Multiyear or "continuing" contracts

A multiyear contract is a contract covering the needs or requirements of more than one fiscal year.

We start with some very basic propositions:

A fixed-term appropriation (fiscal year or multiple year) may be obligated only during its period of availability.

A fixed-term appropriation may be validly obligated only for the bona fide needs of that fixed term.

The Antideficiency Act prohibits the making of contracts which exceed currently available appropriations or which purport to obligate appropriations not yet made.

Performance may extend into a subsequent fiscal year in certain situations. Also, as long as a contract is properly obligated against funds for the year in which it was made, actual payment can extend into subsequent years. Apart from these situations, and unless the agency either has specific multiyear contracting authority (e.g., 62 Comp. Gen. 569 (1983)), is contracting in compliance with the multiyear contracting provisions of the Federal Acquisition Streamlining Act of 1994, or is operating under a no-year appropriation (e.g., 43 Comp. Gen. 657 (1964)), the Antideficiency Act, together with the bona fide needs rule, prohibits contracts purporting to bind the government beyond the obligational duration of the appropriation. This is because the current appropriation is not available for future needs, and appropriations for those future needs have not yet been made. Citations to support this proposition are numerous. The rule applies to any attempt to obligate the government beyond the end of the fiscal year, even where the contract covers a period of only a few months. 24 Comp. Gen. 195 (1944).

An understanding of the principles applicable to multiyear contracting begins with a discussion of a 1926 decision of the United States Supreme Court. An agency had entered into a long-term lease for office space with 1-year (i.e., fiscal year) funds, but its contract specifically provided that payment for periods after the first year was subject to the availability of future appropriations. In Leiter v. United States, 271 U.S. 204 (1926), the Supreme Court specifically rejected that theory. The Court held that the lease was binding on the government only for one fiscal year, and it ceased to exist at the end of the fiscal year in which the obligation was incurred. It takes affirmative action to bring the obligation back to life. The Court stated its position as follows:

"It is not alleged or claimed that these leases were made under any specific authority of law. And since at the time they were made there was no appropriation available for the payment of rent after the first fiscal year, it is clear that in so far as their terms extended beyond that year they were in violation of the express provisions of the [Antideficiency Act]; and, being to that extent executed without authority of law, they created no binding obligation against the United States after the first year. [Citations omitted.] A lease to the Government for a term of years, when entered into under an appropriation available for but one fiscal year, is binding on the Government only for that year. [Citations omitted.] And it is plain that, to make it binding for any subsequent year, it is necessary, not only that an appropriation be made available for the payment of the rent, but that the Government, by its duly authorized officers, affirmatively continue the lease for such subsequent year; thereby, in effect, by the adoption of the original lease, making a new lease under the authority of such appropriation for the subsequent year."

Id. at 206-07.

The Federal Acquisition Streamlining Act of 1994 (FASA) supplied the "specific authority of law" missing in Leiter to enable agencies to enter into multiyear contracts using fiscal year funds. The multiyear contracts provision, codified at 41 U.S.C. § 254c, authorizes executive agencies, using fiscal year funds, to enter into multiyear contracts (defined as contracts for more than 1 but not more than 5 years) for the acquisition of property or services.

To take advantage of FASA, the agency must either (1) obligate the full amount of the contract to the appropriation current at the time it enters into the contract, or (2) obligate the costs of the first year of the contract plus termination costs. Of course, if the agency elects to obligate only the costs of the individual years for each year of the contract, the agency needs to obligate the costs of each such year against the appropriation current for that year. Contracts relying on FASA must provide that the contract will be terminated if funds are not made available for the continuation of the contract in any fiscal year covered by the contract. Funds available for termination costs remain available for such costs until the obligation for termination costs has been satisfied. 41 U.S.C. § 254c(b).

Importantly, FASA does not apply to all contracts that are intended to meet the needs of more than one fiscal year. Obviously, if multiple year or no-year appropriations are legally available for the full contract period, an agency need not rely on FASA. Also, certain contract forms do not constitute multiyear contracts within the scope of FASA. For example, in B-302358, Dec. 27, 2004, GAO determined that a Bureau of Customs and Border Protection procurement constituted an "indefinite-delivery, indefinite-quantity" (IDIQ) contract that was not subject to FASA. The decision explained that, unlike a contract covered by FASA, an IDIQ contract does not obligate the government beyond its initial year. Rather, it obligates the government only to order a minimum amount of supplies or services. The cost of that minimum amount is recorded as an obligation against the appropriation current when the contract is entered into.

Leiter provides the general framework governing the legality of contracts carrying potential liabilities beyond the fiscal year availability of the appropriations that funded them. While FASA provides the necessary authority to avoid the Leiter problems, the Leiter analysis remains relevant to the extent that FASA does not apply. Thus, GAO decisions interpreting Leiter before enactment of FASA still need to be considered. For example, GAO refused to approve an automatic, annual renewal of a contract for repair and storage of automotive equipment, even though the contract provided that the government had a right to terminate. The reservation of a right to terminate does not save the contract from the prohibition against binding the government in advance of appropriations. 28 Comp. Gen. 553 (1949).

The Post Office wanted to enter into a contract for services and storage of government-owned highway vehicles for periods up to 4 years because it could obtain a more favorable flat rate per mile of operations instead of an item by item charge required if the contract was for 1 year only.

GAO held that any contract for continuous maintenance and storage of the vehicles would be prohibited by 31 U.S.C. § 1341 because it would obligate the government beyond the extent of the existing appropriation. However, there would be no legal objection to including a provision that gave the government an affirmative option to renew the contract from year to year, not to exceed 4 years as specified in the statute authorizing the Postmaster to enter into these types of contracts. 29 Comp. Gen. 451 (1950).

Where a contract gives the government a renewal option, it may not be exercised until appropriations for the subsequent fiscal year actually become available. 61 Comp. Gen. 184, 187 (1981). Under a 1-year contract with renewal options, the fact that funds become available in subsequent years does not place the government under an obligation to exercise the renewal option. Government Systems Advisors, Inc. v. United States, 13 Cl. Ct. 470 (1987), aff'd, 847 F.2d 811 (Fed. Cir. 1988).

Note that, in Leiter, the inclusion of a contract provision conditioning the government's obligation on the subsequent availability of funds was to no avail. In this regard, see also 67 Comp. Gen. 190, 194 (1988); 42 Comp. Gen. 272, 276 (1962); 36 Comp. Gen. 683 (1957). If a "subject to availability" clause were sufficient to permit multiyear contracting, the effect would be automatic continuation from year to year unless the government terminated. If funds were not available and the government nevertheless permitted or acquiesced in the continuation of performance, the contractor would obviously be performing in the expectation of being paid. Apart from questions of legal liability, the failure by Congress to appropriate the money might be viewed as a serious breach of faith. Congress, as a practical if not a legal matter, would have little real choice but to appropriate funds to pay the contractor. This is another example of a type of "coercive deficiency" the Antideficiency Act was intended to prohibit. Thus, it is not enough for the government to retain the option to terminate at any time if sufficient funds are not available. Under Leiter and its progeny, the contract "dies" at the end of the fiscal year, and may be revived only by affirmative action by the government. This "new" contract is then chargeable to appropriations for the subsequent year.

Although today FASA and the Federal Acquisition Regulation recognize "subject to availability" clauses, such a clause, by itself, is not sufficient. FASA provides that a multiyear contract for purposes of FASA:

> "may provide that performance under the contract during the second and subsequent years of the contract is contingent upon the appropriation of funds and (if it does so provide) may provide for a cancellation payment to be made to the contractor if such appropriations are not made."

41 U.S.C. § 254c(d). If an agency decides to include a "subject to availability" clause for the second and subsequent years, the agency also has to provide for possible termination. Availability clauses are required by the Federal Acquisition Regulation in several situations.

While the prescribed contract clauses vary in complexity, they all have one thing in common—each requires the contracting officer to specifically notify the contractor in writing that the contractor may resume performance. For example: (1) contract actions initiated prior to the availability of funds; (2) certain requirements and indefinite-quantity contracts: (3) fully funded cost-reimbursement contracts; (4) facilities acquisition and use; and (5) incrementally funded cost-reimbursement contracts. See 48 C.F.R. subpt. 32.7. The objective of these clauses is compliance with the Antideficiency Act and other fiscal statutes. See ITT Federal Laboratories, ASBCA No. 12987, 69-2 BCA ¶ 7,849 (1969), rev'd and remanded on other grounds, ITT v. United States, 453 F.2d 1283 (1972). What is not sufficient is a simple "subject to availability" clause which would permit automatic continuation subject to the government's right to terminate.

In B-259274, May 22, 1996, the Air Force exercised an option to a severable service contract that extended the contract from September 1, 1994, to August 31, 1995, using fiscal year 1994 funds. However, the Air Force only had enough fiscal year 1994 budget authority to finance 4 months of the option period, leaving the remaining 8 months unfunded. The Air Force modified the agreement by adding a clause stating that the government's obligation beyond December 31, 1994, was subject to the availability of appropriations. Significantly, however, the clause further stated that no legal liability on the part of the government would arise for contract performance beyond December 31, 1994, unless and until the contractor received notice in writing from the Air Force contracting officer that the contractor could continue work. GAO held that this clause converted the government's obligation for the remaining 8 months to no more than a negative obligation not to procure services elsewhere should such services be needed. Since this contractual obligation created no financial exposure on the part of the government, the Air Force had not violated the Antideficiency Act.

It may be useful at this point to reiterate the basic principle that, in the context of contractual obligations, compliance with the Antideficiency Act is determined first on the basis of when an obligation occurs, not when actual payment is scheduled to be made. In the case of a contract with an option to renew, for example, as long as sufficient funds are available to cover the initial contract, there is no violation at the time the contract is made. No obligation accrues for future option years unless and until the government exercises its option.

Another issue to consider with respect to multiyear contracts is the relationship between termination charges and the Antideficiency Act. As a general proposition, the government has the right to terminate a contract "for the convenience of the government" if that action is determined to be in the government's best interests. The Federal Acquisition Regulation prescribes the required contract clauses. 48 C.F.R. subpt. 49.5. Under a termination for convenience, the contractor is entitled to be compensated, including a reasonable profit, for the performed portion of the contract, but may not recover anticipatory profits on the terminated portion. E.g.,48 C.F.R. §§ 49.201, 49.202. Total recovery may not exceed the contract price. Id. § 49.207.

In the typical contract covering the needs of only one fiscal year, termination does not pose a problem. Under 48 C.F.R. § 49.207, the contractor's recovery cannot exceed the contract price; thus, the basic contract obligation will be sufficient to cover potential termination costs. Under a contract with options to renew, however, the situation may differ. A contractor who must incur substantial capital costs at the outset has a legitimate concern over recovering these costs if the government does not renew. A device sometimes used to address this problem, albeit with limited success, is a clause requiring the government to pay termination charges or "separate charges" upon early termination. Separate charges have been found to violate the bona fide needs rule to the extent they do not reasonably relate to the value of current fiscal year requirements. E.g., 36 Comp. Gen. 683 (1957), affd, 37 Comp. Gen. 155 (1957).

Separate charges also have been held to violate the Antideficiency Act. The leading case in this area is 56 Comp. Gen. 142 (1976), affil, 56 Comp. Gen. 505 (1977). The Burroughs Corporation protested the award of a contract to the Honeywell Corporation to provide automatic data processing (ADP) equipment to the Mine Enforcement and Safety Administration. If all renewal options were exercised, the contract would run for 60 months after equipment installation. The contract included a "separate charges" provision under which, if the government failed to exercise any renewal option or otherwise terminated prior to the end of the 60-month systems life, the government would pay a percentage of all future years' rentals based on Honeywell's "list prices" at the time of failure to renew or of termination. This provision violated the Antideficiency Act for two reasons. First, it would amount to an obligation of fiscal year funds for the requirements of future years. And second, it would commit the government to indeterminate liability because the contractor could raise its list or catalog prices at any time. The government had no way of knowing the amount of its commitment. Similar cases involving separate charges are 56 Comp. Gen. 167 (1976); B-216718.2, Nov. 14, 1984; and B-190659, Oct. 23, 1978.

The Burroughs decision also offers guidance on when separate charges may be acceptable. One instance is where it is the only way the government can obtain its needs. Cited in this regard was 8 Comp. Gen. 654 (1929), a case involving the installation of equipment and the procurement of a water supply from a town. There, however, the town was the only source of a water supply, a situation clearly inapplicable to a competitive industry like ADP. 56 Comp. Gen. at 157. In addition, separate charges are permissible if they, together with payments already made, reasonably represent the value of requirements actually performed. Thus, where the contractor has discounted its price based on the government's stated intent to exercise all renewal options, separate charges may be based on the "reasonable value (e.g., ADP schedule price) of the actually performed work at termination based upon the shortened term." Id. at 158. However, termination charges may not be inconsistent with the termination for convenience clause remedy; for example, they may not exceed the value of the contract or include costs not cognizable under a "T for C." Id. at 157.

Where termination charges are otherwise proper, the Antideficiency Act also requires that the agency have sufficient funds available to pay them if and when the contingency materializes. E.g., 62 Comp. Gen. 143 (1983); 8 Comp. Gen. 654, 657 (1929). See also Aerolease Long Beach v. United States, 31 Fed. Cl. 342, 362 (1994), aff'd, 39 F.3d 1198 (Fed. Cir. 1994) (agency complied with Antideficiency Act requirements by including termination costs as current obligations). This requirement is sometimes specified in multiyear contracting legislation. An example is 40 U.S.C. § 322, the Information Technology Fund. In operating the Fund, the General Services Administration is authorized to enter into information technology multiyear contracts if "amounts are available and adequate to pay the costs of the contract for the first fiscal year and any costs of cancellation or termination." Id. § 322(e)(1)(A). Congress may also, of course, provide exceptions. E.g.,B-174839, Mar. 20, 1984.

c. Indemnification

Under an indemnification agreement, one party promises, in effect, to cover another party's losses. It is no surprise that the government is often asked to enter into indemnification agreements. The problem is that such agreements create a risk that the government, at some point in the future, may have to pay amounts in excess of available funds. Consequently, with one very limited exception discussed below, GAO and numerous courts have adhered to the rule that, absent express statutory authority, the government may not enter into an agreement to indemnify where the amount of the government's liability is indefinite, indeterminate, or potentially unlimited. Such an agreement would violate both the Antideficiency Act, 31 U.S.C. § 1341, and the Adequacy of Appropriations Act, 41 U.S.C. § 11, since it can never be said that sufficient funds have been appropriated to cover the government's indemnification exposure. As discussed in this section, indemnity clauses have been upheld under certain conditions:

- where the potential liability of the government was limited to a definite amount known at the time of the agreement, was within the amount of available appropriations, and was not otherwise prohibited by statute;

- where the indemnification agreement is a legitimate object of an appropriation, the agreement specifically provides that the amount of liability is limited to available appropriations, and there is no implication that Congress will, at a later date, appropriate funds to meet deficiencies; or;

- where Congress has specifically authorized the agency to indemnify.

Although a provision limiting liability to appropriations available at the time a loss arises would prevent any overt Antideficiency Act or Adequacy of Appropriations Act violation by removing the "unlimited liability" objection, it could have disastrous fiscal consequences for the agency as well as present other, practical problems. For example, payment of an especially large indemnity obligation at the beginning of a fiscal year could wipe out the entire unobligated balance of the agency's appropriation for the rest of the fiscal year, forcing the agency to seek a supplemental appropriation to finance basic program activities. Conversely, if a liability arises toward the end of the fiscal year it is quite possible that no unobligated balance would be available for an indemnity payment, which means indemnification could prove largely illusory from the standpoint of the contractor or other "beneficiary."

Another practical problem concerns recording the obligations that may arise under indemnity clauses. The indemnity is a potential liability that may become an actual liability when some event outside of the government's control is triggered, at which point the liability becomes a recordable obligation. This creates a fiscal dilemma, however. While the liability is not sufficiently definite at the time the indemnity agreement is made to formally record an obligation, good financial management requires that the agency recognize its contingent liability. Although most of our cases do not directly address this issue, the ones that do, discussed below, have recommended either the obligation or administrative reservation of sufficient funds to cover the potential liability. Clearly, however, this could create a fiscal nightmare where an estimate of potential liability could encompass the entire appropriation for the agency for that fiscal year, and tying up that entire sum would prevent the agency from meeting its mission.

What follows is a discussion of indemnification proposals in decisions issued over the years. As you will see, we have struggled with the practical problems posed by the inclusion of indemnity clauses in government contracts and agreements. For the past several years it has been our view that even if indemnification clauses are rewritten to meet the minimum requirements of the Antideficiency Act or Adequacy of Appropriations Act, there should be a clear governmentwide policy restricting their use. Given the potential liability of the government created by such clauses, exceptions to this policy should not be made without express congressional acquiescence, as has been done whenever Congress has decided that it was in the best interests of the government to assume the risks of having to pay off on an indemnity obligation. See, for example, 10 U.S.C. § 2354, 42 U.S.C. § 2210, and other examples given below.

(1) Prohibition against unlimited liability

As noted above, absent specific statutory authority, the government generally may not enter into an indemnification agreement which would impose an indefinite or potentially unlimited liability on the government. In plain English, you cannot purport to bind the government to unlimited liability. The rule is not some arcane GAO concoction. The Court of Claims stated in California-Pacific Utilities Co. v. United States, 194 Ct. Cl. 703, 715 (1971)):

"The United States Supreme Court, the Court of Claims, and the Comptroller General have consistently held that absent an express provision in an appropriation for reimbursement adequate to make such payment, [the Antideficiency Act, 31 U.S.C. § 1341] proscribes indemnification on the grounds that it would constitute the obligation of funds not yet appropriated. [Citations omitted.]"

For example, in an early case, the Interior Department, as licensee, entered into an agreement with the Southern Pacific Company under which the Department was to lay telephone and telegraph wires on property owned by the licensor in New Mexico. The agreement included a provision that the Department was to indemnify the Company against any liability resulting from the operation. Upon reviewing the indemnity provision, the Comptroller General found that it purported to impose indeterminate contingent liability on the government in violation of Revised Statutes § 3732, the predecessor to the Adequacy of Appropriations Act, 41 U.S.C. § 11. By including the indemnity provision, the contracting officer had exceeded his authority, and the provision was held void. 16 Comp. Gen. 803 (1937).

Similarly, an indefinite and unlimited indemnification provision in a lease entered into by the General Services Administration without statutory authority was held to impose no legal liability on the government since it violated the provisions of 31 U.S.C. § 1341 and 41 U.S.C. § 11. 35 Comp. Gen. 85 (1955).

In 59 Comp. Gen. 369 (1980), the National Oceanic and Atmospheric Administration (NOAA) desired to undertake a series of hurricane seeding experiments off the coast of Australia in cooperation with its Australian counterpart. The State Department, as negotiator, sought GAO's opinion on an Australian proposal under which the United States would agree to indemnify Australia against all damages arising from the activities. State recognized that an unlimited agreement would violate the Antideficiency Act and asked whether the proposal would be acceptable if it specified that the government's liability would be subject to the appropriation of funds by Congress for that purpose. GAO expressed dissatisfaction with this proposal because, even though it would impose no legal obligation unless or until funds are appropriated, it would impose a moral obligation on the United States to make good on its promise. There was a way out, however—insurance. Ordinarily, appropriations are not available to acquire insurance, but GAO concluded that the government's policy of self-insurance did not apply here since the insurance would not be for the purpose of protecting against a risk to which the United States would be exposed but rather is the price exacted by Australia, as the United States' partner in an international venture, to protect Australia's interests. GAO said that NOAA could therefore purchase private insurance, with the premiums to be shared by the government of Australia, provided that the United States' liability under the agreement was limited to its share of the insurance premiums. NOAA's use of its appropriation for the United States' share of the insurance premium would simply be a necessary expense of the project.

Another decision applying the general rule held that the Federal Emergency Management Agency could not agree to provide indeterminate indemnification to agents and brokers under the National Flood Insurance Act. B-201394, Apr. 23, 1981. If the agency considered indemnification necessary to the success of its program, it could either insert a provision limiting the government's liability to available appropriations or seek broader authority from Congress.

In B-201072, May 3, 1982, the Department of Health and Human Services questioned the use of a contract clause entitled "Insurance—Liability to Third Persons," found in the Federal Procurement Regulations (predecessor to the Federal Acquisition Regulation). The clause purported to permit federal agencies to agree to reimburse contractors, without limit, for liabilities to third persons for death, personal injury, or property damage, arising out of performance of the contract and not compensated by insurance, whether or not caused by the contractor's negligence. Since the clause purported to commit the government to an indefinite liability which could exceed available appropriations, the Comptroller General found it in violation of the Antideficiency Act and the Adequacy of Appropriations Act. This decision was affirmed upon reconsideration in 62 Comp. Gen. 361 (1983), one of GAO's more comprehensive discussions of the indemnification problem.

For other cases applying or discussing the general rule, see B-260063, June 30, 1995; 35 Comp. Gen. 85 (1955); 20 Comp. Gen. 95, 100 (1940); 7 Comp. Gen. 507 (1928); 15 Comp. Dec. 405 (1909); B-242146, Aug. 16, 1991; B-117057, Dec. 27, 1957; A-95749, Oct. 14, 1938; 8 Op. Off. Legal Counsel 94 (1984); 2 Op. Off. Legal Counsel 219, 223-24 (1978). A brief letter report making the same point is GAO, Agreements Describing Liability in Undercover Operations Should Limit the Government's Liability, GGD-83-53 (Washington, D.C.: Mar. 15, 1983).

In some of the earlier GAO cases-—for example, 7 Comp. Gen. 507 and 16 Comp. Gen. 803 (1937)-—the Comptroller General offered as furthersupport for the indemnification prohibition the then-existing principle that the United States was not liable for the tortious conduct of its employees. Of course, since the enactment of the Federal Tort Claims Act in 1946, this is no longer true. Thus, the reader should disregard any discussion of the government's lack of tort liability appearing in the earlier cases. The thrust of those cases, namely, the prohibition against open-ended liability, remains valid.

The Comptroller General recognized a limited exception to the rule in59 Comp. Gen. 705 (1980). In that decision, the Comptroller General held that the General Services Administration could agree to certain indemnity provisions in procuring public utility services for government agencies under the Federal Property and Administrative Services Act, 40 U.S.C. § 501. To apply the general rule against indemnification in this situation, the Comptroller General suggested, would constitute "an overly technical and literal reading of the Anti-Deficiency Act." Id. at 707. The decision reasoned as follows:

"The procurement of goods or services from state-regulated utilities which are virtually monopolies is unique in important ways. As a practical matter, there is no other source for the needed goods or services. Moreover, the tariff requirements, such as this indemnification undertaking, are applicable generally to all of the same class of customers of the utility, and are included in the tariff only after administrative proceedings in which the government has the opportunity to participate. The United States is not being singled out for discriminatory treatment nor, presumably, can it complain that the objectionable provision was imposed without notice and the opportunity for a hearing."

"Under the circumstances, we have not objected in the past to the procurement of power by GSA under tariffs containing the indemnity clause and there is no reason to object to the purchase of power under contracts containing essentially the same indemnity clause. As noted already, this has of necessity been the practice in the past. The possibility of liability under the clause is in our judgment remote. In any event, we see little purpose to be served by a rule which prevents the United States from procuring a vital commodity under the same restrictions as other customers are subject to under the tariff if the utility insists that the restrictions are non-negotiable. However, because the possibility exists, however remote, that these agreements could result in future liability in excess of available appropriations, GSA should inform the Congress of the situation."

Id.

Subsequent decisions emphasize that the extent of the exception carved out by 59 Comp. Gen. 705 is limited to its facts. See, e.g., B-260063, June 30, 1995; 62 Comp. Gen. 361 (1983); B-242146, Aug. 16, 1991. In B-197583, Jan. 19, 1981, GAO once again applied the general rule and held that the Architect of the Capitol could not agree to indemnify the Potomac Electric Power Company (PEPCO) for loss or damages resulting from PEPCO's performance of tests on equipment installed in government buildings or from certain other equipment owned by PEPCO which could be installed in government buildings to monitor electricity use for conservation purposes. GAO pointed to two distinguishing factors that justified—and limited—the exception in 59 Comp. Gen. 705. First, in 59 Comp. Gen. 705, there was no other source from which the government could obtain the needed utility services. Here, the testing and monitoring could be performed by government employees. The second factor is summarized in the following excerpt from B-197583, Jan. 19, 1981:

"An even more important distinction, though, is that unlike the situation in the GSA case [59 Comp. Gen. 705], the Architect has not previously been accepting the testing services or using the impulse device from PEPCO and has therefore not previously agreed to the liability represented by the proposed indemnity agreements. In the GSA case, GSA merely sought to enter a contract accepting the same service and attendant liability, previously secured under a non-negotiable tariff, at a rate more advantageous to the Government. Here, however, the Government has other means available to provide the testing and monitoring desired."

Thus, the case did not fall within the "narrow exception created by the GSA decision," and the proposed indemnity agreement was improper.

More recent decisions likewise reaffirm the general rule against open-ended indemnification agreements and reemphasize the limited application of the exception in 59 Comp. Gen. 705. In B-242146, Aug. 16, 1991, GAO held that the United States Park Police could not include in mutual assistance agreements with local law enforcement agencies a clause that the United States would indemnify the latter agencies against claims arising from police actions they took in national parks. Citing 62 Comp. Gen. 361 (1983) and other cases, the decision observed:

"This Office has long held that absent statutory authority, indemnity provisions which subject the United States to indefinite or potentially unlimited contingent liability contravene the Antideficiency Act, 31 U.S.C. § 1341(a) ...since it can never be said that sufficient funds have been appropriated to cover the contingency."

"Here, the potential liability of the Park Police is unknown because the clause in question provides an indemnity for property damage and personal injury. There is no possible way to know at the time the [mutual assistance] memoranda are signed whether there are sufficient funds in the appropriation to cover a liability or when it arises under the indemnification clause because no one knows in advance how much the liability may be." (Footnote omitted.)

The decision rejected the argument that 59 Comp. Gen. 705 supported the indemnification clause in this case, stating:

"We were careful to point out in 62 Comp. Gen. at 364 ... that 59 Comp. Gen. 705 should not serve as a precedent. Indeed, except for 59 Comp. Gen. 705, the accounting officers of the Government have never issued a decision sanctioning the incurring of an obligation for an open-ended indemnity in the absence of statutory authority to the contrary.' 62 Comp. Gen. 364-365."

In B-260063, June 30, 1995, GAO again distinguished 59 Comp. Gen. 705 in holding that a federal agency should not agree to indemnify a utility company for providing electricity to one of the agency's remote facilities. The decision pointed out that, unlike the situation in 59 Comp. Gen. 705, the indemnity clause proposed here was not part of a generally applicable tariff but would discriminate against the agency.

As indicated previously, the general rule against open-ended indemnity agreements has received consistent acceptance by the courts. Examples of court cases endorsing the general rule against open-ended indemnification are Frank v. United States, 797 F.2d 724, 727 (9th Cir. 1986); Union Pacific Railroad Corp. v. United States, 52 Fed. Cl. 730, 732-735 (2002); Lopez v. Johns Manville, 649 F. Supp. 149 (WD. Wash. 1986), aff'd on other grounds, 858 F.2d 712 (Fed. Cir. 1988); In re All Asbestos Cases, 603 F. Supp. 599 (D. Hawaii 1984); Johns-Manville Corp. v. United States, 12 Cl. Ct. 1 (1987). Several of these are asbestos cases in which the courts rejected claims of an implied agreement to indemnify. In Johns-Manville Corp., the court stated:

"Contractual agreements that create contingent liabilities for the Government serve to create obligations of funds just as much as do agreements creating definite or certain liabilities. The contingent nature of the liability created by an indemnity agreement does not so lessen its effect on appropriations as to make it immune to the limitations of [the Antideficiency Act]."

12 Cl. Ct. at 25.

In Hercules, Inc. v. United States, 516 U.S. 417 (1996), the Supreme Court rejected the argument by a manufacturer of the Vietnam War-era defoliant "Agent Orange" that it had an implied-in-fact contract with the United States to indemnify it for tort damages arising from third-party claims against it. The Court noted that an implied-in-fact contract depends upon a meeting of the minds, and that such a meeting of the minds was unlikely given the rule against open-ended indemnity contracts:

"There is ... reason to think that a contracting officer would not agree to the open-ended indemnification alleged here. The Anti-Deficiency Act bars a federal employee or agency from entering into a contract for future payment of money in advance of, or in excess of, an existing appropriation. 31 U.S.C. § 1341. Ordinarily no federal appropriation covers contractors' payments to third-party tort claimants in these circumstances, and the Comptroller General has repeatedly ruled that Government procurement agencies may not enter into the type of open-ended indemnity for third-party liability that petitioner Thompson claims to have implicitly received under the Agent Orange contracts. We view the Anti-Deficiency Act, and the contracting officer's presumed knowledge of its prohibition, as strong evidence that the officer would not have provided, in fact, the contractual indemnification [petitioner] claims."

516 U.S. at 426-427 (footnotes omitted).

The Court cited several instances in which Congress had enacted statutory authorizations for indemnification, and noted that the existence of these statutory authorizations further militated against finding an implied contract to indemnify in this case:

"These statutes [authorizing indemnification], set out in meticulous detail and each supported by a panoply of implementing regulations, ... would be entirely unnecessary if an implied agreement to indemnify could arise from the circumstances of contracting. We will not interpret the [Agent Orange] contracts so as to render these statutes and regulations superfluous."

Id. at 429.

The Federal Circuit's recent decision in E.I. DuPont De Nemours & Company, Inc. v. United States, 365 F.3d 1367 (Fed. Cir. 2004), provides an interesting twist. The issue in that case was whether an indemnity clause contained in a World War II-era contract required the United States to reimburse the contractor for environmental cleanup costs it incurred at the contract site as a result of liability imposed on it under the Comprehensive Environmental Response, Compensation, and Liability Act of 1980 (popularly known as "CERCLA" or the "Superfund" law), 42 U.S.C. §§ 9601-9675. The Court of Federal Claims had viewed the contract's indemnity clause as extending to CERCLA liability, but concluded that the general rule against open-ended indemnification applied to invalidate the clause under the Antideficiency Act:

> "Even though the Indemnification Clause was included in this contract and it is quite reasonable to assume that both the contracting officer and the contractor believed this Clause to place the risk of virtually all liabilities on the government rather than the contractor, the state of the law compels us to hold this clause to be void and unenforceable...."

> "Although we are of the opinion that the current state of the law compels the result expressed, this result is so totally at odds with the agreement the parties clearly made concerning reimbursement and indemnity, and plaintiff is so clearly entitled to the indemnity it seeks under the plain language of the contract it had with the government, made during truly emergency, wartime conditions, we suggest that plaintiff may want to consider the avenue for potential relief available in a Congressional Reference case pursuant to 28 U.S.C. §§ 1492 & 2509."

E.I. DuPont De Nemours & Company, Inc. v. United States, 54 Fed. Cl. 361, 372-373 (2002).

The Federal Circuit reversed in E.I. DuPont De Nemours & Company, Inc., 365 F.3d 1367. The court did not question the general rule against open-ended indemnity provisions; nor did it dispute the lower court's conclusion that the indemnity clause in the DuPont contract was originally invalid under that rule. However, the court concluded that the government in effect ratified the clause through actions taken under a subsequent statute—the Contract Settlement Act of 1944, at 41 U.S.C. §§ 101, 120(a)—that did permit such indemnity provisions. Thus, the court reasoned, the indemnity clause in this case satisfied the "otherwise authorized by law" exception in the Antideficiency Act, 31 U.S.C. § 1341(a)(1)(B). E.I. DuPont De Nemours & Company, Inc., 365 F.3d at 1375-80.

Executive branch adjudicative bodies such as boards of contract appeals and the Federal Labor Relations Authority have also applied the general anti-indemnity rule. See Appeals of National Gypsum Co., ASBCA No. 53259, 03-1 B.C.A. ¶ 32,054 (2002) (indemnity provision of World War II contract unenforceable because in violation of the Antideficiency Act and the Executive Order under which the contract was entered into); KMS Development Co. v. General Services Administration, GSBCA No. 12584, 95-2 B.C.A. ¶ 27, 663 (1995) (no implied-in-fact contract of indemnity since such a contract would be ultra vires as a violation of the Antideficiency Act); National Federation of Federal Employees and U.S. Department of the Interior, 35 F.L.R.A. 1034 (1990) (proposal to indemnify union against judgments and litigation expenses resulting from drug testing program held contrary to law and therefore nonnegotiable); American

Federation of State, County and Municipal Employees and U.S. Department of Justice, 42 F.L.R.A. 412, 515-17 (1991) (similar proposal for drug testing indemnification).

In sum, the GAO decisions, court cases, and other administrative decisions reflect a clear rule against open-ended indemnification agreements (absent statutory authority). Indeed, the Supreme Court's opinion in Hercules, Inc. v. United States, 516 U.S. 417 (1996), discussed previously, commented upon the nearly uniform line of Comptroller General decisions on this point, noting that 59 Comp. Gen. 705 stood as the "one peculiar exception." 516 U.S. at 428.

(2) When indemnification may be permissible

Indemnification agreements may be proper if they are limited to available appropriations and are otherwise authorized. Before ever getting to the question of amount, for an indemnity agreement to be permissible in the first place, it must be authorized either expressly or under a necessary expense theory. 59 Comp. Gen. 369 (1980). The determination as to whether an expense is necessary as incident to the object of the applicable funding source is determined on a case-by-case basis. Although GAO generally affords agencies broad discretion in determining whether a specific expenditure is reasonably related to the accomplishment of an authorized purpose, an agency's discretion in such matters is not unlimited. 18 Comp. Gen. 285, 292 (1938). GAO has had occasion both to approve and to disapprove contract indemnification provisions as necessary or incident to the object of the applicable funding source. See, e.g., 63 Comp. Gen. 145, 150 (1984) (all but one indemnity provision in contracts for vessels were approved as incidental expenses under the Navy's authorized prepositioning ship chartering program); 59 Comp. Gen. 369 (disapproved—general statutory authority to carry out international programs did not provide authority for the United States to agree to provide complete indemnification of another country for all damages resulting from an international weather modification project); 42 Comp. Gen. 708, 712 (1963) (approved—obligation of an agency for damage or destruction that might arise under an indemnity clause in an aircraft rental contract was a necessary expense incident to the hiring of aircraft for which the agency's appropriation was expressly available); B-201394, Apr. 23, 1981 (disapproved—no specific appropriation was available to pay costs arising under a clause indemnifying agents and brokers under the National Flood Insurance program); B-137976, Dec. 4, 1958 (disapproved—an obligation arising under an indemnity provision in an agency's agreement for training with a nongovernment facility was not a necessary expense under the statute authorizing such training agreements).

Once you cross the purpose hurdle—that is, once you determine that the indemnification proposal you are considering is a legitimate object on which to spend your appropriations—you are ready to grapple with the unlimited liability issue.

One way to deal with this issue is to specifically limit the amount of the liability assumed. Such a limitation of an indemnity agreement may come about in either of two ways: it may follow necessarily from the nature of the agreement itself or it may be expressly written into the agreement, coupled with an appropriate obligation or administrative reservation of funds. The latter alternative is the only acceptable one where the government's liability would otherwise be potentially unlimited.

For example, where the government rented buses to transport Selective Service registrants for physical examination or induction, there was no objection to the inclusion of an indemnity provision for damage to the buses caused by the registrants. This was a standard provision in the applicable motor carrier charter coach tariff. 48 Comp. Gen. 361 (1968). Potential liability was not indefinite since it was necessarily limited to the value of the motor carrier's equipment.

Similarly, under a contract for the lease of aircraft, the Federal Aviation Administration (FAA) could agree to indemnify the owner for loss or damage to the aircraft in order to eliminate the need to reimburse the owner for the cost of "hull insurance" and thereby secure a lower rental rate. The liability could properly be viewed as a necessary expense incident to hiring the aircraft, FAA had no-year appropriations available to pay for any such liability, and, as in the Selective Service case, the agreement was not indefinite because maximum liability was measurable by the fair market value of the aircraft. 42 Comp. Gen. 708 (1963). See also 22 Comp. Gen. 892 (1943) (Maritime Commission could amend contract to agree to indemnify contractor against liability to third parties, in lieu of reimbursing contractor for cost of liability insurance premiums, to the extent of available appropriations and provided liability was limited to the amount of coverage of the discontinued insurance policies replaced by the indemnity agreement).

In B-114860, Dec. 19, 1979, the Farmers Home Administration asked whether it could purchase surety bonds or enter into an indemnity agreement in order to obtain the release of deeds of trust for borrowers in Colorado where the original promissory notes had been lost while in the Administration's custody. Colorado law required one or the other where the canceled original note could not be delivered to the Colorado public trustee. GAO concluded that the indemnity agreement was permissible as long as it was limited to an amount not to exceed the original principal amount of the trust deed. The decision further advised that the Administration should reserve sufficient funds to cover its potential liability. The latter aspect of the decision was reconsidered in B-198161, Nov. 25, 1980. Reviewing the particular circumstances involved, GAO was unable to foresee situations in which the government might be required to indemnify the public trustee, and accordingly advised the Administration that the reservation of funds would not be necessary. While reservation of the funds may not have been necessary, GAO did state: "Although the liability which arises from an indemnity agreement to secure the release of a trust deed may be contingent, the maximum cost of liquidating that liability would normally be a recordable expense limited by the administration's annual budget authority."

In 63 Comp. Gen. 145 (1984), certain indemnification provisions in a ship-chartering agreement were found not to impose indefinite or potentially unlimited contingent liability because liability could be avoided by certain separate actions solely under the government's control.

In cases like the Selective Service bus case (48 Comp. Gen. 361) and the FAA aircraft case (42 Comp. Gen. 708), even though the government's potential liability is limited and determinable, this fact alone does not guarantee that the agency will have sufficient funds available should the contingency ripen into an obligation. This concern is met in one of two ways. The first is either to obligate or to reserve administratively sufficient funds to cover the potential liability, although this point has not been completely explored in past decisions. In particular cases, reservation may be determined unnecessary, as in B-198161, Nov. 25, 1980, discussed above. Also, naturally, a specific directive from Congress will render reservation of funds unnecessary. See B-159141, Aug. 18, 1967 (reservation of termination costs for supersonic aircraft contract). The second way is for the agreement to expressly limit the government's liability to appropriations available at the time of the loss with no implication that Congress will appropriate funds to make up any deficiency.

This second device—the express limitation of the government's liability to available appropriations—is sufficient to cure an otherwise fatally defective (i.e., unlimited) indemnity proposal. For example, the government may in limited circumstances assume the risk of loss to contractor-owned property. While the maximum potential liability would be determinable, it could be very large and the administrative reservation of funds is not feasible. Thus, without some form of limitation, such an agreement could result in obligations in excess of available appropriations. The rules concerning the government's assumption of risk on property owned by contractors and used in the performance of their contracts are set forth in 54 Comp. Gen. 824 (1975), modifying B-168106, July 3, 1974. The rules are summarized below:

- If administratively determined to be in the best interest of the government, the government may assume the risk for contractor-owned property which is used solely in the performance of government contracts.

- The government may not assume the risk for contractor-owned property which is used solely for nongovernment work. If the property is used for both government and nongovernment work and the nongovernment portion is separable, the government may not assume the risk relating to the nongovernment work.

- Where the amount of a contractor's commercial work is so insignificant when compared to the amount of the contractor's government work that the government is effectively bearing the entire risk of loss by in essence paying the full insurance premiums, the government may assume the risk if administratively determined to be in the best interest of the government.

Any agreement for the assumption of risk by the government under the above rules must contain a clause to clearly provide that, in the event the government has to pay for losses, payments may not exceed appropriations available at the time of the losses, and that nothing in the contract may be considered as implying that Congress will at a later date appropriate funds sufficient to meet deficiencies. 54 Comp. Gen. at 827.

A somewhat different situation was discussed in 60 Comp. Gen. 584 (1981), involving an "installment purchase plan" for automatic data processing equipment. Under the plan, the General Services Administration would make monthly payments until the entire purchase price was paid, at which time GSA would acquire unencumbered ownership of the equipment. GSM obligation was conditioned on its exercising an option at the end of each fiscal year to continue payments for the next year. The contract contained a risk of loss provision under which GSA would be required to pay the full price for any equipment lost or damaged during the term of the contract. GAO concluded that the equipment should be treated as contractor-owned property for purposes of the risk of loss provision, and that the provision would be improper unless one of the following conditions were met:

- The contract includes the clause specified in 54 Comp. Gen. 824 limiting GSA's liability to appropriations available at the time of the loss and expressly precluding any inference that Congress would appropriate sufficient funds to meet any deficiency; or;

- If the contract does not include these restrictions, then GSA must obligate sufficient funds to cover its possible liability under the risk of loss provision.

If neither of these conditions is met, the assumption of risk clause could violate the Antideficiency Act by creating an obligation in excess of available appropriations if any equipment is lost or damaged during the term of the contract.

In 1982, the Defense Department and the state of New York entered into a contract for New York to provide certain support functions for the 1980 Winter Olympic Games at Lake Placid. The contract provided for federal reimbursement of any disability benefits which New York might be required to pay in case of death or injury of persons participating in the operation. The contract specified that the government's liability could not exceed appropriations for assistance to the Games available at the time of a disabling event, and that the contract did not imply that Congress would appropriate funds sufficient to meet any deficiencies. Since these provisions satisfied the test of 54 Comp. Gen. 824, the indemnity agreement was not legally objectionable. B-202518, Jan. 8, 1982. Under this type of arrangement, GAO noted that an estimated amount should have been recorded as an obligation when the agency was notified that a disabling event had occurred. However, no violation of the Antideficiency Act actually occurred in this case because sufficient funds remained available for obligation at the time New York filed its claim for indemnification under the contract.

Also, the decision in the National Flood Insurance Act case mentioned above (B-201394, Apr. 23, 1981) noted that the defect could have been cured by inserting a clause along the lines of the clause in 54 Comp. Gen. 824. The same point was made in B-201072, May 3, 1982, also discussed earlier. See also National Railroad Passenger Corp. v. United States, 3 CL Ct. 516, 521 (1983) (indemnification agreement between the Federal Railroad Administration and Amtrak did not violate Antideficiency Act where liability was limited to amount of appropriation).

However, as noted in the introduction to this section, over the years GAO has expressed the view that indemnity agreements, even with limiting language, should not be entered into without congressional approval in view of their potentially disruptive fiscal consequences to the agency. 63 Comp. Gen. 145, 147 (1984); 62 Comp. Gen. 361, 368 (1983); B-242146, Aug. 16, 1991. If an agency thinks that indemnification agreements in a particular context are sufficiently in the government's interest, the preferable approach is for the agency to go to Congress and seek specific statutory authority. See B-201394, Apr. 23, 1981.

As discussed below, Congress has seen fit to enact legislation authorizing indemnification agreements when warranted by the circumstances. In 1986, the Chairman of the Subcommittee on Nuclear Regulation, Senate Committee on Environment and Public Works, in connection with proposed Price-Anderson Act amendments the committee was considering, asked GAO to identify possible funding options for a statutory indemnification provision. GAO's response, B-197742, Aug. 1, 1986, listed several options and noted the benefits and drawbacks of each from the perspective of congressional flexibility. The options ranged from creating a statutory entitlement with a permanent indefinite appropriation for payment (indemnity guaranteed but no congressional flexibility), to making payment fully dependent on the appropriations process (full congressional flexibility but no guarantee of payment). In between were various other devices such as contract authority, use of contract provisions such as those in 54 Comp. Gen. 824, and various forms of limited funding authority.

The discussion in B-197742 highlights the essence of the indemnification funding problem:

> "An indemnity statute should generally include two features—the indemnification provisions and a funding mechanism. Indemnification provisions can range from a legally binding guarantee to a mere authorization. Funding mechanisms can similarly vary in terms of the degree of congressional control and flexibility retained. It is impossible to maximize both the assurance of payment and congressional flexibility. Either objective is enhanced only at the expense of the other.... "

> "If payment is to be assured, Congress must yield control over funding, either in whole or up to specified ceilings .... Conversely, if Congress is to retain funding control, payment cannot be assured in any legally binding form and the indemnification becomes less than an entitlement."

B-197742 at 9, 11.

(3) Statutorily authorized indemnification

When we first stated the anti-indemnity rule at the outset of this discussion, we noted that the rule applies in the absence of express statutory authority to the contrary. Naturally, an indemnification agreement, however open-ended it may be, will be "legal" if it is expressly authorized by statute.

One statutory exception to the indemnification rules exists for certain defense-related contracts by virtue of 50 U.S.C. § 1431, often referred to by its Public Law designation, Public Law 85-804. The statute evolved from a temporary wartime measure, section 201 of the First War Powers Act, 1941, ch. 493, 55 Stat. 838, 839 (Dec. 18, 1941). The implementing details on indemnification are found in Executive Order No. 10789, as amended, and Federal Acquisition Regulation (FAR), 48 C.F.R. part 50 (2005). For example, while the decision to indemnify under Public Law 85-804 is discretionary, B-287121, Mar. 20, 2001, such discretion must be exercised by the agency head and cannot be delegated. B-257139, Aug. 30, 1994, citing FAR, 48 C.F.R. § 50.201(d).

Other examples of statutory exceptions are:

- section 4 of the Price-Anderson Act, 42 U.S.C. § 2210, which provides contract authority permitting, among other things, indemnification agreements with Nuclear Regulatory Commission licensees and Department of Energy contractors to pay claims resulting from nuclear accidents;

- section 119 of the Comprehensive Environmental Response, Compensation, and Liability Act, 42 U.S.C. § 9619, which authorizes indemnification of certain Superfund cleanup contractors against negligence (but not gross negligence or intentional misconduct);

- section 308 of the National Aeronautics and Space Act, 42 U.S.C. § 2458b, which authorizes the Administrator of the National Aeronautics and Space Administration (NASA) to indemnify users of NASA space vehicles against third party claims that are not covered by insurance;

- section 2354 of title 10, United States Code, which authorizes the military departments to indemnify research and development contractors against liability not covered by insurance; and;

- section 7423(2) of title 26, United States Code, which authorizes indemnification of federal employees for damages awarded in suits involving their performance of duties under the Internal Revenue Code.

Congress also may enact legislation to provide indemnification for a specific or one-time event. For example, Congress specifically indemnified the manufacturers, distributors, and those who administered the swine flu vaccine purchased and used as part of the National Swine Flu Immunization Program of 1976 against liability for other than their own negligence to persons alleging personal injury or death arising out of the administration of such vaccine. Pub. L. No. 94-380, 90 Stat. 1113 (Aug. 12, 1976).

d. Specific Appropriation Limitations/Purpose Violations

31 U.S.C. § 1301(a) prohibits the use of appropriations for purposes other than those for which they were appropriated. Violations of purpose availability can arise in a wide variety of contexts—charging an obligation or expenditure to the wrong appropriation, making an obligation or expenditure for an unauthorized purpose, violating a statutory prohibition or restriction, etc. The question we explore in this section is the relationship of purpose availability to the Antideficiency Act. In other words, when and to what extent does a purpose violation also violate the Antideficiency Act?

Why does it matter whether you have violated one statute or two statutes? One reason is that, if the second statute is the Antideficiency Act, there are statutory reporting requirements and potential penalties to consider in addition to any administrative sanctions that agencies may impose through internal processes for violations of section 1301 alone.

A useful starting point is the following excerpt from 63 Comp. Gen. 422, 424 (1984):

> "Not every violation of 31 U.S.C. § 1301(a) also constitutes a violation of the Antideficiency Act.... Even though an expenditure may have been charged to an improper source, the Antideficiency Act's prohibition against incurring obligations in excess or in advance of available appropriations is not also violated unless no other funds were available for that expenditure. Where, however, no other funds were authorized to be used for the purpose in question (or where those authorized were already obligated), both 31 U.S.C. § 1301(a) and § 1341(a) have been violated. In addition, we would consider an Antideficiency Act violation to have occurred where an expenditure was improperly charged and the appropriate fund source, although available at the time, was subsequently obligated, malting readjustment of accounts impossible."

First, suppose an agency charges an obligation or expenditure to the wrong appropriation account, either charging the wrong appropriation for the same time period, or charging the wrong fiscal year. The above passage from 63 Comp. Gen. 422 provides the answer—if the appropriation that should have been charged in the first place has sufficient available funds to enable the adjustment of accounts, there is no Antideficiency Act violation. The decision in 73 Comp. Gen. 259 (1994) illustrates this point. In that case, an agency had erroneously charged a furniture order to the wrong appropriation account, but had sufficient funds in the proper account to support an adjustment correcting the error. Thus, GAO concluded, there was no violation of the Antideficiency Act. Id. at 261. On the other hand, a violation exists if the proper account does not have enough money to permit the adjustment, and this includes cases where sufficient funds existed at the time of the error but have since been obligated or expended. See also 70 Comp. Gen. 592 (1991); B-222048, Feb. 10, 1987; B-95136, Aug. 8, 1979.

Other cases illustrating or applying this principle are 57 Comp. Gen. 459 (1978) (grant funds charged to wrong fiscal year); B-224702, Aug. 5, 1987 (contract modifications charged to expired accounts rather than current appropriations); and B-208697, Sept. 28, 1983 (items charged to General Services Administration Working Capital Fund which should have been charged to other operating appropriations). Actually, the concept of "curing" a violation by malting an appropriate adjustment of accounts is not new See, e.g., 16 Comp. Dec. 750 (1910); 4 Comp. Dec. 314, 317 (1897). The Armed Services Board of Contract Appeals also has followed this principle. New England Tank Industries of New Hampshire, Inc., ASBCA No. 26474, 88-1 BCA ¶ 20,395 (1987).

The next situation to consider is an obligation or expenditure in excess of a statutory ceiling. This may be an earmarked maximum in a more general appropriation or a monetary ceiling imposed by some other legislation. An obligation or expenditure in excess of the ceiling violates 31 U.S.C. § 1341(a). See, for example, the following:

- Monetary ceilings on minor military construction (10 U.S.C. § 2805): 63 Comp. Gen. 422 (1984); GAO, Continuing Inadequate Control Over Programming and Financing of Construction, B-133316 (Washington, D.C.: July 23, 1964); Review of Programming and Financing of Selected Facilities Constructed at Army, Navy, and Air Force Installations, B-133316 (Washington, D.C.: Jan. 24, 1961).

- Monetary ceiling on lease payments for family housing units in foreign countries (10 U.S.C. § 2828(e)): 66 Comp. Gen. 176 (1986); B-227527, B-227325, Oct. 21, 1987 (nondecision letter); GAO, Leased Military Housing Costs in Europe Can Be Reduced by Improving Acquisition Practices and Using Purchase Contracts, GAO/NSIAD-85-113 (Washington, D.C.: July 24, 1985), at 7-8.

- Ceiling in supplemental appropriation: B-204270, Oct. 13, 1981 (dollar limit on Standard Level User Charge payable by agency to General Services Administration).

- Ceiling in authorizing legislation: 64 Comp. Gen. 282 (1985) (dollar limit on two Small Business Administration direct loan programs).

In a statutory ceiling case, the account adjustment concept described above may or may not come into play. If the ceiling represents a limit on the amount available for a particular object, then there generally will be no other funds available for that object and hence no "correct" funding source from which to reimburse the account charged. If, however, the ceiling represents only a limit on the amount available from a particular appropriation and not an absolute limit on expenditures for the object, as in the minor military construction cases, for example, then it may be possible to cure violations by an appropriate adjustment. 63 Comp. Gen. at 424.

The final situation is an obligation or expenditure for an object that is prohibited or simply unauthorized. In 60 Comp. Gen. 440 (1981), a proviso in the Customs Service's 1980 appropriation expressly prohibited the use of the appropriation for administrative expenses to pay any employee overtime pay in an amount in excess of $20,000. By allowing employees to earn overtime pay in excess of that amount, the Customs Service violated 31 U.S.C. § 1341. The Comptroller General explained the violation as follows:

"When an appropriation act specifies that an agency's appropriation is not available for a designated purpose, and the agency has no other funds available for that purpose, any officer of the agency who authorizes an obligation or expenditure of agency funds for that purpose violates the Antideficiency Act. Since the Congress has notappropriated funds for the designated purpose, the obligation may be viewed either as being in excess of the amount (zero) available for that purpose or as in advance of appropriations made for that purpose. In either case the Antideficiency Act is violated."

Id. at 441.

In B-201260, Sept. 11, 1984, the Comptroller General advised that expenditures in contravention of the Boland Amendment would violate the Antideficiency Act (although none were found in that case). The Boland Amendment, an appropriation rider, provided that "[n]one of the funds provided in this Act may be used" for certain activities in Central America. In B-229732, Dec. 22, 1988, GAO found the Antideficiency Act violated when the Department of Housing and Urban Development used its funds for commercial trade promotion activities in the Soviet Union, an activity beyond its statutory authority. Similarly, a nonreimbursable interagency detail of an employee, contrary to a specific statutory prohibition, produced a violation in B-247348, June 22, 1992 (letter to Public Printer). All three cases also involved purpose violations and are consistent with 60 Comp. Gen. 440, the rationale being that expenditures would be in excess of available appropriations, which were zero.

More recent GAO decisions likewise consistently apply the principle that the use of appropriated funds for unauthorized or prohibited purposes violates the Antideficiency Act (absent an alternative funding source) since zero funds are available for that purpose. B-302710, May 19, 2004 (use of funds in violation of statutory prohibition against publicity or propaganda); B-300325, Dec. 13, 2002 (appropriations used for unauthorized technical assistance purposes); B-300192, Nov. 13, 2002 (violation of appropriation rider prohibiting use of funds to implement an Office of Management and Budget memorandum); B-290005, July 1, 2002 (appropriation used to procure unauthorized legal services); 71 Comp. Gen. 402, 406 (1992) (unauthorized use of Training and Employment Services appropriation); B-246304, July 31, 1992 (potential violation of appropriation act "Buy American" provision); B-248284, Sept. 1, 1992 (nondecision letter) (reprogramming of funds to an unauthorized purpose).

One court reached a result that appears to interpret the Antideficiency Act somewhat differently. In Southern Packaging and Storage Co. v. United States, 588 F. Supp. 532 (D.S.C. 1984), the court found that the Defense Department had purchased certain combat meal products ("MRE") in violation of a "Buy American" appropriation rider, which provided that "no part of any appropriation contained in this Act ... shall be available" to procure items not grown or produced in the United States. The court rejected the contention that the violation also contravened the Antideficiency Act, stating:

> "There is no evidence in this case to show that [the Defense Personnel Supply Center] authorized expenditures beyond the amount appropriated by Congress for the procurement of the MRE rations and the component foods thereof."

Id. at 550.

Given the sparse discussion in the decision, the fact that Congress does not make specific appropriations for MRE rations, and the fact that the Antideficiency Act regulates both obligations and expenditures in excess of available authority, it is difficult to discern precisely how the Southern Packaging court would apply the Antideficiency Act. In any event, we have found no subsequent judicial or administrative decision that cites this aspect of the Southern Packaging opinion.

e. Amount of Available Appropriation or Fund

Questions occasionally arise over precisely what assets an agency may count for purposes of determining the amount of available resources against which it may incur obligations.

The starting point, of course, is the unobligated balance of the relevant appropriation. Subdivisions of a lump-sum appropriation appearing in legislative history are not legally binding on the agency. They are binding only if carried into the appropriation act itself, or are made binding by some other statute. Thus, the entire unobligated balance of an unrestricted lump-sum appropriation is available for Antideficiency Act purposes. 55 Comp. Gen. 812 (1976).

Where an agency is authorized to retain certain receipts or collections for credit to an appropriation or fund under that agency's control, those receipts are treated the same as direct appropriations for purposes of obligation and the Antideficiency Act, subject to any applicable statutory restrictions. E.g., 71 Comp. Gen. 224 (1992) (National Technical Information Service may use subscription payments to defray its operating expenses but, under governing legislation, may use customer advances only for costs directly related to firm orders).

In addition, certain other assets may be "counted" as available budget authority, that is, obligated against. For example, OMB Circular No. A-11 includes certain spending authority from offsetting collections as a form of "budget authority." See also B-134474-0.M., Dec. 18, 1957. This does not mean anticipated receipts from transactions that have not yet occurred or orders that have not yet been placed. Thus, the Library of Congress could not retain in a revolving fund advances from federal agencies in excess of amounts needed to cover current orders in anticipation of applying the excess amounts to future orders. B-288142, Sept. 6, 2001. Obligations cannot be charged against anticipated proceeds from an anticipated sale of property. See, e.g., B-209758, Sept. 29, 1983 (nondecision memorandum) (sale of assets seized from embezzler). Thus, the Customs Service violated the Antideficiency Act by obligating against anticipated receipts from future sales of seized property unless it had sufficient funds available from other sources to cover the obligation. B-237135, Dec. 21, 1989. Similarly, the Comptroller General found that the Air Force violated the Antideficiency Act by overobligating its Industrial Fund based on estimated or anticipated customer orders. See GAO, The Air Force Has Incurred Numerous Overobligations in its Industrial Fund, AFMD-81-53 (Washington, D.C.: Aug. 14, 1981); 62 Comp. Gen. 143, 147 (1983). Even where receivables are properly included as budgetary resources, an agency may not incur obligations against receipts expected to be received after the end of the current fiscal year without specific statutory authority. 51 Comp. Gen. 598, 605 (1972).

In 60 Comp. Gen. 520 (1981), GAO considered whether the General Services Administration (GSA) could obligate against the value of inventory in the General Supply Fund. GSA buys furniture and other equipment for other agencies through the General Supply Fund, a revolving fund established by statute. Agencies pay GSA either in advance or by reimbursement. For reasons of economy, GSA normally makes consolidated and bulk purchases of commonly used items. Concern over the application of the Antideficiency Act arose when, for several reasons, the Fund began experiencing cash flow problems. To help remedy its "cash flow" problems GSA wanted to consider the amount of available budget authority to include inventory as well as cash assets and advances.

The Comptroller General held that inventory in the General Supply Fund did not constitute a budgetary resource against which obligations could be incurred. The items in the inventory had already been purchased and could not be counted again as a new budgetary resource. Thus, for Antideficiency Act purposes, GSA could not incur obligations using the value of inventory as an available "budgetary resource."

Supplemental appropriations requested but not yet enacted obviously may not be counted as a budgetary resource. B-230117-0.M., Feb. 8, 1989.

f. Intent/Factors beyond Agency Control

A violation of the Antideficiency Act does not depend on intent or lack of good faith on the part of contracting or other officials who obligate or pay in advance or in excess of appropriations. Although these factors may influence the applicable penalty, they do not affect the basic determination of whether a violation has occurred. 64 Comp. Gen. 282, 289 (1985). The Comptroller General once expressed the principle in the following passage which, although stated in a slightly different context, is equally applicable here:

> "Where a payment is prohibited by law, the utmost good faith on the part of the officer, either in ignorance of the facts or in disregard of the facts, in purporting to authorize the incurring of an obligation the payment of which is so prohibited, cannot take the case out of the statute, otherwise the purported good faith of an officer could be used to nullify the law."

A-86742, June 17, 1937.

To illustrate, a contracting officer at the United States Mission to the North Atlantic Treaty Organization accepted an offer for installation of automatic telephone equipment at twice the amount of the unobligated balance remaining in the applicable account. The Department of State explained that the contracting officer had misinterpreted GAO regulations and implementing State Department procedures. But for this misinterpretation, additional funds could have been placed in the account. State therefore felt that the transaction should not be considered in violation of the Act. GAO did not agree and held that the overobligation must be immediately reported as required by 31 U.S.C. § 1517(b). The official's state of mind was not relevant in deciding whether a violation had occurred. 35 Comp. Gen. 356 (1955).

An overobligation may result from external factors beyond the agency's control. Whether this will produce an Antideficiency Act violation depends on the particular circumstances. In 58 Comp. Gen. 46 (1978), the Army asked whether it could make payments to a contractor under a contract requiring payment in local (foreign) currency where the original dollar obligation was well within applicable funding limitations but, due to subsequent exchange rate fluctuations, payment would exceed those limitations. The Army argued that a payment under these circumstances should not be considered a violation of the Act because currency fluctuations are totally beyond the control of the contracting officer or any other agency official. GAO disagreed. The fact that the contracting officer was a victim of circumstances does not make a payment in excess of available appropriations any less illegal. (It is, of course, as with state of mind, relevant in assessing penalties for the violation.) See also 38 Comp. Gen. 501 (1959) (severe adverse weather conditions or prolonged employee strikes generally are not sufficient to justify overobligation by former Post Office Department, but facts in a particular case could justify deficiency apportionment).

In apparent contrast, the Comptroller General stated in 62 Comp. Gen. 692, 700 (1983) that an overobligation resulting from a judicial award of attorney's fees under 28 U.S.C. § 2412(d), the Equal Access to Justice Act, would not violate the Antideficiency Act. See also 63 Comp. Gen. 308, 312 (1984) (judgments or board of contract appeals awards under Contract Disputes Act, same answer); B-227527, B-227325, Oct. 21, 1987 (nondecision letter) (amounts awarded by court judgment not counted in determining whether statutory ceiling on lease payments has been exceeded and Antideficiency Act thereby violated).

The distinction is based on the extent to which the agency can act to avoid the overobligation even though it is imposed by some external force beyond its control. Thus, the currency fluctuation decision stated:

> "When a contracting officer finds that the dollars required to continue or make final payment on a contract will exceed a statutory limitation he may terminate the contract, provided the termination costs will not exceed the statutory limitations. Alternatively, the contracting officer may issue a stop work order and the agency may ask Congress for a deficiency appropriation citing the currency fluctuation as the reason for its request."

58 Comp. Gen. at 48. Similarly, the Postmaster General could curtail operations if necessary. 38 Comp. Gen. 501, 504 (1959). See also 66 Comp. Gen. 176 (1986) (Antideficiency Act would not preclude Air Force from entering into lease for overseas family housing without provision limiting annual payments to statutory ceiling, even though certain costs could conceivably escalate above ceiling, where good faith cost estimates were well below ceiling and lease included termination for convenience clause). Where the agency could have acted to avert the overobligation but did not, there will be a violation. In contrast, in the case of a payment ordered by a court, comparable options (apart from seeking a deficiency appropriation) are not available. (Curtailing activities after the overobligation has occurred to avoid compounding the violation is a separate question.)

g. Exceptions

The Antideficiency Act by its own terms recognizes that Congress can and may grant exceptions. 31 U.S.C. § 1341(a). The statute prohibits contracts or other obligations in advance or excess of available appropriations, "unless authorized by law." This is nothing more than the recognition that Congress can authorize exceptions to the statutes it enacts.

(1) Contract authority

At the outset, it is necessary to distinguish between "contract authority" and the "authority to enter into contracts." A contract is simply a legal device employed by two or more parties to create binding and legally enforceable obligations in furtherance of some objective. The federal government uses contracts every day to procure a wide variety of goods and services. An agency does not need specific statutory authority to enter into contracts. It has long been established that a government agency has the inherent authority to enter into binding contracts in the execution of its duties. Van Brocklin v. Tennessee, 117 U.S. 151, 154 (1886); United States v. Maurice, 26 F. Case 1211, 1216-17 (No. 15,747) (C.C.D. Va. 1823). It should be apparent that these contracts, "authorized by law" though they may be, are not sufficient to constitute exceptions to the Antideficiency Act, else the Act would be meaningless.

For purposes of the Antideficiency Act exception, a contract authorized by law requires not only authority to enter into a contract, but authority to do so without regard to the availability of appropriations. While the former may be inherent, the latter must be conferred by statute. The most common example of this is "contract authority"—statutory authority to enter into binding contracts without the funds adequate to make payments under them.

In some cases, the "exception" language will be unmistakably explicit. An example is the Price-Anderson Act, which provides authority to "make contracts in advance of appropriations and incur obligations without regard to" the Antideficiency Act. 42 U.S.C. § 2210(j). Other examples of clear authority, although perhaps not as explicit as the Price-Anderson Act, are discussed in 27 Comp. Gen. 452 (1948) (long-term operating-differential subsidy agreements under the Merchant Marine Act); B-211190, Apr. 5, 1983 (contracts with states under the Federal Boat Safety Act); B-164497.3, June 6, 1979 (certain provisions of the Federal-Aid Highway Act of 1973); and B-168313, Nov. 21, 1969 (interest subsidy agreements with educations institutions under the Housing Act of 1950).

In an earlier case involving contract authority, GAO insisted that the Corps of Engineers had to include a "no liability unless funds are later made available" clause for any work done in excess of available funds. 2 Comp. Gen. 477 (1923). The Corps later had trouble with this clause because a Court of Claims decision, C.H. Leavell & Co. v. United States, 530 F.2d 878 (Ct. Cl. 1976), allowed the contractor an equitable adjustment for suspension of work due to a delay in enacting an appropriation to pay him, notwithstanding the "availability of funds" clause. In 56 Comp. Gen. 437 (1977), GAO overruled 2 Comp. Gen. 477, deciding that section 10 of the River and Harbor Act of 1922, 33 U.S.C. § 621, by expressly authorizing the Corps to enter into large multiyear civil works projects without seeking a full appropriation in the first year, constituted the necessary exception to the Antideficiency Act and a "funds available" clause was not necessary. This applies as well to contracts financed from the Corps' Civil Works Revolving Fund. B-242974.6, Nov. 26, 1991 (internal memorandum). The rationale of 56 Comp. Gen. 437 also has been applied to long-term fuel storage facilities contracts authorized by 10 U.S.C. § 2388. New England Tank Industries of New Hampshire, Inc., ASBCA No. 26474, 88-1 BCA ¶ 20,395 (1987), vacated on other grounds, New England Tank Industries of New Hampshire v. United States, 861 F.2d 685 (Fed. Cir. 1988).

In 28 Comp. Gen. 163 (1948), the Comptroller General considered whether the Commissioner of Reclamation had budget authority to enter into certain contracts in advance of appropriations (contract authority). Congress had authorized the contract authority in an appropriation act but made it subject to a monetary ceiling. Since the contract authority was explicit, with no language making it contingent on appropriations being made at some later date, the Comptroller General concluded that the statute authorized the Commissioner to enter into a firm and binding contract.

The Bureau of Mines was authorized to enter into a contract (in advance of the appropriation) to construct and equip an anthracite research laboratory. The Bureau asked the General Services Administration (GSA) to enter into the contract on its behalf pursuant to section 103 of the Federal Property and Administrative Services Act of 1949, ch. 288, 63 Stat. 377, 380 (June 30, 1949), which provided that "funds appropriated to ...other Federal agencies for the foregoing purposes [execution of contracts and supervision of construction] shall be available for transfer to and expenditure by the [GSA]." GAO held that the Bureau's contract authority provided a sufficient legal basis for GSA to enter into contracts for construction of the laboratory pursuant to section 103. 29 Comp. Gen. 504 (1950).

A somewhat different kind of contract authority is found in 41 U.S.C. § 11, the so-called Adequacy of Appropriations Act. An exception to the requirement to have adequate appropriations—or any appropriation at all—is made for procurements by the military departments for "clothing, subsistence, forage, fuel, quarters, transportation, or medical and hospital supplies, which, however, shall not exceed the necessities of the current year." By administrative interpretation, the Defense Department has limited this authority to emergency circumstances where immediate action is necessary. Department of Defense Financial Management Regulation 7000.14-R, vol. 3, ch. 12, ¶ 120201 (Jan. 31, 2001).

It should again be emphasized that to constitute an exception to 31 U.S.C. § 1341(a), the "contract authority" must be specific authority to incur the obligation in excess or advance of appropriations, not merely the general authority any agency has to enter into contracts to carry out its functions. Also, an appropriation obviously is needed to liquidate the contract obligation.

Congress may grant authority to contract beyond the fiscal year in terms which amount to considerably less than the type of contract authority described above. An example is 43 U.S.C. § 388, which authorizes the Secretary of the Interior to enter into certain contracts relating to reclamation projects "which may cover such periods of time as the Secretary may consider necessary but in which the liability of the United States shall be contingent upon appropriations being made therefore." See PCL Construction Services, Inc. v. United States, 41 Fed. Cl. 242, 257 (1998), aff'd, 96 Fed. Appx. 672 (Fed. Cir. 2004) (pursuant to 43 U.S.C. § 388, firm fixed-price contract awarded by the Bureau of Reclamation to construct a visitors center and parking structure at Hoover Dam could be incrementally funded without violating the Antideficiency Act). While this provision has been referred to as an exception to the Antideficiency Act (B-72020, Jan. 9, 1948), it authorizes only "contingent contracts" under which there is no legal obligation to pay unless and until appropriations are provided. 28 Comp. Gen. 163 (1948). A similar example, discussed in B-239435, Aug. 24, 1990, is 38 U.S.C. § 230(c) (Supp. II 1990) (subsequently recodified at 38 U.S.C. § 316) which authorized the Department of Veterans

Affairs to enter into certain leases for periods of up to 35 years but further provided that the government's obligation to make payments was "subject to the availability of appropriations for that purpose." For another example, see B-248647.2, Apr. 24, 1995, which discussed the Federal Triangle Development Act, 40 U.S.C. §§ 1101-1109. This act directed GSA to enter into a long-term lease and required the lease agreement to recognize that GSA could obligate funds for lease payments only on an annual basis. 40 U.S.C. § 1105. Therefore, the GSA multiyear lease agreement at issue was specifically "authorized by law" and did not violate the Antideficiency Act. B-248647.2 at fn. 3.

(2) Other obligations "authorized by law"

The "authorized by law" exception in 31 U.S.C. § 1341(a) applies to noncontractual obligations as well as to contracts. The basic approach is the same. The statutory authority must be more than just authority to undertake the particular activity. For example, statutory authority to acquire land and to pay for it from a specified fund is not an exception to the Antideficiency Act. 15 Comp. Gen. 662 (1921). It merely authorizes acquisitions to the extent of funds available in the specified source at the time of purchase. Id. Similarly, the authority to conduct hearings, without more, does not confer authority to do so without regard to available appropriations. 16 Comp. Dec. 750 (1910). Provisions in the District of Columbia Code requiring Saint Elizabeth's Hospital to treat all patients who meet admission eligibility requirements were held not to authorize the Hospital to operate beyond the level of its appropriations. If mandatory expenditures, together with nonmandatory expenditures, would cause a deficiency, the Hospital would have to reduce nonmandatory expenditures. 61 Comp. Gen. 661 (1982).

Congress may expressly state that an agency may obligate in excess of the amounts appropriated, or it may implicitly authorize an agency to do so by virtue of a law that necessarily requires such obligations. See B-262069, Aug. 1, 1995. Several cases have considered the effect of various statutory salary or compensation increases. If a statutory increase is mandatory and does not vest discretion in an administrative office to determine the amount, or if it gives some administrative body discretion to determine the amount, payment of which then becomes mandatory, the obligation is deemed "authorized by law" for Antideficiency Act purposes. See, e.g., 39 Comp. Gen. 422 (1959) (salary increases for Wage Board employees); B-168796, Feb. 2, 1970 (mandatory statutory increase in retired pay for Tax Court judges); B-107279, Jan. 9, 1952 (mandatory increases for certain legislative personnel). GAO has not treated the granting of increases retroactively to correct past administrative errors as creating the same type of exception. See 24 Comp. Gen. 676 (1945). Increases which are discretionary do not permit the incurring of obligations in excess or advance of appropriations. 31 Comp. Gen. 238 (1951) (discretionary pension increases); 28 Comp. Gen. 300 (1948).

Some other examples of obligations authorized by law for Antideficiency Act purposes are:

- Defense Health Program obligations for medical services. B-287619, July 5, 2001.

- Mandatory pilot program in Vermont under Farms for the Future Act of 1990 (loan guarantees and interest assistance). B-244093, July 19, 1991.

- Mandatory transfer from one appropriation account to another where "donor" account contained insufficient unobligated funds. 38 Comp. Gen. 93 (1958).

- Provision in Criminal Justice Act of 1964 imposing unequivocal legislative directive for commencement of certain programs which would necessarily involve creation of financial obligations. B-156932, Aug. 17, 1965.

- Provision in District of Columbia Criminal Justice Act of 1974 (CJA), as amended, malting attorney representation in CJA cases a mandatory expense. B-283599, Sept. 15, 1999. See also B-284566, Apr. 3, 2000.

- Statute authorizing Interstate Commerce Commission to order a substitute rail carrier to serve shippers abandoned by their primary carrier in emergency situations, and to reimburse certain costs of the substitute carrier. B-196132, Oct. 11, 1979.

What are perhaps the outer limits of the "authorized by law" exception are illustrated in B-159141, Aug. 18, 1967. The Federal Aviation Administration (FAA) had entered into long-term, incrementally funded contracts for the development of a civil supersonic aircraft (SST). To ensure compliance with the Antideficiency Act, the FAA each year budgeted for, and obligated, sufficient funds to cover potential termination liability. The appropriations committees became concerned that unnecessarily large amounts were being tied up this way, especially in light of the highly remote possibility that the SST contracts would be terminated. In considering the FAA's 1968 appropriation, the House Appropriations Committee reduced the FAA's request by the amount of the termination reserve, and in its report directed the FAA not to obligate for potential termination costs. The Comptroller General advised that if the Senate Appropriations Committee did the same thing—a specific reduction tied to the amount requested for the reserve, coupled with clear direction in the legislative history—then an overobligation resulting from a termination would be regarded as authorized by law and not in violation of the Antideficiency Act.

3. Voluntary Services Prohibition

a. Introduction

We previously discussed the Antideficiency Act prohibitions contained in section 1341 of title 31, United States Code. The next section of theAntideficiency Act is 31 U.S.C. § 1342:

> "An officer or employee of the United States Government or of the District of Columbia government may not accept voluntary services for either government or employ personal services exceeding that authorized by law except for emergencies involving the safety of human life or the protection of property...."

This provision first appeared, in almost identical form, in a deficiency appropriation act enacted in 1884. Although the original prohibition read "hereafter, no department or officer of the United States shall accept ...," it was included in an appropriation for the then Indian Office of the Interior Department, and the Court of Claims held that it was applicable only to the Indian Office. Glavey v. United States, 35 Ct. Cl. 242, 256 (1900), rev'd on other grounds, 182 U.S. 595 (1901). The Comptroller of the Treasury continued to apply it across the board. See, e.g., 9 Comp. Dec. 181 (1902). In any event, the applicability of the 1884 statute soon became moot because Congress reenacted it as part of the Antideficiency Act in 1905 and again in 1906.

Prior to the 1982 recodification of title 31, section 1342 was subsection (b) of the Antideficiency Act, while the basic prohibitions of section 1341, previously discussed, constituted subsection (a). The proximity of the two provisions in the United States Code reflects their relationship, as section 1342 supplements and is a logical extension of section 1341. If an agency cannot directly obligate in excess or advance of its appropriations, it should not be able to accomplish the same thing indirectly by accepting ostensibly "voluntary" services and then presenting Congress with the bill, in the hope that Congress will recognize a "moral obligation" to pay for the benefits conferred—another example of the so-called "coercive deficiency. In this connection, the chairman of the House committee responsible for what became the 1906 reenactment of the voluntary services prohibition stated:

> "It is a hard matter to deal with. We give to Departments what we think is ample, but they come back with a deficiency. Under the law they can [not] make these deficiencies, and Congress can refuse to allow them; but after they are made it is very hard to refuse to allow them ...."

In addition, as we have noted previously, the Antideficiency Act was intended to keep an agency's level of operations within the amounts Congress appropriates for that purpose. The unrestricted ability to use voluntary services would permit circumvention of that objective. Thus, without section 1342, section 1341 could not be fully effective. Note that 31 U.S.C. § 1342 contains two distinct although closely related prohibitions: It bans, first, the acceptance of any type of voluntary services for the United States, and second, the employment of personal services "exceeding that authorized by law."

b. Appointment without Compensation and Waiver of Salary

(1) The rules—general discussion

One of the evils that the "personal services" prohibition was designed to correct was a practice existing in 1884, whereby lower-grade government employees were being asked to "volunteer" their services for overtime periods in excess of the periods allowed by law. This enabled the agency to economize at the employees' expense but nevertheless generated claims by the employees. Currently, 31 U.S.C. § 1342 serves a number of other purposes and is relevant in a number of contexts involving services by government employees or services which would otherwise have to be performed by government employees. For example, one court suggested that 31 U.S.C. § 1342 also is based in part on the principle that only public officials should be allowed to perform governmental functions. See Suss v. American Society for the Prevention of Cruelty to Animals, 823 F. Supp. 181, 189 (S.D.N.Y. 1993) ("The risks of abuse of power by private parties exercising functions involving [the] exercise of sovereign compulsion is one reason for the limitations imposed by federal law on the use of volunteers in implementing public sector programs."). However, as mentioned previously, the fundamental purposes embodied in section 1342 are to preserve the integrity of the appropriations process by avoiding "coercive deficiencies" and augmentations.

One of the earliest questions to arise under 31 U.S.C. § 1342—and an issue that has generated many cases—was whether a government officer or employee, or an individual about to be appointed to a government position, could voluntarily work for nothing or for a reduced salary. Initially, the Comptroller of the Treasury ducked the question on the grounds that it did not involve a payment from the Treasury, and suggested that the question was appropriate to take to the Attorney General. 19 Comp. Dec. 160, 163 (1912).

The very next year, the Attorney General tackled the question when asked whether a retired Army officer could be employed as superintendent of an Indian school without additional compensation. In what has become the leading case construing 31 U.S.C. § 1342, the Attorney General replied that the appointment would not violate the voluntary services prohibition. 30 Op. Att'y Gen. 51 (1913). In reaching this conclusion, the Attorney General drew a distinction that the Comptroller of the Treasury thereafter adopted, and that GAO and the Justice Department continue to follow to this day—the distinction between "voluntary services" and "gratuitous services." The key passages from the Attorney General's opinion are set forth below:

"[I]t seems plain that the words 'voluntary service' were not intended to be synonymous with 'gratuitous service' and were not intended to cover services rendered in an official capacity under regular appointment to an office otherwise permitted by law to be non-salaried. In their ordinary and normal meaning these words refer to service intruded by a private person as a 'volunteer' and not rendered pursuant to any prior contract or obligation .... It would be stretching the language a good deal to extend it so far as to prohibit official services without compensation in those instances in which Congress has not required even a minimum salary for the office."

"The context corroborates the view that the ordinary meaning of 'voluntary services' was intended. The very next words 'or employ personal service in excess of that authorized by law' deal with contractual services, thus making a balance between 'acceptance' of 'voluntary service' (i.e., the cases where there is no prior contract) and `employment' of 'personal service' (i.e., the cases where there is such prior contract, though unauthorized by law)."

"Thus it is evident that the evil at which Congress was aiming was not appointment or employment for authorized services without compensation, but the acceptance of unauthorized services not intended or agreed to be gratuitous and therefore likely to afford a basis for a future claim upon Congress...."

Id. at 52-53, 55.

The Comptroller of the Treasury agreed with this interpretation:

"[The statute] was intended to guard against claims for compensation. A service offered clearly and distinctly as gratuitous with a proper record made of that fact does not violate this statute against acceptance of voluntary service. An appointment to serve without compensation which is accepted and properly recorded is not a violation of [31 U.S.C. § 1342], and is valid if otherwise lawful."

27 Comp. Dec. 131, 132-33 (1920).

Two main rules emerge from 30 Op. Att'y Gen. 51 and its progeny. First, if compensation for a position is fixed by law, an appointee may not agree to serve without compensation or to waive that compensation in whole or in part. Id. at 56. This portion of the opinion did not break any new ground. The courts had already held, based on public policy, that compensation fixed by law could not be waived. Second, and this is really just a corollary to the rule just stated, if the level of compensation is discretionary, or if the relevant statute prescribes only a maximum (but not a minimum), the compensation can be set at zero, and an appointment without compensation or a waiver, entire or partial, is permissible. Id.; 27 Comp. Dec. at 133.

Both GAO and the Justice Department have had frequent occasion to address these issues, and there are numerous decisions illustrating and applying the rules.

In a 1988 opinion, the Justice Department's Office of Legal Counsel considered whether the Iran-Contra Independent Counsel could appoint Professor Laurence Tribe as Special Counsel under an agreement to serve without compensation. Applying the rules set forth in 30 Op. Att'y Gen. 51, the Office of Legal Counsel concluded that the appointment would not contravene the Antideficiency Act since the statute governing the appointment set a maximum salary but no minimum. Memorandum Opinion for the Acting Associate Attorney General, Independent Counsel's Authority to Accept Voluntary Services—Appointment of Laurence H. Tribe, OLC Opinion, May 19, 1988.

Similarly, the Comptroller General held in 58 Comp. Gen. 383 (1979) that members of the United States Metric Board could waive their salaries since the relevant statute merely prescribed a maximum rate of pay. In addition, since the Board had statutory authority to accept gifts, a member who chose to do so could accept compensation and then return it to the Board as a gift. Both cases make the point that compensation is not "fixed by law" for purposes of the "no waiver" rule where the statute merely sets a maximum limit for the salary.

A good illustration of the kind of situation 31 U.S.C. § 1342 is designed to prevent is 54 Comp. Gen. 393 (1974). Members of the Commission on Marihuana and Drug Abuse had, apparently at the chairman's urging, agreed to waive their statutory entitlement to $100 per day while engaged in Commission business. The year after the Commission ceased to exist, one of the former members changed his mind and filed a claim for a portion of the compensation he would have received but for the waiver. Since the $100 per day had been a statutory entitlement, the purported waiver was invalid and the former commissioner was entitled to be paid. Similar claims by any or all of the other former members would also have to be allowed. If insufficient funds remained in the Commission's now-expired appropriation, a deficiency appropriation would be necessary.

A few earlier cases deal with fact situations similar to that considered in 30 Op. Att'y Gen. 51— the acceptance by someone already on the federal payroll of additional duties without additional compensation. In 23 Comp. Gen. 272 (1943), for example, GAO concluded that a retired Army officer could serve, without additional compensation, as a courier for the State Department. The voluntary services prohibition, said the decision, does not preclude "the assignment of persons holding office under the Government to the performance of additional duties or the duties of another position without additional compensation." Id. at 274. Another World War II era decision held that American Red Cross Volunteer Nurses' Aides who also happened to be full-time federal employees could perform volunteer nursing services at Veterans Administration hospitals. 23 Comp. Gen. 900 (1944).

One thing the various cases discussed above have in common is that they involve the appointment of an individual to an official government position, permanent or temporary. Services rendered prior to appointment are considered purely voluntary and, by virtue of 31 U.S.C. § 1342, cannot be compensated. Lee v. United States, 45 Ct. Cl. 57, 62 (1910); B-181934, Oct. 7, 1974. It also follows that post-retirement services, apart from appointment as a reemployed annuitant, are not compensable. 65 Comp. Gen. 21 (1985). In that case, an alleged agreement to the contrary by the individual's supervisor was held unauthorized and therefore invalid.

It also has been held that experts and consultants employed under authority of 5 U.S.C. § 3109 (the basic governmentwide authority for procuring expert and consultant services) may serve without compensation without violating the Antideficiency Act as long as it is clearly understood and agreed that no compensation is expected.27 Comp. Gen. 194 (1947); 6 Op. Off. Legal Counsel 160 (1982). Cf. B-185952, Aug. 18, 1976 (uncompensated participation in pre-bid conference, on-site inspection, and bid opening by contractor engineer who had prepared specifications regarded as "technical violation" of 31 U.S.C. § 1342).

Several of the decisions note the requirement for a written record of the agreement to serve without compensation. Proper documentation is important for evidentiary purposes should a claim subsequently be attempted. E.g., 27 Comp. Gen. at 195; 26 Comp. Gen. 956, 958 (1947);27 Comp. Dec. 131, 132-33 (1920); 2 Op. Off. Legal Counsel 322, 323 (1977). Specifically, the decisions state that the individuals should acknowledge in writing and in advance that they will receive no compensation and that they should explicitly waive any and all claims against the government on account of their service.

The rule that compensation fixed by statute may not be waived does not apply if the waiver or appointment without compensation is itself authorized by statute. The Comptroller General stated the principle as follows in 27 Comp. Gen. at 195:

"[E]ven where the compensation for a particular position is fixed by or pursuant to law, the occupant of the position may waive his ordinary right to the compensation fixed for the position and thereafter forever be estopped from claiming and receiving the salary previously waived, if there be some applicable provision of law authorizing the acceptance of services without compensation."

As noted above, the decision in 27 Comp. Gen. 194 cited as the provision authorizing the acceptance of services without compensation in that case what is now section 3109(b) of title 5, United States Code. Under section 3109(b), agencies may, when authorized by an appropriation or other act, procure the services of experts or consultants for up to 1 year without regard to other provisions of title 5 governing appointment and compensation. This authority is subject to a maximum rate of compensation in some cases, but there is no minimum rate.

In B-139261, June 26, 1959, GAO reiterated the above principle, and gave several additional examples of statutes sufficient for this purpose. The examples included the following statutory provisions that remain essentially the same in substance as they were in 1959:

- section 204(b) of title 29, United States Code, which authorizes the Administrator of the Labor Department's Wage and Hour Division to utilize voluntary and uncompensated services;

- section 401(7) of title 39, United States Code, which authorizes the Postal Service to accept gifts or donations of services or property; and;

- section 210(b) of title 47, United States Code, which states that no provision of law shall be construed to prohibit common carriers from rendering free service to any agency of the government in connection with preparation for the national defense, subject to rules prescribed by the Federal Communications Commission.

At this point a 1978 case, 57 Comp. Gen. 423, should be noted. The decision held that a statute authorizing the Agency for International Development (MD) to accept gifts of "services of any kind" (22 U.S.C. § 2395(d)) did not permit waiver of salary by MD employees whose compensation was fixed by statute. Section 2395(d) is very similar to one of the examples given in B-139261, June 26, 1959, discussed above, of statutes that would authorize the acceptance of voluntary services. See 39 U.S.C. § 401(7). However, 57 Comp. Gen. 423 is distinguishable from B-139261, 27 Comp. Gen. 194, and the other voluntary services cases discussed previously. The question in 57 Comp. Gen. 423 was whether MD could invoke its gift-acceptance authority to justify paying regular federal employees less than the salaries prescribed by law. The decision held that it did not:

"Section 2395(d) ... authorizes the acceptance of gifts. Therefore, MD may accept services from private sources either gratuitously or at a fraction of their value. However, section 2395(d) does not authorize individuals to be appointed to regular positions having compensation rates fixed by or pursuant to statute at rates less than those specified. It, therefore, differs from the statute, which was the subject of 27 Comp. Gen. 194, supra, and accordingly is not a provision of law authorizing employees whose compensation is fixed by or pursuant to statute to waive any part of such compensation."

57 Comp. Gen. at 424-25.

As noted earlier, 27 Comp. Gen. 194 concerned temporary experts or consultants. B-139261 concerned civilian volunteers who sought to provide services for an Air Force reserve center. Likewise, the other statutory examples cited in B-139261 clearly were aimed at individuals other than regular federal employees. Thus, 57 Comp. Gen. 423 appears to represent the sensible caveat that general statutory authorities to accept voluntary services or "gifts" of services do not supersede statutes providing for the compensation of federal employees and cannot be invoked to avoid the consequences of those statutes.

The rules for waiver of salary or appointment without compensation may be summarized as follows:

- If compensation is not fixed by statute, that is, if it is fixed administratively or if the statute merely prescribes a maximum but no minimum, it may be waived as long as the waiver qualifies as "gratuitous." There should be an advance written agreement waiving all claims.

- If compensation is fixed by statute, it may not be waived, the voluntary versus gratuitous distinction notwithstanding, without specific statutory authority. This authority generally may take the form of authority to accept donations of services or to employ persons without compensation.

- If the employing agency has statutory authority to accept gifts, the employee can accept the compensation and return it to the agency as a gift. Even if the agency has no such authority, the employee can still accept the compensation and donate it to the United States Treasury.

(2) Student interns

In 26 Comp. Gen. 956 (1947), the then Civil Service Commission asked whether an agency could accept the uncompensated services of college students as part of a college's internship program. The students "would be assigned to productive work, that is, to the regular work of the agency in a position which would ordinarily fall in the competitive civil service." The answer was no. Since the students would be used in positions the compensation for which was fixed by law, and since compensation fixed by law cannot be waived, the proposal would require legislative authority.

Thirty years later, the Justice Department's Office of Legal Counsel considered another internship program and provided similar advice. Without statutory authority, uncompensated student services that furthered the agency's mission, that is, "productive work," could not be accepted. 2 Op. Off. Legal Counsel 185 (1978).

In view of the long-standing rule, supported by decisions of the Supreme Court, prohibiting the waiver of compensation for positions required by law to be salaried, GAO and Justice had little choice but to respond as they did. Clearly, however, this answer had its downside. It meant that uncompensated student interns could be used only for essentially "make-work" tasks, a benefit to neither the students nor the agencies.

The solution, apparent from both cases, was legislative authority, which Congress provided later in 1978 by the enactment of 5 U.S.C. § 3111. The statute authorizes agencies, subject to regulations of the Office of Personnel Management, to accept the uncompensated services of high school and college students, "notwithstanding section 1342 of title 31," if the services are part of an agency program designed to provide educational experience for the student, if the student's educational institution gives permission, and if the services will not be used to displace any employee. 5 U.S.C. § 3111(b).

A paper entitled A Part-Time Clerkship Program in Federal Courts for Law Students by the Honorable Jack B. Weinstein and William B. Bonvillian, written in 1975 and printed at 68 F.R.D. 265, considered the use of law students as part-time law clerks, without pay, to mostly supplement the work of the regular law clerks in furtherance of the official duties of the courts. Based on the statute's legislative history and 30 Op. Att'y Gen. 51 (1913), previously discussed, Judge Weinstein concluded that the program did not violate the Antideficiency Act. Although this aspect of the issue is not explicitly discussed in the paper, it appears that the compensation of regular law clerks is fixed administratively. See 28 U.S.C. § 604(a)(5). In any event, the Administrative Office of the United States Courts was given authority in 1978 to "accept and utilize voluntary and incompensated (gratuitous) services." 28 U.S.C. § 604(a)(17).

(3) Program beneficiaries

Programs are enacted from time to time to provide job training assistance to various classes of individuals. The training is intended, among other things, to enable participants to enter the labor market at a higher level of skill. Questions have arisen under programs of this nature as to the authority of federal agencies to serve as employers.

A 1944 case, 24 Comp. Gen. 314, considered a vocational rehabilitation program for disabled war veterans. GAO concluded that 31 U.S.C. § 1342 did not preclude federal agencies from providing on-the-job training, without payment of salary, to program participants. The decision is further discussed in 26 Comp. Gen. 956, 959 (1947). In 51 Comp. Gen. 152 (1971), GAO concluded that 31 U.S.C. § 1342 precluded federal agencies from accepting work by persons hired by local governments for public service employment under the Emergency Employment Act of 1971. Four years later, GAO modified the 1971 decision, holding that a federal agency could provide work without payment of compensation to (i.e., accept the free services of) trainees sponsored and paid by nonfederal organizations from federal grant funds under the Comprehensive Employment and Training Act of 1973. 54 Comp. Gen. 560 (1975). The decision stated:

> "Considering that the services in question will arise out of a program initiated by the Federal Government, it would be anomalous to conclude that such services are proscribed as being voluntary within the meaning of 31 U.S.C. § [1342]. That is to say, it is our opinion that the utilization of enrollees or trainees by a Federal agency under the circumstances here involved need not be considered the acceptance of 'voluntary services' within the meaning of that phrase as used in 31 U.S.C. § [1342]." Id. at 561.

In B-211079.2, Jan. 2, 1987, the relevant program legislation expressly authorized program participants to perform work for federal agencies "notwithstanding section 1342 of title 31." The decision suggests that the statutory authority was necessary not because of the Antideficiency Act but to avoid an impermissible augmentation of appropriations. It is in any event consistent in result with 24 Comp. Gen. 314 and 54 Comp. Gen. 560.

(4) Applicability to legislative and judicial branches

The applicability of 31 U.S.C. § 1342 to the legislative and judicial branches of the federal government does not appear to have been seriously questioned.

The salary of a Member of Congress is fixed by statute and therefore cannot be waived without specific statutory authority. B-159835, Apr. 22, 1975; B-123424, Mar. 7, 1975; B-123424, Apr. 15, 1955; A-8427, Mar. 19, 1925; B-206396.2, Nov. 15, 1988 (nondecision letter). However, as each of these cases points out, nothing prevents a Senator or Representative from accepting the salary and then, as several have done, donate part or all of it back to the United States Treasury.

In 1977, GAO was asked by a congressional committee chairman whether section 1342 applies to Members of Congress who use volunteers to perform official office functions. GAO responded, first, that section 1342 seems clearly to apply to the legislative branch. GAO then summarized the rules for appointment without compensation and advised that, to the extent that a particular employee's salary could be fixed administratively by the Member in any amount he or she chooses to set, that employee's salary could be fixed at zero. This once again was essentially an application of the rules set down decades earlier in 30 Op. Att'y Gen. 51 (1913) and 27 Comp. Dec. 131 (1920). See also B-69907, Feb. 11, 1977.

The salary of a federal judge is also "fixed by law"—even more so because of the constitutional prohibition against diminishing the compensation of a federal judge while in office. U.S. Const. art III, § 1. A case applying the standard "no waiver" rules to a federal judge is B-157469, July 24, 1974.

c. Other Voluntary Services

Before entering the mainstream of the modern case law, two very earlydecisions should be noted. In 12 Comp. Dec. 244 (1905), the Comptroller of the Treasury held that an offer by a meat-packing firm to pay the salaries of Department of Agriculture employees to conduct a pre-export pork inspection could not be accepted because of the voluntary services prohibition. Similar cases have since come up, but they have been decided under the augmentation theory without reference to 31 U.S.C. § 1342. See 59 Comp. Gen. 294 (1980) and 2 Comp. Gen. 775 (1923).

To restate, apart from the 1905 decision, which has not been followed since, the voluntary services prohibition has not been applied to donations of money. In another 1905 decision, a vendor asked permission to install an appliance on Navy property for trial purposes at no expense to the government. Presumably, if the Navy liked the appliance, it would then buy it. The Comptroller of the Treasury pointed out an easily overlooked phrase in the voluntary service prohibition—the services that are prohibited are voluntary services "for the United States." Here, temporary installation by the vendor for trial purposes amounted to service for his own benefit and on his own behalf, "as an incident to or necessary concomitant of a proper exhibition of his appliance for sale." Therefore, the Navy could grant permission without violating the Antideficiency Act as long as the vendor agreed to remove the appliance at his own expense if the Navy chose not to buy it. 11 Comp. Dec. 622 (1905). This case has not been cited since.

For the most part, the subsequent cases have been resolved by applying the "voluntary versus gratuitous" distinction first enunciated by the Attorney General in 1913 in 30 Op. Att'y Gen. 51, discussed above. The underlying philosophy is perhaps best conveyed in the following statement by the Justice Department's Office of Legal Counsel:

> "Although the interpretation of § [1342] has not been entirely consistent over the years, the weight of authority does support the view that the section was intended to eliminate subsequent claims against the United States for compensation of the 'volunteer,' rather than to deprive the government of the benefit of truly gratuitous services."

6 Op. Off. Legal Counsel 160, 162 (1982).

In an early formulation that has often been quoted since, the Comptroller General noted that:

> "The voluntary service referred to in [31 U.S.C. § 1342] is not necessarily synonymous with gratuitous service, but contemplates service furnished on the initiative of the party rendering the same without request from, or agreement with, the United States therefor. Services furnished pursuant to a formal contract are not voluntary within the meaning of said section."

7 Comp. Gen. 810, 811 (1928). In 7 Comp. Gen. 810, a contractor had agreed to prepare stenographic transcripts of Federal Trade Commission public proceedings and to furnish copies to the Commission without cost, in exchange for the exclusive right to report the proceedings and to sell transcripts to the public. The decision noted that consideration under a contract does not have to be monetary consideration, and held that the contract in question was supported by sufficient legal consideration. While the case is thus arguably not a true "voluntary services" case, it has often been cited since, not so much for the actual holding but for the above-quoted statement of the rule.

For example, in B-13378, Nov. 20, 1940, the Comptroller General held that the Secretary of Commerce could accept gratuitous services from a private agency, created by various social science associations, which had offered to assist in the preparation of official monographs analyzing census data. The services were to be rendered under a cooperative agreement which specified that they would be free of cost to the government. The Commerce Department agreed to furnish space and equipment, but the monographs would not otherwise have been prepared.

Applying the same approach, GAO found no violation of 31 U.S.C. § 1342 for the Commerce Department to accept services by the Business Advisory Council, which were agreed in advance to be gratuitous. B-125406, Nov. 4, 1955. Likewise, the Commission on Federal Paperwork could accept free services from the private sector as long as they were agreed in advance to be gratuitous. B-182087-0.M., Nov. 26, 1975.

In a 1982 decision, the American Association of Retired Persons wanted to volunteer services to assist in crime prevention activities (distribute literature, give lectures, etc.) on Army installations. GAO found no Antideficiency Act problem as long as the services were agreed in advance, and so documented, as gratuitous. B-204326, July 26, 1982.

In B-177836, Apr. 24, 1973, the Army had entered into a contract with a landowner under which it acquired the right to remove trees and other shrubs from portions of the landowner's property incident to an easement. A subsequent purchaser of the property complained that some tree stumps had not been removed, and the Army proceeded to contract to have the work done. The landowner then submitted a claim for certain costs he had incurred incident to some preliminary work he had done prior to the Army's contract. Since the landowner's actions had been purely voluntary and had been taken without the knowledge or consent of the government, 31 U.S.C. § 1342 prohibited payment.

In 7 Comp. Gen. 167 (1927), a customs official had stored, in his own private boathouse, a boat which had been seized for smuggling whiskey. The customs official later filed a claim for storage charges. Noting that "the United States did not expressly or impliedly request the use of the premises and therefore did not by implication promise to pay therefor," GAO concluded that the storage had been purely a voluntary service, payment for which would violate 31 U.S.C. § 1342.

As if to prove the adage that there is nothing new under the sun, GAO considered another storage case over 50 years later, B-194294, July 12, 1979. There, an Agriculture Department employee had an accident while driving a government-owned vehicle assigned to him for his work. A Department official ordered the damaged vehicle towed to the employee's driveway, to be held there until it could be sold. Since the government did have a role in the employee's assumption of responsibility for the wreck, GAO found no violation of 31 U.S.C. § 1342 and allowed the employee's claim for reasonable storage charges on a quantum meruit basis.

Section 1342 covers any type of service which has the effect of creating a legal or moral obligation to pay the person rendering the service. Naturally, this includes government contractors. See PCL Construction Services, Inc. v. United States, 41 Fed. CL 242, 257-260 (1998), quoting with approval from the second edition of Principles of Federal Appropriations Law on this point. The prohibition includes arrangements in which government contracting officers solicit or permit—tacitly or otherwise—a contractor to continue performance on a "temporarily unfunded" basis while the agency, which has exhausted its appropriations and cannot pay the contractor immediately, seeks additional appropriations. This was one of the options considered in 55 Comp. Gen. 768 (1976), discussed previously in connection with 31 U.S.C. § 1341(a). The Army proposed a contract modification which would explicitly recognize the government's obligation to pay for any work performed under the contract, possibly including reasonable interest, subject to subsequent availability of funds. The government would use its best efforts to obtain a deficiency appropriation. Certificates to this effect would be issued to the contractor, including a statement that any additional work performed would be done at the contractor's own risk. In return, the contractor would be asked to defer any action for breach of contract.

GAO found this proposal "of dubious validity at best." Although the certificate given to the contractor would say that continued performance was at the contractor's own risk, it was clear that both parties expected the contract to continue. The government expected to accept the benefits of the contractor's performance and the contractor expected to be paid--eventually—for it. This is certainly not an example of a clear written understanding that work for the government is to be performed gratuitously. Also, the proposal to pay interest was improper as it would compound the Antideficiency Act violation. Although 55 Comp. Gen. 768 does not specifically discuss 31 U.S.C. § 1342, the relationship should be apparent.

GAO's opinion in B-302811, July 12, 2004, provides a recent example of an appropriate "gratuitous services" type contract that did not run afoul of the 31 U.S.C. § 1342 prohibition against voluntary services. This decision concerned the General Services Administration's (GSA) proposed National Brokers Contract, under which GSA would award four real estate brokers exclusive rights to represent the United States with respect to all GSA real property leases. The brokers would be required to provide a range of services commonly offered in commercial leasing transactions such as assisting federal agencies in developing their space requirements, surveying the rental market, and negotiating and preparing leases. The proposal took the form of a "no-cost" contract in which GSA would make no payments to the brokers for their services. Rather, the brokers would collect commissions from the landlords who leased property to the federal agencies. In approving the legality of this proposed arrangement, the decision observed:

> "Because the contract was constructed as a no cost contract, GSA will have no financial liability to brokers, and brokers will have no expectation of a payment from GSA. The acceptance of services without payment pursuant to a valid, binding no-cost contract does not augment an agency's appropriation nor does it violate the voluntary services prohibition. Although the brokers contract clearly expects that brokers will be remunerated by commissions from landlords, as is a common practice in the real estate industry, GSA does not require landlords to pay commissions. If a landlord were to fail to pay a broker, the broker would have no claim against GSA." Id. at 7.

d. Exceptions

Two kinds of exceptions to 31 U.S.C. § 1342 have already been discussed—where acceptance of services without compensation is specifically authorized by law, and where the government and the volunteer have a written agreement that the services are to be rendered gratuitously with no expectation of future payment.

There is a third exception, written into the statute itself: "emergencies involving the safety of human life or the protection of property." The cases dealing with this statutory exception have arisen in a variety of contexts and are discussed below, along with recent developments.

(1) Safety of human life

In order to invoke this exception, the services provided to protect human life must have been rendered in a true emergency situation. What constitutes an emergency was discussed in several early decisions.

In 12 Comp. Dec. 155 (1905), a municipal health officer disinfected several government buildings to prevent the further spread of diphtheria. Several cases of diphtheria had already occurred at the government compound, including four that resulted in deaths. The Comptroller of the Treasury found that the services had been rendered in an emergency involving the loss of human life, and held accordingly that the doctor could be reimbursed for the cost of materials used and the fair value of his services.

In another case, the S.S. Rexmore, a British vessel, deviated from its course to London to answer a call for help from an Army transport ship carrying over 1,000 troops. The ship had sprung a leak and appeared to be in danger of sinking. The Comptroller General allowed a claim for the vessel's actual operating costs plus lost profits attributable to the services performed. The Rexmore had rendered a tangible service to save the lives of the people aboard the Army transport, as well as the transport vessel itself. 2 Comp. Gen. 799 (1923).

On the other hand, GAO denied payment to a man who was boating in the Florida Keys and saw a Navy seaplane make a forced landing. He offered to tow the aircraft over two miles to the nearest island, and did so. His claim for expenses was denied. The aircraft had landed intact and the pilot was in no immediate danger. Rendering service to overcome mere inconvenience or even to avoid a potential future emergency is not enough to overcome the statutory prohibition. 10 Comp. Gen. 248 (1930).

(2) Protection of property

The main thing to remember here is that the property must be either government-owned property or property for which the government has some responsibility. The standard was established by the Comptroller of the Treasury in 9 Comp. Dec. 182, 185 (1902) as follows:

"I think it is clear that the statute does not contemplate property in which the Government has no immediate interest or concern; but I do not think it was intended to apply exclusively to property owned by the Government. The term 'property' is used in the statute without any qualifying words, but it is used in connection with the rendition of services for the Government. The implication is, therefore, clear that the property in contemplation is property in which the Government has an immediate interest or in connection with which it has some duty to perform."

In the cited decision, an individual had gathered up mail scattered in a train wreck and delivered it to a nearby town. The government did not "own" the mail but had a responsibility to deliver it. Therefore, the services came within the statutory exception and the individual could be paid for the value of his services.

Applying the approach of 9 Comp. Dec. 182, the Comptroller General held in B-152554, Feb. 24, 1975, that section 1342 did not permit the Agency for International Development to make expenditures in excess of available funds for disaster relief in foreign countries. A case clearly within the exception is 3 Comp. Gen. 979 (1924), allowing reimbursement to a municipality which had rendered firefighting assistance to prevent the destruction of federal property where the federal property was not within the territory for which the municipal fire department was responsible.

An exception was also recognized in 53 Comp. Gen. 71 (1973), where a government employee brought in food for other government employees in circumstances which would justify a determination that the expenditure was incidental to the protection of government property in an extreme emergency. In this case, the General Services Administration had to assemble and maintain for 5 days a cadre of approximately 175 special police in connection with the unauthorized occupation of a Bureau of Indian Affairs building. The police officers were required to perform tours of duty that sometimes extended to 24 hours. They were kept at the ready to reoccupy the building and they were not permitted to leave the marshaling area because of the imminence of court orders and administrative directives.

(3) Recent developments

During the past two decades, cases addressing the "emergencies involving the safety of human life or the protection of property" exception to 31 U.S.C. § 1342 have arisen primarily in the context of "funding gaps" where an agency is faced with an appropriations lapse (or potential lapse) usually at the outset of a fiscal year. In 1990, Congress amended 31 U.S.C. § 1342 by adding the following language:

"As used in this section, the term 'emergencies involving the safety of human life or the protection of property' does not include ongoing, regular functions of government the suspension of which would not imminently threaten the safety of human life or the protection of property."

Two recent GAO decisions have considered the emergency exception to 31 U.S.C. § 1342 (including its 1990 amendment) in a context other than a funding gap. The question in B-262069, Aug. 1, 1995, was whether the District of Columbia could exceed its appropriation for certain programs, including Aid to Families with Dependent Children and Medicaid, without violating the Antideficiency Act. The main issue in that decision was whether the "unless authorized by law exception" to the Antideficiency Act in 31 U.S.C. § 1341(a)(1)(A) applied. GAO held that it did not. The decision also noted the existence of the emergencies exception to 31 U.S.C. § 1342, but held that it was likewise inapplicable:

> "An 'emergency' under section 1342 'does not include ongoing, regular functions of government the suspension of which would not imminently threaten the safety of human life or the protection of property.' We are not presently aware of any facts or circumstances that would make this limited exception available to the District. See, 5 Op.O.L.C. 1, 7-11 (1981)."

B-262069 at 3, fn. 1.

The decision in B-262069 addressed a hypothetical situation; the District had not actually exceeded its appropriation there. Unfortunately, a subsequent opinion, B-285725, Sept. 29, 2000, involved the real thing. In that case, the District of Columbia Health and Hospitals Public Benefit Corporation (PBC) had incurred obligations and made payments in excess of its appropriations. The PBC maintained that the emergency exception to 31 U.S.C. § 1342 as construed by the Attorney General applied; thus, there was no violation. GAO disagreed:

> "The funding gap situations discussed by the Attorney General arise typically at the beginning of a fiscal year because of the absence or expiration of budget authority under circumstances that are beyond an agency's control. In the present situation, the exhaustion of appropriations occurred during the fiscal year because of a rate of operations and obligations in excess of available resources. Viewed in this light, PBC's failure to regulate its activities and spending so as to operate within its available budget resources is not the type of 'emergency' covered either by the Attorney General's earlier opinions or 31 U.S.C. § 1342."

B-285725, Enclosure at 9.

The opinion acknowledged that PBC's ongoing functions of operating a hospital and clinics involved the provision of services essential to the protection of human life. However, the opinion observed that PBC, like many federal agencies engaged in protecting human life and safety, requested and received appropriations to cover these functions. It added:

"Once the Congress enacts appropriation[s], it is incumbent on the PBC (and similarly situated federal agencies) to manage its resources to stay within the authorized level. Nothing in the District's Submission demonstrates that the PBC's exhaustion of appropriations prior to the end of the fiscal year was caused by some unanticipated event or events (e.g., mass injuries resulting from hurricane, flood or other natural disasters) requiring PBC to provide services for the protection of life beyond the level it should have reasonably been expected to anticipate when it prepared its budget."

Id. By way of summary, the opinion observed:

"While the failure of Congress to enact appropriations at the beginning of the fiscal year may qualify as an emergency event for purposes of section 1342, it would be a novel proposition, one that we are unwilling to endorse, to conclude that an agency's failure to manage and live within the resources provided for an activity involved in protecting human life permits it to incur obligations in excess of amounts provided. Nothing that we have been provided warrants the conclusion that the overobligations resulted from an unanticipated emergency rather than from the PBC's failure to manage and live within its budgetary resources during the fiscal year."

B-285725 at 3.

In essence, B-285725 held that the emergencies exception to 31 U.S.C. § 1342 does not apply where an agency exceeds its appropriations—at least absent events beyond the agency's control that the agency (and presumably the Congress) could not have foreseen in determining the agency's funding levels.

In two opinions to the United States Marshals Service (USMS) in 1999 and 2000, the Office of Legal Counsel addressed a potential exhaustion of USMS appropriations, which never materialized: Memorandum Opinion for the General Counsel, United States Marshals Service, USMS Obligation To Take Steps To Avoid Anticipated Appropriations Deficiency, OLC Opinion, May 11, 1999, and Memorandum Opinion for the General Counsel, United States Marshals Service, Continuation of Federal Prisoner Detention Efforts in the Face of a USMS Appropriations Deficiency, OLC Opinion, Apr. 5, 2000. The opinions dealt with a potential exhaustion of appropriations for USMS prisoner-detention functions, but did not describe the circumstances giving rise to the potential exhaustion. While these opinions recognized the "affirmative obligation" on the part of agencies to manage available appropriations in order to avoid deficiencies, they did not address the important distinction between an exhaustion of appropriations (or funding gap) resulting from unforeseen circumstances and an exhaustion of appropriations resulting from the agency's failure to manage its operations within the limits of enacted appropriations. We would disagree with the Office of Legal Counsel opinions to the extent they could be read to suggest that regardless of the reasons for the exhaustion of appropriations, whenever an agency like USMS, whose statutory mission involves the protection of life and property, runs out of money, it has open-ended authority to continue to incur obligations under the Antideficiency Act's emergencies exception. This is exactly the "coercive deficiency" that the Congress legislated against in enacting the Antideficiency Act. See B-285725, Sept. 29, 2000. The Antideficiency Act was intended to keep agency operations at a level within the amounts that Congress appropriates for that purpose. If an agency concludes that it needs more funds than Congress has appropriated for a fiscal year, the agency should ask Congress to enact a supplemental appropriation; it should not continue operations without regard to the Antideficiency Act.

e. Voluntary Creditors

A related line of decisions are the so-called "voluntary creditor" cases. A voluntary creditor is an individual, government or private, who pays what he or she perceives to be a government obligation from personal funds. The rule is that the voluntary creditor cannot be reimbursed, although there are significant exceptions. For the most part, the decisions have not related the voluntary creditor prohibition to the Antideficiency Act, with the exception of one very early case (17 Comp. Dec. 353 (1910)) and two more recent ones (53 Comp. Gen. 71 (1973) and 42 Comp. Gen. 149 (1962)).

4. Apportionment of Appropriations

Because of the apportionment and related provisions of the Antideficiency Act, 31 U.S.C. §§ 1511-1519, an agency generally does not have the full amount of its appropriations available to it at the beginning of the fiscal year. Apportionment is an administrative process by which, as its name suggests, appropriated funds are distributed to agencies in portions over the period of their availability. The Office of Management and Budget (OMB) apportions funds for executive branch agencies. 31 U.S.C. § 1513(b); Exec. Order No. 6166, § 16 (June 10, 1933), at 5 U.S.C. § 901 note. Appropriations for legislative branch agencies, the judicial branch, the District of Columbia, and the International Trade Commission are apportioned by officials having administrative control of those funds. 31 U.S.C. § 1513(a). In addition to apportionment, appropriations are subject to further administrative subdivision by the heads of the agencies to which the appropriations are made. 31 U.S.C. § 1514.

Section 1517(a) of title 31 prohibits officers and employees of the federal and District of Columbia governments from making or authorizing an expenditure or obligation that exceeds an apportionment or the amount permitted under certain other subdivisions of appropriated funds. Agencies must report violations of section 1517(a) to the Congress and the President. Those who violate section 1517(a) are subject to administrative discipline as well as criminal penalties in the case of willful violations. See 31 U.S.C. §§ 1517(b), 1518, and 1519.

a. Statutory Requirement for Apportionment

Subsection (a) of section 1512 establishes the basic requirement for the apportionment of appropriations:

> "(a) Except as provided in this subchapter, an appropriation available for obligation for a definite period shall be apportioned to prevent obligation or expenditure at a rate that would indicate a necessity for a deficiency or supplemental appropriation for the period. Anappropriation for an indefinite period and authority to make obligations by contract before appropriations shall be apportioned to achieve the most effective and economical use. An apportionment may be reapportioned under this section."

Although apportionment was first required legislatively in 1905, the current form of the statute derives from a revision enacted in 1950 in section 1211 of the General Appropriation Act, 1951. The 1950 revision was part of an overall effort by Congress to amplify and enforce the basic restrictions against incurring deficiencies in violation of the Antideficiency Act, 31 U.S.C. § 1341.

Section 1512(a) requires that all appropriations be administratively apportioned so as to ensure their obligation and expenditure at a controlled rate which will prevent deficiencies from arising before the end of a fiscal year. Although section 1512 does not tell you who is to make the apportionment, section 1513 names the President as the apportioning official for most executive branch agencies. The President delegated the function to the Director of the Bureau of the Budget in 1933, and it now reposes in the successor to that office, the Director of the Office of Management and Budget (OMB). Legislative and judicial branch appropriations are apportioned by officials in those branches. 31 U.S.C. § 1513(a).

The term "apportionment" may be defined as follows:

> "The action by which [the apportioning official] distributes amounts available for obligation, including budgetary reserves established pursuant to law, in an appropriation or fund account. An apportionment divides amounts available for obligation by specific time periods (usually quarters), activities, projects, objects, or a combination thereof. The amounts so apportioned limit the amount of obligations that may be incurred. An apportionment may be further subdivided by an agency into allotments, suballotments, and allocations. In apportioning any account, some funds may be reserved to provide for contingencies or to effect savings made possible pursuant to the Antideficiency Act. Funds apportioned to establish a reserve must be proposed for deferral or rescission pursuant to the Impoundment Control Act of 1974 (2 U.S.C. §§ 681-688)."

> "The apportionment process is intended to (1) prevent the obligation of amounts available within an appropriation or fund account in a manner that would require deficiency or

supplemental appropriations and (2) achieve the most effective and economical use of amounts made available for obligation."

Apportionment is required not only to prevent the need for deficiency or supplemental appropriations, but also to ensure that there is no drastic curtailment of the activity for which the appropriation is made. 36 Comp. Gen. 699 (1957). See also 38 Comp. Gen. 501 (1959). In other words, the apportionment requirement is designed to prevent an agency from spending its entire appropriation before the end of the fiscal year and then putting Congress in a position in which it must either enact an additional appropriation or allow the entire activity to come to a halt. 64 Comp. Gen. 728, 735 (1985). See also Memorandum Opinion for the General Counsel, United States Marshals Service, USMS Obligation To Take Steps To Avoid Anticipated Appropriations Deficiency, OLC Opinion, May 11, 1999 (opining that 31 U.S.C. § 1512(a) imposes "an affirmative obligation" on federal agencies to take steps to use their available funds in a way that will avoid the need for a deficiency or supplemental appropriations, citing 64 Comp. Gen. 728 and 36 Comp. Gen. 699).

In 36 Comp. Gen. 699, Post Office funds had been reapportioned in such a way that the fourth quarter funds were substantially less than those for the third quarter. The Comptroller General stated:

"A drastic curtailment toward the close of a fiscal year of operations carried on under a fiscal year appropriation is a prima facie indication of a failure to so apportion an appropriation 'as to prevent obligation or expenditure thereof in a manner which would indicate a necessity for deficiency or supplemental appropriations for such period.' In our view, this is the very situation the amendment of the law in 1950 was intended to remedy."

36 Comp. Gen. at 703. See also 64 Comp. Gen. 728, 735-36 (1985). However, the mere fact that an agency faces a severe lack of funds and needs to curtail services late in a fiscal year does not necessarily mean that the apportioning authority has violated 31 U.S.C. § 1512(a). Programmatic factors that could not reasonably be foreseen at the time of an apportionment or reapportionment may affect the pattern or pace of spending over the course of the year. Also, as discussed hereafter in section C.4.e, the statute itself permits apportionments indicating the need for a deficiency or supplemental appropriation in certain limited circumstances.

A 1979 decision involved the Department of Agriculture's Food Stamp Program. The program was subject to certain spending ceilings which it seemed certain, given the rate at which the Department was incurring expenditures, which the Department was going to exceed. The Department feared that, if it was bound by a formula in a different section of its authorizing act to pay the mandated amount to each eligible recipient, it would have to stop the whole program when the funds were exhausted. Based on both the Antideficiency Act and the program legislation, GAO concluded that there had to be an immediate pro rata reduction for all participants. Discontinuance of the program when the funds ran out would violate the purpose of the apportionment requirement. A-51604, Mar. 28, 1979.

This is not to say that every subactivity or project must be carried out for the full fiscal year, on a reduced basis, if necessary. Section 1512(a) applies to amounts made available in an appropriation or fund. Where, for example, the then Veterans Administration (VA) nursing home program was funded from moneys made available in a general, lump-sum VA medical care appropriation, the agency was free to discontinue the nursing home program and reprogram the balance of its funds to other programs also funded under that heading. B-167656, June 18, 1971. (The result would be different if the nursing home program had received a line-item appropriation.)

The general rule against apportionments that indicate the need for a deficiency or supplemental appropriation does not preclude an agency from requesting an apportionment of all or most of its existing appropriations at the same time that it is seeking a supplemental so long as the agency has in place a plan that would enable it to function through the end of the fiscal year should Congress not enact the supplemental. 64 Comp. Gen. 728, 735 (1985). See also B-255529, Jan. 10, 1994. In 64 Comp. Gen. 728, the former Interstate Commerce Commission (ICC) had requested an apportionment of the full annual amount available to it under a continuing resolution at the outset of fiscal year 1985. At the same time, the ICC voted to seek a supplemental appropriation in order to avoid severe staffing cuts that would have been required without it. The Comptroller General held that the apportionment was not improper:

"As we have indicated, at the recommendation of its Managing Director the ICC adopted an operating plan for fiscal year 1985 which included a request for a supplemental appropriation. However, part of that operating plan was an emergency plan which would enable the ICC to operate for the entire fiscal year even without a supplemental. Under the plan, if the Congress did not enact a supplemental appropriation by the end of March, the Commission was to furlough all its employees for 1 day per week for the remainder of the year. This would allow the Commission to operate through the end of the fiscal year within the $48 million already appropriated. In fact a supplemental was not passed by the end of March and the furlough was implemented...."

"The actions taken by the ICC ...demonstrate that from the time at which the Congress and the President approved legislation reducing ICC's funding below the requested level, every decision related to expenditures was made to avoid violation of the Antideficiency Act."

64 Comp. Gen. at 735.

The requirement to apportion applies not only to 1-year appropriations and other appropriations limited to a fixed period of time, but also to "no-year" money and even to contract authority (authority to contract in advance of appropriations). 31 U.S.C. §§ 1511(a), 1512(a). In the case of indefinite appropriations and contract authority, the requirement states only that the apportionment is to be made in such a way as "to achieve the most effective and economical use" of the budget authority. Id. § 1512(a).

Prior to the 1982 recodification of title 31 of the United States Code, the apportionment requirement applied explicitly to government corporations which are instrumentalities of the United States. While the applicability of the requirement has not changed, the recodification dropped the explicit language, viewing it as covered by the broad definition of "executive agency" in 31 U.S.C. § 102. The authority of some government corporations to determine the necessity of their expenditures and the manner in which they shall be incurred is not sufficient to exempt a corporation from the apportionment requirement. 43 Comp. Gen. 759 (1964).

The apportionment process provides a set of administrative controls over the use of appropriations in addition to those Congress has imposed through the appropriations act itself. The apportionment process cannot alter or otherwise affect the operation of statutory requirements concerning the availability or use of appropriated funds. In this regard, OMB's guidance on apportionments states:

> "... The apportionment of funds should not be used as a means of resolving any question dealing with the legality of using funds for the purposes for which they are appropriated. Any questions as to the legality of using funds for a particular purpose must be resolved through legal channels."

OMB Circ. No. A-11, pt. 4, § 120.17.

Furthermore, an apportioning official cannot apportion funds in advance of their availability for obligation or expenditure. In B-290600, July 10, 2002, OMB had apportioned certain budget authority for loan guarantees to the Air Transportation Stabilization Board pursuant to the Board's request. The statute enacting this budget authority had conditioned its availability such that the budget authority "shall be available only to the extent that a request... that includes designation of such amount as an emergency requirement... is transmitted by the President to Congress." The President had not transmitted this designation at the time of the apportionment. Therefore, GAO concluded that OMB and the Board had violated the Antideficiency Act. OMB and the Board recognized the violation and had already taken steps to avoid a recurrence.

b. Establishing Reserves

Section 1512(c) of 31 U.S.C. provides as follows:

> "(c)(1) In apportioning or reapportioning an appropriation, a reserve may be established only:

> > "(A) to provide for contingencies;

"(B) to achieve savings made possible by or through changes in requirements or greater efficiency of operations; or;

"(C) as specifically provided by law.

"(2) A reserve established under this subsection may be changed as necessary to carry out the scope and objectives of the appropriation concerned. When an official designated in section 1513 of this title to make apportionments decides that an amount reserved will not be required to carry out the objectives and scope of the appropriation concerned, the official shall recommend the rescission of the amount in the way provided in chapter 11 of this title for appropriation requests. Reserves established under this section shall be reported to Congress as provided in the Impoundment Control Act of 1974 (2 U.S.C. 681 et seq.)."

Section 1512(c) seeks to limit the circumstances in which the full appropriation is not apportioned or utilized and a reserve fund is established. Under this provision, the apportioning official is authorized to establish reserves only to provide for contingencies or to effect savings, unless the reserve is specifically authorized by statute.

At one time, this section was a battleground between the executive and legislative branches. The executive branch had relied on this portion of the Antideficiency Act to impound funds for general fiscal or economic policy reasons such as containment of federal spending and executive judgment of the relative merits, effectiveness, and desirability of competing federal programs (often referred to as "policy impoundments"). See 54 Comp. Gen. 453, 458 (1974); B-135564, July 26, 1973.

Prior to 1974, the predecessor of 31 U.S.C. § 1512(c) contained rather expansive language to the effect that a reserve fund could be established pursuant to "other developments subsequent to the date on which [the] appropriation was made available." 31 U.S.C. § 665(c)(2) (1970 ed.).

Despite this expansive language, the Comptroller General's position had been that the authority to establish reserves under the Antideficiency Act was limited to providing for contingencies or effecting savings which are in furtherance of, or at least consistent with, the purposes of an appropriation. B-130515, July 10, 1973. The Comptroller General did not interpret the law as authorizing a reserve of funds (i.e., an impoundment) based upon general economic, fiscal, or policy considerations that were extraneous to the individual appropriation or were in derogation of the appropriation's purpose. B-125187, Sept. 11, 1973; B-130515, July 10, 1973. See also State Highway Commission of Missouri v. Volpe, 479 F.2d 1099, 1118 (8th Cir. 1973), which held that the right to reserve funds in order to "effect savings" or due to "subsequent events," etc., must be considered in the context of the applicable appropriation statute.

The Impoundment Control Act of 1974 amended section 1512(c) by eliminating the "other developments" clause and by prohibiting the establishment of appropriation reserves except as provided under the Antideficiency Act for contingencies or savings, or as provided in other specific statutory authority. The intent was to preclude reliance on section 1512(c) as authority for "policy impoundments." City of New Haven v. United States, 809 F.2d 900, 906 (D.C. Cir. 1987); 54 Comp. Gen. 453 (1974); B-148898-0.M., Aug. 28, 1974.

The executive branch, however, continued to defer for policy reasons, arguing that section 1013 of the Impoundment Control Act provided authority, independent of the Antideficiency Act, to withhold funds from obligation temporarily for fiscal policy reasons. GAO agreed that this interpretation was consistent with the language of the Impoundment Control Act and with the statutory scheme, pointing out that Congress had reserved the power under the Impoundment Control Act to disapprove any deferral, particularly deferrals for fiscal policy reasons, as a counterweight to the President's power to defer. 54 Comp. Gen. at 455. At that time, the Impoundment Control Act provided for disapproval using a one-house veto. This counterweight vanished when the Supreme Court held one-house legislative veto provisions unconstitutional. Immigration & Naturalization Service v. Chadha, 462 U.S. 919 (1983). Accordingly, in a decision issued on January 20, 1987, the U.S. Court of Appeals for the District of Columbia invalidated section 1013, which was the sole general legislative authority for policy deferrals. City of New Haven, 809 F.2d at 902, 905-09. In September of 1987, Congress reenacted section 1013(b) of the Impoundment Control Act, 2 U.S.C. § 684(b), without the unconstitutional legislative veto provision and reiterated that the same limits on appropriation reserves that appear in 31 U.S.C. § 1512(c) are the sole justifications for deferrals. See Pub. L. No. 100-119, § 206, 101 Stat. 754, 785 (Sept. 29, 1987).

The Comptroller General discussed examples of permissible (i.e., nonpolicy) reserves in 51 Comp. Gen. 598 (1972) and 51 Comp. Gen. 251 (1971). The first decision concerned the provisions of a long-term charter of several tankers for the Navy. The contract contained options to renew the charter for periods of 15 years. In the event that the Navy declined to renew the charter short of a full 15-year period, the vessels were to be sold by a Board of Trustees, acting for the owners and bondholders. Any shortfall in the proceeds over the termination value was to be unconditionally guaranteed by the Navy. GAO held that it would not violate the Antideficiency Act to cover this contingent liability by setting up a reserve. 51 Comp. Gen. 598 (1972). In 51 Comp. Gen. 251 (1971), GAO said that it was permissible to provide in regulations for a clause to be inserted in future contracts for payment of interest on delayed payments of a contractor's claim. Reserving sufficient funds from the appropriation used to support the contract to cover these potential interest costs would protect against potential Antideficiency Act violations.

In 1981, the Community Services Administration established a reserve as a cushion against Antideficiency Act violations while the agency was terminating its operations. Grantees argued that the reserve improperly reduced amounts available for discretionary grants. In Rogers v. United States, 14 Cl. Ct. 39, 46-47 (1987), aff'd, 801 F.2d 729 (Fed. Cir. 1988), cert. denied, 490

U.S. 1034 (1989), the court held that a reasonable reserve for contingencies was properly within the agency's discretion.

c. Method of Apportionment

The remaining portions of 31 U.S.C. § 1512 are subsections (b) and (d), set forth below:

"(b)(1) An appropriation subject to apportionment is apportioned by:

"(A) months, calendar quarters, operating seasons, or other time periods;

"(B) activities, functions, projects, or objects; or;

"(C) a combination of the ways referred to in clauses (A) and (B) of this paragraph...

"(d) An apportionment or reapportionment shall be reviewed at least 4 times a year by the official designated in section 1513 of this title to make apportionments."

Subsection (b) and (d) are largely technical, implementing the basic apportionment requirement of 31 U.S.C. § 1512(a). Section 1512(b) makes it clear that apportionments need not be made strictly on a monthly, quarterly, or other fixed time basis, nor must they be for equal amounts in each time period. The apportioning officer is free to take into account the "activities, functions, projects, or objects" of the program being funded and the usual pattern of spending for such programs in deciding how to apportion the funds. Absent some statutory provision to the contrary, OMB's determination is controlling. Thus, in Maryland Department of Human Resources v. United States Department of Health & Human Services, 854 F.2d 40 (4th Cir. 1988), the court upheld OMB's quarterly apportionment of social services block grant funds, rejecting the state's contention that it should receive its entire annual allotment at the beginning of the fiscal year. Section 1512(d) requires a minimum of four reviews each year to enable the apportioning officer to make reapportionments or other adjustments as necessary.

Conversely, OMB may decide to apportion all or most of an available appropriation at the outset of a fiscal year. In B-255529, Jan. 10, 1994, GAO held that OMB's apportionments at the beginning of the fiscal year of the full amounts available for two State Department appropriation ("Contributions to International Organizations" and "Contributions for International Peacekeeping Activities") constituted an appropriate exercise of OMB's discretion. Quoting from an earlier opinion, B-152554, Feb. 17, 1972, the decision then observed that the amounts to be apportioned depended on the needs of the programs as determined by OMB:

"It must be recognized that, with respect to a number of programs, particularly where grant or other assistance funds are involved, a large portion of the funds normally are obligated during the early part of the fiscal year. The pattern of obligations is much different than where, for example, an appropriation is primarily available for salaries and administrative expenses. In such case the expenditures would be comparatively constant throughout the year. The pattern of obligations, however, is primarily an administrative matter ... [for resolution through] the apportionment process."

The decision pointed out that, according to the State Department, payments under the Contributions to International Organizations account traditionally were made in the first quarter of the fiscal year. Payments under the Peacekeeping account usually occurred as bills were received and funds were available, but the Department advised GAO that there was a large backlog of bills at the time funds became available, thereby justifying immediate apportionment of the entire annual appropriation.

d. Control of Apportionments

Section 1513 of title 31, United States Code, specifies the authorities and timetables for making the apportionments or reapportionments of appropriations required by section 1512. Section 1513(a) applies to appropriations of the legislative and judicial branches of the federal government, as well as appropriations of the International Trade Commission and the District of Columbia government. It assigns authority to apportion to the "official having administrative control" of the appropriation. Apportionment must be made 30 days before the start of the fiscal year for which the appropriation is made, or within 30 days after the enactment of the appropriation, whichever is later. The apportionment must be in writing.

Section 1513(b) deals with apportionments for the executive branch. The President is designated as the apportioning authority. As we have seen, the function has been delegated to the Director, Office of Management and Budget (OMB). The Director of OMB has up to 20 days before the start of the fiscal year or 30 days after enactment of the appropriation act, whichever is later, to make the actual apportionment and notify the agency of the action taken. 31 U.S.C. § 1513(b)(2). Again, the apportionments must be in writing. Although primary responsibility for a violation of section 1512 lies with the Director of OMB, the head of the agency concerned also may be found responsible if he or she fails to send the Director accurate information on which to base an apportionment.

In B-163628, Jan. 4, 1974, GAO responded to a question from the chairman of a congressional committee about the power of OMB to apportion the funds of independent regulatory agencies, such as the Securities and Exchange Commission (SEC). The Comptroller General agreed with the chairman that independent agencies should generally be free from executive control or interference. The response then stated:

"The apportionment power may not lawfully be used as a form of executive control or influence over agency functions. Rather, it may only be exercised by OMB in the manner and for the purposes prescribed in 31 U.S.C. § [1512]—i.e., to prevent obligation or expenditure in a manner which would give rise to a need for deficiency or supplemental appropriations, to achieve the most effective and economical use of appropriations and to establish reserves either to provide for contingencies or to effect savings which are in furtherance of or at least consistent with, the purposes of an appropriation.

"As thus limited, the apportionment process serves a necessary purpose—-the promotion of economy and efficiency in the use of appropriations.

"Since a useful purpose is served by OMB's proper exercise of the apportionment power, we do not believe that the potential for abuse of the power is sufficient to justify removing it from OMB."

Thus, the appropriations of independent regulatory agencies like the Securities and Exchange Commission (SEC) are subject to apportionment by OMB, but OMB may not lawfully use its apportionment power to compromise the independence of those agencies.

The Impoundment Control Act may permit OMB, in effect, to delay the apportionment deadlines prescribed in 31 U.S.C. § 1513(b). For example, when the President sends a rescission message to Congress, the budget authority proposed to be rescinded may be withheld for up to 45 days pending congressional action on a rescission bill. 2 U.S.C. §§ 682(3), 683(b). In B-115398.33, Aug. 12, 1976, GAO responded to a congressional request to review a situation in which an apportionment had been withheld for more than 30 days after enactment of the appropriation act. The President had planned to submit a rescission message for some of the funds but was late in drafting and transmitting his message. If the full amount contained in the rescission message could be withheld for the entire 45-day period, and Congress ultimately declined to enact the full rescission, release of the funds for obligation would occur only a few days before the budget authority expired. The Comptroller General suggested that, where Congress has completed action on a rescission bill rescinding only a part of the amount proposed, OMB should immediately apportion the amounts not included in the rescission bill without awaiting the expiration of the 45-day period. See also B-115398.33, Mar. 5, 1976.

e. Apportionments Requiring Deficiency Estimate

In our discussion of the basic requirement for apportionment, we quoted31 U.S.C. § 1512(a) to the effect that appropriations must be apportioned "to prevent obligation or expenditure at a rate that would indicate a necessity for a deficiency or supplemental appropriation." The requirement that appropriations be apportioned so as to avoid the need for deficiency or supplemental appropriations is fleshed out in 31 U.S.C. § 1515 (formerly subsection (e) of the Antideficiency Act):

"(a) An appropriation required to be apportioned under section 1512 of this title may be apportioned on a basis that indicates the need for a deficiency or supplemental appropriation to the extent necessary to permit payment of such pay increases as may be granted pursuant to law to civilian officers and employees (including prevailing rate employees whose pay is fixed and adjusted under subchapter IV of chapter 53 of title 5) and to retired and active military personnel.

"(b)(1) Except as provided in subsection (a) of this section, an official may make, and the head of an executive agency may request, an apportionment under section 1512 of this title that would indicate a necessity for a deficiency or supplemental appropriation only when the official or agency head decides that the action is required because of:

"(A) a law enacted after submission to Congress of the estimates for an appropriation that requires an expenditure beyond administrative control; or;

"(B) an emergency involving the safety of human life, the protection of property, or the immediate welfare of individuals when an appropriation that would allow the United States Government to pay, or contribute to, amounts required to be paid to individuals in specific amounts fixed by law or under formulas prescribed by law, is insufficient.

"(2) If an official making an apportionment decides that an apportionment would indicate a necessity for a deficiency or supplemental appropriation, the official shall submit immediately a detailed report of the facts to Congress. The report shall be referred to in submitting a proposed deficiency or supplemental appropriation."

Section 1515 thus provides certain exceptions to the requirement of section 1512(a) that apportionments be made in such manner as to assure that the funds will last throughout the fiscal year and there will be no necessity for a deficiency appropriation. Under subsection 1515(a), deficiency apportionments are permissible if necessary to pay salary increases granted pursuant to law to federal civilian and military personnel. Under subsection 1515(b), apportionments can be made in an unbalanced manner (e.g., an entire appropriation could be obligated by the end of the second quarter) if the apportioning officer determines that (1) a law enacted subsequent to the transmission of budget estimates for the appropriation requires expenditures beyond administrative control, or (2) there is an emergency involving safety of human life, protection of property, or immediate welfare of individuals in cases where an appropriation for mandatory payments to those individuals is insufficient.

Prior to 1957, what is now subsection 1515(b) prohibited only the making of an apportionment indicating the need for a deficiency or supplemental appropriation, so the only person who could violate this subsection was the Director of OMB. An amendment in 1957 made it equally a violation for an agency to request such an apportionment. See 38 Comp. Gen. 501 (1959). The exception in subsection 1515(b)(1)(A) for expenditures "beyond administrative control" required by a statute enacted after submission of the budget estimate may be illustrated by statutory increases in compensation, although many of the cases would now be covered by subsection (a). We noted several of the cases in our consideration of when an obligation or expenditure is "authorized by law" for purposes of 31 U.S.C. § 1341. Those cases established the rule that a mandatory increase is regarded as "authorized by law" so as to permit overobligation, whereas a discretionary increase is not. The same rule applies in determining when an expenditure is "beyond administrative control" for purposes of 31 U.S.C. § 1515(b). Thus, statutory pay increases for Wage Board employees granted pursuant to a wage survey meet the test. 39 Comp. Gen. 422 (1959); 38 Comp. Gen. 538, 542 (1959). See also 45 Comp. Gen. 584, 587 (1966) (severance pay in fiscal year 1966). Discretionary increases, just as they are not "authorized by law" for purposes of 31 U.S.C. § 1341, are not "beyond administrative control" for purposes of section 1515(b). 44 Comp. Gen. 89 (1964) (salary increases to Central Intelligence Agency employees); 31 Comp. Gen. 238 (1951) (pension increases to retired District of Columbia police and firefighters).

The Wage Board exception was separately codified in 1957 and now appears at 31 U.S.C. § 1515(a), quoted above. Subsection 1515(a) reached its present form in 1987 when Congress expanded it to include pay increases granted pursuant to law to non-Wage Board civilian officers and employees and to retired and active military personnel.

The "emergency" exceptions in subsection 1515(b)(1)(B) have not been discussed in GAO decisions, although a 1989 internal memorandum suggested that the exception would apply to Forest Service appropriations for fighting forest fires. B-230117-O.M., Feb. 8, 1989. The exceptions for safety of human life and protection of property appear to be patterned after identical exceptions in 31 U.S.C. § 1342 (acceptance of voluntary services), so the case law under that section would likely be relevant for construing the scope of the exceptions under section 1515(b). See 43 Op. Att'y Gen. 293, 5 Op. Off. Legal Counsel 1, 9-10 (1981) ("as provisions containing the same language, enacted at the same time, and aimed at related purposes, the emergency provisions or sections 1342 and 1515(b)(1)(B) "should be deemed in pari materia and given a like construction"); Memorandum for the General Counsel, United States Marshals Service, Continuation of Federal Prisoner Detention Efforts in the Face of a USMS Appropriation Deficiency, OLC Opinion, Apr. 5, 2000 ("we think it clear that, if an agency's functions fall within § 1342's exception for emergency situations, the standard for the 'emergency' exception under§ [1515(b)(1)(B)] also will be met"). See also Memorandum for the Director, Office of Management and Budget, Government Operations in the Event of a Lapse in Appropriations, OLC Opinion, Aug. 16, 1995, at 7, fn. 6.

It is less obvious that the converse would necessarily be true—that is, that an "emergency" for purposes of subsection 1515(b)(1)(B) automatically qualifies as an "emergency" for purposes of section 1342. As we pointed out in discussing section 1342, this section was amended in 1990 to add the following language:

"As used in this section, the term 'emergencies involving the safety of human life or the protection of property' does not include ongoing, regular functions of government the suspension of which would not imminently threaten the safety of human life or the protection of property."

Such language was not added to subsection 1515(b)(1)(B). Thus, on its face, subsection 1515(b)(1)(B) may embody at least a slightly more flexible standard of "emergency" than section 1342, although we have found no cases addressing this point.

Importantly, the exceptions in 31 U.S.C. § 1515(b) are exceptions only to the prohibition against malting or requesting apportionments requiring deficiency estimates; they are not exceptions to the basic prohibitions in 31 U.S.C. § 1341 against obligating or spending in excess or advance of appropriations. The point was discussed at some length in B-167034, Sept. 1, 1976. Legislation had been proposed in the Senate to repeal 41 U.S.C. § 11 (the Adequacy of Appropriations Act), which prohibits the malting of a contract, not otherwise authorized by law, unless there is an appropriation "adequate to its fulfillment," except in the case of contracts made by a military department for "clothing, subsistence, forage, fuel, quarters, transportation, or medical and hospital supplies." The question was whether, if 41 U.S.C. § 11 were repealed, the military departments would have essentially the same authority under section 1515(b).

The Defense Department expressed the view that section 1515(b) would not be an adequate substitute for the 41 U.S.C. § 11 exception which allows the incurring of obligations for limited purposes even though the applicable appropriation is insufficient to cover the expenses at the time the commitment is made. Defense commented as follows:

"The authority to apportion funds on a deficiency basis in [31 U.S.C. § 1515(b)] does not, as alleged, provide authority to incur a deficiency. It merely authorizes obligating funds at a deficiency rate under certain circumstances, e.g., a $2,000,000 appropriation can be obligated in its entirety at the end of the third quarter, but it does not provide authority to obligate one dollar more than $2,000,000."

Letter from the Deputy Secretary of Defense to the Chairman, House Armed Services Committee, Apr. 2, 1976 (quoted in B-167034, Sept. 1, 1976).

The Comptroller General agreed with the Deputy Secretary, stating:

"[Section 1515(b)] in no way authorizes an agency of the Government actually to incur obligations in excess of the total amount of money appropriated for a period. It only provides an exception to the general apportionment rule set out in [31 U.S.C. § 1512(a)] that an appropriation be allocated so as to insure that it is not exhaustedprematurely. [Section 1515(b)] says nothing about increasing the total amount of the appropriation itself or authorizing the incurring of obligations in excess of the total amount appropriated. On the contrary, as noted above, apportionment only involves the subdivision ofappropriations already enacted by Congress. It necessarily follows that the sum of the parts, as apportioned, could not exceed the total amount of the appropriations being apportioned.

"Any deficiency that an agency incurs where obligations exceed total amounts appropriated, including a deficiency that arises in a situation where it was determined that one of the exceptions set forth in [section 1515(b)] was applicable, would constitute a violation of 31 U.S.C. § [1341(a)] ...."

B-167034, Sept. 1, 1976.

f. Exemptions from Apportionment Requirement

A number of exemptions from the apportionment requirement, formerly found in subsection (f) of the Antideficiency Act, are now gathered in 31 U.S.C. § 1516

"An official designated in section 1513 of this title to make apportionments may exempt from apportionment:

"(1) a trust fund or working fund if an expenditure from the fund has no significant effect on the financial operations of the United States Government;

"(2) a working capital fund or a revolving fund established for intragovernmental operations;

"(3) receipts from industrial and power operations available under law; and;

"(4) appropriations made specifically for:

"(A) interest on, or retirement of, the public debt;

"(B) payment of claims, judgments, refunds, and drawbacks;

"(C) items the President decides are of a confidential nature;

"(D) payment under a law requiring payment of the total amount of the appropriation to a designated payee; and;

"(E) grants to the States under the Social Security Act (42 U.S.C. 301 et seq.)."

Section 1516 is largely self-explanatory and the various enumerated exceptions appear to be readily understood. Note that the statute does not make the exemptions mandatory. It merely authorizes them, within the discretion of the apportioning authority (OMB). OMB's implementing instructions, OMB Circular No. A-11, Preparation, Submission, and Execution of the Budget, part 4, § 120 (June 21, 2005), have not adopted all of the exemptions permitted under the statute. For example, the Circular's list of funds exempted from apportionment pursuant to 31 U.S.C. § 1516 does not include trust funds or intragovernmental revolving funds. See OMB Cir. No. A-11, at § 120.7.

In addition, 10 U.S.C. § 2201(a) authorizes the President to exempt appropriations for military functions of the Defense Department from apportionment upon determining "such action to be necessary in the interest of national defense."

Another exemption, this one mandatory, is contained in 31 U.S.C.§ 1511(b)(3): appropriations for "the Senate, the House of Representatives, a committee of Congress, a member, officer, employee, or office of either House of Congress, or the Office of the Architect of the Capitol or an officer or employee of that Office" are exempt from the apportionment requirement. The remainder of the legislative branch along with the judicial branch are subject to apportionment. See 31 U.S.C. § 1513(a).

g. Administrative Division of Apportionments

Thus far, we have reviewed the provisions of the Antideficiency Act directed at the appropriation level and the apportionment level. The law also addresses agency subdivisions.

The first provision to note is 31 U.S.C. § 1513(d):

"An appropriation apportioned under this subchapter maybe divided and subdivided administratively within the limits of the apportionment."

Thus, administrative subdivisions are expressly authorized. The precise pattern of subdivisions will vary based on the nature and scope of activities funded under the apportionment and, to some extent, agency preference. The levels of subdivision below the apportionment level are, in descending order, allotment, suballotment, and allocation. See OMB Circular No. A-11, Preparation, Submission, and Execution of the Budget, § 20.3 (June 21, 2005), which notes under its definition of apportionment: "An apportionment may be further subdivided by an agency into allotments, suballotments, and allocations." As we will see later in our discussion of 31 U.S.C. § 1517(a), there are definite Antideficiency Act implications flowing from how an agency structures its fund control system.

The next relevant statute is 31 U.S.C. § 1514:

"(a) The official having administrative control of anappropriation available to the legislative branch, the judicial branch, the United States International Trade Commission, or the District of Columbia government, and, subject to the approval of the President, the head of each executive agency (except the Commission) shall prescribe by regulation a system of administrative control notinconsistent with accounting procedures prescribed under law. The system shall be designed to:

"(1) restrict obligations or expenditures from each appropriation to the amount of apportionments or reapportionments of the appropriation; and;

"(2) enable the official or the head of the executive agency to fix responsibility for an obligation or expenditure exceeding an apportionment or reapportionment.

"(b) To have a simplified system for administratively dividing appropriations, the head of each executive agency (except the Commission) shall work toward the objective of financing each operating unit, at the highest practical level, from not more than one administrative division for each appropriation affecting the unit."

Section 1514 is designed to ensure that the agencies in each branch of the government keep their obligations and expenditures within the bounds of each apportionment or reapportionment. The official in each agency who has administrative control of the apportioned funds is required to set up, by regulation, a system of administrative controls to implement this objective. The system must be consistent with any accounting procedures prescribed by or pursuant to law, and must be designed to (1) prevent obligations and expenditures in excess of apportionments or reapportionments, and (2) fix responsibility for any obligation or expenditure in excess of an apportionment or reapportionment. Agency fund control regulations in the executive branch must be approved by OMB. See OMB Cir. No. A-11, pt. 4, § 150.7.

Subsection (b) of 31 U.S.C. § 1514 was added in 1956 and was intended to simplify agency allotment systems. Prior to 1956, it was not uncommon for agencies to divide and subdivide their apportionments into numerous "pockets" of obligational authority called "allowances." Obligating or spending more than the amount of each allowance was a violation of the Antideficiency Act as it then existed. The Second Hoover Commission (Commission on Organization of the Executive Branch of the Government) had recommended simplification in 1955. The Senate and House Committees on Government Operations agreed. Both committees reported as follows:

"The making of numerous allotments which are further divided and suballotted to lower levels leads to much confusion and inflexibility in the financial control of appropriations or funds as well as numerous minor violations of [the Antideficiency Act]."

S. Rep. No. 84-2265, at 9 (1956); H.R. Rep. No. 84-2734, at 7 (1956). The result was what is now 31 U.S.C. § 1514(b).

As noted, one of the objectives of 31 U.S.C. § 1514 is to enable the agency head to fix responsibility for obligations or expenditures in excess of apportionments. The statute encourages agencies to fix responsibility at the highest practical level, but does not otherwise prescribe precisely how this is to be done. Apart from subsection (b), the substance of section 1514 derives from a 1950 amendment to the Antideficiency Act. In testimony on that legislation, the Director of the then Bureau of the Budget stated:

"At the present time, theoretically, I presume the agency head is about the only one that you could really hold responsible for exceeding [an] apportionment. The revised section provides for going down the line to the person who creates the obligation against the fund and fixes the responsibility on the bureau head or the division head, if he is the one who creates the obligation."

Thus, depending on the agency regulations and the level at which administrative responsibility is fixed, the violating individual could be the person in charge of a major agency bureau or operating unit, or it could be a contracting officer or finance officer.

Identifying the person responsible for a violation will be easy in probably the majority of cases. However, where there are many individuals involved in a complex transaction, and particularly where the actions producing the violation occurred over a long period of time, pinpointing responsibility can be much more difficult. Hopkins and Nutt, in their study of the Antideficiency Act, present the following as a sensible approach:

"Generally, [the individual to be held responsible] will be the highest ranking official in the decision-making process who had knowledge, either actual or constructive, of (1) precisely what actions were taken and (2) the impropriety or at least questionableness of such actions. There will be officials who had knowledge of either factor. But the person in the best and perhaps only position to prevent the ultimate error—and thus the one who must be held accountable—is the highest one who is aware of both.

Thus, Hopkins and Nutt conclude, where multiple individuals are involved in a violation, the individual to be held responsible "must not be too remote from the cause of the violation and must be in a position to have prevented the violation from occurring."

h. Expenditures in Excess of Apportionment

The former subsection (h) of the Antideficiency Act, now 31 U.S.C. § 1517(a), provides:

"(a) An officer or employee of the United States Government or of the District of Columbia government may not make or authorize an expenditure or obligation exceeding:

"(1) an apportionment; or;

"(2) the amount permitted by regulations prescribed under section 1514(a) of this title."

Section 1517(a) must be read in conjunction with sections 1341, 1512, and 1514, previously discussed.

Subsection 1517(a)(1) prohibits obligations or expenditures in excess of an apportionment. Thus, an agency must observe the limits of its apportionments just as it must observe the limits of its appropriations. It follows that an agency cannot obligate or expend appropriations before they have been apportioned. Thus, GAO stated in B-290600, July 10, 2002:

"The Antideficiency Act prohibits ... the making or the authorizing of obligations or expenditures in advance of, or in excess of, available appropriations. 31 U.S.C. § 1341. An agency may obligate an appropriation only after OMB has apportioned it to the agency."

Since the Antideficiency Act requires an apportionment before an agency can obligate the appropriation, 31 U.S.C. § 1512(a), an obligation in advance of an apportionment violates the Act. See B-255529, Jan. 10, 1994. In other words, if zero has been apportioned, zero is available for obligation or expenditure. When an agency anticipates a need to obligate appropriations upon their enactment, it may request (but not receive) an apportionment before a regular appropriation or continuing resolution has been enacted. Typically, for regular appropriation acts, agencies submit their apportionment requests to OMB by August 21 or within 10 calendar days after enactment of the appropriation, whichever is later. See OMB Circular No. A-11, Preparation, Submission, and Execution of the Budget, § 120.30 (June 21, 2005). OMB permits agencies to submit requests on the day Congress completes action on the appropriation bill. Id. § 120.34. OMB encourages agencies to begin their preparation of apportionment requests as soon as the House and Senate have reached agreement on funding levels (id. § 120.30) and to discuss the proposed request with OMB representatives (id. § 120.34). OMB will entertain expedited requests and, for emergency funding needs, may approve the apportionment request by telephone or fax Id. For continuing resolutions, OMB typically expedites the process by malting "automatic" apportionments under continuing resolutions. See B-255529, Jan. 10, 1994; OMB Cir. No. A-11, § 123.5.

Under some circumstances, an agency may have a legal duty to seek an additional apportionment from OMB. Blackhawk Heating & Plumbing Co. v. United States, 622 F.2d 539, 552 n.9 (Ct. Cl. 1980); Berends v. Butz, 357 E Supp. 143, 155-56 (D. Minn. 1973). In Berends v. Butz, the Secretary of Agriculture had terminated an emergency farm loan program, allegedly due to a shortage of funds. The court found the termination improper and directed reinstatement of the program. Since the shortage of funds related to the amount apportioned and not the amount available under the appropriation, the court found that the Secretary had a duty to request an additional apportionment in order to continue implementing the program. The case does not address the nature and extent of any duty OMB might have in response to such a request.

Subsection 1517(a)(2) makes it a violation to obligate or expend in excess of an administrative subdivision of an apportionment to the extent provided in the agency's fund control regulations prescribed under section 1514. The importance of 31 U.S.C. § 1514 becomes much clearer when it is read in conjunction with 31 U.S.C. § 1517(a)(2). Section 1514 does not prescribe the level of fiscal responsibility for violations below the apportionment level. It merely recommends that the agency set the level at the highest practical point and suggests no more than one subdivision below the apportionment level. The agency thus, under the statute, has a measure of discretion. If it chooses to elevate overobligations or overexpenditures of lower-tier subdivisions to the level of Antideficiency Act violations, it is free to do so in its fund control regulations.

At this point, it is important to return to OMB Circular No. A-11. Since agency fund control regulations must be approved by OMB (id. § 150.7), OMB has a role in determining what levels of administrative subdivision should constitute Antideficiency Act violations. Under OMB

Circular No. A-11, § 145.2, overobligation or overexpenditure of an allotment or suballotment are always violations. Overobligation or overexpenditure of other administrative subdivisions are violations only if and to the extent specified in the agency's fund control regulations. See 31 U.S.C. §§ 1514(a), 1517(a)(2).

In 37 Comp. Gen. 220 (1957), GAO considered proposed fund control regulations of the Public Housing Administration. The regulations provided for allotments as the first subdivision below the apportionment level. They then authorized the further subdivision of allotments into "allowances," but retained responsibility at the allotment level. The "allowances" were intended as a means of meeting operational needs rather than an apportionment control device. GAO advised that this proposed structure conformed to the purposes of 31 U.S.C. § 1514, particularly in light of the 1956 addition of section 1514(b), and that expenditures in excess of an "allowance" would not constitute Antideficiency Act violations.

For further illustration, see 35 Comp. Gen. 356 (1955) (overobligation of allotment stemming from misinterpretation of regulations); B-95136, Aug. 8, 1979 (overobligation of regional allotments would constitutereportable violation unless sufficient unobligated balance existed at central account level to adjust the allotments); B-179849, Dec. 31, 1974 (overobligation of allotment held a violation of section 1517(a) where agency regulations specified that allotment process was the "principal means whereby responsibility is fixed for the conduct of program activities within the funds available"); B-114841.2-0.M., Jan. 23, 1986 (no violation in exceeding allotment subdivisions termed "work plans"); B-242974.6, Nov. 26, 1991 (nondecision memorandum) (under Defense Department regulations, overobligations of administrative subdivisions of funds that are exempt from apportionment do not constitute Antideficiency Act violations.).

5. Penalties and Reporting Requirements:

a. Administrative and Penal Sanctions

Violations of the Antideficiency Act are subject to sanctions of two types, administrative and penal. The Antideficiency Act is the only one of the title 31, United States Code, fiscal statutes to prescribe penalties of both types, a fact which says something about congressional perception of the Act's importance.

An officer or employee who violates 31 U.S.C. § 1341(a) (obligate/expend in excess or advance of appropriation), section 1342 (voluntary services prohibition), or section 1517(a) (obligate/expend in excess of an apportionment or administrative subdivision as specified by regulation) "shall be subject to appropriate administrative discipline including, when circumstances warrant, suspension from duty without pay or removal from office." 31 U.S.C. §§ 1349(a), 1518. For a case in which an official was reduced in grade and reassigned to other duties, see Duggar v. Thomas, 550 F. Supp. 498 (D.D.C. 1982) (upholding the agency's action against a charge of discrimination).

In addition, an officer or employee who "knowingly and willfully" violates any of the three provisions cited above "shall be fined not more than $5,000, imprisoned for not more than 2 years, or both." 31 U.S.C. §§ 1350, 1519. As far as GAO is aware, it appears that no officer or employee has ever been prosecuted, much less convicted, for a violation of the Antideficiency Act as of this writing. The knowing and willful failure to record an overobligation in order to conceal an Antideficiency Act violation is also a criminal offense. See 71 Comp. Gen. 502, 509-10 (1992) (discussing several relevant criminal provisions in title 18, United States Code).

Factors such as the absence of bad faith or the lack of intent to commit a violation are irrelevant for purposes of determining whether a violation has occurred. However, intent is relevant in evaluating the assessment of penalties. Note that the criminal penalties are linked to a determination that the law was "knowingly and willfully" violated, but the administrative sanction provisions do not contain similar language. Thus, intent or state of mind may (and probably should) be taken into consideration when evaluating potential administrative sanctions (whether to assess them and, if so, what type), but must be taken into consideration in determining applicability of the criminal sanctions. Understandably, the provisions for fines and/or jail are intended to be reserved for particularly flagrant violations.

Finally, the administrative and penal sanctions apply only to violations of the three provisions cited-31 U.S.C. §§ 1341(a), 1342, and 1517(a). They do not, for example, apply to violations of 31 U.S.C. § 1512 (requiring that all appropriations be administratively apportioned so as to ensure obligation and expenditure at a controlled rate which will prevent deficiencies from arising before the end of a fiscal year). 36 Comp. Gen. 699 (1957).

b. Reporting Requirements

Once it is determined that there has been a violation of 31 U.S.C. § 1341(a), 1342, or 1517(a), the agency head "shall report immediately to the President and Congress all relevant facts and a statement of actions taken." 31 U.S.C. §§ 1351, 1517(b). Further instructions on preparing the reports may be found in OMB Circular No. A-11, Preparation, Submission, and Execution of the Budget, § 145 (June 21, 2005). The reports are to be signed by the agency head. Id. § 145.7. The report to the President is to be forwarded through the Director of OMB. Id.

In the Consolidated Appropriations Act, 2005, Congress amended the Antideficiency Act to add that the heads of executive branch agencies and the Mayor of the District of Columbia shall also transmit "[a] copy of each report ... to the Comptroller General on the same date the report is transmitted to the President and Congress."

The report is to include all pertinent facts and a statement of all actions taken to address and correct the Antideficiency Act violation (any administrative discipline imposed, referral to the

Justice Department where appropriate, new safeguards imposed, etc.). An agency also should include a request for a supplemental or deficiency appropriation when needed. It is also understood that the agency will do everything it can lawfully do to correct or mitigate the financial effects of the violation. For example, when the Fish and Wildlife Service improperly entered into contracts for legal services, we explained that there were a number of ways the Department of Interior could correct the Service's Antideficiency Act violations if unable to obtain a deficiency appropriation of the budget authority needed to cover amounts the Service paid to these contractors, including ratifying the contracts and covering their costs out of unobligated balances of the applicable fiscal year appropriation, or paying the contractors on a quantum meruit basis out of unobligated balances. B-290005, July 1, 2002. See also B-255831, July 7, 1995; 55 Comp. Gen. 768, 772 (1976); B-223857, Feb. 27, 1987; B-114841.2-O.M., Jan. 23, 1986. In view of the explicit provisions of 31 U.S.C. § 1351, there is no private right of action for declaratory, mandatory, or injunctive relief under the Antideficiency Act. Thurston v. United States, 696 E Supp. 680 (D.D.C. 1988).

Factors such as mistake, inadvertence, lack of intent, or the minor nature of a violation do not affect the duty to report. For example, the Office of Management and Budget (OMB) and the Air Transportation Stabilization Board (ATSB) were required to report an Antideficiency Act violation when OMB erroneously apportioned, and ATSB erroneously obligated, funds to cover the subsidy cost of a loan guarantee prior to the availability of budget authority. B-290600, July 10, 2001. Of course, if the agency feels there are extenuating circumstances, it is entirely appropriate to include them in the report. 35 Comp. Gen. 356 (1955).

What if GAO uncovers a violation but the agency thinks GAO is wrong? The agency must still make the required reports, and must include an explanation of its disagreement. OMB Cir. No. A-11, § 145. See also GAO, Anti-Deficiency Act: Agriculture's Food and Nutrition Service Violates the Anti-Deficiency Act, GAO/AFMD-87-20 (Washington, D.C.: Mar. 17, 1987).

6. Funding Gaps

The term "funding gap" refers to a period of time between the expiration of an appropriation and the enactment of a new one. A funding gap is one of the most difficult fiscal problems a federal agency may have to face. As our discussion here will demonstrate, the case law reflects an attempt to forge a workable solution to a bad situation.

Funding gaps occur most commonly at the end of a fiscal year when new appropriations, or a continuing resolution, have not yet been enacted. In this context, a gap may affect only a few agencies (if, for example, only one appropriation act remains unenacted as of October 1), or the entire federal government. A funding gap may also occur if a particular appropriation becomes exhausted before the end of the fiscal year, in which event it may affect only a single agency or a single program, depending on the scope of the appropriation. In the latter case the lack of funds occurs as a consequence of unforeseen circumstances beyond the agency's control as opposed to the exhaustion of appropriations as a result of poor management.

Funding gaps occur for a variety of reasons. For one thing, the complexity of the budget and appropriations process makes it difficult at best for Congress and the President to get everything done on time. Add to this the enormity of some programs and the need to address budget deficits, and the scope of the problem becomes more apparent. Also, funding gaps are perhaps an inevitable reflection of the political process.

As GAO has pointed out, funding gaps, actual or threatened, are both disruptive and costly. They also produce difficult legal problems under the Antideficiency Act. The basic question, easy to state but not quite as easy to answer, is—what is an agency permitted or required to do when faced with a funding gap? Can it continue with "business as usual," must it lock up and go home, or is there some acceptable middle ground?

In 1980, a congressional subcommittee asked GAO whether agency heads could legally permit employees to come to work when the applicable appropriation for salaries had expired and Congress had not yet enacted either a regular appropriation or a continuing resolution for the next fiscal year. The Comptroller General replied in B-197841, Mar. 3, 1980, that 31 U.S.C. §§ 1341(a) and 1342 were both violated if agency employees reported for work under those circumstances. Permitting the employees to come to work would result in an obligation to pay salary for the time worked, an obligation in advance of appropriations in violation of section 1341(a). With respect to section 1342, no one was suggesting that the employees were offering to work gratuitously, even assuming they could lawfully do so, which for the most part they cannot. The fact that employees were willing to take the risk that the necessary appropriation would eventually be enacted did not avoid the violation. Clearly, the employees still expected to be paid eventually. "During a period of expired appropriations," the Comptroller General stated, "the only way the head of an agency can avoid violating the Antideficiency Act is to suspend the operations of the agency and instruct employees not to report to work until an appropriation is enacted." B-197841, at 3.

Notwithstanding the literal effect of the Antideficiency Act, however, the Comptroller General went on to observe in B-197841, "[W]e do not believe that the Congress intends that federal agencies be closed during periods of expired appropriations." In this regard, the opinion pointed out that at the beginning of fiscal year 1980, GAO had prepared an internal memorandum to address its own operations in the event of a funding gap. The memorandum said, in effect, that employees could continue to come to work, but that operations would have to be severely restricted. No new obligations could be incurred for contracts or small purchases of any kind, and of course the employees could not actually be paid until appropriations were enacted. The opinion further noted that the then chairman of the Senate Appropriations Committee had placed the 1980 GAO memorandum in the Congressional Record, and had described it as providing "common sense guidelines." The opinion also pointed to the fact that when Congress enacted appropriations following a funding gap, it generally made the appropriations retroactive to the beginning of the fiscal year and included language ratifying obligations incurred during the funding gap.

"It thus appears," the opinion concluded, "that the Congress expects that the various agencies of the Government will continue to operate and incur obligations during a period of expired appropriations." Nevertheless, the opinion conceded that this approach would "legally produce widespread violations of the Antideficiency Act." B-197841, at 4. Therefore, the opinion reiterated GAO's support at that time for legislation then pending that would provide permanent statutory authority to continue the pay of federal employees during funding gaps. Id.

Less than two months after GAO issued B-197841, the Attorney General issued his opinion to the President. The Attorney General essentially agreed with GAO's analysis that permitting employees to work during a funding gap would violate the Antideficiency Act, but concluded further that the approach outlined in the GAO internal memorandum went beyond what the Act permitted. 43 Op. Att'y Gen. 224, 4A Op. Off. Legal Counsel 16 (1980). The opinion stated:

"There is nothing in the language of the Antideficiency Act or in its long history from which any exception to its terms during a period of lapsed appropriations may be inferred....

"First of all ..., on a lapse in appropriations, federal agencies may incur no obligations that cannot lawfully be funded from prior appropriations unless such obligations are otherwise authorized by law. There are no exceptions to this rule under current law, even where obligations incurred earlier would avoid greater costs to the agencies should appropriations later be enacted.

"Second, the Department of Justice will take actions to enforce the criminal provisions of the Act in appropriate cases in the future when violations of the Antideficiency Act are alleged. This does not mean that departments and agencies, upon a lapse in appropriations, will be unable logistically to terminate functions in an orderly way.... Authority may be inferred from the Antideficiency Act itself for federal officers to incur those minimal obligations necessary to closing their agencies."

4A Op. Off. Legal Counsel at 19, 20.

This opinion stands for the proposition that agencies had little choice but to lock up and go home. A second opinion, 43 Op. Att'y Gen. 293, 5 Op. Off. Legal Counsel 1 (1981), went into much more detail on possible exceptions and should be read in conjunction with the 1980 opinion.

As set forth in the 1981 Attorney General opinion, the exceptions fall into two broad categories.

The first category is obligations "authorized by law." Within this category, there are four types of exceptions:

- Activities funded with appropriations that do not expire at the end of the fiscal year, that is, multiple year and no-year appropriations.

- Activities authorized by statutes that expressly permit obligations in advance of appropriations, such as contract authority.

- Activities "authorized by necessary implication from the specific terms of duties that have been imposed on, or of authorities that have been invested in, the agency." To take the example given in the opinion, there will be cases where benefit payments under an entitlement program are funded from other than 1-year appropriations (e.g., a trust fund), but the salaries of personnel who administer the program are funded by 1-year money. As long as money for the benefit payments remains available, administration of the program is, by necessary implication, "authorized by law," unless the entitlement legislation or its legislative history provides otherwise or Congress takes affirmative measures to suspend or terminate the program.

- Obligations "necessarily incident to presidential initiatives undertaken within his constitutional powers," for example, the power to grant pardons and reprieves. This same rationale would apply to legislative branch agencies that incur obligations "necessary to assist the Congress in the performance of its constitutional duties." B-241911, Oct. 23, 1990 (nondecision letter).

The second broad category reflected the exceptions authorized under 31 U.S.C. § 1342—emergencies involving the safety of human life or the protection of property. The Attorney General suggested the following rules for interpreting the scope of this exception:

"First, there must be some reasonable and articulable connection between the function to be performed and the safety of human life or the protection of property. Second, there must be some reasonable likelihood that the safety of human life or the protection of property would be compromised, in some degree, by delay in the performance of the function in question."

5 Op. Off. Legal Counsel at 8.

The Attorney General then cited the identical exception language in the deficiency apportionment prohibition of 31 U.S.C. § 1515, and noted that the Office of Management and Budget followed a similar approach in granting deficiency apportionments over the years. Given the wide variations in agency activities, it would not be feasible to attempt an advance listing of functions or activities that might qualify under this exception. Accordingly, the Attorney General made the following recommendation:

"To erect the most solid foundation for the Executive Branch's practice in this regard, I would recommend that, in preparing contingency plans for periods of lapsed appropriations, each government department or agency provide for the Director of the Office of Management and Budget some written description, that could be transmitted to Congress, of what the head of the agency, assisted by its general counsel, considers to be the agency's emergency functions."

5 Op. Off. Legal Counsel at 11.

Lest this approach be taken too far, Congress added the following sentence to 31 U.S.C. § 1342:

"As used in this section, the term 'emergencies involving the safety of human life or the protection of property' does not include ongoing, regular functions of government the suspension of which would not imminently threaten the safety of human life or the protection of property."

Omnibus Budget Reconciliation Act of 1990, Pub. L. No. 101-508, § 13213(b), 104 Stat. 1388, 1388-621 (Nov. 5, 1990).

The conference report on the 1990 legislation explained the intent:

"The conference report also makes conforming changes to title 31 of the United States Code to make clear that... ongoing, regular operations of the Government cannot be sustained in the absence of appropriations, except in limited circumstances. These changes guard against what the conferees believe might be an overly broad interpretation of an opinion of the Attorney General issued on January 16, 1981, regarding the authority for the continuance of Government functions during the temporary lapse of appropriations, and affirm that the constitutional power of the purse resides with Congress."

H.R. Conf. Rep. No. 101-964, at 1170 (1990).

The Ninth Circuit Court of Appeals added to the list of exceptions, holding the suspension of the civil jury trial system for lack of funds unconstitutional. Armster v. United States District Court, 792 F.2d 1423 (9th Cir. 1986). Faced with the potential exhaustion of appropriations for juror fees, the Administrative Office of the United States Courts, at the direction of the Judicial Conference of the United States, had sent a memorandum to all district court judges advising that civil jury trials would have to be suspended until more money was available. Basing its holding on the Constitution and expressly declining to rule on the Antideficiency Act, the court held that a suspension for more than a "most minimal" time violated the seventh amendment. Id. at 1430. See also Hobson v. Brennan, 637 E Supp. 173 (D.D.C. 1986). The court said that "we do not hold that the Anti-Deficiency Act requires the result suggested by the Administrative Office. If it did, its commands would, of course, have to yield to those of the Constitution." Armster, 792 F.2d at 1430 n.13.

Since the appropriation was not yet actually exhausted, and since there was still ample time for Congress to provide additional funds, the court noted that its decision did not amount to ordering Congress to appropriate money. The court noted, but did not address, the far more difficult question of what would happen if the appropriation became exhausted and Congress refused to appropriate additional funds. Armster, 792 F.2d at 1430-31 and 1431 n.14.

This, then, is the basic framework. There are a number of exceptions to the Antideficiency Act which would permit certain activities to continue during a funding gap. For activities not covered by any of the exceptions, however, the agency must proceed with prompt and orderly termination or violate the Act and risk invocation of the criminal sanctions. A very brief restatement may be found in 6 Op. Off. Legal Counsel 555 (1982).

Within this framework, GAO and the Justice Department addressed a number of specific problems agencies encountered in coming to grips with funding gaps during the 1980s and early 1990s. For example, toward the end of fiscal year 1982, the President vetoed a supplemental appropriations bill. As a result, the Defense Department did not have sufficient funds to meet the military payroll. The total payroll obligation consisted of (1) the take-home pay of the individuals, and (2) various items the employing agency was required to withhold and transfer to someone else, such as federal income tax and Social Security contributions. The Treasury Department published a change to its regulations permitting a temporary deferral of the due date for payment of the withheld items, and the Defense Department, relying on the "safety of human life or protection of property" exception, used the funds it had available to pay military personnel their full take-home pay. The Attorney General upheld the legality of this action. 43 Op. Att'y Gen. 369, 6 Op. Off. Legal Counsel 27 (1982). The Comptroller General agreed, but questioned the blanket assumption that all military personnel fit within the exception. B-208985, Oct. 29, 1982; B-208951, Oct. 5, 1982. The extent to which this device might be available to civilian agencies would depend on (1) Treasury's willingness to grant a similar deferral, and (2) the extent to which the agency could legitimately invoke the emergency exception.

Additional cases dealing with funding gap problems are:

- Salaries of commissioners of Copyright Royalty Tribunal attach by virtue of their status as officers without regard to availability of funds. Salary obligation is therefore viewed as "authorized by law" for purposes of Antideficiency Act, and commissioners could be retroactively compensated for periods worked without pay during a funding gap. 61 Comp. Gen. 586 (1982).

- Richmond district office of Internal Revenue Service shut down for half a day in October 1986 due to a funding gap. Subsequent legislation authorized retroactive compensation of employees affected. GAO concluded that the legislation applied to intermittent as well as regular full-time employees, and held that the intermittent employees could be compensated in the form of administrative leave for time lost during the half-day furlough. B-233656, June 19, 1989.

- Witness who had been ordered to appear in federal court was stranded without money to return home when court did not convene due to funding gap. Cash disbursement to permit witness to return home or secure overnight lodging was held permissible since hardship circumstances indicated reasonable likelihood that safety of witness would be jeopardized. 5 Op. Off. Legal Counsel 429 (1981).

There are also a few cases addressing actions an agency has taken to forestall the effects of a funding gap. In 62 Comp. Gen. 1 (1982), the Merit Systems Protection Board, faced with a substantial cut in its appropriation, placed most of its employees on half-time, half-pay status in an attempt to stretch its appropriation through the end of the fiscal year. A subsequent supplemental appropriation provided the necessary operating funds. GAO advised that it was within the Board's discretion, assuming the availability of sufficient funds, to grant retroactive administrative leave to the employees who had been affected by the partial shutdown.

GAO reviewed another furlough plan in 64 Comp. Gen. 728 (1985). The Interstate Commerce Commission had determined that if it continued its normal rate of operations, it would exhaust its appropriation six weeks before the end of the fiscal year. To prevent this from happening, it furloughed its employees for one day per week. GAO found that the Commission's actions were in compliance with the Antideficiency Act. While the ICC was thus able to continue essential services, the price was financial hardship for its employees, plus "serious backlogs, missed deadlines and reduced efficiency." Id. at 732.

During the 1980s and early 1990s, GAO also issued several reports on funding gaps. The first was Funding Gaps Jeopardize Federal Government Operations, PAD-81-31 (Washington, D.C.: Mar. 3, 1981). In that report, GAO noted the costly and disruptive effects of funding gaps, and recommended the enactment of permanent legislation to permit federal agencies to incur obligations, but not disburse funds, during a funding gap. In the second report, Continuing Resolutions and an Assessment of Automatic Funding Approaches, GAO/AFMD-86-16 (Washington, D.C.: Jan. 29, 1986), GAO compared several possible options but this time made no specific recommendation. The Office of Management and Budget had pointed out, and GAO agreed, that automatic funding legislation could have the undesirable effects of (1) reducing pressure on Congress to make timely funding decisions, and (2) permitting major portions of the government to operate for extended periods without action by either House of Congress or the

President. The ideal solution, both agencies agreed, is the timely enactment of the regular appropriation bills.

In Managing the Cost of Government: Proposals for Reforming Federal Budgeting Practices, GAO/AFMD-90-1 (Washington, D.C.: Oct. 1, 1989) at 28-29, GAO reiterated its support for the concept of an automatic continuing resolution in a form that does not reduce the incentive to complete action on the regular appropriation bills. A 1991 GAO report analyzed the impact of a funding gap which occurred over the 1990 Columbus Day weekend and again renewed the recommendation for permanent legislation to, at a minimum, allow agencies to incur obligations to compensate employees during temporary funding gaps but not pay them until enactment of the appropriation. Government Shutdown: Permanent Funding Lapse Legislation Needed, GAO/GGD-91-76 (Washington, D.C.: June 6, 1991). The report stated:

"In our opinion, shutting down the government during temporary funding gaps is an inappropriate way to encourage compromise on the budget. Beyond being counterproductive from a financial standpoint, a shutdown disrupts government services. In addition, forcing agency managers to choose who will and will not be furloughed during these temporary funding lapses severely tests agency management's ability to treat its employees fairly."

Id. at 9.

The history of funding gaps over recent decades reveals several distinct phases, which were captured in an analysis by a Congressional Research Service report to Congress entitled Preventing Federal Government Shutdowns: Proposals for an Automatic Continuing Resolution,No. RL30339 (Washington, D.C.: May 19, 2000) (hereafter "CRS Report"). The first phase, covering fiscal years 1977 through 1980, was a period in which agencies reacted to funding gaps along the lines suggested in GAO's opinion in B-197841, Mar. 3, 1980, described previously, by curtailing operations but not shutting down. During this period, there were 6 funding gaps that lasted from 8 to 17 days. See the CRS Report at 4, Table 1. The second phase, covering fiscal years 1981 through 1995, occurred under the stricter approach to funding gaps reflected in the Attorney General opinions described above. As the CRS Report notes, funding gaps during this period were less frequent and shorter. There were 11 funding gaps in all over this period, many of which took place over weekends. None lasted more than 3 days. Id.

The string of shorter funding gaps came to an abrupt halt in fiscal year 1996. As CRS reported, the unusually difficult and acrimonious budget negotiations for that year led to two funding gaps: the first was 5 days and the second, the longest in history, lasted for 21 days. Id. at 3, 5. Both of these funding gaps resulted in widespread shutdowns of government operations. During the first funding gap, an estimated 800,000 federal employees were furloughed. During the second, about 284,000 employees were furloughed and another 475,000 continued to work in a nonpay status under the emergency exception to the Antideficiency Act.

Not surprisingly, the events of 1995-1996 spawned additional legal opinions from the Office of Legal Counsel. These opinions essentially followed the legal framework described previously and did not break much new ground. However, they do illustrate the scope and application of the Antideficiency Act in different funding gap contexts. See, e.g., Memorandum for the Attorney General, Effect of Appropriations for Other Agencies and Branches on the Authority To Continue Department of Justice Functions During the Lapse in the Department's Appropriations, OLC Opinion, Dec. 13, 1995 (if a suspension of the Justice Department's functions during the period of anticipated funding lapse would prevent or significantly damage the execution of those functions, the Department's functions and activities may continue); Memorandum for the Attorney General, Participation in Congressional Hearings During An Appropriations Lapse, OLC Opinion, Nov. 16, 1995 (Justice Department officials may testify at congressional hearings during a lapse in funding for the Department); Memorandum for the Counsel to the President, Authority To Employ the Services of White House Office Employees During An Appropriations Lapse, OLC Opinion, Sept. 13, 1995 (outlined the authorities that permitted White House employees to continue to work, but not actually be paid, during a funding gap); Memorandum for the Director of the Office of Management and Budget, Government Operations in the Event of a Lapse in Appropriations, OLC Opinion, Aug. 16, 1995 (reinforced the Justice Department's existing narrow interpretation that the emergency exception applied only in the case of an imminent threat or set of circumstances requiring immediate action).

The 1995-1996 funding gaps also produced at least one lawsuit, although it did not reach a final decision on the merits. In American Federation of Government Employees v. Rivlin, Civ. A. No. 95-2115 (EGS) (D.D.C. Nov. 17, 1995), the plaintiffs sought a temporary restraining order to prevent the executive branch from requiring federal employees who had been designated "emergency" personnel to work during the funding gap. They contended that forcing employees to work without pay violated several personnel statutes and also constituted a misapplication of 31 U.S.C. § 1342 since many of the employees did not meet the emergency criteria under section 1342. The court denied the requested relief, observing:

"The court is not convinced at this juncture that plaintiffs will either suffer irreparable harm in the event a temporary restraining order is not issued or that the interests of the public will be best served by the issuance of a temporary restraining order. Plaintiffs essentially concede that if the court were to issue a TRO, the government would indeed be shut down, because the Executive Branch could not require its employees to work without compensation. Although undoubtedly the public has an interest in having the budget impasse resolved and indeed has an interest in the outcome of this judicial proceeding, one could easily imagine the chaos that would be attendant to a complete governmental shutdown. It is inconceivable, by any stretch of the imagination, that the best interests of the public at large would somehow be served by the creation of that chaos."

American Federation of Government Employees, slip. op. at 4.

The court further observed that it was "purely speculative" whether any employees would actually go without pay since Congress had always appropriated funds to compensate employees for services rendered during a government shutdown. Id. The lawsuit was eventually dismissed as moot following resolution of the budget impasse. American Federation of Government Employees v. Rivlin, 995 F. Supp. 165 (D.D.C. 1998).

The current phase in the history of funding gaps commenced on the heels of the 1995-1996 government shutdowns and has featured, thus far, the total absence of funding gaps. While there have been delays in the enactment of regular appropriations, there has been no funding gap since 1996.

Of course, the potential for future funding gaps still exists and proposals for legislation to cushion their impact have been raised again in recent years. However, such proposals have met with little enthusiasm. GAO was more cautionary in its most recent comments on this subject. See GAO, Budget Process: Considerations for Updating the Budget Enforcement Act, GAO-01-991T (Washington, D.C.: July 19, 2001), at 12:

> "The periodic experience of government `shutdowns'—or partial shutdowns when appropriations bills have not been enacted—has led to proposals for an automatic continuing resolution. The automatic continuing resolution, however, is an idea for which the details are critically important. Depending on the detailed structure of such a continuing resolution, the incentive for policymakers—some in the Congress and the President—to negotiate seriously and reach agreement may be lessened."

For example, GAO pointed out that some negotiators might find the "default position" specified in an automatic continuing resolution to be preferable to proposals on the table.

Likewise, several efforts to enact an automatic continuing resolution in recent years have been unsuccessful. In 1997, President Clinton vetoed a supplemental appropriations bill that contained such a provision. In 2000, the House of Representatives rejected such a proposal in a floor vote.

Chapter 8: Continuing Resolutions

A. Introduction

1. Definition and General Description

The term "continuing resolution" may be defined as follows:

> "An appropriation act that provides budget authority for federal agencies, specific activities, or both to continue in operation when Congress and the President have not completed action on the regular appropriation acts by the beginning of the fiscal year."

For the most part, continuing resolutions are temporary appropriation acts. With a few exceptions to be noted later, they are intended by Congress to be stop-gap measures enacted to keep existing federal programs functioning after the expiration of previous budget authority and until regular appropriation acts can be enacted. B-300673, July 3, 2003. Congress resorts to the continuing resolution when there is no regular appropriation for a program or agency, perhaps because the two houses of Congress have not yet agreed on common language, because authorizing legislation has not yet been enacted, or because the President has vetoed an appropriation act passed by Congress. 58 Comp. Gen. 530, 532 (1979). Also, given the size and complexity of today's government, the consequent complexity of the budget and appropriations process, and the occasionally differing policy objectives of the executive and legislative branches, it sometimes becomes difficult for Congress to enact all of the regular appropriation acts before the fiscal year ends.

Continuing resolutions are nothing new GAO has found administrative decisions discussing them as far back as the 1880s. At one time, they were called "temporary resolutions." The term "continuing resolution" came into widespread use in the early 1960s.

In the 20 years from fiscal years 1962 to 1981, 85 percent of the appropriation bills for federal agencies were enacted after the start of the fiscal year and thus necessitated continuing resolutions. GAO has discussed the problems inherent in this situation in several reports. See, e.g., GAO, Updated Information Regarding Funding Gaps and Continuing Resolutions, GAO/PAD-83-13 (Washington, D.C.: Dec. 17, 1982); Funding Gaps Jeopardize Federal Government Operations, PAD-81-31 (Washington, D.C.: Mar. 3, 1981). In 24 of the fiscal years between fiscal years 1977 and 2004, Congress and the President did not complete action on a majority of the 13 regular appropriations by the start of the fiscal year. In eight of those years, they did not finish any of the bills by the start of the new fiscal year. Twenty-one continuing resolutions were enacted for fiscal year 2001.

The periodic experience of government "shutdowns," or partial shutdowns, when appropriations bills have not been enacted has led to proposals for an automatic continuing resolution. The automatic continuing resolution, however, is an idea for which the details are critically important. Depending on the detailed structure of such a continuing resolution, the incentive for policymakers—some in the Congress and the President—to negotiate seriously and reach agreement may be lessened. If the goal of the automatic continuing resolution is to provide a little more time for resolving issues, it could be designed to permit the incurrence of obligations to avoid a funding gap, but not the outlay of funds to liquidate the new obligations. This would allow agencies to continue operations for a period while the Congress completes appropriations actions. GAO, Budget Process: Considerations for Updating the Budget Enforcement Act, GAO-01-991T (July 19, 2001).

Continuing resolutions are enacted as joint resolutions making continuing appropriations for a certain fiscal year or portion of the fiscal year. Although enacted in this form rather than as an "act," once passed by both houses of Congress and approved by the President, a continuing resolution becomes a public law and has the same force and effect as any other statute. Oklahoma v. Weinberger, 360 F. Supp. 724, 726 (WD. Okla. 1973); B-152554, Dec. 15, 1970. Since a continuing resolution is a form of appropriation act, it often will include the same types of restrictions and conditions that are commonly found in regular appropriation acts. See, e.g., B-210603, Feb. 25, 1983 (ship construction appropriation in continuing resolution making funds available "only under a firm, fixed price type contract"). Indeed, continuing resolutions typically incorporate by reference restrictions and conditions from regular appropriations acts. See, e.g., Pub. L. No. 108-309, § 102, 118 Stat. 1137, 1138 (Sept. 30, 2004). Having said this, however, it is necessary to note that continuing resolutions, at least those in what GAO considers the "traditional form," differ considerably from regular appropriation acts.

Continuing resolutions may take different forms. The "traditional" form, used consistently except for a few years in the 1980s, employs essentially standard language and is clearly a temporary measure. An example of this form is Public Law 108-309, the first continuing resolution for fiscal year 2005, which provided funding authority from October 1 through November 20, 2004. Section 101 appropriates:

> "Such amounts as may be necessary under the authority and conditions provided in the applicable appropriations Act for fiscal year 2004 for continuing projects or activities including the costs of direct loans and loan guarantees (not otherwise specifically provided for in this joint resolution) which were conducted in fiscal year 2004, at a rate for operations not exceeding the current rate, and for which appropriations, funds, or other authority was made available in the following appropriations Acts ..."

Section 101 then references most of the regular appropriation acts for fiscal year 2004.

Public Law 108-309 also contains a number of additional typical provisions, including the following:

"SEC. 102. Appropriations made by section 101 shall be available to the extent and in the manner which would be provided by the pertinent appropriations Act."

"SEC. 104. No appropriation or funds made available or authority granted pursuant to section 101 shall be used to initiate or resume any project or activity for which appropriations, funds, or other authority were not available during fiscal year 2004."

"SEC. 107. Unless otherwise provided for in this joint resolution or in the applicable appropriations Act, appropriations and funds made available and authority granted pursuant to this joint resolution shall be available until (a) enactment into law of an appropriation for any project or activity provided for in this joint resolution, or (b) the enactment into law of the applicable appropriations Act by both Houses without any provision for such project or activity, or (c) November 20, 2004, whichever first occurs."

When enacting continuing resolutions in this form, there is clear indication that Congress intends and expects that the normal authorization and appropriation process will eventually produce appropriation acts which will replace or terminate the budget authority contained in the resolution. Thus, a continuing resolution of this type generally provides that funds appropriated for an activity by the resolution will no longer be available for obligation if the activity is later funded by a regular appropriation act, or Congress indicates its intent to end the activity by enacting an applicable appropriation act without providing for the activity. 58 Comp. Gen. at 532. See also section 107 of Public Law 108-309, quoted above. Obligations already incurred under the resolution, however, may be liquidated.

GAO's decision in B-300673, July 3, 2003, illustrates the interplay between funding under a continuing resolution and a later-enacted regular appropriation. The fiscal year 2003 appropriation act for the legislative branch authorized the House of Representatives Chief Administrative Officer to use that Office's salaries and expenses appropriation to pay certain expenses of the House Child Care Center for "fiscal year 2003 and each succeeding fiscal year." Pub. L. No. 108-7, § 108, 117 Stat. 11, 355 (Feb. 20, 2003). Previously, a revolving fund paid those expenses. However, since Public Law 108-7 was not enacted until February 20, 2003, fiscal year 2003 expenses for the Child Care Center were initially charged to the revolving fund under continuing resolutions. With enactment of Public Law 108-7, GAO held that the Chief Administrative Officer's salaries and expenses appropriation should fund the Child Care Center expenses retroactive to the beginning of fiscal year 2003 and that this appropriation should reimburse the revolving fund for the fiscal year 2003 expenses initially charged to it under the continuing resolutions. The decision stated that the fact that payments were initially made during a period covered by a continuing resolution was not significant since the regular appropriation, once enacted, supersedes the continuing resolution and governs the amount and period of availability.

Unlike regular appropriation acts, continuing resolutions in their traditional form do not usually appropriate specified sums of money. Rather, they usually appropriate "such amounts as may be necessary" for continuing projects or activities at a certain "rate for operations." The rate for operations may be the amount provided for the activity in an appropriation act that has passed both houses of Congress but has not become law; the lower of the amounts provided when each house has passed a different act; the lower of the amounts provided either in an act which has passed only one house or in the administration's budget estimate; the amount specified in a particular conference report; the lower of either the amount provided in the budget estimate or the "current rate"; or simply the current rate. Therefore, in order to determine the sum of money appropriated for any given activity by this type of continuing resolution, it is necessary to examine documents other than the resolution itself. Some continuing resolutions have used a combination of "formula appropriations" of the types described in this paragraph and appropriations of specific dollar amounts. An example is the fiscal year 1996 continuing resolution, Pub. L. No. 104-69, 109 Stat. 767 (Dec. 22, 1995).

There are times when Congress acknowledges at the outset that it is not likely to enact one or more regular appropriation acts during the current fiscal year. See, for example, the 1980 continuing resolution, Pub. L. No. 96-86, 93 Stat. 656 (Oct. 12, 1979), which provided budget authority for the legislative branch for the entire fiscal year.

For a few years in the 1980s, Congress used a very different form of continuing resolution, simply stringing together the complete texts of appropriation bills not yet enacted and enacting them together in a single "omnibus" package. This approach reached its extreme in the 1988 continuing resolution, Pub. L. No. 100-202, 101 Stat. 1329 (Dec. 22, 1987), which included the complete texts of all 13 of the regular appropriation bills. This form of continuing resolution differs from the traditional form in two key respects:

- Unlike the traditional continuing resolution, the "full text" version amounts to an acknowledgment that no further action on the unenacted bills will be forthcoming, and consequently provides funding for the remainder of the fiscal year.

- When the entire text of an appropriation bill is incorporated into a continuing resolution, the appropriations are in the form of specified dollar amounts, the same as if the individual bill had been enacted.

The "full text" format generally does not raise the same issues of statutory interpretation that arise under the traditional format. However, it produces new ones. For example, in a continuing resolution which consolidates the full texts of what would otherwise have been several separate appropriation acts, GAO has construed the term "this act" as referring only to the individual "appropriation act" in which it appears rather than to the entire continuing resolution. B-230110, Apr. 11, 1988.

While the omnibus approach of the 1988 resolution may appear convenient, it generated considerable controversy because, among other reasons, it is virtually "veto-proof—the President has little choice but to sign the bill or bring the entire government to an abrupt halt. See Presidential Remarks on the Signing of the Continuing Appropriations for Fiscal Year 1988 and the Omnibus Budget Reconciliation Act of 1987 Into Law, 23 Weekly Comp. Pres. Doc. 1546, 1547 (Dec. 22, 1987).

There was no continuing resolution for fiscal year 1989. All 13 of the appropriation bills were enacted on time, for what was reported to be the first time in 12 years. For fiscal year 1990, Congress reverted to the traditional type of continuing resolution. See Pub. L. No. 101-100, 103 Stat. 638 (Sept. 29, 1989). Nor were there any continuing resolutions for fiscal years 1995 and 1997. The start of the 1997 fiscal year was met with an omnibus appropriations act which added five regular appropriations bills to a sixth regular appropriations bill. Pub. L. No. 104-208, 110 Stat. 3009 (Sept. 30, 1996). The remaining seven bills were enacted separately.

Questions arising under continuing resolutions can be grouped loosely into two broad categories. First are questions in which the fact that a continuing resolution is involved is purely incidental, in other words, questions which could have arisen just as easily under a regular appropriation act. For example, one of the issues considered in B-230110, Apr. 11, 1988, was whether certain provisions in the 1988 resolution constituted permanent legislation. Cases in this category are included with their respective topics throughout this workbook.

Second are issues that are unique to continuing resolutions. For the most part, the material deals with the traditional form of continuing resolution as it is this form that uses concepts and language found only in continuing resolutions.

One point that should emerge from the GAO decisions and opinions is the central role of legislative intent. To be sure, legislative intent cannot change the plain meaning of a statute; Congress must enact what it intends in order to make it law. However, there are many cases in which the statutory language alone does not provide a clear answer, and indications of congressional intent expressed in well-established methods, viewed in light of the purpose of the continuing resolution, will tip the balance.

In one case, for example, a continuing resolution provided a lump-sum appropriation for the National Oceanic and Atmospheric Administration's research and facilities account, and provided further for the transfer of $1.8 million from the Fisheries Loan Fund. The first continuing resolution for 1987 included the transfer provision and was signed into law on October 1, 1986. The Fisheries Loan Fund was scheduled to expire at "the close of September

30, 1986." Under a strictly technical reading, the $1.8 million ceased to be available once the clock struck midnight on September 30. However, the Comptroller General found the transfer provision effective, noting that a contrary result would "frustrate the obvious intent of Congress." B-227658, Aug. 7, 1987.

Similarly, appropriations for the United States Commission on Civil Rights contained in a fiscal year 1992 continuing resolution were found to have extended the existence of the Commission beyond its termination on September 30, 1991. "When viewed in their entirety, legislative actions on the Commission's reauthorization and appropriation bills, together with their legislative history, clearly manifest an intent by Congress for the Commission to continue to operate after September 30, 1991." 71 Comp. Gen. 378, 381 (1992).

While many of the continuing resolution provisions to be discussed will appear highly technical (because they are highly technical), there is an essential logic to them, evolved over many years, which is more readily seen from the perspective not of a specific case or problem, but of the overall goals and objectives of continuing resolutions and their relationship to the rest of the budget and appropriations process.

2. Use of Appropriation Warrants

Funds, including funds appropriated under a continuing resolution, are drawn from the Treasury by means of an appropriation warrant (FMS Form 6200). A warrant is the official document issued pursuant to law by the Secretary of the Treasury upon enactment of an appropriation that establishes the amount of money authorized to be withdrawn from the Treasury. Under 31 U.S.C. § 3323(a), warrants authorized by law are to be signed by the Secretary of the Treasury and countersigned by the Comptroller General. However, under the authority of section 3326(a) of title 31, United States Code, the Secretary of the Treasury and the Comptroller General have issued several joint regulations phasing out the countersignature requirement. First, Department of the Treasury-General Accounting Office Joint Regulation No. 5 (Oct. 18, 1974) waived the requirement for all appropriations except continuing resolutions. Next, Treasury-GAO Joint Regulation No. 6 (Oct. 1, 1983) further simplified the process by requiring issuance of a warrant and countersignature under a continuing resolution only once, for the total amount appropriated, unless a subsequent resolution changed the annual amount. Finally, Treasury-GAO Joint Regulation No. 7, effective January 1, 1991, eliminated the countersignature requirement completely.

B. Rate for Operations

1. Current Rate:

The current rate, as that term is used in continuing resolutions, is equivalent to the total amount of money which was available for obligation for an activity during the fiscal year immediately prior to the one for which the continuing resolution is enacted.

The term "current rate" is used in continuing resolutions to indicate the level of spending which Congress desires for a program. For example, a resolution may appropriate sufficient funds to enable a program to operate at a rate for operations "not in excess of the current rate," or at a rate "not in excess of the lower of the current rate" or the rate provided in a certain bill. It is possible to read the term "current rate" as referring to either the amount of money available for the program in the preceding year, or an amount of money sufficient to enable continuation of the program at the level of the preceding year. The two can be very different.

As a general proposition, GAO regards the term "current rate" as referring to a sum of money rather than a program level. See, e.g., 58 Comp. Gen. 530, 533 (1979); B-194362, May 1, 1979. Thus, when a continuing resolution appropriates in terms of the current rate, the amount of money available under the resolution will be limited by that rate, even though an increase in the minimum wage may force a reduction in the number of people participating in an employment program (B-194063, May 4, 1979), or an increase in the mandatory level of assistance will reduce the number of meals provided under a meals for the elderly program (B-194362, May 1, 1979).

The term "current rate" refers to the rate of operations carried on within the appropriation for the prior fiscal year. B-152554, Dec. 6, 1963. The current rate is equivalent to the total appropriation, or the total funds which were available for obligation, for an activity during the previous fiscal year. Edwards v. Bowen, 785 F.2d 1440 (9th Cir. 1986); B-300167, Nov. 15, 2002; B-255529, Jan. 10, 1994; 64 Comp. Gen. 21 (1984); 58 Comp. Gen. 530, 533 (1979); B-194063, May 4, 1979; B-194362, May 1, 1979. Funds administratively transferred from the account during the fiscal year, under authority contained in substantive legislation, should not be deducted in determining the current rate. B-197881, Apr. 8, 1980; B-152554, Nov. 4, 1974. It follows that funds transferred into the account during the fiscal year pursuant to statutory authority should be excluded. B-197881, Apr. 8, 1980.

In those instances in which the program in question has been funded by 1-year appropriations in prior years, the current rate is equal to the total funds appropriated for the program for the previous fiscal year. See, e.g., B-271304, Mar. 19, 1996; 64 Comp. Gen. at 22; 58 Comp. Gen. 530; B-194362, May 1, 1979. In those instances in which the program has been funded by multiple year or no-year appropriations in prior years, the current rate is equal to the total funds appropriated for the previous fiscal year plus the total of unobligated budget authority carried over into that year from prior years. 58 Comp. Gen. 530; B-152554, Oct. 9, 1970.

One apparent deviation from this calculation of current rate occurred in 58 Comp. Gen. 530, a case involving the now obsolete Comprehensive Employment and Training Act program. In that decision, the Comptroller General, in calculating the current rate under the 1979 continuing resolution, included funds appropriated in a 1977 appropriation act and obligated during 1977. Ordinarily, only funds appropriated by the fiscal year 1978 appropriation act, and carry-over funds unobligated at the beginning of fiscal year 1979, would have been included in the current rate. However, Congress did not appropriate funds for this activity in the fiscal year 1978 appropriation act. In this instance the funds appropriated in 1977 were included because it was clear from the legislative history of the appropriation act that Congress intended these funds to be an advance of appropriations for fiscal year 1978. Thus, in order to ascertain the actual amount available for the activity for fiscal year 1978, it was necessary to include the advance funding provided by the 1977 appropriation act. The rationale used in this decision would apply only when it is clear that Congress was providing advance funding for the reference fiscal year in an earlier year's appropriation act.

Where funding for the preceding fiscal year covered only a part of that year, it may be appropriate to "annualize" the previous year's appropriation in order to determine the current rate. This was the result in 61 Comp. Gen. 473 (1982), in which the fiscal year 1981 appropriation for a particular program had been contained in a supplemental appropriation act and was intended to cover only the last quarter of the fiscal year. The current rate for purposes of the fiscal year 1982 continuing resolution was four times the fiscal year 1981 figure.

Prior year supplemental appropriations also count in calculating the current rate. In this regard, section 103 of Public Law 108-309, 118 Stat. 1137, 1138 (Sept. 30, 2004), discussed above, provides:

"The appropriations Acts listed in section 101 shall be deemed to include miscellaneous and supplemental appropriation laws enacted during fiscal year 2004."

There are exceptions to the rule that current rate means a sum of money rather than a program level. For example, GAO construed the fiscal year 1980 continuing resolution as appropriating sufficient funds to support an increased number of Indochinese refugees in view of explicit statements by both the Appropriations and the Budget Committees that the resolution was intended to fund the higher program level. B-197636, Feb. 25, 1980. Also, the legislative history of the fiscal year 1981 continuing resolution (Pub. L. No. 96-369, 94 Stat. 1351 (Oct. 1, 1980)) indicated that in some instances current rate must be interpreted so as to avoid reducing existing program levels.

It is always preferable for the exception to be specified in the resolution itself. Starting with the first continuing resolution for fiscal year 1983 (Pub. L. No. 97-276, 96 Stat. 1186 (Oct. 2, 1982)), Congress began appropriating for the continuation of certain programs "at a rate to maintain current operating levels." GAO has construed this language as meaning sufficient funds to maintain the program in question at the same operating level as at the end of the immediately preceding fiscal year. B-209676, Apr. 14, 1983; B-200923, Nov. 16, 1982 (nondecision letter). Recent continuing resolutions have included similar language for entitlement and other mandatory payments: "activities shall be continued at the rate to maintain program levels under current law."

2. Rate Not Exceeding Current Rate

When a resolution appropriates funds to continue an activity at a rate for operations "not in excess of the current rate," the amount of funds appropriated by the resolution is equal to the current rate less any unobligated balance carried over into the present year.

As discussed in the preceding section, the current rate is equivalent to the total amount of funds that was available for obligation for a project or activity in the preceding fiscal year. When the continuing resolution appropriates funds to continue an activity at a rate for operations "not in excess of the current rate," it is the intent of Congress that the activity have available for obligation in the present fiscal year no more funds than it had available for obligation in the preceding fiscal year. Therefore, if there is a balance of unobligated funds which can be carried over into the present fiscal year because the funds are multiple year or no-year funds, this balance must be deducted from the current rate in determining the amount of funds appropriated by the continuing resolution. If this were not done, the program would be funded at a higher level in the present year than it was in the preceding year, which is not permitted by the language of the resolution. See 58 Comp. Gen. 530, 535 (1979).

For example, suppose a continuing resolution for fiscal year 2006 were to appropriate sufficient funds to continue an activity at a rate not exceeding the current rate, and the current rate, or the total amount which was available for obligation in fiscal year 2005, is $1,000,000. Of this amount, suppose $100,000 of multiple year funds remains unobligated at the end of fiscal year 2005, and is available for obligation in fiscal year 2006. If the activity is to operate at a rate not to exceed the current rate, $1,000,000, then the resolution appropriates no more than the difference between the current rate and the carryover from 2005 to 2006, or $900,000. If the resolution were interpreted as appropriating the full current rate, then a total of $1,100,000 would be available for fiscal year 2006, and the activity would be able to operate at a rate in excess of the current rate, a result prohibited by the language of the resolution.

An unobligated balance which does not carry over into the present fiscal year (the more common situation) does not have to be deducted. B-152554, Nov. 4, 1974.

A commonly encountered form of continuing resolution formula appropriation is an amount not in excess of the current rate or the rate provided in some reference item, whichever is lower. The reference item may be an unenacted bill, a conference report, the President's budget estimate, etc. When the current rate produces the lower figure—the situation encountered in 58 Comp. Gen. 530—the above rule applies and an unobligated carryover balance must be deducted to determine the amount appropriated by the continuing resolution. However, when the current rate is not the lower of the two referenced items, the rule does not necessarily apply.

To illustrate, a continuing resolution appropriated funds for the Office of Refugee Resettlement at a rate for operations not in excess of the lower of the current rate or the rate authorized by a bill as passed by the House of Representatives. The rate under the House- passed bill was $50 million. The current rate was $77.5 million, of which $39 million remained unobligated at the end of the preceding fiscal year and was authorized to be carried over into the current fiscal year. If the continuing resolution had simply specified a rate not in excess of the current rate, or if the rate in the House-passed bill had been greater than the current rate, it would have been necessary to deduct the $39 million carryover balance from the $77.5 million current rate to determine the maximum funding level for the current year. Here, however, the rate in the House-passed bill was the lower of the two.

Reasoning that the current rate already includes an unobligated carryover balance, if any, whereas the rate in the House-passed bill did not include a prior year's balance, and supported by the legislative history of the continuing resolution, the Comptroller General concluded that the amount available for the current year was the amount appropriated by the resolution, $50 million, plus the unobligated carryover balance of $39 million, for a total of $89 million. 64 Comp. Gen. 649 (1985). The decision distinguished 58 Comp. Gen. 530, stating that "the rule with respect to deduction of unobligated balances in 58 Comp. Gen. 530 is not applicable where the lower of two referenced rates is not the current rate." Id. at 652-53. The case went to court, and the Ninth Circuit Court of Appeals reached the same result. Edwards v. Bowen, 785 F.2d 1440 (9th Cir. 1986).

In sum, if a continuing resolution appropriates the lower of the current rate or the rate in some reference item, you compare the two numbers to determine which is lower before taking any unobligated carryover balance into account. If the current rate is lower, you then deduct the carryover balance to determine the funding level under the continuing resolution. If the rate in the reference item is lower, the funding level is the reference rate plus the carryover balance unless it is clear that this is not what was intended.

3. Spending Pattern under Continuing Resolution

a. Pattern of Obligations

An agency may determine the pattern of its obligations under a continuing resolution so long as it operates under a plan which will keep it within the rate for operations limit set by the resolution. If an agency usually obligates most of its annual budget in the first month or first quarter of the fiscal year, it may continue that pattern under the resolution. If an agency usually obligates funds uniformly over the entire year, it will be limited to that pattern under the resolution, unless it presents convincing reasons why its pattern must be changed in the current fiscal year.

Continuing resolutions are often enacted to cover a limited period of time, such as a month or a calendar quarter. The time limit stated in the resolution is the maximum period of time during which funds appropriated by the resolution are available for obligation.

However, this limited period of availability does not affect the amount of money appropriated by the resolution. The rate for operations specified in the resolution, whether in terms of an appropriation act which has not yet become law, a budget estimate, or the current rate, is an annual amount. The continuing resolution, in general, regardless of its period of duration, appropriates this full annual amount. See B-271304, Mar. 19, 1996; B-152554, Nov. 4, 1974.

Because the appropriation under a continuing resolution is the full annual amount, an agency may generally follow any pattern of obligating funds, so long as it is operating under a plan which will enable continuation of activities throughout the fiscal year within the limits of the annual amount appropriated. Thus, under a resolution with a duration of one month, and which appropriates funds at a rate for operations not in excess of the current rate, the agency is not necessarily limited to incurring obligations at the same rate it incurred them in the corresponding month of the preceding year if the agency can establish that it is operating under a flexible plan that would enable continuation of activities throughout the fiscal year. B-152554, Dec. 6, 1963. The same principle applies when the resolution appropriates funds at a rate to maintain current operating levels. B-209676, Apr. 14, 1983.

However, the pattern of obligations in prior years does provide a framework for determining the proper pattern of obligations under the continuing resolution. For example, if the activity is a formula grant program in which nearly all appropriated funds are normally obligated at the beginning of the fiscal year, then the full annual amount should be made available to the agency under the resolution, even though the resolution may be in effect for only 1 month. However, if the activity is salaries and expenses, in which funds are normally obligated uniformly throughout the year, then the amount made available to the agency should be only one-twelfth of the annual amount under a 1-month resolution or one-fourth of the annual amount under a calendar quarter resolution. B-152554, Feb. 17, 1972.

For example, GAO determined that OMB properly apportioned, and the State Department properly obligated, 75 percent of funds appropriated by a fiscal year 1994 continuing resolution (Pub. L. No. 103-88, 107 Stat. 977 (Sept. 30, 1993)) for payments to the United Nations. It was State Department policy to defer payment of the United States' general assessment of United Nations contributions to the fourth quarter of the calendar year, which is the first quarter of the fiscal year. As a matter of normal practice, the State Department also made peacekeeping payments when bills were received to the extent funds were available. We found that the advance apportionment and obligation for the United Nations assessment and peacekeeping payments with funds appropriated by the fiscal year 1994 continuing resolution did not violate either the continuing resolution or the provisions of title 31, United States Code, controlling apportionment of funds. B-255529, Jan. 10, 1994.

Congress can, of course, alter the pattern of obligations by the language of the resolution. For example, if the resolution limits obligations in any calendar quarter to one-fourth of the annual rate, the agency is limited to that one-fourth rate regardless of its normal pattern of obligations. B-152554, Oct. 16, 1973. Further, even if the resolution itself does not have such limitations, but the legislative history clearly shows the intent of Congress that only one-fourth of the annual rate be obligated each calendar quarter, only this amount should be made available unless the agency can demonstrate a real need to exceed that rate. B-152554, Nov. 4, 1974.

Beginning with fiscal year 1996, Congress to date has included the following two provisions in continuing resolutions:

> "... for those programs that had high initial rates of operation or complete distribution of funding at the beginning of the fiscal year in fiscal year [1995] because of distributions of funding to States, foreign countries, grantees, or others, similar distributions of funds for fiscal year [1996] shall not be made and no grants shall be awarded for such programs funded by this resolution that would impinge on final funding prerogatives."

> "This joint resolution shall be implemented so that only the most limited funding action of that permitted in the resolution shall be taken in order to provide for continuation of projects and activities."

Pub. L. No. 104-31, §§ 113, 114, 109 Stat. 278, 281 (Sept. 30, 1995).

GAO considered these provisions in B-300167, Nov. 15, 2002. That decision involved the Federal Highway Administration's (FHWA) distribution of federal aid to highways funds to the states under a continuing resolution for fiscal year 2003, Pub. L. No. 107-229, 116 Stat. 1465 (Sept. 30, 2002).

FHWA had determined its distributions to the states at 4/365ths of the current rate of $31.8 billion since that was the previous fiscal year's obligation limitation under the 2002 Department of Transportation appropriations act referenced by the continuing resolution. FHWA's consistent

Federal Appropriations Law

historical practice was to allocate funds to the states on a pro-rata basis by multiplying the percentage of the year covered by the continuing resolution by the rate for the continuing resolution (at the time the anticipated length of the continuing resolution was 4 days, hence FHWA's 4/365ths distribution).

OMB, however, apportioned a total amount of $27.7 billion to FHWA during the term of the continuing resolution to refrain from "impinging on final funding prerogatives" per the first provision quoted above, thereby reducing the amount FHWA had available for allocation to the states from 4/365ths of $31.8 billion to 4/365ths of $27.7 billion. OMB reasoned that because the program traditionally makes available all of the budgetary resources subject to limitation for allocation to the states at the beginning of the fiscal year, had OMB apportioned the full amount of the fiscal year 2002 level, then any subsequent effort by Congress to enact an obligation limitation of less than $31.8 billion could have been compromised.

GAO found that OMB had no basis to further reduce the level of highway spending below the current rate established in fiscal year 2002. Based on the plain language of the first provision above, it only applies to programs that (1) had "high initial rates of operation or a complete distribution" of funds at the beginning of the prior fiscal year (assuming the normal appropriations process), and where (2) a "similar distribution of funds" under the continuing resolution would impinge on Congress's final funding prerogatives. In other words, the provision can only be applied to reduce or limit the distribution of the current rate for a program (as defined in the continuing resolution) if both prongs of the two-part test are met. Since FHWA's long-standing practice of distributing highway funds under a continuing resolution on a pro-rata basis fully protects congressional funding prerogatives, and does so in a manner that is consistent with the second provision (and is far more restrictive than would be true under the first provision), GAO concluded that OMB was not justified under the two provisions to set the level of highway spending at $27.7 billion.

Congress subsequently resolved the dispute between OMB and FHWA by including a specific provision in its second amendment to the continuing resolution establishing an annual rate of operations of $31.8 billion for FHWA provided that total obligations for the program not exceed $27.7 billion while operating under the resolution, Pub. L. No. 107-240, § 137, 116 Stat. 1492, 1495 (Oct. 11, 2002).

b. Apportionment

The requirement that appropriations be apportioned by the Office of Management and Budget, imposed by the Antideficiency Act, applies to funds appropriated by continuing resolution as well as regular appropriations. See generally OMB Circular No. A-11, Preparation, Submission, and Execution of the Budget, pt. 4, § 120.1 (June 21, 2005).

Typically, OMB has permitted some continuing resolution funds to be apportioned automatically. OMB Cir. No. A-11, § 123.5. For example, if a given continuing resolution covers 10 percent of a fiscal year, OMB may permit 10 percent of the appropriation to be apportioned automatically, meaning that the agency can obligate this amount without seeking a specific apportionment. Under such an arrangement, if program requirements produced a need for additional funds, the agency would have to seek an apportionment from OMB for the larger amount.

Apportionment requirements may vary from year to year because of differences in duration and other aspects of applicable continuing resolutions. A device OMB has commonly used to announce its apportionment requirements for a given fiscal year is an OMB Bulletin reflecting the particular continuing resolution for that year.

4. Liquidation of Contract Authority

When in the preceding fiscal year Congress has provided an agency with contract authority, the continuing resolution must be interpreted as appropriating sufficient funds to liquidate that authority to the extent it becomes due during the period covered by the continuing resolution.

When an activity operates on the basis that in one year Congress provides contract authority to the agency and in the next year appropriates funds to liquidate that authority, then a continuing resolution in the second year must be interpreted as appropriating sufficient funds to liquidate the outstanding contract authority. The term "contract authority" means express statutory authority to incur contractual obligations in advance of appropriations. Thus, there is no "rate for operations" limitation in connection with the liquidation of due debts based on validly executed contracts entered into under statutory contract authority. In this context, rate for operations limitations apply only to new contract authority for the current fiscal year. B-114833, Nov. 12, 1974.

5. Rate for Operations Exceeds Final Appropriation

If an agency operating under a continuing resolution incurs obligations within the rate for operations limit, but Congress subsequently appropriates a total annual amount less than the amount of these obligations, the obligations remain valid. B-152554, Feb. 17, 1972.

For example, a continuing resolution for a period of 1 month may have a rate for operations limitation of the current rate. The activity being funded is a grant program and the agency obligates the full annual amount during the period of the resolution. Congress then enacts a regular appropriation act which appropriates for the activity an amount less than the obligations already incurred by the agency. Under these circumstances, the obligations incurred by the agency remain valid obligations of the United States.

Having established that the "excess" obligations remain valid, the next question is how they are to be paid. At one time, GAO took the position that an agency finding itself in this situation must not incur any further obligations and must attempt to negotiate its obligations downward to come within the amount of the final appropriation. B-152554, Feb. 17, 1972. If this is not possible, the agency would have to seek a supplemental or deficiency appropriation. This position was based on a provision commonly appearing in continuing resolutions along the following lines:

"Expenditures made pursuant to this joint resolution shall be charged to the applicable appropriation, fund, or authorization whenever a bill in which such applicable appropriation, fund, or authorization is contained is enacted into law."

However, the 1972 opinion failed to take into consideration another provision commonly included in continuing resolutions:

"Appropriations made and authority granted pursuant to this joint resolution shall cover all obligations or expenditures incurred for any program, project, or activity during the period for which funds or authority for such project or activity are available under this joint resolution."

When these two provisions are considered together, it becomes apparent that the purpose of the first provision is merely to emphasize that the funds appropriated by the continuing resolution are not in addition to the funds later provided when the applicable regular appropriation act is enacted. Accordingly, GAO modified the 1972 opinion and held that funds made available by a continuing resolution remain available to pay validly incurred obligations which exceed the amount of the final appropriation. 62 Comp. Gen. 9 (1982). See also 67 Comp. Gen. 474 (1988); B-207281, Oct. 19, 1982.

Thus, obligations under a continuing resolution are treated as follows

"When an annual appropriation act provides sufficient funding for an appropriation account to cover obligations previously incurred under the authority of a continuing resolution, any unpaid obligations are to be charged to and paid from the applicable account established under the annual appropriation act. Similarly, to the extent the annual act provides sufficient funding, those obligations which were incurred and paid during the period of the continuing resolution must be charged to the account created by the annual appropriation act. On the other hand, to the extent the annual appropriation act does not provide sufficient funding for the appropriation account to cover obligations validly incurred under a continuing resolution, the obligations in excess of the amount provided by the annual act should be charged to and paid from the appropriation account established under authority of the continuing resolution. Thus the funds made available by the resolution must remain available to pay these obligations."

62 Comp. Gen. 9, 11-12 (1982). Thus, as GAO had advised in 1972, agencies are still required to make their best efforts to remain within the amount of the final appropriation. The change recognized in 62 Comp. Gen. 9 is that, to the extent an agency is unable to do so, the

appropriation made by the continuing resolution remains available to liquidate the "excess" obligations.

C. Projects or Activities

"Projects or activities" as used in continuing resolutions may have two meanings. When determining which government programs are covered by the resolution, and the rate for operations limit, the term "project or activity" refers to the total appropriation rather than to specific activities. When determining whether an activity was authorized or carried out in the preceding year, the term "project or activity" may refer to the specific activity. The following paragraphs will elaborate.

The term "projects or activities" is sometimes used in continuing resolutions to indicate which government programs are to be funded and at what rate. Thus a resolution might appropriate sufficient funds to continue "projects or activities provided for" in a certain appropriation bill "to the extent and in the manner" provided in the bill or as provided for in prior year appropriation acts. See, e.g., Pub. L. No. 108-309, §§ 101, 102, 118 Stat. 1137-38 (Sept. 30, 2004).

Occasionally Congress will use only the term "activities" by appropriating sufficient funds "for continuing the following activities, but at a rate for operations not in excess of the current rate." See, e.g., Pub. L. No. 97-51, § 101(d), 95 Stat. 958, 961 (Oct. 1, 1981). When used in this context, "projects or activities" or simply "activities" does not refer to specific items contained as activities in the administration's budget submission or in a committee report. Rather, the term refers to the appropriation for the preceding fiscal year. B-204449, Nov. 18, 1981. Thus, if a resolution appropriates funds to continue projects or activities under a certain appropriation at a rate for operations not exceeding the current rate, the agency is operating within the limits of the resolution so long as the total of obligations under the appropriation does not exceed the current rate. Within the appropriation, an agency may fund a particular activity at a higher rate than that activity was funded in the previous year and still not violate the current rate limitation, assuming of course that the resolution itself does not provide to the contrary.

An exception to the interpretation that projects or activities refers to the appropriation in existence in the preceding fiscal year occurred in 58 Comp. Gen. 530 (1979). In prior years, Comprehensive Employment and Training Act (CETA) programs had been funded in two separate appropriations, Employment and Training Assistance and Temporary Employment Assistance. The individual programs under the two appropriations differed only in that the number of jobs provided under Temporary Employment Assistance depended on the condition of the national economy.

Concurrently with the enactment of the 1979 continuing resolution, Congress amended the CETA authorizing legislation so that certain programs previously operating under the Temporary Employment Assistance appropriation were to operate in fiscal year 1980 under the Employment and Training Assistance appropriation. Under these circumstances, if the phrase "activities under the Comprehensive Employment and Training Act" in the continuing resolution had been interpreted as referring to the two separate appropriations made in the preceding year, and the current rates calculated accordingly, there would have been insufficient funds available for the now increased programs under the Employment and Training Assistance appropriation, and a surplus of funds available for the decreased programs under the Temporary Employment Assistance appropriation. To avoid this result, the Comptroller General interpreted the 1979 continuing resolution as appropriating a single lump-sum amount for all CETA programs, based on the combined current rates of the two appropriation accounts for the previous year. See 58 Comp. Gen. at 535- 36.

Of course, as we noted earlier, continuing resolutions are really just short term appropriations that bridge the gaps that occasionally arise between the end of appropriations for one fiscal year and the start of appropriations for the next. For this reason, continuing resolutions usually refer only to those projects and activities for which annual funding has expired—on account of which funding is being provided. It should be remembered that most, but not all, of the government is funded under annual appropriations. Those projects and activities which are funded by multiple year and no-year appropriations are not usually directly affected by continuing resolutions. Thus, it would be a mistake to read the failure of a continuing resolution to address funding for the rest of the government as an implicit prohibition on undertaking other projects or activities that are, in fact, funded from other appropriations not covered by the continuing resolution.

The term "projects or activities" has also been used in continuing resolutions to prohibit the use of funds to start new programs. Thus, many resolutions have contained a section stating that no funds made available under the resolution shall be available to initiate or resume any project or activity which was not conducted during the preceding fiscal year. When used in this context, the term "projects or activities" refers to the individual program rather than the total appropriation. See 52 Comp. Gen. 270 (1972); 35 Comp. Gen. 156 (1955).

One exception to this interpretation occurred in B-178131, Mar. 8, 1973. In that instance, in the previous fiscal year funds were available generally for construction of buildings, including plans and specifications. However, a specific construction project was not actually under way during the previous year. Nonetheless it was decided that, because funds were available generally for construction in the previous year, this specific project was not a new project or activity and thus could be funded under the continuing resolution.

In more recent years, Congress has resolved the differing interpretations of "project or activity" by altering the language of the new program limitation. Rather than limiting funds to programs which were actually conducted in the preceding year, the more recent resolutions prohibit use of funds appropriated by the resolution for "any project or activity for which appropriations, funds, or other authority were not available" during the Continuing Resolutions preceding fiscal year. Thus, if an agency had authority and sufficient funds to carry out a particular program in the preceding year, that program is not a new project or activity regardless of whether it was actually operating in the preceding year.

A variation occurred in 60 Comp. Gen. 263 (1981). A provision of the Higher Education Act authorized loans to institutions of higher education from a revolving fund, not to exceed limitations specified in appropriation acts. Congress had not released money from the loan fund since 1978. The fiscal year 1981 continuing resolution provided funds to the Department of Education based on its regular fiscal year 1981 appropriation bill as passed by the House of Representatives. The House-passed version included $25 million for the higher education loans. Since the continuing resolution did not include a general prohibition against using funds for projects not funded during the preceding fiscal year, the $25 million from the loan fund was available under the continuing resolution, notwithstanding that the program had not been funded in the preceding year.

Another variation can be seen in In re Uncle Bud's, Inc., 206 B.R. 889 (Bankr. M.D. Tenn., 1997). In a fiscal year 1997 continuing resolution, Pub. L. No. 104-99, title II, § 211, 110 Stat. 26, 37-38 (Jan. 26, 1996), Congress amended the Bankruptcy Code to require the U.S. Trustee to impose and collect a new quarterly fee as part of the bankruptcy process. Uncle Bud's, 206 B.R. at 897. Some debtors argued that the new fee was barred because it constituted a "new activity." The bankruptcy court disagreed, noting that, while the fee itself was new, the U.S. Trustee had long been required to collect other fees imposed by law. The court reasoned that the continuing resolution language was intended to limit spending to previous year levels. The new fee did not require the expenditure of additional funds—rather, it brought in more revenues. Accordingly, the bankruptcy court concluded that collection of the new fee represented, not a new project or activity, but the continuation of activities undertaken in the previous year. Id. On appeal, while other parts of the bankruptcy court's ruling were reversed, this part was upheld and even expanded when the district court gave retroactive effect to the provision imposing the new fees. See Vergos v. Uncle Bud's, Inc., No. 3-97-0296 (M.D. Tenn., Aug. 17, 1998).

Under the right set of circumstances, the projects or activities limitation can also have the effect of blocking existing programs. For example, in Environmental Defense Center v. Babbitt, 73 F.3d 867 (9th Cir. 1995), the Secretary of the Interior was sued for failing to determine whether to list the California red-legged frog under the Endangered Species Act, 16 U.S.C. § 1533(b)(6)(A). The Secretary acknowledged that the only actions that remained to be taken before the frog's status could be settled were the agency's in-house review and its final decision-making. Babbitt, 73 F.3d at 871-72. However, the Secretary argued he could not take those steps because, in 1995, Congress had enacted an appropriations rider which rescinded some of that fiscal year's funds and barred the remaining funds for that year from being used to make any determination that a species was threatened or endangered. See Emergency Supplemental Appropriations and Rescissions for the Department of Defense to Preserve and Enhance Military Readiness Act of 1995, Pub. L. No. 104- 6, 109 Stat. 73, 86 (Apr. 10, 1995). Although the supplemental rider applied only to fiscal year 1995 funds, the ban was effectively continued into fiscal year 1996 by the projects or activities limitation in the continuing resolution under which the government was being funded when the lawsuit was brought. Babbitt, 73 F.3d at 870.

Continuing Resolutions can carry over restrictions on projects and activities that applied under prior year appropriations riders. The court held that neither the appropriations rider nor the projects or activities limitation repealed the Secretary's duty to determine whether the California red-legged frog is endangered, but they did bar the Secretary from complying with that duty by denying him funding for that purpose. Id. at 871-72. As the court explained

"Even though completion of the process may require only a slight expenditure of funds, ... taking final action on the California red- legged frog listing proposal would necessarily require the use of appropriated funds. The use of any government resources—whether salaries, employees, paper, or buildings—to accomplish a final listing would entail government expenditure. The government cannot make expenditures, and therefore cannot act, other than by appropriation." Id.

D. Relationship to other Legislation

1. Not Otherwise Provided For

Continuing resolutions often appropriate funds to continue projects "not otherwise provided for." This language limits funding to those programs which are not funded by any other appropriation act. Programs which received funds under another appropriation act are not covered by the resolution even though the authorizing legislation which created the program is mentioned specifically in the continuing resolution. See B-183433, Mar. 28, 1979. For example, if a resolution appropriates funds to continue activities under the Social Security Act, and a specific program under the Social Security Act has already been funded in a regular appropriation act, the resolution does not appropriate any additional funds for that program.

2. Status of Bill or Budget Estimate Used as Reference

When a continuing resolution appropriates funds at a rate for operations specified in a certain bill or in the administration's budget estimate, the status of the bill or estimate on the date the resolution passes is controlling, unless the resolution specifies some other reference date.

A continuing resolution will often provide funds to continue activities at a rate provided in a certain bill that has passed one or both houses of Congress, or at the rate provided in the administration's budget estimate. In such instances, the resolution is referring to the status of the bill or budget estimate on the date the resolution became law. B-164031(2).17, Dec. 5, 1975; B-152098, Jan. 30, 1970.

For example, the resolution may provide that activities are to be continued at the current rate or at the rate provided in the budget estimate, whichever is lower. The budget estimate referred to is the one in existence at the time the resolution is enacted, and the rate for operations cannot be increased by a subsequent upward revision of the budget estimate. B-164031(2).17, Dec. 5, 1975.

Similarly, if a resolution provides that activities are to continue at the rate provided in a certain appropriation bill, the resolution is referring to the status of the bill on the date the resolution is enacted. A later veto of the bill by the President would not affect the continuation of programs under the resolution. B-152098, Jan. 15, 1973.

Where a continuing resolution provides funds based on a reference bill, this includes restrictions or limitations contained in the reference bill, as well as the amounts appropriated, unless the continuing resolution provides otherwise. 33 Comp. Gen. 20 (B-116069, July 10, 1953); B-199966, Sept. 10, 1980. In National Treasury Employees Union v. Devine, 733 F.2d 114 (D.C. Cir. 1984), the court construed a provision in a reference bill prohibiting the implementation of certain regulations, accepting without question the restriction as having been "enacted into law" by a continuing resolution which provided funds "to the extent and in the manner provided for" in the reference bill. See also Environmental Defense Center v. Babbitt, 73 F.3d 867 (9th Cir. 1995); Connecticut v. Schweiker, 684 F.2d 979 (D.C. Cir. 1982), cert. denied, 459 U.S. 1207 (1983). Obviously, the same result applies under a "full text" continuing resolution, that is, a continuing resolution that enacts the full text of a reference bill "to be effective as if" the reference bill "had been enacted into law as the regular appropriation Act." B-221694, Apr. 8, 1986.

A provision in a continuing resolution using a reference bill may incorporate legislative history, in which event the specified item of legislative history will determine the controlling version of the reference bill. For example, an issue in American Federation of Government Employees v. Devine, 525 F. Supp. 250 (D.D.C. 1981), was whether the 1982 continuing resolution prohibited the Office of Personnel Management from funding coverage of therapeutic abortions in government health plans. The resolution funded employee health benefits "under the authority and conditions set forth in H.R. 4121 as reported to the Senate on September 22, 1981." An earlier version of H.R. 4121 had included a provision barring the funding of therapeutic abortions. However, the bill as reported to the full Senate by the Appropriations Committee on September 22, 1981, dropped the provision. Accordingly, the court held that the continuing resolution could not form the basis for refusing to fund therapeutic abortions in the plaintiff's 1982 health plan. Devine, 525 F. Supp. at 254.

In previous years, it was also not uncommon for a continuing resolution to appropriate funds as provided in a particular reference bill at a rate for operations provided for in the conference report on the reference bill. See, e.g., Pub. L. No. 99-103, § 101(c), 99 Stat. 471, 472 (Sept. 30, 1985). At a minimum, this will include items on which the House and Senate conferees agreed, as reflected in the conference report. If the resolution also incorporates the "joint explanatory statement" portion of the conference report, then it will enact those amendments reported in "technical disagreement" as well. See B-221694, Apr. 8, 1986; B-205523, Nov. 18, 1981; B-204449, Nov. 18, 1981.

3. More Restrictive Authority

The "more restrictive authority," as that term is used in continuing resolutions, is the version of a bill which gives an agency less discretion in obligating and disbursing funds under a certain program.

Continuing resolutions will often appropriate funds to continue projects or activities at the rate provided in either the version of an appropriation act that has passed the House or the version that has passed the Senate, whichever is lower, "or under the more restrictive authority." Under this language, the version of the bill which appropriates the lesser amount of money for an activity will be controlling. If both versions of the bill appropriate the same amount, the version which gives the agency less discretion in obligating and disbursing funds under a program is the more restrictive authority and will be the reference for continuing the program under the resolution. B-210922, Mar. 30, 1984; B-152098, Mar. 26, 1973; B-152554, Dec. 15, 1970.

However, this provision may not be used to amend or nullify a mandatory provision of prior permanent law. To illustrate, the Federal Housing Administration was required by a provision of permanent law to appoint an Assistant Commissioner to perform certain functions. The position subsequently became controversial. For the first month of fiscal year 1954, the agency operated under a continuing resolution which included the "more restrictive authority" provision. Language abolishing the position had been contained in one version of the reference bill, but not both. The bill, when subsequently enacted, abolished the position.

Under a strict application of the "more restrictive authority" provision, it could be argued that there was no authority to continue the employment of the Assistant Commissioner during the month covered by the continuing resolution. Noting that "laws are to be given a sensible construction where a literal application thereof would lead to unjust or absurd consequences, which should be avoided if a reasonable application is consistent with the legislative purpose," the Comptroller General held that the Assistant Commissioner could be paid his salary for the month in question. B-116566, Sept. 14, 1953. The decision concluded:

"Manifestly the [more restrictive authority] language... was not designed to amend or nullify prior permanent law which theretofore required, or might thereafter require, the continuance of a specific project or activity during July 1953....

"Accordingly, it is concluded that the words 'the lesser amount or the more restrictive authority' as used in [the continuing resolution] had reference to such funds and authority as theretofore were provided in appropriations for [the preceding fiscal year], and which might be changed, enlarged or restricted from year to year."

In addition, continuing resolutions frequently provide that a provision "which by its terms is applicable to more than one appropriation" and which was not included in the applicable appropriation act for the preceding fiscal year, will not be applicable to funds or authority under the resolution unless it was included in identical form in the relevant appropriation bill as passed by both the House and the Senate. Thus, in 52 Comp. Gen. 71 (1972), a provision in the House version of the 1973 Labor Department appropriation act prohibited the use of "funds appropriated by this Act" for Occupational Safety and Health Act (OSHA) inspections of firms employing 25 persons or less. The Senate version contained the identical version except that "15" was substituted for "25." The continuing resolution for that year contained both the "more restrictive authority" and the "applicable to more than one appropriation" provisions. The Comptroller General concluded that, even though the House provision was more restrictive, the OSHA provision did not apply to funds under the continuing resolution since it had not been contained in the 1972 appropriation act and by its terms it was applicable to more than one appropriation (i.e., it applied to the entire appropriation act). See also B-210922, Mar. 30, 1984; B-142011, Aug. 6, 1969.

For purposes of the "applicable to more than one appropriation" provision, GAO has construed the "applicable appropriation act for the preceding fiscal year" as meaning the regular appropriation act for the preceding year and not a supplemental. B-210922, Mar. 30, 1984. (The cited decision also illustrates some of the complexities encountered when the appropriation act for the preceding year was itself a continuing resolution.)

4. Lack of Authorizing Legislation

In order for a government agency to carry out a program, the program must first be authorized by law and then funded, usually by means of regular appropriations. This section deals with the relationship of continuing resolutions to programs whose authorization has expired or is about to expire. The common issue is the extent to which a continuing resolution provides authority to continue the program after expiration of the underlying authorization.

As the following discussion will reveal, there are no easy answers. The cases frequently involve a complex interrelationship of various legislative actions (or inactions) and are not susceptible to any meaningful formulation of simple rules. For the most part, the answer is primarily a question of intent, circumscribed of course by statutory language and aided by various rules of statutory construction.

We start with a fairly straightforward case. Toward the end of fiscal year 1984, Congress was considering legislation (S. 2456) to establish a commission to study the Ukrainian famine of 1932-33. The bill passed the Senate but was not enacted into law before the end of the fiscal year. The fiscal year 1985 continuing resolution provided that "there are hereby appropriated $400,000 to carry out the provisions of S. 2456, as passed by the Senate on September 21, 1984. If this provision were not construed as authorizing the establishment and operation of the commission as well as the appropriation of funds, it would have been absolutely meaningless. Accordingly, GAO concluded that the appropriation incorporated the substantive authority of S. 2456. B-219727, July 30, 1985. The result was supported by clear and explicit legislative history.

In a 1975 case, GAO held that the specific inclusion of a program in a continuing resolution will provide both authorization and funding to continue the program despite the expiration of the appropriation authorization legislation. Thus, for example, if the continuing resolution specifically states that the School Breakfast Program is to be continued under the resolution, the program may be continued although funding authorization legislation for the program expires prior to or during the period the resolution is in effect. 55 Comp. Gen. 289 (1975). The same result would follow if the intent to continue the program was made particularly clear in legislative history. 65 Comp. Gen. 318, 320-21 (1986).

The result in 55 Comp. Gen. 289 flows from two concepts. First, the continuing resolution, as the later enactment, is the more recent expression of congressional intent. Second, if Congress can appropriate funds in excess of a specific ceiling in authorizing legislation, which it can, then it should be able to appropriate funds to continue a program whose funding authorization is about to expire, at least where the authorization of appropriations is not a legal prerequisite to the appropriation itself.

However, the "rule" of 55 Comp. Gen. 289 is not an absolute and the result in any given case will depend on several variables. Although not spelled out as such in any of the decisions, the variables may include: the degree of specificity in the continuing resolution; the apparent intent of Congress with respect to the expired program; whether what has expired is an authorization of appropriations or the underlying program authority itself; and the duration of the continuing resolution (short-term versus full fiscal year).

In one case, for example, "all authority" under the Manpower Development and Training Act (MDTA) terminated on June 30, 1973. The program was not specifically provided for in the 1974 continuing resolution, and the authority in fact was not reestablished until enactment of the Comprehensive Employment and Training Act (CETA)[Footnote 30] six months later. Under these circumstances, the Claims Court held that, in the absence of express language in the continuing resolution or elsewhere, contracts entered into during the gap between expiration of the MDTA and enactment of CETA were without legal authority and did not bind the government. Consortium Venture Corp. v. United States, 5 Cl. Ct. 47 (1984), aff'd mem., 765 F.2d 163 (Fed. Cir.1985).

In another case, recent Defense Department authorization acts, including the one for fiscal year 1985, had authorized a test program involving payment of a price differential to "labor surplus area" contractors. The test program amounted to an exemption from permanent legislation prohibiting the payment of such differentials. The 1985 provision expired, of course, at the end of fiscal year 1985. The 1986 continuing resolution made no specific provision for the test program nor was there any evidence of congressional intent to continue the test program under the resolution. (This lack of intent was confirmed when the 1986 authorization act was subsequently enacted without the test program provision.) GAO found that the Defense Logistics Agency's failure to apply the price differential in evaluating bids on a contract awarded under the continuing resolution (even though the differential had been included in the solicitation issued prior to the close of fiscal year 1985) was not legally objectionable. 65 Comp. Gen. 318 (1986).

A more difficult case was presented in B-207186, Feb. 10, 1989. Congress enacted two pieces of legislation on December 22, 1987. One was a temporary extension of the Solar Bank, which had been scheduled to go out of existence on September 30, 1987. Congress had enacted several temporary extensions while it was considering reauthorization, the one in question extending the Bank's life to March 15, 1988. The second piece of legislation was the final continuing resolution for 1988 which funded the government for the remainder of the fiscal year. The resolution included a specific appropriation of $1.5 million for the Solar Bank, with a 2-year period of availability.

If the concept of 55 Comp. Gen. 289 were applied, the result would have been that the specific appropriation in the continuing resolution, in effect, reauthorized the Solar Bank as well. However, the "later enactment of Congress" concept has little relevance when both laws are enacted on the same day. In addition, in contrast to 55 Comp. Gen. 289, there was no indication of congressional intent to continue the Solar Bank beyond the March 1988 expiration date. Therefore, GAO distinguished prior cases, found that the two pieces of legislation could be reconciled, and concluded that the resolution merely appropriated funds for the Bank to use during the remainder of its existence.

Another case involving a sunset provision is 71 Comp. Gen. 378 (1992). The legislation establishing the United States Commission on Civil Rights provided for the Commission to terminate on September 30, 1991. During fiscal year 1991, Congress was working on the Commission's reauthorization and its regular fiscal year 1992 appropriation. Although both bills passed both houses of Congress, neither was enacted into law by September 30. The first continuing resolution for fiscal year 1992, with a cutoff date of October 29, 1991, expressly provided funds for activities included in the Commission's yet- unenacted 1992 appropriations bill. It was clear from all of this that Congress intended the Commission to continue operating beyond September 30. Thus, the continuing resolution effectively suspended the sunset date and authorized the Commission to operate until October 28, 1991, when the regular 1992 appropriation act was enacted, at which time the regular appropriation provided similar authority until November 26, when the reauthorization was enacted.

Appropriation bills sometimes contain provisions malting the availability of the appropriations contingent upon the enactment of additional authorizing legislation. If a continuing resolution used a bill with such a provision as a reference, and if the authorizing legislation was not enacted, the amount contained in the appropriation bill, and therefore the amount appropriated by the continuing resolution, would be zero. To avoid this possibility, a continuing resolution may contain a provision suspending the effectiveness of such "contingency" provisions for the life of the resolution. Such a suspension provision will be applicable only until the referenced appropriation bill is enacted into law. 55 Comp. Gen. at 294.

E. Duration

1. Duration of Continuing Resolution

Continuing resolutions generally provide that the budget authority provided for an activity by the resolution shall remain available until (a) enactment into law of a regular appropriation for the activity, (b) enactment of the applicable appropriation by both houses of Congress without provision for the activity, or (c) a fixed cutoff date, whichever occurs first. Once either of the first two conditions occurs, or the cutoff date passes, funds appropriated by the resolution are no longer available for obligation and new obligations may be incurred only if a regular appropriation is made or if the termination date of the resolution is extended.

The period of availability of funds under a continuing resolution can be extended by Congress by amending the fixed cutoff date stated in the resolution. B-165731(1), Nov. 10, 1971; B-152098, Jan. 30, 1970.

The extension may run beyond the session of Congress in which it is enacted. B-152554, Dec. 15, 1970. Thus, some fiscal years have seen a series of continuing resolutions, informally designated "first," "second," etc., up to "final." This happens as Congress extends the fixed cutoff date for short time periods until either all the regular appropriation acts are enacted or Congress determines that some or all of the remaining bills will not be enacted individually, in which event relevant portions of the resolution will continue in effect for the remainder of the fiscal year.

The second condition of the standard duration provision—enactment of the appropriation by both houses of Congress without provision for the activity—will be considered to have occurred only when it is clear that Congress intended to terminate the activity. Thus, in B-164031(1), Mar. 14, 1974, although regular and supplemental appropriation acts had been enacted without provision for a program, the Comptroller General decided that funds for the program were still available under the continuing resolution. In this case, the legislative history indicated that in enacting the regular appropriation act, Congress was providing funding for only some of the programs normally funded by this act and was deferring consideration of other programs, including the one in question. Therefore, the second condition was not applicable. Moreover, because supplemental appropriations are intended to provide funding only for new or additional needs, omission of the program from the supplemental did not trigger the second cutoff provision. As discussed previously, once the applicable appropriation is enacted into law, expenditures made under the continuing resolution are charged to that appropriation, except that valid obligations incurred under the continuing resolution in excess of the amount finally appropriated are charged to the account established under the continuing resolution.

2. Duration of Appropriations

For the most part, the duration (period of obligational availability) of an appropriation under a short-term continuing resolution does not present problems. If you have, say, only 1 month to incur obligations under a continuing resolution, it matters little that the corresponding appropriation in a regular appropriation act might be a multiple year or no-year appropriation. Also, once the regular appropriation is enacted, it supersedes the continuing resolution and governs the period of availability. B-300673, July 3, 2003. Questions may arise, however, under continuing resolutions whose duration is the balance of the fiscal year.

For example, the continuing resolution for fiscal year 1979 included the standard duration provision described above, with a cutoff date of September 30, 1979, the last day of the fiscal year. However, a provision in the Comprehensive Employment and Training Act (CETA), 29 U.S.C. § 802(B) (1976), stated that "notwithstanding any other provision of law, unless enacted in specific limitation of the provisions of this subsection," appropriations to carry out the CETA program shall remain available for 2 years. Applying the principle that a specific provision governs over a more general one, it was held that funds appropriated for CETA under the continuing resolution were available for obligation for 2 years in accordance with the CETA provision. B-194063, May 4, 1979; B-115398.33, Mar. 20, 1979.

A few years earlier, the United States District Court for the District of Columbia had reached the same result in a case involving grants to states under the Elementary and Secondary Education Act. Pennsylvania v. Weinberger, 367 E Supp. 1378, 1384-85 (D.D.C. 1973). The court stated, "it is a basic premise of statutory construction that in such circumstances the more specific measure ... is to be held controlling over the general measure where inconsistencies arise in their application." Id. at 1385.

Application of the same principle produced a similar result in B- 199966, Sept. 10, 1980. The 1980 continuing resolution appropriated funds for foreign economic assistance loans by referencing the regular 1980 appropriation bill which had passed the House but not the Senate. For that type of situation, the resolution provided for continuation of projects or activities "under the appropriation, fund, or authority granted by the one House [which had passed the bill]." The House- passed bill gave the economic assistance loan funds a 2-year period of availability. The continuing resolution also included the standard duration provision with a cutoff date of September 30, 1980. Since the duration provision applied to the entire resolution whereas the provision applicable to the loan funds had a narrower scope, the latter provision was the more specific one and the loan funds were therefore held to be available for 2 years. See also 60 Comp. Gen. 263 (1981) for further discussion of similar continuing resolution language.

In some instances, an extended period of availability is produced by a specific exemption from the standard duration provision. For example, the 1983 continuing resolution provided foreign assistance funds "under the terms and conditions" set forth in the Foreign Assistance Appropriation Act of 1982, and further exempted that appropriation from the duration provision. Since under the 1982 act, appropriations for the African Development Fund were to remain available until expended, appropriations to the Fund under the continuing resolution were also no-year funds. B-212876, Sept. 21, 1983. In view of the express exemption from the duration provision, there was no need to apply the "specific versus general" rule because there was no conflict. See also B-210922, Mar. 30, 1984.

3. Impoundment

The duration of a continuing resolution is relevant in determining the application of the Impoundment Control Act. Impoundment in the context of continuing resolutions was discussed in a letter to the Chairman of the House Budget Committee, B-205053, Dec. 31, 1981. Generally, a withholding from obligation of funds provided under a continuing resolution would constitute an impoundment. Where the continuing resolution runs for only part of the fiscal year, the withholding, even if proposed for the duration of the continuing resolution, should be classified as a deferral rather than a rescission. Withholding funds during a temporary continuing resolution is different from withholding them for the life of a regular annual appropriation in that, in the former situation, Congress is still deliberating over the regular funding levels. Also, deferred funds are not permanently lost when a continuing resolution expires if a subsequent funding measure is passed.

Under this interpretation, classification as a rescission would presumably still be appropriate where a regular appropriation is never passed, the agency is operating under continuing resolution authority for the entire fiscal year, and the timing of a withholding is such that insufficient opportunity would remain to utilize the funds. See B- 115398, May 9, 1975.

Impoundment issues under continuing resolutions may arise in other contexts as well. See, e.g., 64 Comp. Gen. 649 (1985) (failure to make funds available based on good faith disagreement over treatment of carryover balances in calculating rate for operations held not to constitute an illegal rescission); B-209676, Apr. 14, 1983 (no improper impoundment where funds were apportioned on basis of budget request although continuing resolution appropriated funds at rate to maintain program level, as long as apportionment was sufficient to maintain requisite program level).

This page intentionally left blank

www. congress. gov.
↓
you can get a sens of
how appropriations. are going on.

Federal Appropriations Law

Exercise 1

Necessary Expense

The Dodd-Frank Wall Street Reform and Consumer Protection Act (Dodd-Frank) requires the Commodity Futures Trading Commission to implement whistleblower incentive and customer education programs. The law established the Fund, which is available to the Commission without fiscal year limitation for two purposes: (1) "the payment of awards to whistleblowers" who provides original information that leads to the successful resolution of a covered judicial or administration action, or related action and (2) "the funding of customer education initiatives." A covered judicial or administrative action is one brought by the Commission under the Commodity Exchange Act or its rules and regulations and results in monetary sanctions exceeding $1,000,000. Customer education initiatives are designed to help market participants and the public protect themselves against fraud or other violations of the Commodity Exchange Act or its rules and regulations.

The Commission asks if it may use the Fund to establish an office and hire personnel to carry out whistleblower incentive and customer education programs. The Commission explains that the office will "design, implement, and oversee the customer education initiatives; will intake and track whistleblower tips and complaints; make whistleblower eligibility determinations at the beginning and throughout the claims process; and perform related ministerial functions."

1. Comment on the ability of the Commission to use the funds as it seeks.

2. What factors are relevant to this inquiry?

[Handwritten annotations: "office — GAO approved.", "education", "awards", "3-part test:", "specific office is better + not the existing community Acp"]

Exercise 2

Voluntary Services

The Federal Election Commission (Commission) seeks to appoint a single individual, John Jeffries, to two positions within the Commission. The individual would hold positions both as a Staff Director and also as the Chief Information Officer. The Commission seeks to pay him only for the CIO position.

The Staff Director reports directly to the Commission and is the highest-ranking employee of the Commission other than the presidentially-appointed Commissioners. The incumbent serves as the chief administrative and management officer of the Commission and supervises the operation of all divisions, except the Office of General Counsel, the Office of Inspector General, and the Office of the Chief Financial Officer. The current compensation for the Staff Director position is $155,500 per year.

Unlike the Staff Director position, the CIO position is not established by statute. The CIO is responsible for the Commission's information technology strategy and architecture, and manages all aspects of the work of the Commission's Information Technology Division. The CIO is compensated under the Senior Level system. This system allows a minimum of $119,554 per year and a maximum of $165,300 per year.

The Commission seeks to pay Mr. Jeffries only for the CIO position, but to pay him at the maximum amount.

1. Would this be considered Voluntary Services? Would it be prohibited?

2. Is it allowable to pay Mr. Jeffries at the maximum amount?

Exercise 3

Bona Fide Needs

[handwritten timeline: Bas yr → yr2 → yr3 → yr4 → yr5]

The Small Business Administration has an IDIQ Contract, which provides for one base year and four one-year options and includes a list of computer hardware and software that SBA intended to purchase, as necessary, by the issuance of task orders. When initially executed in 2009, the SBA IDIQ Contract provided for a $290,000 guaranteed minimum for the base year. On September 28 2009, SBA unilaterally executed a contract modification that increased the base year minimum from $290,000 to $1,315,000. SBA obligated the additional $1,025,000 in the guaranteed minimum two months later and did so against its fiscal year 2009 appropriation. *[handwritten: Nov 2009]*

In September 2010, SBA exercised option year one and modified the SBA IDIQ Contract on three separate occasions during a span of two weeks. As a result of these contract modifications, SBA obligated an aggregate of $1,860,000 in fiscal year 2010 funds.

1. Are there any possible issues with the SBA's actions?

2. What additional information would be relevant to these concerns?

[handwritten notes:]
Too many mod within 3 wks.
g min amt – drastically
SBA – didn't follow purpose of need
violation bonafide needs rule statute.
– needs not justified

Federal Appropriations Law

Exercise 4

Cost Reimbursement Contracts

The Financial Crimes Enforcement Network (FinCEN) of the Department of the Treasury entered into a cost-reimbursement contract for the design, development, and deployment of a computer system. The contract included a cost ceiling of $8.9 million for the estimated cost and fixed fee. However, the contract also stated that the "total funds currently available for payment and allotted to this contract are $2,000,000" and that the contract was "subject to incremental funding," and "no legal liability on the part of the Government for payment of money in excess of $2,000,000 shall arise, unless and until additional funds are made available by the Contracting Officer through a modification of the contract."

FinCEN obligated $2 million to the contract at the time it was signed. Subsequently, in the next fiscal year, the agency obligated additional funds to reach the ceiling of $8.9 million. During the second fiscal year, FinCEN made a number of modifications to the contract that increased its cost beyond the initial $8.9 million ceiling established in the contract. Although FinCEN charged most of these modifications to its second fiscal year appropriations, it charged two of the modifications to its third fiscal year appropriations.

1. What are the issues in this situation?

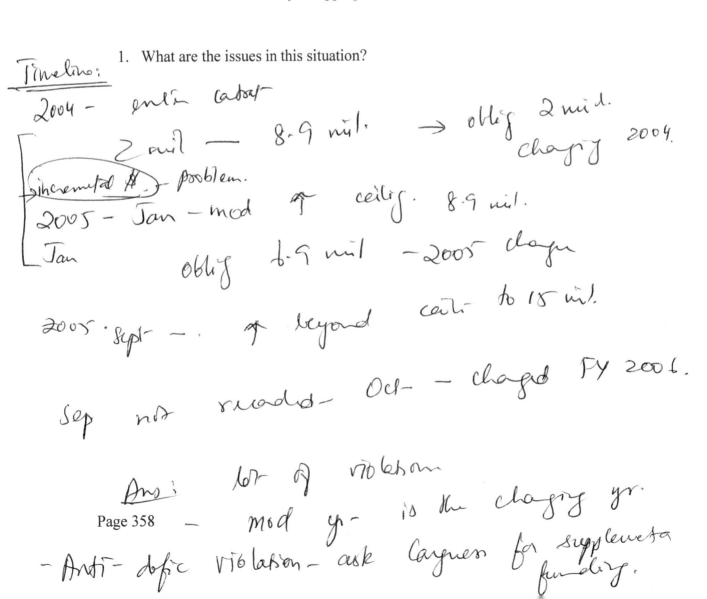

Timeline:

2004 - enter contract
    2 mil — 8.9 mil. → oblig 2 mil.
                              charging 2004.
incremental $ - problem.
2005 - Jan - mod ↑ ceiling. 8.9 mil.
    Jan   oblig 6.9 mil — 2005 charge

2005 · Sept - . ↑ beyond ceiling to 15 mil.

Sep not recorded — Oct — charged FY 2006.

Ans: lot of violation
Page 358 — mod yr - is the charging yr.
- Anti-defic violation - ask Congress for supplementa funding.

Federal Appropriations Law

Exercise 5

Settlements and Ratifications

In September 2003, The National Science Board Office (NSBO), a part of the National Science Foundation (NSF) issued a cost reimbursement level-of-effort contract to SAI for science and engineering policy support to the contract was a one-year base contract with three 1-year options. On August 26, 2005, NSF issued a Task Order The Task Order required SAI to develop and implement an electronic Web based process to assess the impact of NSB policy recommendations, activities, and other products. During February and March of 2006, an NSBO Senior Scientist directed SAI to change the order of deliverables under the Task Order and SAI agreed to adjust the schedule to accommodate such changes. Neither NSF nor NSBO had granted the NSBO Senior Scientist, who initiated these changes, the authority to enter into contracts on behalf of NSBO or to modify or amend contracts.

On January 10, 2007, SAI submitted a Request for Equitable Adjustment/Certified Claim, pursuant to the Contract Disputes Act to NSF's contracting officer requesting $188,640 for additional costs incurred because of changes to the contract initiated by the NSBO Senior Scientist. In negotiations that concluded on March 23, 2007, SAI and NSF agreed to settle SAI's claim for $88,000.

(handwritten notes:)
x3
+ 1 yr. 9
2003 – ban
2005 – opp TO
2006 – mod.
2007 – claim
(100,000 yr)

1. To which fiscal year would the settlement money be properly charged?

   2006 = delivery yr.

2. Would it change if the government had ratified the change in 2006?

   Yes

   Not a ratification = treat as mod.

   This is just a settlement.

   does not relate to 2005-06 funds.

   2007 = charging year because it was just a settlement.

Page 359

Exercise 6

Personal Expenses

The National Telecommunications and Information Administration (NTIA) was responsible for implementing a program to provide vouchers to the public for use towards purchase of analog-to-digital television signal converter boxes, as part of the federal government's transition to all-digital television transmissions. NTIA planned to conduct a pilot program of the voucher program prior to the program's nationwide launch.

NTIA intended to ask pilot program participants to complete a survey regarding their experience. NTIA will review these questionnaires to gather information regarding the efficacy of the converter box coupon program. Using this information, NTIA hopes to fix problems with the coupon program before beginning the full-scale launch of the program. In an effort to increase the survey response rate, NTIA seeks to give out $25 gift cards to participants who complete the survey.

1. Can NTIA use appropriated funds for the purchase of the gift cards?